Technologies for Business Information Systems

Technologies
for Business Information
Systems

edited by

Witold Abramowicz
Poznan University of Economics,
Poznan, Poland

and

Heinrich C. Mayr
Alpen-Adria-University,
Klagenfurt, Austria

 Springer

A C.I.P. Catalogue record for this book is available from the Library of Congress.

ISBN-13 978-90-481-7415-7
ISBN-10 1-4020-5634-6 (e-book)
ISBN-13 978-1-4020-5634-5 (e-book)

Published by Springer,
P.O. Box 17, 3300 AA Dordrecht, The Netherlands.

www.springer.com

Printed on acid-free paper

Contents

Business Process Management

e-Government

Information Systems

Information Retrieval and Filtering

Ontologies

Software Engineering

Preface

Technologies for Business Information Systems

The material collected in this book covers a broad range of applications of computer science methods and algorithms in business practice. It presents a research cutting edge in development, implementation, and improvement of computer systems. We publish this book with intention that it helps to establish strong foundations for further development of research in this area and support people involved in business computer applications, those implementing computer technology in industry. The computer science and information systems topics covered in the book include data warehouses, ERP, XML, ontologies, rule languages, Web services. We divided the chapters into several areas of applications of the above. There are parts on modeling business processes, devoted to applications of formal methods and metrics that assist this crucial step for contemporary heavy-IT oriented enterprises. This is accompanied by chapters on information systems considered both from engineering and social perspectives. Particular topics on software engineering have been placed in a separate book part. We addressed also advancements in information retrieval and formal representation of knowledge using ontologies and rule languages. These topics are worth of interest due to their reemergence in recent years, significant advances and broad range of potential as well as actual applications. Last but not least comes the other area of applying IT – e-government. Several authors elaborate on methods and experiences of IT adoption for administrative purposes. We hope that with their conclusions applied our slightly unwieldy, yet necessary e-gov systems are improved.

We hope that you will find this book useful for practical and research purposes – that would be the best satisfaction for our authors, to whom we are very thankful.

The book could not be published without enormous amount of work that the colleagues from Poznan University of Economics, Poland, Agata Filipowska, Tomasz Kaczmarek and Krzysztof Węcel put in it.

Witold Abramowicz and Heinrich C. Mayr

Poznań, September 2006

ix

List of Contributors

Adamus, Radoslaw
Computer Engineering Department, Technical University of Lodz
ul. Stefanowskiego 18/22
90-924 Lodz, Poland

Ahonen, Jarmo J.
Department of Computer Science, University of Kuopio
P.O. Box 1627
70211 Kuopio, Finland

Bartoszek, Jerzy
Technical University of Poznań, Institute of Control and Information Engineering
Pl. M. Skłodowskiej-Curie 5
60-965 Poznań, Poland

Baškarada, Saša
School of Computer and Information Science, University of South Australia
Mawson Lakes, SA 5095
Australia

Bassara, Andrzej
Poznań University of Economics, Department of Management Information Systems
Al. Niepodległości 10
60-967 Poznań, Poland

Begier, Barbara
Poznań University of Technology
Pl. M. Sklodowskiej-Curie 5,
60-965 Poznan, Poland

Bernroider, Edward
Vienna University of Economics and Business Administration
Augasse 2-6, 1090
Vienna A-1090, Austria

Brzykcy, Grażyna
Technical University of Poznań, Institute of Control and Information Engineering
Pl. M. Skłodowskiej-Curie 5, 60-965 Poznań, Poland
Poznań, Poland

Buddendick, Christian
European Research Center for Information Systems (ERCIS),
University of Muenster Leonardo-Campus 3
48149 Muenster, Germany

Budzowski, Roman
Uniwersytet Szczeciński, Instytut Informatyki w Zarządzaniu
ul. Mickiewicza 64
71-101 Szczecin, Poland

Campos, Cristina
Grupo de Investigación en Integración y Re-Ingeniería de Sistemas (IRIS),
Dept. de Llenguatges i Sistemes Informatics, Universitat Jaume I,
Campus del Riu Sec s/n
12071 Castelló, Spain

Ceglarek, Dariusz
Poznan University of Economics, Department of Management Information Systems
Al. Niepodległości 10
60-967 Poznan, Poland

Chalmeta, Ricardo
Grupo de Investigación en Integración y Re-Ingeniería de Sistemas (IRIS),
Dept. de Llenguatges i Sistemes Informatics, Universitat Jaume I,
Campus del Riu Sec s/n
12071 Castelló, Spain

Choroś, Kazimierz
Institute of Applied Informatics, Wroclaw University of Technology
Wyb. S. Wyspianskiego 27
50-370 Wroclaw, Poland

Cichon, Pawel
Wrocław Institute of Technology
Wybrzeze Wyspiańskiego 27
50-370 Wrocław, Poland

Ciorăscu, Iulian
Information Management Institute, University of Neuchâtel
Pierre-à-Mazel 7
CH-2000 Neuchâtel, Switzerland

Concepcion, Arturo I.
Department of Computer Science, California State University
San Bernardino
CA 92407, USA

Cybulka, Jolanta
Institute of Control and Information Engineering, Poznań University of Technology,
Poznań, Poland
ul. Piotrowo 3A
60-965 Poznan, Poland

De Beer, Jan
Legal Informatics and Information Retrieval group,
Interdisciplinary Center for Law and ICT, Katholieke Universiteit Leuven
Tiensestraat 41
B-3000 Leuven, Belgium

Esichaikul, Vatcharaporn
School of Engineering and Technology, Asian Institute of Technology
PO Box 4, Klong Luang
Pathumthani 12120, Thailand

Filipowska, Agata
Poznań University of Economics, Department of Management Information Systems
Al. Niepodległości 10
Poznań, Poland

Gao, Jing
School of Computer and Information Science, University of South Australia
Mawson Lakes, SA 5095
Australia

Governatori, Guido
School of Information Technology and Electrical Engineering,
The University of Queensland
Brisbane QLD 4072, Australia

Grangel, Reyes
Grupo de Investigación en Integración y Re-Ingeniería de Sistemas (IRIS),
Dept. de Llenguatges i Sistemes Informatics, Universitat Jaume I,
Campus del Riu Sec s/n
12071 Castelló, Spain

Gruhn, Volker
Computer Science Faculty, University of Leipzig
Klostergasse 3
04109 Leipzig, Germany

Gulla, Jon Atle
Norwegian University of Science and Technology,
Department of Computer and Information Science
Sem Saelands vei 7-9
NO-7491 Trondheim, Norway

Honkaranta, Anne
University of Jyväskylä, Faculty of Information Technology
P.O. Box 35
40014 Jyväskylä, Finland

Huzar, Zbigniew
Wrocław Institute of Technology
Wybrzeze Wyspiańskiego 27
50-370 Wrocław, Poland

Ingvaldsen, Jon Espen
Norwegian University of Science and Technology,
Department of Computer and Information Science
Sem Saelands vei 7-9
NO-7491 Trondheim, Norway

Jauhiainen, Eliisa
University of Jyväskylä
P.O. Box 35
40014 Jyväskylä, Finland

Kankaanpää, Irja
Information Technology Research Institute, University of Jyväskylä
P.O. Box 35
40014 Jyväskylä, Finland

Kaschek, Roland
Department of Information Systems, Massey University
Wellington Campus, Private Box 756
Wellington, New Zealand

Koch, Stefan
Institute for Information Business, Vienna University
of Economics and Business Administration
Augasse 2-6
Wien 1090, Austria

Koronios, Andy
School of Computer and Information Science, University of South Australia
Mawson Lakes, SA 5095
Australia

Koskinen, Jussi
Information Technology Research Institute, University of Jyväskylä
P.O. Box 35
40014 Jyväskylä, Finland

Kowalkiewicz, Marek
Department of Management Information Systems,
The Poznan University of Economics Al. Niepodległości 10
60-967 Poznan, Poland

Kowalska, Justyna
Institute of Applied Informatics, Wroclaw University of Technology
Wyb. S. Wyspiańskiego 27
50-370 Wroclaw, Poland

Król, Dariusz
Wrocław University of Technology, Institute of Applied Informatics
Wyb. Wyspiańskiego 27, 50-370 Wrocław, Poland
Wrocław, Poland

Kuliberda, Kamil
Computer Engineering Department, Technical University of Lodz
ul. Stefanowskiego 18/22
90-924 Lodz, Poland

Kulpa, Artur
Uniwersytet Szczeciński, Instytut Informatyki w Zarządzaniu
ul. Mickiewicza 64
71-101 Szczecin, Poland

Kumar, Nishant
Research Center for Management Informatics, Katholieke Universiteit Leuven,
Belgium Naamsestraat 69
B-3000 Leuven, Belgium

Lægreid, Tarjei
Norwegian University of Science and Technology,
Department of Computer and Information Science
Sem Saelands vei 7-9, NO-7491 Trondheim, Norway
Trondheim, Norway

Laue, Ralf
Computer Science Faculty, University of Leipzig, Germany
Klostergasse 3, 04109 Leipzig, Germany, fax: +49 341 973 23 39
Leipzig, Germany

Lintinen, Heikki
Information Technology Research Institute, University of Jyväskylä
P.O. Box 35
40014 Jyväskylä, Finland

Lu, Ruopeng
School of Information Technology and Electrical Engineering,
The University of Queensland
Brisbane QLD 4072, Australia

Ma, Chunyan
Department of Computer Science, California State University
San Bernardino
CA 92407, USA

Mazur, Zygmunt
Wrocław Institute of Technology
Wybrzeze Wyspiańskiego 27
50-370 Wrocław, Poland

Meissner, Adam
Institute of Control and Information Engineering,
Poznań University of Technology, Poznań, Poland
ul. Piotrowo 3A
60-965 Poznan, Poland

Mitlöhner, Johann
Vienna University of Economics and Business Administration
Augasse 2-6
Vienna A-1090, Austria

Mochol, Malgorzata
Free University Berlin
Takustr. 9
14195 Berlin, Germany

Moens, Marie-Francine
Legal Informatics and Information Retrieval group,
Interdisciplinary Center for Law and ICT, Katholieke Universiteit Leuven
Tiensestraat 41
B-3000 Leuven, Belgium

Mrozowski, Adam
Wrocław Institute of Technology
Wybrzeze Wyspiańskiego 27
50-370 Wrocław, Poland

Oleksy, Jacek
Siemens, Software Development Center
Poland

Pankowski, Tadeusz
Institute of Control and Information Engineering,
Poznań University of Technology, Faculty of Mathematics and Computer Science,
Adam Mickiewicz University ul. Piotrowo 3A
60-965 Poznań, Poland

Pavlov, Roman
Department of Computer-Aided Management Systems,
National Technical University Kharkov, Ukraine

Picard, Willy
The Poznań University of Economics
Al. Niepodległości 10
60-967 Poznań, Poland

Piskorski, Jakub
Department of Management Information Systems, The Poznan University of Economics
Al. Niepodległości 10
60-967 Poznan, Poland

Podyma, Małgorzata
Computer Association of Information Bogart Ltd.
Poland

Puhlmann, Frank
Business Process Technology Group Hasso-Plattner-Institute
for IT Systems Engineering at the University of Potsdam
Prof.-Dr.-Helmert-Str. 2-3
D-14482 Potsdam, Germany

Rutkowski, Wojciech
Poznań University of Economics, Department of Management Information Systems
Al. Niepodległości 10
60-967 Poznan, Poland

Sadiq, Shazia
School of Information Technology and Electrical Engineering,
The University of Queensland
Brisbane QLD 4072, Australia

Sandal, Paul Christian
*Norwegian University of Science and Technology, Department of Computer
and Information Science
Sem Saelands vei 7-9
NO-7491 Trondheim, Norway*

Schnieders, Arnd
*Business Process Technology Group Hasso-Plattner-Institute
for IT Systems Engineering at the University of Potsdam
Prof.-Dr.-Helmert-Str. 2-3
D-14482 Potsdam, Germany*

Shekhovtsov, Vladimir A.
*Department of Computer-Aided Management Systems,
National Technical University Kharkov, Ukraine*

Simon, Eric
*Information Management Institute University of Neuchâtel,
Switzerland Pierre-à-Mazel 7
CH-2000 Neuchâtel, Switzerland*

Simperl, Elena Paslaru Bontas
*Free University Berlin
Takustr. 9
14195 Berlin, Germany*

Sivula, Henna
*Information Technology Research Institute, University of Jyväskylä
P.O. Box 35
40014 Jyväskylä, Finland*

Statkiewicz, Izydor
*Main Library and Scientific Information Center,
Wroclaw University of Technology Wyb. S. Wyspiańskiego 27
50-370 Wroclaw, Poland*

Stoffel, Kilian
*Information Management Institute University of Neuchâtel, Switzerland
Pierre-à-Mazel 7
CH-2000 Neuchâtel, Switzerland*

Subieta, Kazimierz
*Computer Engineering Department, Technical University of Lodz,
Institute of Computer Science PAS, Warsaw, Poland, Polish-Japanese Institute
of Information Technology ul. Stefanowskiego 18/22
90-924 Lodz, Poland*

Sulčič, Viktorija
University of Primorska, Faculty of Management Koper
Cankarjeva 5
SI-6000 Koper, Slovenia

Swacha, Jakub
Uniwersytet Szczeciński, Instytut Informatyki w Zarządzaniu
ul. Mickiewicza 64
71-101 Szczecin, Poland

Szymański, Michał
Wrocław University of Technology, Institute of Applied Informatics
Wyb.Wyspianskiego 27
50370 Wrocław, Poland

Tempich, Christoph
Institute AIFB, University of Karlsruhe
76128 Karlsruhe, Germany

Thomas, Oliver
Institute for Information Systems (IWi), German Research Center
for Artificial Intelligence (DFKI), Saarbruecken
Stuhlsatzenhausweg 3
66123 Saarbruecken, Germany

Tilus, Tero
Information Technology Research Institute, University of Jyväskylä
P.O. Box 35
40014 Jyväskylä, Finland

Trawiński, Bogdan
Wrocław University of Technology, Institute of Applied Informatics
Wyb. Wyspiańskiego 27
50-370 Wrocław, Poland

Urbański, Andrzej P.
Institute of Computer Science, Department of Computer Science and Management,
Poznań University of Technology
ul.Piotrowo 3a
60-965 Poznań, Poland

Vanthienen, Jan
Research Center for Management Informatics, Katholieke Universiteit Leuven,
Belgium Naamsestraat 69
B-3000 Leuven, Belgium

Varavithya, Wanchai
School of Engineering and Technology, Asian Institute of Technology
PO Box 4, Klong Luang
Pathumthani 12120, Thailand

vom Brocke, Jan
European Research Center for Information Systems (ERCIS),
University of Muenster Leonardo-Campus 3
48149 Muenster, Germany

Węcel, Krzysztof
Poznań University of Economics, Department of Management Information Systems
Al. Niepodległości 10
Poznań, Poland

Wieloch, Karol
Poznań University of Economics, Department of Management Information Systems
Al. Niepodległości 10
Poznań, Poland

Wislicki, Jacek
Computer Engineering Department, Technical University of Lodz
ul. Stefanowskiego 18/22
90-924 Lodz, Poland

Zlatkin, Sergiy
Department of Information Systems, Massey University
Wellington Campus, Private Box 756
Wellington, New Zealand

1 Conceptual Modelling for Grid Computing: Applying Collaborative Reference Modelling[*]

Jan vom Brocke[1], Oliver Thomas[2], Christian Buddendick[1]

[1] European Research Center for Information Systems (ERCIS)
University of Muenster (Germany)
{jan.vom.brocke|christian.buddendick}@ercis.uni-muenster.de
[2] Institute for Information Systems (IWi)
at the German Research Center for Artificial Intelligence (DFKI),
Saarland University, Saarbruecken (Germany)
oliver.thomas@iwi.dfki.de

1.1 Introduction

With the evolution of grid computing, powerful means have been developed that enable virtual organizations by sharing resources in networks. Therefore underlying business processes need to be questioned regarding the technological potentials offered. In addition, the evolution of grid computing needs to consider the business needs of virtual organizations. Methods of Business Engineering can be applied in order to align business processes of virtual organizations and grid technology. In this article, we first give a brief insight into both, grid computing and business engineering. On that basis, we argue that particularly collaborative reference modelling, as means of business engineering might be a promising approach for this kind of alignment. The potentials of collaborative reference modelling in this area are illustrated by an example. We then conclude with a short summary and an outlook for further research opportunities.

[*] This publication is based on work done in cooperation between the "Center for Internet Economy" at ERCIS (grant number 01AK704) and the research project "Reference Model-Based Customizing with Vague Data" at DFKI (grant number SCHE 185/25−1). The authors wish to thank the German Federal Ministry of Education and Research (BMBF) and the German Research Foundation (DFG).

W. Abramowicz and H.C. Mayr (eds.), Technologies for Business Information Systems, 1–11.
© 2007 Springer.

1.2 Grid Computing and Business Engineering

1.2.1 Foundations of Grid Computing

The term "the Grid" evolved the mid 1990s to denote a proposed distributed computing infrastructure for advanced science and engineering [9]. Nowadays first applications of grid computing can be found in scientific as well as in company's practice, for example the development of an operational grid for the Large Hadron Collider (LHC) at CERN (http://lcg.web.cern.ch/LCG/) and SETI@Home [7] (http://setiathome.berkeley.edu/). As its predecessor, distributed computing, the field of grid computing deals with the potential of resource sharing for computing in networks [10]. A computational grid is an infrastructure that provides dependable, consistent, pervasive, and inexpensive access to high-end computational capabilities [9]. The infrastructure is not limited to hardware and software but also includes people or intuitions as part of a Grid. Grid technologies enable large-scale sharing of resources within formal or informal consortia of individuals and/or institutions [4]. From a user perspective, the distributed heterogeneous resources are perceived as homogenous resources. Grid technologies are a basic precondition for the successful implementation of virtual organizations [16]. Virtual organizations offer potentials of flexibility and standardization at the same time by a mixture of market and hierarchy based coordination mechanisms [20]. Therefore, they are often referred to as hybrid organization forms [20, 34].

In order to realise the potentials of virtual organisations by grid computing, technological, methodological and organisational issues have to be taken into account. Business engineering concepts can integrate these three perspectives [35, 36] and be applied as a promising means for the design of grid based virtual organisations.

1.2.2 Foundations of Business Engineering

The field of "business engineering" emerged at the start of the 1990ies as a management trend. It aims at enriching existing approaches with respect to both the development of operational information systems and business strategies for process design [3, 21, 27]. From today's perspective, business engineering can be seen as a method and model-based design theory for businesses in the information age [28]. Using the methods and models made available by business engineering, business information systems can be designed, implemented, and adapted according to specific business needs. At the same time, improvements to business operations made possible by innovations in information technology (IT) are also targeted. Thus, the goal of business engineering is to systematically align business applications and operations with the help of engineering principles. These principles can be applied for the alignment of grids on the technological level and virtual organizations on the business logic level.

Nowadays, business processes have established themselves as the organizational objects of design for business engineering [6, 14]. Thus, with regard to corporate strategy, both the design of business processes and the analysis of the demands for their IT-support are of importance in business engineering projects aiming at the design of a grid based virtual organization. The design of business processes must follow a comprehensive approach encompassing the planning and the control, as well as the management of the operational workflows.

Information modelling has proved useful in supporting the systematic procedure in process design [11, 15, 19, 37]. Modelling techniques such as, for example, the "unified modeling language" (UML) [29] or the "event-driven process chain" (EPC) [18], serve as methodological approaches for the construction of models. Software tools for business process modelling, such as IBM Rational or the ARIS-Toolset, can support the business engineer by way of system components for the collection, design, analysis, and simulation of business process models for grid based virtual organizations.

The extensive demand for information models in business engineering warrants the need for reference modelling concepts. The intention of reference modelling is to systematically reuse information models in systems reengineering [32, 33]. To give a definition, a reference model is a special information model that can be reused in the design process of other business process models [33]. The approach is based on the finding that, despite various differences between design processes, general design patterns can be identified capable of solving design problems for a wide range of applications. Thus, the goal of reference models is to cover these general patterns in order to raise the efficiency and effectiveness of specific modelling processes [1, 8, 23, 30]. The reuse of reliable patterns in the context of grid based virtual organisations can enhance the flexibility to reconfigure a virtual organisation and at the same time safeguard the effectiveness and efficiency of the organisation and its grid infrastructure. To achieve these potentials for grid-based organisations, specific requirements have to be met by reference modelling approaches.

1.3 Reference Modelling as means of Business Engineering for Grid based Virtual Organizations

1.3.1 Requirements for Reference Modelling

The support of distributed actors within virtual organizations is a central requirement to be met by reference modelling in this context. The need for integrating infrastructure, methods and organization in reference models is another important requirement. In order to derive relevant fields of action in design projects of reference models for grid based virtual organisations, a specific framework can be applied [33]. Figure 1 presents an overview of this framework along with the fields of action for building an reference modelling infrastructure enabling the reuse of conceptual models in business engineering projects for grid based virtual organizations. The framework emphasizes the fact that the implementation of design processes is an interdisciplinary task. Thus, the work calls for contributions from various perspectives that must be integrated according to specific requirements and opportunities. This model particularly shows that apart from the methodological aspects of model design focused on in theory, contributions in the field of technological and organizational infrastructure are needed.

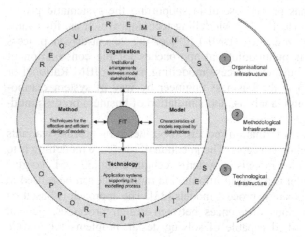

Fig. 1. Framework for the Design of Reference Modelling Infrastructures

Seen against the background of this framework, we can identify three fields of action for the design of an infrastructure for reference modelling:

Organizational Infrastructure: Relevant stakeholders in the modelling process must be identified and efficient ways of coordination between them established. In detail, this indicates the need to take into account the user's perspective at an early stage in the modelling process and provide coordination mechanism for distributed users and designers of reference models for grid based virtual organizations.

Methodological Infrastructure: Appropriate guidelines for describing business processes using models are needed. These guidelines should focus on certain characteristics which models should have in order to meet the requirements of grid based virtual organisations. Thus, rules are derived describing ways of building models accordingly.

Technological Infrastructure: In order to make use of reference modelling in practice, application systems supporting the settings considered relevant within the other fields are needed. From a methodological perspective, it is mainly the functionality of case tools that is addressed. Thus, available tools must be examined and used accordingly. In addition, seen from an organizational perspective, systems supporting various ways of cooperation are needed, e.g. knowledge management systems, work group systems, or project management systems.

Reference modelling situations are characterized by certain requirements and opportunities which direct the settings in the fields. In order to meet the situation properly, various interdependencies between the settings in the different fields must be taken into account. For example, the technological conditions in a grid have an effect as an enabler or as a restriction for both organizational and technical settings. Thus, the design follows a balanced manner, aiming at a so-called "fit of design". In the following, an example of a reference modelling infrastructure for grid based virtual organizations is introduced.

1.3.2 Collaborative Reference Modelling as an Infrastructure for Business Engineering

Introduction to Collaborative Reference Modelling

"Collaborative reference modelling" is a specific concept addressing reference modelling primarily from an organizational perspective. This reconciles with the intended purpose the design of patterns for grid based virtual organizations. Based on the organizational aspects, consecutive settings in the field of technological and methodological infrastructure can be derived. The essential idea of collaborative reference modelling is to share models with a greater range of shareholders in order to both continuously check and improve them from various perspectives. Accordingly, the infrastructure should provide efficient ways of transferring and discussing modelling results during the entire life cycle of certain business areas. Given such an infrastructure, both a division of labour and an increase in model quality could be achieved. As a result, an essential contribution to business engineering for grid based virtual organizations could be achieved in practice.

In order to design an appropriate infrastructure for collaborative reference modelling, efficient means of collaboration from an organizational perspective must first be analyzed. These findings then set the main requirements for the design of the technical infrastructure which is then used to implement the organizational processes in practice. In addition, findings in the field of methodological infrastructures can be derived which make the collaborative design of reference models in practice easier. The following passage briefly introduces these perspectives.

Organizational Infrastructure: Networking of Stakeholders

Corresponding to the intended application domain, grid based virtual organizations, mechanisms of network organizations [13, 20] can be applied in the organizational infrastructure of reference modelling. In particular, preliminary work in the field of organizing reuse-based engineering delivers insights on the organizational design [24, 26]. According to the transaction cost theory, the arrangements may be carried out by hierarchy, market or hybrid forms of coordination [2]. A deeper analysis of the alternatives to reference modelling [34] shows that the network organization, as a hybrid mode, is a promising means for reference modelling. On the one hand, it guarantees certain standardization necessary for developing shared mental models, while on the other, it leaves a critical degree of flexibility important for involving a wide range of stakeholders and possible network partners. On the basis of the AGIL-scheme [20], a brief outline of the underlying mechanisms can be given.

A strong impact on coordination comes from the individual return each stakeholder expects from his or her participation in the network. In particular, suppliers of reference models face a wide range of customers, whereas the customers themselves profit from transparency over a greater range of models. The design of reference models can focus on highly specialized solutions which significantly contribute to model quality. Thanks to a stronger coupling compared to markets, people tend to establish a common understanding of their business in networks. In reference modelling, this gives way to the establishment of shared mental models pertaining to the semantic context of an application domain. Whereas the information system infrastructure provides a methodology for describing the semantic context, its design and application are carried out on an organizational level. This shared context is vital for efficient collaboration, because the understanding of models is strongly influenced by personal perception. Due to the history of shared experiences, social relations evolve in networks. These relations are helpful in order in modelling projects. Assets, such as the reputation of stakeholders, give ground for vague requirements specifications which facilitate flexible responses in a dynamically changing environment. This way, both the quality and the efficiency of the design, are supported.

The actual organizational design of a specific design project for grid based virtual organization has to be determined on the coordination structures within the network. Depended on the distribution of power in the network (e.g. centre focused networks) a suitable mix of coordination mechanisms has to be incorporated.

Technological Infrastructure: Collaborative Platforms

To support distributed stakeholders within a network, information systems which support model sharing need to be implemented [12]. In particular, this means the support of processes for both exchanging and discussing models within a shared semantic context. The essential functionality is illustrated in Figure 2 with an example for a prototypical implementation (see www.herbie-group.de).

Features for exchanging models, i.e. the up- and downloading of models on a shared repository, build the foundation for the collaborative design. Internet-technology offers promising means for accessing the repository in a flexible manner via a web-browser. Based on standard exchange-formats like XML, higher-level formats complying with the syntax of modelling languages are path leading. For the language of EPC for example, the format EPML is provided [22]. Standards like WebDAV make it possible to integrate the platform with local file-servers which facilitate the processes of model exchange. Beyond the technical aspects, it is essential to capture the semantics of the models to be shared on the platform [25]. For this purpose, feature-based techniques can be applied. Apart from the area of domain engineering [17], these techniques are subject to the field of knowledge management, especially information retrieval. In this field, quite a number of appropriate techniques are being developed, ranging from simple taxonomies to more complex anthologies [5, 38]. However, the appropriate application of these methods in practice still seems to be challenging.

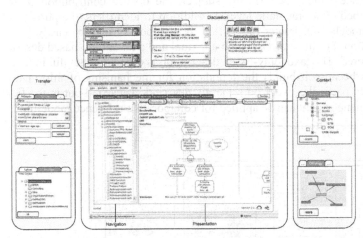

Fig. 2. Elements of a Collaborative Platform for Reference Modelling

Services for discussing models are needed in order to support the continuous improvement of the reference models disseminated on the platform. In contrast to conventional community platforms, these services should be made available in relation to each single model. In reference modeling, such a close connection is essential for directing the discussion towards special contributions and thereby, increasing the efficiency of the collaboration. To support individual preferences, various channels of communication should be offered for each model, including newsgroups (asynchronous communication) and chat rooms (synchronous communication).

Methodological Infrastructure: The Encapsulation of Models

Based on the organizational structure and the technology in use, methodological aspects have to be taken into account as well when designing reference models for grid based virtual organizations. To integrate the different relevant perspectives on virtual organizations (infrastructure, methods and organization) also different model types have to be integrated in a reference model. For example, UML and EPC models can be distributed one by one. However, the efficiency of sharing the models could be increased by encapsulating them according to certain standards [33]. An example of such a standard is shown in Figure 3. The framework incorporates principles from component-based software engineering [24, 31]. Essentially multiple models must be structured in such a way that a combination of them fulfils a certain modelling purpose. In addition, a description of the collection is given which serves to hide implementation details and to identify models by their essential semantic contribution. For this purpose, the framework provides interfaces on multiple layers: in detail, there are interfaces which specify the overall subject, the content provided to cover it and the representation available describing the content.

In the interface which specifies the subject, the overall contribution of the model is described on a pragmatic level. In addition to identifiers, the purpose of the collected models is characterized so that the component may be easily found by its contribution. For this purpose, both a textual and a taxonomy-based description are considered. The taxonomy-based description is especially helpful in large-scale networks because it builds the foundation for mechanisms of information retrieval [24]. In particular, work on semantic descriptions carried out in the field of knowledge management can be applied for collaborative reference modelling.

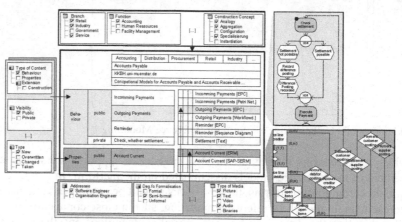

Fig. 3. Encapsulating Reference Models as Components

According to this type of specification, the component shown in Figure 3 is characterized by the framework to provide "Conceptual Models for Accounts Payable and Accounts Receivable..." a pattern that can be applied for a large variety of grid based virtual organizations.

The content that is necessary for fulfilling the overall purpose of the component is specified by an additional interface on a more detailed layer. In this interface, items of the taxonomy serve to differentiate content regarding various views in information modelling. On the basis of systems-thinking, focusing on either the behaviour or the properties of a described system can differentiate models. Further differentiations can be implemented by the taxonomy, including either a wider or a more detailed set of views. The component describing "accounts payable", for example, needs descriptions of behavioural aspects from the processing of "Incoming Payments" and "Outgoing Payments", as well as from "Reminders". As a foundation, properties described in the "Account Current" are needed.

In a collaborative environment, the content of each type can be represented in various modelling languages because stakeholders have different preferences. Therefore, a special interface must be created which specifies the representations available. The semantic description serves to characterize the stockholder's perspective for which a representation is made. The ERM representing the "Account

Current", for example, addresses "Software Engineers". Additional rules are required to support the integration of models in order to ensure a consistency in construction.

1.4 Conclusion and Further Research

Grid computing enables the evolvement of virtual organizations by delivering an appropriate infrastructure. Concepts of Business Engineering especially conceptual business process modelling can be applied in order to link the technological infrastructure with the business logic of a virtual organization. In order to enhance flexibility and safeguard effectiveness and efficiency of cooperation at the same time reference modelling is a promising means by reusing reliable patterns. Based on the specific design situation certain requirements have to be met by infrastructures for reference modelling in this context. Two requirements are essential to be met: (1) support of distributed actors and (2) integration of technological, methodological and organizational aspects. Both requirements can be met by applying collaborative reference modelling for purposes of business engineering for grid based virtual organizations. The application of collaborative reference modelling for this specific purpose is illustrated by an example in this article. By this, an integration of design and use processes of grid infrastructures and virtual organizations can be achieved.

Beside this integration, an integration of semantic structures can facilitate the design and application of reference models for virtual organizations. These structures can be applied as blueprints for collaborative knowledge management processes within virtual organizations and enhance the efficiency of cooperative business processes. Further research should focus on this integration and its automated support by application systems. Alike questions of profitability in reference modelling should be addressed in future work.

References

1. Becker J, et al (2004) Configurative Process Modeling – Outlining an Approach to Increased Business Process Model Usability. in Proceedings of the 2004 Information Resources Management Association Conference
2. Coase RH (1937) The Nature of the Firm. Economica, 4 (11): pp 386–405
3. Cornes R (1990) Business systems design and development. NY: Prentice Hall
4. Czajkowski K, Fitzgerald S, Foster I, Kesselman C (2001) Grid Information Services for Distributed Resource Sharing. Proceedings of the Tenth IEEE International Symposium on High-Performance Distributed Computing (HPDC–10), IEEE Press, August 2001
5. Daconta MC, Obrst LJ, Smith KT (2003) The Semantic Web: A Guide to the Future of XML, Web Services and Knowledge Management. Indianapolis
6. Davenport TH (1993) Process Innovation: Reengineering Work through Information Technology. Boston, MA: Harvard Business School Press

7. David P, Anderson J, Cobb E, Korpela M, Lebofsky, Werthimer D (2002) SETI@home An Experiment in Public-Resource Computing. *COMMUNICATIONS OF THE ACM*, November 2002/Vol. 45, No. 11
8. Fettke P, Loos P (2003) Classification of reference models – a methodology and its application. Information Systems and e-Business Management, 1(1): pp 35–53
9. Foster I, Kesselman C (eds.) (1999) The Grid: Blueprint for a New Computting Infrastructure. Morgan Kaufmann
10. Foster I, Kesselman C, Tuecke S (2001) The Anatomy of the Grid: Enabling Scalable Virtual Organizations International J. Supercomputer Applications, 15(3)
11. Fowler M (1997) Analysis patterns: Reusable object models. Menlo Park CA: Addison Wesley
12. Gomaa H (1995) Domain modeling methods and environments. ACM SIGSOFT Software Engineering Notes, 20(SI): pp 256–258
13. Håkansson H (1989) Corporate Technological Behaviour, Co-operation and Networks. London et al
14. Hammer M, Champy J (1993) Reengineering the corporation: A manifesto for business revolution. London: Brealey
15. Hay DC (2003) Requirements analysis: from business views to architecture. Upper Saddle River, NJ: Prentice Hall PTR
16. Joseph J, Fellenstein C (2004) Grid Computing. Prentice Hall, Upper Saddle River (NJ)
17. Kang K, C, et al (1998) FORM: A feature-oriented reuse method with domain-specific reference architectures. Annals of Software Engineering, 5: pp 143–168
18. Keller G, Nüttgens M, Scheer AW (1992) Semantische Prozeßmodellierung auf der Grundlage "Ereignisgesteuerter Prozeßketten (EPK), in Veröffentlichungen des Instituts für Wirtschaftsinformatik der Universität des Saarlandes (in German). AW Scheer: Saarbrücken
19. Kilov H (2002) Business models: a guide for business and IT. Upper Saddle River: Prentice Hall
20. Klein S (1993) A Conceptual Model of Interorganizational Networks – A Parsonsian Perspective. In ESF-Conference "Forms of Inter-Organizational Networks: Structures and Processes". Berlin
21. Kruse C, et al (1993) Ways of Utilizing Reference Models for Data Engineering. CIM, International Journal of Flexible Automation and Integrated Manufacturing, 1(1): pp 47–58
22. Mendling J, Nüttgens M (2004) XML-based Reference Modelling: Foundations of an EPC Markup Language, in Referenzmodellierung, Becker J and Delfmann P (eds). Heidelberg. pp 19–49
23. Mertins K, Bernus P (2006) Reference Models, in Handbook on Architectures of Information Systems, P Bernus, K Mertins, and G Schmidt (eds). Springer-Verlag: Berlin et al. pp 665–667
24. Mili H, et al (2002) Reuse-Based Software Engineering. New York
25. Mili H, Mili F, Mili A (1995) Reusing Software: Issues and Research Directions. IEEE Transactions on Software Engineering, 21(6): pp 528–562
26. Ommering Rv (2002) Building product populations with software components. In Proceedings of the 24th International Conference on Software Engineering. Orlando, Florida: ACM Press
27. Österle H (1995) Business in the information age: Heading for new processes. Berlin: Springer
28. Österle H, Winter R (2003) Business Engineering, in Business Engineering: Auf dem Weg zum Unternehmen des Informationszeitalters, H Österle and R Winter (eds). Springer: Berlin. pp 3–19 (in German)

29. Rumbaugh J, Jacobson I, Booch G (2004) The Unified Modeling Language reference manual. 2nd edn Addison-Wesley Longman Ltd. 550
30. Scheer AW, Nüttgens M (2000) ARIS Architecture and Reference Models for Business Process Management, in Business Process Management – Models, Techniques, and Empirical Studies, Wvd Aalst, J Desel, and A Oberweis (eds). Berlin et al. pp 376–389
31. Szyperski C (1998) Component Software. Beyond Object-Oriented Programming. Vol. 2nd. New York: ACM Press and Addison-Wesley
32. Thomas O (2005) Understanding the Term Reference Model in Information System Research. in First International Workshop on Business Process Reference Models (BPRM′05). Nancy, France
33. vom Brocke J (2003) Referenzmodellierung, Gestaltung und Verteilung von Konstruktionsprozessen (in German). Berlin
34. vom Brocke J, Buddendick C (2004) Organisationsformen in der Referenzmodellierung – Forschungsbedarf und Gestaltungsempfehlungen auf Basis der Transaktionskostentheorie. Wirtschaftsinformatik, 46(5): pp 341–352
35. vom Brocke J, Thomas O (2006) Reference Modeling for Organizational Change: Applying Collaborative Techniques for Business Engineering. in: Proceedings of the 12th AMCIS; Acapulco, México, Atlanta, Georgia, USA: AIS, pp 680–688
36. vom Brocke J; Thomas O (2006) Designing Infrastructures for Reusing Conceptional Models – A General Framework and its Application for Collaborative Reference Modeling. In: Lecture Notes in Informatics, LNI P–85, EDS.: W Abramowicz, HC Mayr, pp 501–514
37. Wand Y, Weber R (2002) Research Commentary: Information Systems and Conceptual Modeling – A Research Agenda. Information Systems Research, 13(4): pp 363–376
38. Whitman L, Ramachandran K, Ketkar V (2001) A taxonomy of a living model of the enterprise. Proceedings of the 33nd conference on Winter simulation. Arlington, Virginia: IEEE Computer Society. pp 848–855

2 Approaches for Business Process Model Complexity Metrics

Volker Gruhn, Ralf Laue

Chair of Applied Telematics / e-Business*
Computer Science Faculty, University of Leipzig, Germany
{gruhn,laue}@ebus.informatik.uni-leipzig.de

2.1 Introduction

One of the main purposes for developing business process models (BPM) is to support the communication between the stakeholders in the software development process (domain experts, business process analysts, software developers to name just a few). To fulfill this purpose, the models should be easy to understand and easy to maintain. If we want to create models that are easy to understand, at first we have to define what "easy to understand" means: We are interested in complexity metrics, i.e. measurements that can tell us whether a model is easy or difficult to understand. In the latter case, we may conclude from the metrics that the model should be re-engineered, for example by decomposing it into simpler modules.

A significant amount of research has been done on the complexity of software programs, and software complexity metrics have been used successfully for purposes like predicting the error rate, estimating maintenance costs or identifying pieces of software that should be re-engineered. In this paper, we discuss how the ideas known from software complexity research can be used for analyzing the complexity of BPMs. To our best knowledge, there is rather few published work about this subject. In 2002, Latva-Koivisto[1] was the first one who suggested to study BPM complexity metrics, but this paper discussed rather simple BPM languages (like process charts) only.

Cardoso[2] (whose approach we discuss in section 2.4) was the first author who addressed the problems of measuring the complexity of more expressive BPM languages. Following this pioneering work, other authors have published about this

---

* The Chair of Applied Telematics / e-Business is endowed by Deutsche Telekom AG.

W. Abramowicz and H.C. Mayr (eds.), Technologies for Business Information Systems, 13–24.

topic recently: [3] presented a suite of metrics for the evaluation of BPMN models. They suggested some counting and relationship metrics (like "total number of tasks"). Cardoso et al. [4] published a paper which has quite a lot of similarities with our work. [5] presented the first extensive quantitative analysis of BPM complexity metrics. They related several complexity metrics to the number of errors found in BPMs in the SAP R/3 reference model. Such results are very valuable for assessing the suitability of complexity metrics. [6] was the first paper that discusses BPM complexity metrics that are related not only to the control flow, but also to the data flow and resource utilization.

In this article, we want to give an overview about factors that have an influence on the complexity of the control flow of a BPM and metrics that can be used to measure these factors. Validation of the proposed metrics in a case study is beyond of the scope of this paper and has to be done in future research. Also we restrict our discussion to the control flow of the BPM, neglecting other aspects like data flow and resource utilization.

In the following sections, we discuss well-known complexity metrics for software programs and their adaptation to BPMs. After introducing the notation of event driven process chains in section 2.2, section 2.3 discusses the *Lines of Code* as the simplest complexity metric. Metrics which take into account the control flow and the structure of a model are discussed in sections 2.4 and 2.5. Section 2.6 presents metrics which measure the cognitive effort to comprehend a model. Metrics for BPMs that are decomposed into modules are discussed in section 2.7. Finally, section 2.8 gives a summary about the metrics and their usage for analyzing the complexity of BPMs.

2.2 The BPM Language EPC

The metrics discussed in this paper are independent from the modeling language. They can be used for models in various formalisms, for example event driven process chains[7], UML activity diagrams[8], BPMN[9] or YAWL[10]. Of course, these graphical languages have different expressiveness. This paper discusses only those elements which can be found in all languages. Additional research would be necessary to address advanced concepts that are supported by some but not all business process modeling languages. In particular, the use of concepts like Exceptions, Cancellation or Compensation can increase the difficulty of a BPM considerably.

If we have to depict a BPM in this article, we use the notation of event driven process chains[7], mainly because of its simplicity. EPCs consist of functions (activities which need to be executed, depicted as rounded boxes), events (pre- and postconditions before / after a function is executed, depicted as hexagons) and connectors (which can split or join the flow of control between the elements). Arcs between these elements represent the control flow. The connectors are used to model parallel and alternative executions. There are two kinds of connectors: Splits have one incoming and at least two outgoing arcs, joins have at least two incoming arcs and one outgoing arc.

AND-connectors (depicted as $\left(\wedge\right)$) are used to model parallel execution. When an AND-split is executed, the elements on all outgoing arcs have to be executed in parallel. The corresponding AND-join connector waits until all parallel control flows that have been started are finished.

XOR-connectors (depicted as $\left(\times\right)$) can be used to model alternative execution: A XOR-split has multiple outgoing arcs, but only one of them will be processed. The corresponding XOR-join waits for the completion of the control flow on the selected arc.

Finally, OR-connectors (depicted as $\left(\vee\right)$) are used to model parallel execution of one or more flows. An OR-split starts the processing of one or more of its outgoing arcs. The corresponding OR-join waits until all control flows that have been started by the OR-split are finished.

2.3 Size of the Model: Lines of Code

The easiest complexity measurement for software is the "lines of code" (LOC) count which represents the program size. While for assembler programs a line of code is the same as an instruction statement, for programs written in a high-level programming language, the LOC count usually refers to the number of executable statements (ignoring comments, line breaks etc.)[11].

For BPMs, the number of activities in the model can be regarded as an equivalent to the number of executable statements in a piece of software. Additionally, [4] suggests variants of this metric that count join and split connectors as well. "Number of Activities" and "Number of Activities and Connectors" are simple, easy to understand measures for the size of a BPM. However, those metrics do not take into account the structure of the model: A BPM with 50 activities may be written using a well-structured control flow which is easy to understand or in an unstructured way which makes understanding very hard. For this reason, we will discuss other metrics which measure the complexity of the control flow.

2.4 Control Flow Complexity of the Model: McCabe-Metric

The cyclomatic number, introduced by McCabe[12], is one of the most widely used software metrics. It is calculated from the control flow graph and measures the number of linearly-independent paths through a program. For a formal definition, we refer to the literature[11, 12]; informally it is sufficient to say that the cyclomatic number is equal to the number of binary decisions (for example IF-statements in a

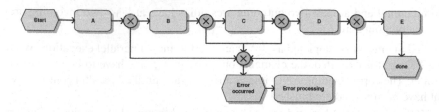

Fig. 1. "almost linear" model with CFC=8

programming language) plus 1. Non-binary decisions (for example `select` or `case`-statements in a programming language) with n possible results are counted as n-1 binary decisions.

The cyclomatic number measures the number of all possible control flows in a program. For this reason, a low cyclomatic number indicates that the program is easy to understand and to modify. The cyclomatic number is also an indicator of testability, because it corresponds to the number of test cases needed to achieve full path coverage. [13] found that there is a significant correlation between the cyclomatic number of a piece of software and its defect level.

Cardoso[2] has suggested a complexity measure for BPMs which is a generalization of McCabe's cyclomatic number. The control-flow complexity of processes (CFC) as defined by Cardoso is the number of mental states that have to be considered when a designer develops a process. Analogously to the cyclomatic number which is equal to the number of binary decisions plus 1, the corresponding CFC metric for BPMs counts the number of decisions in the flow of control. Every split in the model adds to the number of possible decisions as follows:

- AND-split: As always *all* transitions outgoing from an AND-split must be processed, the designer needs only to consider one state as the result of the execution of an AND-split. For this reason, every AND-split in a model adds 1 to the CFC metric of this model.
- XOR-split with n outgoing transitions: Exactly one from n possible paths must be taken, i.e. the designer has to consider n possible states that may arise from the execution of the XOR-split. For this reason, every XOR-split with n outgoing transitions adds n to the CFC metric of this model.
- OR-split with n outgoing transitions: There are $2^n - 1$ possibilities to process at least one and at most n of the outgoing transitions of an OR-split, i.e. every OR-split with n outgoing transitions adds $2^n - 1$ to the CFC metric.

[2] reports the result of a first (yet rather small) experiment to verify the validity of the CFC metric: A correlation was found between the "perceived complexity" as rated by students and the CFC metric. On the other hand, [5] has found that the CFC metric seems to have no impact on the odds of an error in a BMP model. A possible reason for this negative result is that just counting the number of possible decisions

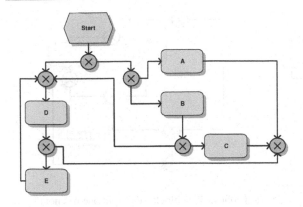

Fig. 2. "unstructured" model with CFC=8

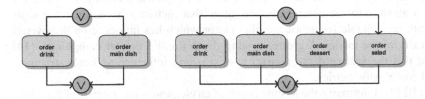

Fig. 3. Two models which different CFC metrics

in a model gives only little information about its structure. For example, compare the BPMs in Fig. 1 and Fig. 2. For both models, the CFC is 8, because they contain the same number of binary decisions. Nevertheless, the "almost linear" model in Fig. 1 is much easier to understand.

As another example, Fig. 3 shows two models with one OR split/join-block. The left one has a CFC of 3, the right one a CFC of 15. If we want to measure the difficulty to comprehend a model, this difference seems to be unjustified.

To overcome these shortcomings, we will discuss other metrics in the next sections. These metrics take into account the structure of the BPM. They can be used additionally to the CFC metric.

2.5 Structure of the Model: Nesting Depth and Jumps out of a Control Structure

Both models depicted in Fig. 1 and Fig. 2 have a CFC metric of 8. However, there should be no doubt that Fig. 1 shows a much less complex model than Fig. 2. One reason for this lies in the fact that that Fig. 1 shows an "almost linear" flow of

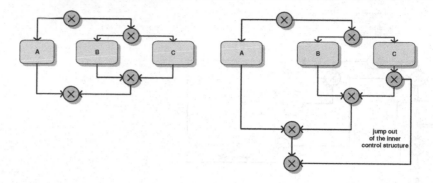

Fig. 4. The left model has properly nested control flow blocks, the right one has not

control while in Fig. 2, there are several nested XOR-splits and XOR-joins. From the research about software complexity, we know that metrics that measure the nesting depth are suitable for measuring this factor which has influence on the overall complexity of the model: A greater nesting depth implies greater complexity. [14] showed that the nesting depth metrics have a strong influence on other structure-related complexity metrics.

For BPMs, informally, the nesting depth of an element is the number of decisions in the control flow that are necessary to reach this element. Formal definitions can be found in [15] and [16].

The maximum nesting depth in Fig. 1 is 1 (every error leads to the error handling process); the model in Fig. 2 has a maximum nesting depth of 3 (because three decisions must be made in order to process action C). Using this metric, we conclude that Fig. 2 shows a more complex model than Fig. 1. The nesting depth metric can be calculated additionally to the CFC metric that has been discussed in the last section.

We have to note that the use of the term "nesting depth" is a little bit misleading. Other than modern structured programming languages, common graph-oriented business modeling languages (for example UML activity diagrams[8] or YAWL[10]) do not require proper nesting, i.e. splits and joins does not have to occur pairwise. This is comparable with programming languages that do not only allow structured loops (like `repeat...until` etc.) but also arbitrary `GOTO`-jumps. Not without a reason, [17] writes that "the current unstructured style of business process modeling, which we can call spaghetti business process modeling, leads to similar problems as spaghetti coding".

If we are asking for the complexity of a BPM, we must take into account these difficulties that arise from splits and joins that do not occur pairwise in well-nested constructs.

As an example, Fig. 4 shows two similar models. The splits and joins in the left one are properly nested – the inner control structure (XOR-split/XOR-join) is contained completely within the outer control structure. In the right model, there is a jump out of the inner control block, and this jumps leads to a target "behind" the outer control structure. For this reason, we call the left model well-structured while the right one is not well-structured. A formal definition of "well-structuredness" in terms of Petri net terminology was given by van der Aalst[18].

For software programs, [19] introduced the *knot count* metric for measuring such (undesirable) jumps out of and into a structured control flow. A control graph of a program has a knot whenever the paths associated with transfer of control interemph. For example, this is the case for the control flow graph shown in Fig. 5.

Fig. 5. Control flow with a knot

Informally, unstructuredness means that there is a misfit between split and join connectors in a BPM. The split-join-ratio (number of splits divided by the number of joins) was proposed in [5] for measuring this misfit. However, a weakness of this metric is that unstructuredness in one part of the BPM that results in a too high (i.e. greater than 1) split-join-ratio can be "corrected" by inserting another unstructured element into the model which has a too small (i.e. smaller than 1) split-join-ratio.

While the split-join-ratio is obviously too simple to serve as a good metric for unstructuredness, a formal definition of a metrics that cover all relevant aspects of unstructuredness is less trivial than expected at a first glance. We are currently preparing a research paper about this topic where we will define a metric that can count the possible reasons for unstructuredness, i.e.

1. Splits without well-defined corresponding join and joins without well-defined corresponding split.
2. Mismatch between the type of a split and its corresponding join (An example is an XOR-split that activates exactly one of many possible branches together with an AND-join that waits for completion of *all* branches.)
3. Cycles with more than one entry point or more than one exit point
4. Cycles with exit- or entry points which are not "XOR" connectors

In general, using not well-structured models as the one in Fig. 4 can be regarded as bad modeling style which makes understanding of the model more complicate. Mostly, it is possible to redesign such models by using well-structured ones[20]. For example, the language BPEL4WS[21] or the workflow management system ADEPT[22] have semantic restrictions which force the modeler to build well-structured models.[1] For such models, the "unstructuredness metric" should always

---

[1] It is worth mentioning that the UML 2.0 specification does not require anymore that forks and joins must occur pairwise, which was necessary in the version 1.0 of the standard. We

be 0, just as the knot count metric is always 0 for programs written in a structured programming language.

2.6 Comprehensiveness of the model: Cognitive Complexity Metrics

In section 2.4, we have used two examples to illustrate shortcomings of the CFC[2] metric. The additional metrics proposed in section 2.5 are helpful for the example depicted in Fig. 1 and Fig. 2. They could be used in addition to the CFC metric.

Now let's have a look at the other example (Fig. 3). Both models show a control structure in which one or more paths are executed in parallel. If we define complexity as "difficulty to test" (i.e. number of test cases needed to achieve full path coverage), the CFC metric does a perfect job. However, we argue that this metric is less useful if we define complexity as "difficulty to *understand* a model": The number of control flow paths between the OR-split and the OR-join has not too much influence on the effort that is necessary to comprehend this control structure. Regardless of whether there are 2, 4 or 10 control flow paths between the split and the join, the person who reads the model will always understand everything between the OR-split and the OR-join as only *one control structure*. We think that this is the main reason behind the result published in [5] where it has been found that the CFC metric seems to have no impact on the odds of an error in a BMP model.

Shao and Wang [23] defined the cognitive weight as a metric to measure the effort required for comprehending a piece of software. They defined *cognitive weights* for basic control structures as a measure for the difficulty to understand this control structure. For example, the call of a user-defined function has a cognitive weight of 2 while the execution of control flows in parallel has a cognitive weight of 4.

The cognitive weight of a software component without nested control structures is defined as the sum of the cognitive weights of its control structures. It seems to be a promising approach to use the ideas from [23] to define cognitive weights for BPMs. If we want to do so, we have to consider the fact that BPMs may be modeled in an unstructured way as discussed in section 2.5. Also, we have to take into account some differences between BPM and software: For example, it is necessary to consider specific concepts like cancellation or the multi-choice-pattern[24]. We have suggested an adaptation of the cognitive metrics to (well-structured) BPMs in [25]. [25] outlines the basic ideas for a cognitive weight for BPMs which still need to be validated in experiments. This will be subject of our further research.

The idea behind cognitive weights is to regard basic control structures as *patterns* that can be understood by the reader as a whole. A similar idea has been proposed by [26]. This approach is based on automatically finding well-known architectural

---

do not think that this can be seen as a progress towards better understandable models with less errors.

patterns (for example from [27]) in a UML model. The idea behind this approach is that well-documented patterns have been found highly mature and using them helps to improve code quality, understandability and maintainability. Obviously, this assertion should be regarded with care: Architectural patterns are only useful if they are used by experienced programmers in the right way, and an extensive use of patterns does not have to mean anything for the quality of the code. So, if the approach from [26] is used, a deep knowledge about the patterns and their correct usage is necessary.

However, [26] does not only discuss the use of "good" design patterns, it also recognizes so called anti-patterns, i.e. commonly occurring solutions to a problem that are known to have negative consequences. If such an anti-pattern is found in the code, this can be regarded as a sign of bad programming.

It seems to be appealing to us to use the ideas from [26] in the context of business process models. In particular, finding anti-patterns should be very useful in order to uncover bad modeling style. An example for such an anti-pattern for BPMs is the *Implicit Termination* pattern as described in [24]. (Implicit Termination means that a process should be terminated if nothing else is to do - without modeling an explicit end state, see [24] for details).

2.7 Modularization of the Model: Fan-in / Fan-out-Metrics

Modular modeling of business processes is supported by all major BPM languages (for example by nested activity diagrams in UML, sub-processes in BPMN, composite tasks in YAWL or hierarchical event-driven process chains).

Dividing a BPM into modular sub-models cannot only help to make the BPM easier to understand, it can also lead to smaller, reusable models.

For analyzing the modularization of a BPM, we can adapt the ideas of Henry and Kafura[28] who developed metrics for reasoning about the structure of modularized software systems. They measure the fan-in and fan out for every module, where *fan-in* is a count of all other modules that call a given module and *fan-out* is a count of all other modules that are called from the model under investigation. Usually, the modules with a large fan-in are small submodules doing some simple job that is needed by a lot of other modules. On the other hand, the modules with a large fan-out are large modules on the higher layers of the design structure. If a module with both large fan-in and fan-out is detected, this may indicate that a re-design could improve the model. [28] suggests the metric $((fan - in) \cdot (fan - out))^2$ in order to measure this kind of structural complexity.

This metric can be used in the same way for analyzing BPMs: If a sub-model of a BPM has a high structural complexity according to the fan-in/fan-out metric, they will be difficult to use and are most likely poorly designed.

Table 1. Complexity metrics for software and BPM

software complexity metric	corresponding metric for BPM	usage, significance
Lines of Code	number of activities (and connectors)	very simple, does not take into account the control-flow
cyclomatic number [12]	CFC as defined by Cardoso [2]	measures the number of possible control flow decisions, well-suited for measuring the number of test cases needed to test the model, does not take into account other structure-related information
nesting depth	nesting depth	provides information about structure
knot-count [19]	counting the "reasons for unstructuredness"	measure of "well-structuredness" (for example jumps out of or into control-flow structures) is always 0 for well-structured models
cognitive weight[23]	cognitive weight (tailored for BPM)[25]	measures the cognitive effort to understand a model, can indicate that a model should be re-designed
(Anti)Patterns [29]	(Anti)Patterns for BPM	experience with the patterns needed counting the usage of anti-patterns in a BPM can help to detect poor modeling
Fan-in / Fan-out [28]	Fan-in / Fan-out	can indicate poor modularization

2.8 Conclusion and Directions for Future Research

Table 1 summarizes the results from the past sections: Metrics for measuring the complexity of *software* are compared to corresponding metrics for *business process models*. Also, we assess the significance of these metrics for BPM. As the metrics in the left column of the table have been proved to be useful for measuring the complexity of software, we expect that the corresponding metrics in the second column will be useful for measuring the complexity of BPMs. It is one aim of our future research to validate this expectation.

Due to the number of factors that contribute to the complexity of a BPM, we cannot identify a single metric that measures all aspects of a model's complexity. This situation is well-known from the measuring of software complexity. A common solution is to associate different metrics within a metrics suite. Each individual metric in the suite measures one aspect of the complexity, and together they give a more accurate overview. For BPMs, the CFC as defined by Cardoso[2] or a cognitive weight metric (tailored to BPM) seems to be suitable to give some kind of "general" information about the complexity of a BPM. Nesting depth can be used complementary to both CFC and cognitive weight. Additionally, measuring unstructuredness and counting anti-patterns are useful to uncover bad modeling style, modeling errors and models that are difficult to understand. The fan-in/fan-out metrics can be used to evaluate the decomposition of the model into sub-models.

All metrics discussed in this article can be easily computed by a machine. Also, they are independent from the modeling language, because they use "high-level" information from the control flow graph of the BPM only.

The layout of a graphical model (for example the alignment of the edges of graphical elements) and the comprehensiveness of the texts used in the model are aspects of complexity that cannot be measured with the metrics discussed in this article.

Some metrics can instantly be used for analyzing BPM, namely the number of activities, Cardoso's CFC[2], the nesting depth and the fan-in/fan-out metrics. For defining and using cognitive weights, patterns and anti-patterns, further tailoring to the demands of BPM is necessary. This will be the subject of our ongoing research.

References

1. A. Latva-Koivisto, "Finding a complexity measure for business process models," tech. rep., Systems Analysis Laboratory, Helsinki University of Technology, 2002.
2. J. Cardoso, "How to measure the control-flow complexity of web processes and workflows," in *The Workflow Handbook*, pp. 199–212, 2005.
3. E. Rolón, F. Ruiz, F. García, and M. Piattini, "Towards a suite of metrics for business process models in BPMN," in *8th International Conference on Enterprise Information Systems, Paphos, Cyprus*, 2006.
4. J. Cardoso, J. Mendling, G. Neumann, and H. Reijers, "A discourse on complexity of process models," in *Proceedings of the BPM 2006 Workshops, Workshop on Business Process Design BPI 2006, Vienna, Austria*, 2006.
5. J. Mendling, M. Moser, G. Neumann, H. Verbeek, B. F. van Dongen, and W. M. van der Aalst, "A quantitative analysis of faulty EPCs in the SAP reference model," Tech. Rep. BPM-06-08, BPM Center Report, BPMcenter.org, 2006.
6. J. Cardoso, "Complexity analysis of BPEL web processes," *Software Process:Improvement and Practice Journal*, to appear 2006.
7. W. M. van der Aalst, "Formalization and verification of event-driven process chains.," *Information & Software Technology*, vol. 41, no. 10, pp. 639–650, 1999.
8. Object Management Group, "UML 2.0 Superstructure Final Adopted Specification," tech. rep., 2003.
9. Business Process Management Initiative, "Business Process Modeling Notation," tech. rep., BPMI.org, 2004.
10. W. M. van der Aalst and A. Hofstede, "YAWL: Yet another workflow language," Tech. Rep. FIT-TR-2002-06, Queensland University of Technology, Brisbane, 2002.
11. S. H. Kan, *Metrics and Models in Software Quality Engineering*. Boston, MA, USA: Addison-Wesley Longman Publishing Co., Inc., 2002.
12. T. J. McCabe, "A complexity measure," *IEEE Trans. Software Eng.*, vol. 2, no. 4, pp. 308–320, 1976.
13. R. B. Grady, "Successfully applying software metrics," *Computer*, vol. 27, no. 9, pp. 18–25, 1994.
14. A. Schroeder, "Integrated program measurement and documentation tools," in *ICSE '84: Proceedings of the 7th international conference on Software engineering*, (Piscataway, NJ, USA), pp. 304–313, IEEE Press, 1984.

15. W. A. Harrison and K. I. Magel, "A complexity measure based on nesting level," *SIGPLAN Not.*, vol. 16, no. 3, pp. 63–74, 1981.

16. P. Piwowarski, "A nesting level complexity measure," *SIGPLAN Not.*, vol. 17, no. 9, pp. 44–50, 1982.

17. A. Holl and G. Valentin, "Structured business process modeling (SBPM)," in *Information Systems Research in Scandinavia (IRIS 27) (CD-ROM)*, 2004.

18. W. M. van der Aalst, "The Application of Petri Nets to Workflow Management," *The Journal of Circuits, Systems and Computers*, vol. 8, no. 1, pp. 21–66, 1998.

19. M. R. Woodward, M. A. Hennell, and D. Hedley, "A measure of control-flow complexity in program text," *IEEE Transactions on Software Engineering*, vol. SE-5, no. 1, pp. 45–50, 1979.

20. B. Kiepuszewski, A. H. M. ter Hofstede, and C. Bussler, "On structured workflow modelling," in *Conference on Advanced Information Systems Engineering*, pp. 431–445, 2000.

21. T. Andrews, "Business process execution language for web services," 2003.

22. M. Reichert and P. Dadam, "ADEPTflex -supporting dynamic changes of workflows without losing control," *Journal of Intelligent Information Systems*, vol. 10, no. 2, pp. 93–129, 1998.

23. J. Shao and Y. Wang, "A new measure of software complexity based on cognitive weights," *IEEE Canadian Journal of Electrical and Computer Engineering*, vol. 28, no. 2, pp. 69–74, 2003.

24. W. M. van der Aalst, A. Hofstede, B. Kiepuszewski, and A. Barros, "Workflow patterns," *Distributed and Parallel Databases*, vol. 14, no. 3, 2003.

25. V. Gruhn and R. Laue, "Adopting the cognitive complexity measure for business process models," in *Fifth IEEE International Conference on Cognitive Informatics, Beijing, China*, pp. 236–241, IEEE Computer Society, 2006.

26. J. Gustafsson, "Metrics calculation in MAISA," 2000.

27. E. Gamma, R. Helm, R. Johnson, and J. Vlissides, "Design patterns: Abstraction and reuse of object-oriented design," *Lecture Notes in Computer Science*, vol. 707, pp. 406–431, 1993.

28. S. Henry and K. Kafura, "Software structure metrics based on information flow," *IEEE Transactions on Software Engineering*, vol. 7(5), pp. 510–518, 1981.

29. J. Paakki, A. Karhinen, J. Gustafsson, L. Nenonen, and A. I. Verkamo, "Software metrics by architectural pattern mining," in *Proc. International Conference on Software: Theory and Practice*, pp. 325–332, 2000.

3 Characterization and Tool Supported Selection of Business Process Modeling Methodologies

Roland Kaschek[1], Roman Pavlov[2], Vladimir A. Shekhovtsov[2], Sergiy Zlatkin[1]

[1] Department of Information Systems, Massey University, New Zealand
{S.Zlatkin,R.H.Kaschek}@massey.ac.nz
[2] Department of Computer-Aided Management Systems, National Technical University
"KPI" Kharkiv, Ukraine
shekvl@kpi.kharkov.ua

3.1 Introduction

Business process modeling faces considerable complexities. There are various reasons for these complexities: conflicting modeling goals; the need for the process simulation or automation by means of a workflow management systems [27], business process management systems ([22], [26]) or other process-aware information systems [9]; wide diversity of modeling stakeholders such as customers, owners, business analysts, system analysts, programmers, and testers.

One of these complexities is the problem of selection of an adequate modeling methodology. In the process of choosing business process modeling methodology (BPMM) most suited for the particular task the responsible decision maker has to act under such conditions as incomplete knowledge, insufficient resources, compatibility requirements, and lack of time. In this situation, responsible persons are often tempted to reduce risk by choosing from the set of familiar methodologies.

The selection problem is further complicated because there are too many methodologies to choose from. The set of currently available BPMMs includes proprietary vendor-specific methodologies (e.g. WDL [12], etc.), de-facto standards created and promoted by various standard bodies (such as UML Activity Diagrams by OMG [21], XPDL by Workflow Management Coalition [28], etc.), well accepted methodologies for process modeling in the particular limited problem area (e.g. Petri Nets [3], Event-driven Process Chains [16], etc.). Usually, better-known BPMMs are

W. Abramowicz and H.C. Mayr (eds.), Technologies for Business Information Systems, 25–37.
© 2007 *Springer.*

accompanied with the instruction material, but it is very difficult to find and assess any recommendations regarding which methodology to use.

During the last decade, large number of works focusing on methodology selection limited for particular problem domains has been published. In [17] and [18] Kaschek and Mayr proposed frameworks for comparing object-oriented modeling (OOM) tools and analysis methods. Using these frameworks, they built detailed characterization taxonomies aimed to accompany the process of selecting these tools and methods. In our opinion, it is possible to apply the general approach to method selection from [18] for selecting BPMMs. We therefore use the basic principles of this approach as a basis for the selection framework described in our paper. Albertyn ([8], [5], [4]) has introduced ontology for the particular class of business modeling processes (e-Processes) intended to aid the development of e-commerce information systems. This ontology provides two-level characteristics of e-Processes, scales thereof, and a conceptual frame-work for quantitative assessment of e-Processes under comparison. Al-Humaidan and Rossiter [6] carried out similar research. Their methodologies taxonomy is intended to aid the development of workflow-oriented information systems. Mansar et.al. [19] proposed a strategy for selecting process redesign knowledge.

Some works also dealt with comparison of BPMMs. An obvious approach to use is pairwise comparisons of the admissible methodologies (e.g. [10] compares UML and EPC, or [24] compares XPDL, BPML and BPEL4WS). Other approaches focus on one particular criterion. For example, van der Aalst et. al. identify a list of control workflow patterns [1] and analyze several BPMM regarding the aid they provide for using these patterns [2]. Running a few steps forward, we suggest that our experts refer to workflow patterns when valuing behavioral perspective (see section 3.3.5). Mendling et. al. have compared how different BPMMs are interchanged between tools and systems [20]. We refer experts to that work when valuing exchangeability (see section 3.3.6).

Apart from those isolated approaches, we are not aware of any general framework for selecting from a set of admissible BPMMs. In this paper we try to build the foundation of such a framework based on a method ranking approach combined with a case based approach (according to [18]). We will also justify each criterion introduced in this framework, and describe the supporting software.

The rest of the paper is organized as follows: in the next section, we explain our selection method. In section 3.3, we introduce the criteria of our framework. In section 3.4, we discuss the tool developed to support the approach. In section 3.5, we make conclusions and discuss the directions for future research.

3.2 The Selection Method

We propose a method for selecting from a set of admissible BPMMs those that are best suited for a set of modeling cases. The method quantitatively assesses the admissible BPMM for each modeling case, aggregates the individual assessment outcomes, and then selects the BPMM that scores highest for the total. In this paper, however, we focus on obtaining the assessments of the admissible BPMMs.

We understand "assessing" metaphorically as measuring, with a person obtaining the data by following a heuristic procedure. Assessing therefore requires defining a quality and a respective scale such that each scale instance represents a specific condition of the quality. The scale values can be figures and then each figure stands for a particular multiple of a unit of the quality. The scale becomes then an ordered set, as it inherits the order of numbers. Alternatively, the scale values can be labels of an arbitrary kind. Such a label being the score of a BPMM means that the BPMM meets a condition that is associated with the label. The quality on which we focus in this paper is the suitability of a BPMM for a modeling task.

We consider the quality of a BPMM to be multi-faceted, as is commonly done for other complex entities such as software systems [13] or software processes [25]. The purpose of a BPMM is to guide a number of individuals in modeling business processes. A BPMM therefore must incorporate knowledge about how to model business processes. We group this knowledge into the following classes:

1. the **modeling system**, i.e. the suggested modeling notions, abstraction concepts, patterns, and anti-patterns;
2. the **representation system**, i.e. the suggested notation for representing business process models;
3. the **cost** for producing the result, including the ability to forecast this cost and the precision and cost of the forecast;
4. the **domain of application**, i.e. the domain regarding which the BPMM claims to be useful;
5. the **usability**, i.e. the ability of BPMM to support multiple views (perspectives) of business processes;
6. the **compatibility** of the BPMM with other methodologies, and
7. the **maturity**, i.e. its stability, theoretical foundation, tool support, documentation, etc.

Please note that in this paper we only consider the selection of a BPMM for a modeling task. Obviously, when focusing on a different task such as (1) implementing a business process with a workflow management system, or (2) using the BPMM until further notice for modeling all business processes, the BPMM suitable for that task might may be different from the one most suitable for the task on which we focus in this paper.

We consider the classes introduced above as characteristics of BPMMs. Scoring a BPMM with respect to these characteristics depends strongly on knowledge of the characteristics. We consider obtaining these scores to be a task requiring business knowledge. It requires case-specific knowledge, which typically is available to business experts but not to method experts. Business experts, on the other the other hand, often would not have a sufficient knowledge of the existing methodologies and their assessment and thus would have difficulties choosing a suitable methodology. Consequently, effective and efficient choice of the BPMM best suited for a set of cases, requires blending the knowledge of business experts and methodology experts. We propose achieving this by using the Analytic Hierarchy Process (AHP) [23].

AHP assessment follows a four-step procedure. First, the main objective is defined (which is "select the best suited BPMM" in our case), followed by **the methodology step, business step, and decision-making step.**[1]

On the methodology step, we first complete the definition of the set of characteristics. Our characteristics form a two-level hierarchy (see section 3.3 for this). We then pick the alternatives, i.e. the admissible BPMMs. Together with the characteristics they build the complete hierarchy. Finally, the methodology experts assess the admissible BPMMs by pairwise comparison in terms of the second-level criteria.

During the business step, the business experts rank the relative importance of the characteristics for the modeling case at hand. They first rank the top-level characteristics and then the second-level characteristics inside the particular branch of hierarchy. For these rankings, the pairwise comparison technique is used as well.

During the decision-making step, the methodology expert knowledge and the business expert knowledge are blended. To calculate the *final priorities* of the admissible BPMM, the "ideal synthesis" AHP mode ([11], pp. 151-174) is used.

For further details on this method including its theoretical foundations, practical limitations and ways to overcome them, examples of calculations and formulas, we refer the reader to our paper [15]]. In this paper, we also addressed and discussed the solutions for two main problems of "classic" AHP, namely (1) ensuring the consistency of the pairwise comparison matrix, and (2) avoiding rank reversals. We also used two case studies to demonstrate our approach in action.

3.3 The BPMM characteristics

As mentioned above, the characteristics for BPMM evaluation are organized into a two-level hierarchy. On the top level, there are general characteristics (BPMM knowledge classes) described in section 2: modeling system, representation system, cost, domain, usability, compatibility, and maturity. In this section, we de-scribe the sub-characteristics of these knowledge classes in detail.

3.3.1 Modeling system

We subdivide this general characteristic into the following sub-characteristics:

- **Completeness,** i.e. the degree to which the BPMM provides a means of expression, such as modeling notions, abstraction concepts, patterns, and anti-patterns,

---

[1] We use a terminology that is different from the original one used in [23].

that enables the business experts to effectively and efficiently solve modeling tasks within the domain of application of the BPMM. The corresponding question is *"does the BPMM provide a means of expression and guidance for efficiently modeling business processes belonging to the BPMM's domain of application?"*

- **Redundancy**, i.e. the ratio of the BPMM provides a means of expression that can be defined by the means of other such entities. The corresponding question is *"what is the relative number of means of expression that can be defined using other such means?"*
- **Concept quality**, i.e. the ratio of ill-defined (ambiguous or unclear) means of expression of the BPMM. The corresponding question is *"what is the relative number of means of expression that are ambiguous or not clearly defined?"*
- **Concept adequacy**, i.e. the suitability of the BPMM-suggested modeling system for modeling tasks within the BPMM's domain of application. The corresponding question is *"how close to the common understanding of domain objects and concepts are the BPMM means of expression?"*
- **Process nesting**, i.e. the degree of support of model and process nesting for the particular methodology. The corresponding question is *"which degree of business process nesting is supported?"* Complex process models can be split onto simpler models that contain more specific routine activities or subprocesses.

3.3.2 Representation system

We subdivide this general characteristic into the following sub-characteristics.

- **Readability**, i.e. the simplicity and clarity of the particular notation, the level of representation of the widely accepted business-oriented concepts. The corresponding question is *"how readable is the notation of the particular BPMM for people that are familiar with the method's domain?"*
- **Granularity** with the corresponding question *"how much detail in business process descriptions is supported?"* Some problems require very fine-grained descriptions for the business activities; some can be used with more abstract, coarse-grained descriptions. For example, for business process re-engineering it would be necessary to specify the exact way of sending the document, e.g. "put the document into an envelope", "put the stamp on the envelope", "send the envelope with the document via priority mail" (later on all of these could be replaced e.g. with "send the document via email"). For other problem areas, it would be sufficient to use a coarser "send the document" description.
- **Learnability**, with the corresponding question *"how steep is the learning curve of this BPMM?"* Sometimes the users have no previous experience working with any BPMM – in this case the simplicity of learning could have high relative merit for them. On the other hand, experienced users (or users with more time and other resources) could treat other characteristics as more important.

3.3.3 Cost

As mentioned above we include here:

- **Ability to forecast** precisely the cost of creating a model using a particular BPMM. This may include such items as hardware and software costs, human resources involved, etc. The corresponding question is *"how precise are the cost forecasts suggested by the BPMM?"*
- **Cost of the forecast**, with the corresponding question *"how expensive is a cost forecast as suggested by this BPMM?"*

3.3.4 Domain of application

We subdivide this characteristic into the following sub-characteristics:

- **Versatility**, with the corresponding question *"how flexible is this BPMM, and what is its ability to cover different problem areas?"*
- **Suitability for the particular problem areas**, with the corresponding question *"how well is this BPMM suited for a given problem area?"* For this paper, we selected three problem areas: real-time process modeling, web services interaction modeling and the process modeling in the communication domain.

3.3.5 Usability

We subdivide this characteristic into the following sub-characteristics according to [14].

- **Functional perspective**, i.e. the estimation of the BPMM's ability to de-scribe and store the general specification of the business process. The corresponding question is *"what is the quality and completeness of the general specification of the business processes implemented in this BPMM?"* The most important part of specification with regard to this criterion is the goal of the process; other valuable components are the process tasks, its general description, etc.
- **Behavioral perspective**, i.e. the estimation of the BPMM's ability to support elements describing the complex behavior of the business process (sequential actions, synchronization, asynchronous execution, loops, exceptions etc.). The most practical way of making this evaluation is to estimate the BPMM capabilities of implementing the common workflow patterns [1] via the following question *"what is the level of implementation of the workflow patterns for this BPMM?"*
- **Resource perspective**, i.e. the estimation of the BPMM's ability to describe and store the resources of the business process: its inputs and outputs, its internal data etc. The corresponding question is *"what is the quality and completeness of the resource descriptions implemented in this BPMM?"*

- **Organizational perspective**, i.e. the estimation of the BPMM's ability to describe the participants of the business process (departments, people, systems etc.) and their roles. The corresponding question is *"what is the quality and completeness of the participant descriptions implemented in this BPMM?"*

3.3.6 Compatibility

We subdivide this characteristic into the following sub-characteristics.

- **Exchangeability**, with the corresponding question *"how well can instantiations of a given BPMM be exchanged between tools implementing the BPMM?"* The survey paper [20] can be useful for the comparison according to the criterion based on this characteristic.
- **Mappability**, with the corresponding question *"how well can instantiations of a given BPMM be mapped onto instantiations of other BPMM?"*

3.3.7 Maturity

We subdivide this characteristic into the following sub-characteristics.

- **Stability**, with the corresponding question *"how stable (or well accepted) in the BPM community is this BPMM?"* Stability can address the quality of the method, the time of its foundation, the reputation of its authors, etc.
- **Theoretical foundation**, i.e. the level of theoretical support for the particular BPMM, the ability of its basic concepts to be mathematically proved, its analytical capabilities (for example, the ability of its models to be converted into simulation models). The corresponding question is *"how satisfactory is the theoretical foundation of a given BPMM?"*
- **Tool support**, i.e. the presence and quality of the current software implementation of the particular methodology. The corresponding question is *"what is the quality and availability of tools to implement a given BPMM?"*
- **Documentation**, i.e. the availability and quality of the respective documentation for the BPMM, its comprehensiveness and relative simplicity. Hence, the question is *"is the required documentation available and how comprehensive is it?"*

3.4 BPMM Selector Tool

To support the heuristics presented in [15] and in this paper, the tool called BPMM Selector was implemented as web-based information system. Experts and all interested users can access this system using any JavaScript-capable web browser. Fig. 1 shows the high-level architecture of the tool.

BPMM Selector has extendable component architecture based on the .NET Framework (using ASP.NET features). All domain logic is implemented as ASP.NET web services. All the expert values are stored in a database.

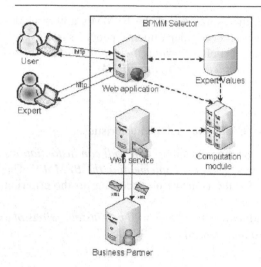

Fig. 1. BPMM Selector Architecture

Interaction of users with the BPMM Selector is performed via the set of views. These views form the presentation tier of the application. Every view is the separate module allowing the user to work with the particular kind of information. Currently these views are implemented as ASP.NET-powered pages with corresponding code-behind components. The views are developed using AJAX technology [7] that is supposed to enrich the user interaction. No page reloads are necessary in process of the user interaction with the view; all interactions are processed on the client side with JavaScript code.

Currently, there are the following views implemented for the BPMM Selector: *criteria view, methodologies view, experts view, users view*, and *decision view*.

Criteria view (Fig. 2) displays the expandable hierarchy of criteria. Users can navigate through hierarchy and make necessary modifications. Every criterion is accompanied with description.

Methodologies view (Fig. 3) displays information about BPM methodologies that are registered with BPMM Selector. It is possible to see further information about each BPMM from this view. This information is linked to the name of the particular methodology in the list and contains the complete methodology description and the list of external links.

Experts view (Fig. 4) is intended to be used by methodology experts. It displays all their results of assessments of the admissible BPMMs by pairwise comparison in terms of the second-level criteria registered into BPMM Selector and al-lows to modify these values. As shown on Fig. 4, to simplify interaction it is possible to filter information of this view by criterion and expert.

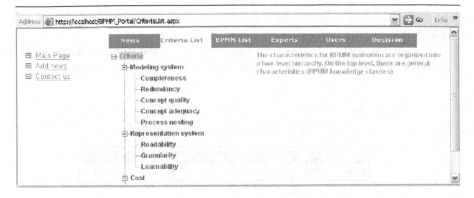

Fig. 2. Criteria view

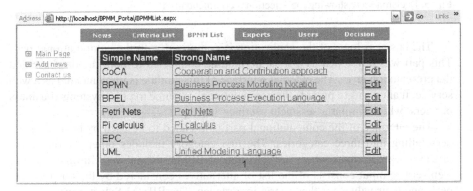

Fig. 3. Methodology view

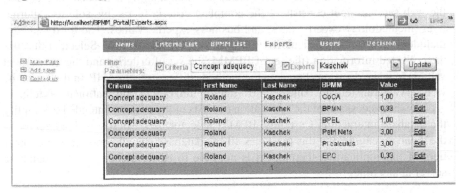

Fig. 4. Expert view

Users view is intended to be used by business experts. They can browse and modify their criteria preferences.

Decision view (Fig. 5) shows the final priorities of the BPM methodologies for the supplied problem. These priorities form the selection recommendation.

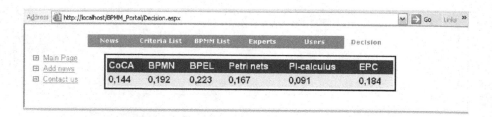

Fig. 5. Decision view showing the selection recommendation

The business logic of the application is comprised with the computational part. This part was developed as a separate module connected to both the database and the presentation layer. The external interface of this module is implemented as a web service. It allows us to provide the computational resource to other systems (business partners) where similar assessment routines are required.

The interface of the computational part is intended to be used by business partners falling into three categories. The first category includes other BP-related or process-aware systems where the selection of BPMM is required. In this case, the web service input consists of the list of alternatives considered by the business experts and their values for the criteria importance. The BPMM Selector provides the criteria and the assessments of the methodology experts. The second category includes arbitrary systems where AHP-based decision-making is needed. In this case, the web service input consists of the complete criteria hierarchy, solution alternatives, methodology expert values, and business experts' values. The third category includes the systems (particularly future versions of the BPMM Selector) that use the collected information (the set of BPMM, the set of criteria, and the assessment values) to make decisions based on the methods different from AHP. In this case, the web service transfers the collected information into other computational module.

The data access tier of the application consists of the routines intended to simplify the database interaction. Currently, BPMM Selector uses Microsoft SQL Server as the database engine, but this tier hides all the database-specific code from the other tiers of the application, therefore it is possible to easily switch to other database server at any time.

3.5 Conclusions and future work

In this paper, we have described the architecture and implementation of the BPMM Selector tool supporting the process of selecting among business process modeling methodologies. The tool applies specific version of the AHP for select-ing the best business process modeling methodology for a given modeling task based on criteria obtained from the two-level hierarchical list of BPMM charac-teristics. To obtain the selection recommendation, BPMM Selector uses blended expert knowledge from both methodology experts and business experts. All the information necessary for making a selection is registered with BPMM Selector using Web-based interface.

The first direction for the future work is related to the fact that the current no-tion of expert needs to be significantly extended. We need to create the directory of experts where every expert is accompanied with some properties (affiliation, area of competence etc). Users should be able to filter experts according to the values of the parameters (for example, all experts from the particular university) and perform calculation with the subset of the expert pool.

Filtering experts according to the values of parameters is the simplest example of choosing the subset of experts. More advanced solution seems to be applying the AHP to the process of selecting the experts. Both these selecting/filtering techniques can be used together so the user can choose one or the other.

The second direction is to implement the internal XML representation of the data, which can be used to perform data exchange between different components of the system. Since the values are organized in a hierarchy, XML appears to be the best choice of format for their transfer. XQuery expressions can be used to perform queries to the data.

Other directions for the future work are as follows: (1) attracting methodology experts to populate the Expert Values database, (2) applying the heuristics and the tool in a number of fully realistic case studies, and (3) comparing the BPMM se-lection method described in this paper with rule-based selection methods as well as case-based selection methods.

References

1. van der Aalst, W.M.P.; ter Hofstede, A.H.M.; Kiepuszewski, B.; Barrios, A.P.: Workflow Patterns. Distributed and Parallel Databases. Vol. 14, No. 1, pp. 5-51, 2003.
2. van der Aalst, W.M.P.: Standard Evaluation, URL: http://is.tm.tue.nl/research/patterns/standards.htm (last accessed 07/01/06), last edited 2005.
3. Van der Aalst, W.M.P.; van Hee, K.: Workflow management: Models, Methods, and Sys-tems, The MIT Press, 2002.
4. Albertyn, F.: Ontology for the Selection of e-Processes, Web Information Systems Engi-neering – WISE 2005 Workshops, LNCS 3807 Springer, pp. 1-10, 2005.

5. Albertyn, F.; Kaschek, R.: E-process selection; In Kotsis G., Bressan S., Taniar D., Ibrahim I. K. (Eds.) The Sixth International Conference on Information Management and Web-based Application & Services, Austrian Computer Society, Books@ocg.at Vol. 183, pp. 143-152, 2004.

6. Al-Humaidan, F.; B.N. Rossiter, B.N.: A Taxonomy and Evaluation for Systems Analysis Methodologies in a Workflow Context: Structured Systems Analysis Design Method (SSADM), Unified Modelling Language (UML), Unified Process, Soft Systems Methodology (SSM) and Organisation Process Modelling, CS-TR: 751, Department of Computing Science, University of Newcastle, 2001.

7. Asleson, R.; Schutta, N., Foundations of Ajax, Apress, 2006.

8. Albertyn, F.; Zlatkin, S.: The Process of Developing a Business Processes Assembler, in Anatoly E. Doroshenko and Terry A. Halpin and Stephen W. Liddle and Heinrich C. Mayr (eds.): Proceedings of ISTA 2004 Conference, LNI P-48, pp. 165-176, GI, 2004.

9. Dumas, M.; van der Aalst, W.M.P.; ter Hofstede, A.: Process-Aware Information Systems: Bridging People and Software Through Process Technology, Wiley, 2005.

10. Ferdian: A Comparison of Event-driven Process Chains and UML Activity Diagram for Denoting Business Processes, Project Work, Technical University Hamburg-Harburg, 2001.

11. Forman, E.H.; Selly, M.A., Decision By Objectives, World Scientific Press, 2001.

12. Groiss Informatics: System Administration, Dokumentversion 6.1.1, URL: http://www.groiss.com (last accessed 07/01/06), 2003.

13. Ghezzi, C.; Jazyeri, M.; Mandrioli, D.: Software Qualities and Principles. Chapter 101 of Tucker, A. B.: Computer Science Handbook Chapman & Hall/CRC, 2nd ed. 2004.

14. Jablonski, S.; Bussler, C.: Workflow Management: Modeling Concepts, Architecture and Implementation, International Thompson Computer Press, 1996.

15. Kaschek, R.; Pavlov, R.; Shekhovtsov, V.; Zlatkin, S.: Towards Selecting Among Business Process Modeling Methodologies. In Witold Abramowicz and Heinrich C. Mayr (eds.:) Proceedings of 9th International Conference on Business Information Systems, BIS 2006, LNI-85, pp. 28-46, GI, 2006.

16. Keller, G.; Nüttgens, M.; Scheer, A.-W.: Semantische Prozeßmodellierung auf der Grundlage "Ereignisgesteuerter Prozeßketten (EPK)", in: Scheer, A.-W. (Hrsg.): Veröffentlichungen des Instituts für Wirtschaftsinformatik, Heft 89, Saarbrücken 1992.

17. Kaschek, R., Mayr, H.C. A characterization of OOA tools. Proceedings of the Fourth International Symposium on Assessment of Software Tools (SAST '96), pp. 59-67, 1996.

18. Kaschek, R., Mayr, H.C. Characteristics of Object Oriented Modeling Methods. EMISA Forum, Vol. 8, No. 2, pp. 10-39, 1998.

19. Mansar, S.L.; Reijers, H.A.; Ounnar, F.: BPR Implementation: a Decision-Making Strategy, Proceedings of the Workshop on Business Process Design 2005.

20. Mendling, J.; Neumann, G.; Nuttgens, M.: A Comparison of XML Interchange Formats for Business Process Modelling. In: F. Feltz, A. Oberweis, B. Otjacques, eds.: Proc. of EMISA 2004 "Informationssysteme im E-Business und E-Government", Luxembourg, Luxembourg, LNI, vo. 56, pages 129-140, 2004.

21. Object Management Group, OMG Unified Modeling Language Specification, Version 2.0, URL: http://www.omg.org/technology/documents/formal/uml.htm (last accessed 07/01/06), March 2003.

22. Ould, M.: Business Process Management: A Rigorous Approach, BCS, Meghan-Kiffer Press, 2005.

23. Saaty T.L.: Multicriteria Decision Making: The Analytic Hierarchy Process: Planning, Priority Setting, Resource Allocation. Pittsburgh: RWS Publications, 1990.

24. Shapiro, R.: A Technical Comparison of XPDL, BPML and BPEL4WS, Cape Vision, 2002.

25. Sommerville, I.: Software Process Models. Chapter 102 of Tucker, A. B.: Computer Science Handbook Chapman & Hall/CRC, 2nd ed., 2004.

26. Smith, H.; Fingar, P.: Business Process Management: The Third Wave, Meghan-Kiffer Press, 2002.

27. Workflow Management Coalition Terminology and Glossary, Document Num-ber WFMC-TC-1011, URL: http://www.wfmc.org (last accessed 07/01/06), 1999.

28. Workflow Management Coalition: Process Definition Interface - XML Process Definition Language, Document Number WFMC-TC-1025, Version 2.00, URL: http://ww.wfmc.org (last accessed 07/01/06), 2005.

4 A Framework for Utilizing Preferred Work Practice for Business Process Evolution

Ruopeng Lu, Shazia Sadiq, Guido Governatori

School of Information Technology and Electrical Engineering
The University of Queensland, Brisbane, Australia
{ruopeng, shazia, guido}@itee.uq.edu.au

4.1 Introduction

Success of BPM systems is predominantly found in the automation of business processes that contain repetitive procedures, and that can be modelled prior to deployment. However, new requirements have risen due to the deployment of BPM systems in non-traditional domains such as collaborative business processes and dynamic applications that demand a high level of flexibility in execution. It is essential that technology supports the business to adapt to changing conditions.

An example can be found in customer inquiry management of a telecommunication company, where inquiry logging and reporting procedures are predictable and repetitive. However, response to individual inquiries and subsequent tests and services performed are prescribed uniquely for each case, but nonetheless have to be coordinated and controlled. Suppose that a number of diagnostic tests (say 8 tests, T1, T2, …,T8) are available. Any number of these tests can be prescribed for a given request, and in a given order. The supervising engineer should have the flexibility to design a plan that best suits the customer request. The knowledge that guides the design of inquiry response is implicit and owned by domain experts, e.g., supervising engineer in this example. Most often, such decisions can only be made based on case specific conditions that cannot be anticipated at design time. This knowledge constitutes the corporate skill base and is found in the experiences and practices of individual workers, who are domain experts in a particular aspect of the overall operations.

There is significant evidence in literature on the difficulties in mapping process logic to process models [11]. With the absence of explicit articulation, the complexity is of increased manifold. We believe this is a limitation in current solutions,

W. Abramowicz and H.C. Mayr (eds.), Technologies for Business Information Systems, 39–50.

and part of the modelling effort needs to be transferred to domain experts who make design decisions based on their expertise and instance specific conditions.

The aim of this paper is to provide a theoretical foundation for designing and implementing a framework for harnessing successful work practice driven by domain experts, and subsequently providing a means of managing this knowledge for business process design and evolution.

The rest of the paper is organised as follows. Section 2 will present the building blocks of the modelling and execution framework. In section 3, details of approach will be presented. Section 4 will discuss related work, followed by conclusions drawn from this work in section 5.

4.2 Framework for Business Process Modelling and Execution

We propose a framework for business process modelling and execution that attempts to achieve a balance between flexibility and control [6, 9]. The framework consists of two major components: (1) A constraint-based process modelling approach, called Business Process Constraint Network (BPCN); and (2) a repository for case specific process models, called Process Variant Repository (PVR).

BPCN provides a descriptive way to build models for business processes where the complete process cannot be prescribed at design time. In BPCN, business process requirements are extracted and transformed into a set of **process constraints**, which are represented in a way that is readable by human and supports analysis and validation for correctness. The process model is constructed (or completed) at runtime and verified against the process constraints [6]. We refer to these individually tailored process instances as **process variants**, which are represent by process graphs. A **process graph** (cf. Fig. 1) presents a typical graphical process model, i.e., $G = <N, E>$ is a direct acyclic graph (DAG), where N is the set of nodes and E is the set of arcs (edges) $E \subseteq N \times N$, where the arcs correspond to flow relations. The set of node is partitioned into a set of task nodes and a set of coordinators where coordinator nodes (ellipses) represent typical semantics [10]. Execution of G can then be done through a typical state-based process execution engine. We will be using this notation to illustrate various examples in this paper.

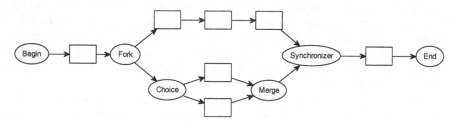

Fig. 1. Modelling constructs of a process variant

The BPCN execution environment allows the generation of potentially a large number of customized process variants, each of which has been constructed with the help of a domain expert utilizing expert knowledge as well as case-specific requirements.

PVR is designed to extract the knowledge and reasoning that led to a particular design. We argue that these design decisions are embedded in various process properties, e.g., process data values. If a significant number of process variants have been designed in a similar way, then it is an indication of a preferred (and likely successful) work practice.

The main contribution of this paper is the proposal of the management framework of PVR. Specifically, its role in managing work practice of domain experts for business process evolution. Fig. 2 illustrates the overall architecture of the framework.

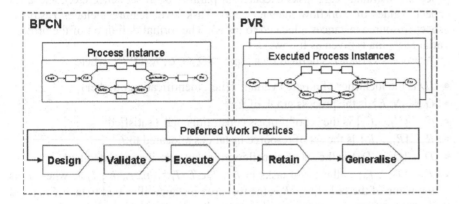

Fig. 2. Framework overview

4.3 Approach

In this section, we present the PVR framework in detail, including the design of case repository schema and the management strategy of PVR. In particular, the case schema defines which case properties to be retained in PVR for future references. The PVR management components include an index structure which defines the organisation of cases, the definition as well as the measure of similarity between precedents and new cases; and lastly the case update approach which specify how PVR is populated by new cases.

4.3.1 Schema of PVR

PVR provides a well-formed structure to store past process designs, as well as an instrument to harness successful work practice for process evolution. When a process variant completes execution, the template that governs the instance (as designed through BPCN) is retained in PVR. The **schema** of PVR defines the structure and data content according to which process variants are stored.

The fundamental goal of PVR is to extract preferred work practices, more specifically to generalise the conditions contributing to the preference. The descriptive information in process variants are the properties of business processes, which can be divided into instance level and task level. In our approach, we classify instance level properties into **temporal** aspect (process execution duration), **control flow** aspect (inter-task dependencies between process tasks restricted by relative process constraints, e.g., tasks executed in parallel or in sequence etc.), and **data** aspect (values of workflow relevant data). Task level feature includes **resource** aspect (resource instances allocated to tasks). The formal definition of the process variant schema is given as follow.

A process variant I is defined by a tuple $<ID, G, C, R, D, T>$, where

- ID is the identifier of process variant I (i.e., identification number);
- $G = <N, E>$ is the process graph of I;
- $C = \{C_1,...,C_k\}$ is the set of process constraints that I satisfied;
- $R = \{R_1,...,R_l\}$ is the set of resource instances allocated to I;
- $D = \{D_1,...,D_m\}$ is the set of workflow-relevant data items related to I;
- $T = \{T_1,...,T_n\}$ is the set of tasks in I. $\forall T_i \in T$, $T_i = <n_i, r_i, T_i^-, T_i^+>$, where n_i is the name of the task T_i; $r_i \in R$ is the resource instance allocated to task T_i; T_i^- and T_i^+ are the time stamps when task T_i started and completed execution. Execution duration dur_i of T_i is given by $dur_i = |T_i^+ - T_i^-|$. Execution duration of a process variant I is the sum of dur_i for all T_i in I, i.e., $Duration(I) = \sum_{i=1}^{n} dur_i$.
  PVR is the set of all process variants, i.e., PVR $= \{I_1,...,I_p\}$.

The above definitions can be illustrated by the following example. In Fig. 3, we provide three process variants I_1, I_2 and I_3. The variants are intended to represent particular test setups in the customer inquiry management scenario as introduced in section 1. All these process variants satisfy the same process constraint C_1: test T1 must always be performed before test T5. For each task T_i, the allocated resource instance r_i, the start and complete time stamps T_i^- and T_i^+ are annotated in the process graphs for illustration purpose.

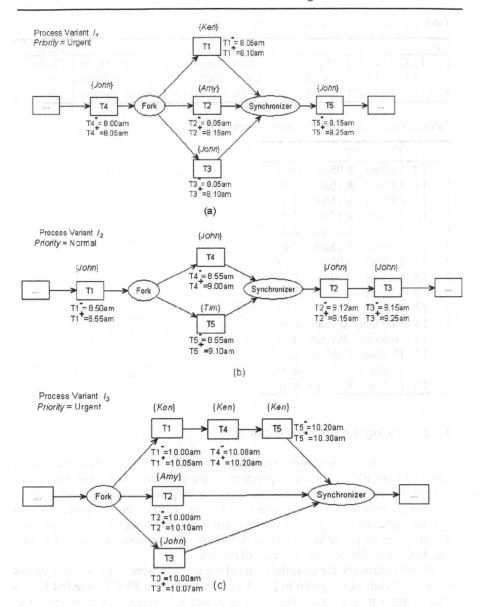

Fig. 3. (Partial) process graphs of process variants (a) I_1, (b) I_2 and (c) I_3

I_1, I_2 and I_3 are stored in PVR according to the schema definition, as shown in Table 1 and 2.

Table 1. Instance level schema of process variants

ID	T	G	C	R	D	Duration
1	$\{T1,T2,T3,T4,T5\}$	$<N_1, E_1>$	$\{C_1\}$	$\{John, Ken, Amy\}$	$\{Priority = \text{urgent}\}$	25min
2	$\{T1,T2,T3,T4,T5\}$	$<N_2, E_2>$	$\{C_1\}$	$\{John, Tim\}$	$\{Priority = \text{normal}\}$	35min
3	$\{T1,T2,T3,T4,T5\}$	$<N_3, E_3>$	$\{C_1\}$	$\{John, Ken, Amy\}$	$\{Priority = \text{urgent}\}$	30min

Table 2. Task level schema of process variants

ID	n	T^r	T^+	r
1	T4	8.00am	8.05am	John
1	T1	8.05am	8.10am	Ken
1	T2	8.05am	8.15am	Amy
1	T3	8.05am	8.12am	John
1	T5	8.15am	8.25am	John
2	T1	8.50am	8.55am	John
2	T4	8.55am	9.00am	John
2	T5	8.55am	9.10am	Tim
2	T2	9.12am	9.15am	John
2	T3	9.15am	9.25am	John
3	T1	10.00am	10.05am	Ken
3	T2	10.00am	10.10am	Amy
3	T3	10.00am	10.07am	John
3	T4	10.08am	10.20am	Ken
3	T5	10.20am	10.30am	Ken

4.3.2 Indexing the process variants

Upon certain design conditions, precedents of similar process variants need to be retrieved from PVR such that experience of the preferred work practices can be utilised. As the number of process variants can be potentially very large, a linear scan for all instances in search for a few "similar" cases is not desirable. As a result, the preferred work practices in PVR are managed through an index structure, which serves as identifiers for process variants sharing some common features, e.g., have been allocated the same set of resources.

We now introduce the essential terms of the index structure. These terms follow the general convention given in [4]. A process variant in PVR is referred to as a **case**. A **descriptor** is an *attribute-value* pair used to describe a case. For example, a simple descriptor is (*Duration, 25min*). **Dimension** refers to the attribute part of a descriptor. The dimension of the abovementioned example is the temporal perspective of business process, because the duration refers to the period of time taken to execute the process instance. Cases can be described in one or more dimensions. A descriptor for a given case is also said to be a case **feature**. PVR uses a hierarchical organisation to index cases. The collection of all features is called the **description** of a case. The index structure in our approach contains features in four dimensions, including control flow, resource, data and performance metric.

Control Flow dimension describes the control flow patterns of a case, which can discriminate different cases by the topological properties of their process graphs. For example, cases I_1 and I_2 (cf. Fig. 3) can be partially distinguished by the feature "$\{T4,T5\}$-*Serial*", which indicates in case I_1 tasks T4 and T5 were executed in serial, while parallel in case I_2. Another control flow feature of I_1 is tasks T1, T2 and T3 are executed in parallel, i.e., "$\{T1,T2,T3\}$-parallel".

Resource dimension concerns with the resource instances allocated to execute the process variants. Note however that resource aspect may constitute complex specifications, beyond a simple overall list [8].

Workflow relevant data, which may affect design decisions for process variants, can be used as **data** dimension features in PVR index.

The **performance metric** dimension uses quantitative scales to discriminate process variants based on their execution duration. These may include absolute values, ranges, or temporal relations.

The description of a case is the union of all features for this case. For example, the description of I_1, I_2 and I_3 (cf. Fig. 3) are shown in Table 3 and 4.

Table 3. Description for cases I_1 and I_3

Feature	
Control Flow	$\{T1, T2, T3\}$- *parallel*
Control Flow	$\{T4, T5\}$- *serial*
Resource	$\{John, Ken, Amy\}$
Data	*Priority* = Urgent
Performance Metric	*Duration* = [0min ~ 30min]

Table 4. Description for case I_2

Feature	
Control Flow	$\{T4, T5\}$-parallel
Resource	$\{John, Tim\}$
Data	*Priority* = Normal
Performance Metric	*Duration* > 30min

Fig. 4 shows the overall index structure for I_1, I_2 and I_3. The index is a tree-structure consists of four types of nodes: *feature*, *description*, *case*, and *exemplar* nodes. Feature nodes are on top level which point to one or more description nodes. A description node points to a case node or an exemplar node. An exemplar node points to one or more case nodes. A case node contains the entry to the storage of a process variant (case). An important concept is the **exemplar**, which is generalised from multiple cases sharing exactly the same description. An exemplar is referred to as a **preferred work practice** when the number of cases in this exemplar exceed the given threshold value (e.g., say 30 cases). Typically, this value is specified by domain experts. This is further described in section 3.4 in repository update procedure.

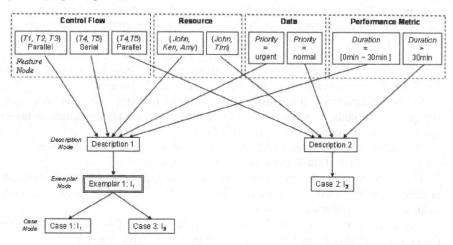

Fig. 4. Overall index structure for cases I_1, I_2 and I_3

4.3.3 Similarity measure

The index in PVR groups similar cases together. Overtime, PVR accumulates a sufficiently large number of process variants, when preferred work practices can be generalised. It is required to determine whether a new case is sufficiently similar to current cases in PVR. The process of determining similarity between two cases I' and I is called **matching**. The case to be compared with is called the base case.

The similarity matching in our approach endorses exact matches along the control, resource, data and performance metric dimensions. If a real number between [0, 1] is assigned to each dimension to indicate the degree of match, then 1 indicates exactly matching features and 0 otherwise. For example, the control flow features of two cases can be either exactly matching each other (e.g., {$T1$, $T2$, $T3$} executed in parallel in both I_1 and I_3), or otherwise not matching at all (e.g., {$T4$, $T5$} executed in serial in I_1 but parallel in I_2). Similarly, for resource and data features, two cases match if the set of resource instances (or workflow-relevant data) are the same. Lastly, we measure the degree of match of performance metric dimension by measuring the distance between two values on a qualitative scale. If two values are within the same qualitative region (e.g., *Duration* = [1hr ~ 5hr]), then they are considered a match.

We use an aggregation function to determine the overall similarity of two cases. For the purpose of illustration, the importance of each dimension is assigned an equal value initially. Let F be the set of all features of the process instance I, we define function *Sim*: $F \times F \rightarrow \{0, 1\}$, which determines the similarity of two features and returns the similarity score 0 or 1. The overall similarity *sim* of process variant *I* and *I'* is given by:

$$sim = \frac{\sum_{i=1}^{m} Sim(F_i, F_i') \bullet W_i}{m} \qquad (3.1)$$

where *m* is the number of features of *I'*; F_i and F_i' are corresponding features of *I* and *I'* respectively; W_i is the weight of feature F_i and F_i'. A new case *I'* is said to be *exactly matching* the base case *I* if and only if the overall similarity *sim* equals 1. For example, supposed a new case *I'* having the following description (Table 5) is to be matched with the base case I_1. Control flow features, as well as resource and data features match each other, thus each having the similarity score 1. However, the performance metric dimensions do not match, as duration of I_1 is between [0min~30min], and the duration of *I'* is >30min, thus the score is 0. The overall similarity is 0.8 (when each dimension has equal weight, i.e., $W_i = 1$ for all *i*). Hence *I'* is not exactly matching I_1.

Table 5. Description of a new case *I'*

Feature	
Control Flow	*{T1, T2, T3}- parallel*
Control Flow	*{T4, T5}- serial*
Resource	*{John, Ken, Amy}*
Data	*Priority* = Urgent
Performance Metric	*Duration* > 30min

However, in certain circumstance, when exact matching is not essential or improbable, a threshold value for similarity can be defined (e.g., 0.8) for partially matching cases. In this sense, I_1 and *I'* *match* each other. Furthermore, some dimensions can be prioritised by assigning a higher weight than the others. In order to do so, the weights must be adjusted properly such that the overall similarity score is always between 0 and 1.

Furthermore, the case matching techniques can be extended to further support case retrieval in process evolution. We have developed a methodology [5] for retrieving both exact and partial matching cases based on complex control flow features against some desired facts (queries with certain features).

4.3.4 PVR update approach

The process of inserting new cases and adjusting the index structure constitutes the repository update approach. PVR update procedure determines the way the case should be indexed by extracting features from the case and computing the index values. The description of the new case is computed by extracting relative information form the process variant according to a preference list of features designed by domain experts, which covers the four dimensions (control, data, resource, performance metric) of features. When the number of matching cases under an exemplar exceeds the preference threshold as a result of the insertion, the exemplar is generalised as a preferred work practice.

The update procedure presented below (Table 6) is adapted from [4], which takes the new case as *input*, produces preferred work practice as *output* (if the number of similar cases in the repository exceeds the predetermined *threshold*).

Table 6. Update approach of PVR

Procedure PVR Update
1. compute index values (description of the new case *I*)
2. **for** each existing description in the index
3.   compare with the description of the new case
4.   **if** no matching description exists
5.   create a new description node
6.   create a new case node under the description node
7.   **else** // *there exists such a description*
8.   **if** is case node underneath
9.   create an exemplar node above the case node
10.   **else** // *is exemplar node underneath*
11.   create a new case node
12.   increase the threshold counter
13.   **if** exceeds threshold
14.   export exemplar as preferred work practice
15.   **end if**
16.   **end if**
17. **end if**

4.4 Related Work

The difficulty in mapping of domain specific knowledge to machine-readable representations is widely recognized in literature. This is a hard problem in general and has been addressed in process modelling through various approaches, e.g., through modular approaches where process logic is divided into different perspectives (informational, functional, organisational etc.), through language expressibility analysis in workflows [1], and through comprehensive methodologies [11]. In this paper, we approach this problem through user's perspective, by providing a mechanism to push successful work practice preferences into process specification. This problem actually translates to finding the "best" practice for a given scenario.

There are several techniques that address similar problems of knowledge acquisition and learning. Case-Based Reasoning (CBR) is one such approach, that we have found to link closely to our problem. CBR has been proven to be useful in weak theory domains and system with a large number unstructured and experiential knowledge [2]. It utilises specific knowledge of previously experienced problems and solutions. The knowledge acquisition is realised by an incremental, sustained learning process, where new experience is retained when a new problem has been solved, which provides references to solve similar problems in future [4].

Our approach applies certain concepts from CBR by following the general design guidelines of case representation and repository (section 3.1), as well as adapting the indexing and case matching techniques (section 3.2–3.4).

In the meantime, there are a number of recent proposals for workflow management approaches based on CBR techniques [3, 7, 12], which have demonstrated the possibilities to apply CBR techniques to achieve certain workflow management goals. However, we believe there are still challenges that the abovementioned proposals yet to overcome: Firstly, as a new problem is solved by adapting similar past cases to meet new demands, the solution proposed by CBR is only as good as the cases it has collected. As a result, in CBR-based workflow systems, precedential models kept in the system needed to be sensible and domain specific. Secondly, since index is essential for efficient case retrievals and updates in a large repository, a proper organisation of case memory is also highly desirable in CBR-based workflow systems. Lastly, a precise definition of similarity is needed if effective case matching is required. These issues have been addressed in our framework appropriately.

4.5 Conclusions and Future Work

In this paper, we have presented an approach for harnessing implicit process knowledge found in successful work practice from a flexible process modelling and execution framework, and using the acquired knowledge for guiding subsequent process design and evolution. The main contribution of this paper relates to the design of functions to manage the process variant repository. The proposed functions address relative aspects of the requirements for PVR management, namely design of PVR, effective indexing, similarity matching and consequent repository update. These functions can be implemented by well-known CBR techniques in literature. However, we anticipate several interesting and challenging extensions to our work, notably in extending the design of the template schema, and more advanced similarity measure that that allow for partial matching within specific dimensions. A query facility has been developed to harness successful work practices based on queries containing complex control flow features [5], where partial matching cases can be handled. Further extensions to this work towards multi-aspect queries are being developed.

References

1. van der Aalst, W.M.P, ter Hofstede A.H.M, Kiepuszewski B, Barros AP (2003) Workflow Patterns. Distributed and Parallel Databases 14(1): 5-51
2. Aamodt A, Plaza E (1994) Case-based reasoning: foundational issues, methodological variations, and system approaches. AI Communications 7(1): 39-59
3. Kim JH, Suh W and Lee H (2002) Document-based workflow modeling: a case-based reasoning approach. Expert Systems with Applications 23(2), 77-93
4. Kolodner J (1993) Case-Based Reasoning. Morgan Kaufmann Publishers
5. Lu R, Sadiq S, Governatori G (2006) Managing Process Variants as an Information Resource. In: 4th International Conference on Business Process Management (BPM2006). Vienna, Austria
6. Lu R, Sadiq S, Padmanabhan V, Governatori G (2006) Using a Temporal Constraint Network for increased flexibility in Business Process Execution. In: Dobbie G, Bailey J (eds) 17th Australasian Database Conference (ADC2006). Hobart, Australia
7. Madhusudan T, Zhao JL, Marshall B (2004) A case-based reasoning framework for workflow model management. Data Knowledge Engineering 50(1): 87-115
8. Russell N, ter Hofstede A.H.M., Edmond D (2005) Workflow Resource Patterns. Technical report, Centre for Information Technology Innovation, Queensland University of Technology
9. Sadiq S, Sadiq W, Orlowska ME (2005) A Framework for Constraint Specification and Validation in Flexible Workflows. Information Systems 30(5): 349-378
10. Sadiq W, Orlowska ME (1999) On Capturing Process Requirements of Workflow Based Business Information System. In: 3rd International Conference on Business Information Systems (BIS '99). Springer-Verlag, Poznan, Poland.
11. Scheer AW (2000) ARIS-Business Process Modeling. 3rd edn, Springer, Berlin Heidelberg New York
12. Weber B, Rinderle S, Wild W, Reichert M (2005) CCBR-Driven Business Process Evolution. In: 6th International Conference on Case-Based Reasoning, (ICCBR2005). Springer, Chicago, USA

5 On the Suitability of the Pi-Calculus for Business Process Management*

Frank Puhlmann

Business Process Technology Group
Hasso-Plattner-Institute for IT Systems Engineering
at the University of Potsdam
D-14482 Potsdam, Germany
frank.puhlmann@hpi.uni-potsdam.de

5.1 Introduction

This chapter discusses the suitability of a process algebra for the description of mobile systems, the π-calculus [2], as a formal foundation for *Business Process Management* (BPM). BPM refers to an integrated set of activities for designing, enacting, managing, analyzing, optimizing, and adapting *business processes*. Since BPM lacks a uniform formal foundation for the technical aspects [3], we investigate requirements that a theory should fulfill and argue why the π-calculus is well suited for them.

Our argumentation complements the work on the π-calculus as a foundation for BPM from an economical viewpoint as investigated by Smith and Fingar [4, 5] by focusing on technical aspects. We therefore analyze three major shifts in the area of BPM, ranging from system description and distribution aspects up to changing environments in which business processes are executed. We argue that the arising requirements for BPM can only be fulfilled by mobile system theory, such as the π-calculus. Mobile systems are a complete new approach to BPM, that have not yet been investigated as a formal foundation for BPM. We discuss concepts like Workflow Patterns [6], service orchestration and choreography as well as correlations [7] using recent work in the area of mobile systems and BPM [8, 9].

The remainder of this chapter is organized as follows. We first introduce the shifting requirements for BPM in section 5.2, followed by a discussion of how the

---

* This chapter is a follow-up extension to a paper originally published in [1].

W. Abramowicz and H.C. Mayr (eds.), Technologies for Business Information Systems, 51–62.
© 2007 *Springer.*

π-calculus supports their representation in section 5.3. The chapter continues with an example in section 5.4 and concludes in section 5.5.

5.2 Shifting Requirements

Today there is an emerging shift in the area of Business Process Management. People are used to state-based Workflow Management Systems (WfMS) that enact static business processes called *workflows*. A workflow consists of several activities or tasks[1] guided by explicit control flow that defines the state the workflow is in [10]. The workflow itself often resembles some kind of office process that is enacted in a well defined and closed environment like the department of an enterprise. Structural change occurs seldom and can be handled in a pre-defined manner [11].

However, things are changing to more agile business processes enacted in distributed environments. These "new" business processes are routed by events instead of documents stored in databases. The events are consumed and produced by activities that have no static connections but event connectors. Events are used as preconditions to trigger activities and produced as an outcome. Some activities are still executed in closed environments, but most are distributed as services over open environments such as the Internet. There is no absolute control of the business process by a single engine, or by any engine, as activities are outsourced and fulfilled not by technical issues but rather by legal contracts. The event-based model allows the flexible integration of activities and processes into other business processes, wherever they are distributed, and however they are executed, as long as their interaction behavior is matching.

These sketched shifts in BPM bring up some very interesting questions regarding the formal representation. In the following subsection we discuss the three most important ones in detail. Each subsection is concluded with a short paragraph summarizing the issues and deriving requirements for formalisms.

5.2.1 From Static to Agile Systems

Current state of the art research in BPM focuses on static system theory for designing and enacting business processes. Examples are Workflow nets [10], the YAWL system [12], Workflow Modules [13], or Production Workflows [14]. Analysis of business processes is focused on Petri nets [15], such as given by different variants of soundness [16, 17]. However, as BPM broadens to inter-organizational business processes between departments, companies, and corporations, static process descriptions as given by Petri nets have come to their limitations. This is especially true with the arrival of service oriented architectures (SOA) [18] as a central realization strategy for BPM.

---

[1] Although sometimes used differently, we use activity and task synonymous here.

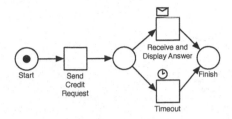

Fig. 1. Sample business process in Workflow net notation [10]

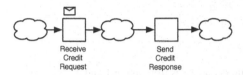

Fig. 2. An abstract process for interaction with the business process shown in figure 1

To underpin these assumption, let's take a closer look at the example shown in figure 1. The simple business process consists of a task that sends a credit request and afterwards waits for either the response or a timeout if no response has been received within a given timeframe. In traditional workflow systems, this process lives alone. Each task appears at the work list of some employee who finally executes it. The first task consists of writing and sending a letter. Afterwards, two exclusive tasks appear at the work list. If an answer is received by mail within the given timeframe, the answer is processed, whereas otherwise the timeout task is selected (which contains some fallback actions).

Next generation BPM incorporates the service oriented computing paradigm, where now all tasks of the example are represented as services. These services interact with other services to fulfill their goals. But what is required for this to take place? Of course, a corresponding process we can interact with. Let's assume this to be an abstract process, meaning that we only know the parts we can use for interaction, shown in figure 2.

We use clouds to denote the hidden parts of the corresponding process and call it a service. All we know about it is the interface description (receive a request, send response with the corresponding parameter format not shown in the visualization), as well as the interaction behavior (first receive a request, then send a response). To denote the interaction between our business process and the service in a static way, we need to introduce additional states that describe incoming requests and outgoing responses. The result contains two Workflow nets which interact by shared places, shown in figure 3.

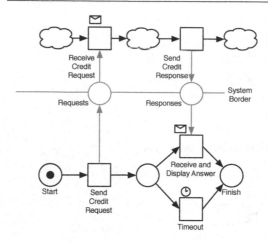

Fig. 3. Static interaction between the business processes from figure 1 and 2

But converting business processes to services by defining their static interaction points is only half the truth of SOA. Beside a *service requester* and a *service provider*, as given by the examples, a third role, called a *service broker* is employed inside a service oriented environment. The task of the service broker is to discover matching services based on a request from the service requester and a list of registered service providers. Matching services can then be dynamically incorporated for usage within the business process of the service requester. Notable, new service providers could register at the service broker even after the business process of the service requester has been deployed. Thus, possible interaction partners could not be anticipated in advance, but furthermore are discovered and dynamically integrated just in time.

As a key result, agile systems based on service oriented architectures require support for dynamic binding of services that was not needed in static systems.

BPM Shift I:

BPM shifts from static to agile business processes as the later supports dynamic binding of interaction partners found in service oriented architectures.

New Requirement I:

A formalism representing the first shift of BPM should support the direct representation of dynamic binding.

5.2.2 From Central Engines to Distributed Services

Service oriented architectures as the primary realization for BPM enforce another shift. Loose coupling between activities of business process also becomes important.

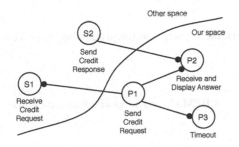

Fig. 4. Dynamic routing and interaction view of figure 3

We adapt the loose coupling paradigm to BPM by utilizing pre- and postconditions for each activity according to [19]. Figure 4 shows the interaction from figure 3 by representing all tasks ask individual services. Each service is represented as a circle with a short name inside (not to be confused with the states, or places of Workflow nets). Dependencies between services are denoted by lines. Each line connects a postcondition of one service with the precondition of another one, where the precondition end is marked with a filled circle. We can detect dependencies between $P1$ and $S1$, $P2$, $P3$ as well as $S2$ and $P2$. The tasks $S1$, $P2$, and $P3$ can only be activated after $P1$ has been executed, thus meaning the preconditions of $S1$, $P2$, and $P3$ depend on the postconditions of $P1$. The task $S2$ has some preconditions linked to $S1$ that are not known to us.

These loose coupling between different activities allows for highly distributed systems. Instead of having a single engine controlling every aspect of a workflow, this knowledge is now spread across the parts of collaborating workflows. Distributed tasks, called services, wait for messages to arrive that trigger the activation and produce new messages to trigger other tasks. Of course, there are some distinctions to be made.

They start with different spaces in the environment for the distributed tasks to live in. In figure 4, this is denoted with *Our Space* and *Other Space*. Our space is usually something like an intranet, where we control things like access conditions, availability, implementation issues and so on. We make some of our services available to the outer world, acting as interaction points, without providing knowledge or access to our internal structures. Indeed, we are free to restructure our internals as wanted. Our workflow incorporates other tasks that are available in the other space, typically in other intranets or the Internet. These other tasks are parts of systems such as ours, and represent interaction interfaces. However, we have only limited control over them, mostly by legal agreements. We cannot enforce their availability, functionality, or implementation. Still, we are free to drop them as interaction partners and bound to others. This high flexibility requires the shift from closed, central engines to open, distributed services for representing workflows.

BPM Shift II:

BPM shifts from central engines to distributed systems as integration becomes a core BPM activity.

New Requirement II:

A formalism supporting the second shift of BPM should support advanced composition and visibility of its parts.

5.2.3 From Closed to Open Environments

In traditional workflow theory, the execution environments are quite static and fore-seeable. We denote this kind of environment closed, as the level of external influences is rather low. However, with shifts from traditional departments and companies up to virtual organizations and agile, customer order-specific collaborations, the execution environment is shifting, too. This new kind of environment is called open and is represented by large intranets as well as the Internet.

Closed environments are usually accessible, deterministic, quite static, and have a limited number of possible actions. Accessibility describes the level of knowledge we have about the execution environment regarding completeness, accuracy, and up-to-dateness of the information. In a single company or department we should be able to exactly capture this knowledge. If we expand the environment to the whole Internet, there is much left in the dark that could be useful or crucial for our business, however we are simply unable to find and incorporate it.

Executing a task in an open environment is more uncertain then in a closed one. This is denoted as the determinism of the actions. In an open environment they are way more possibilities to foresee and handle. However, if the environment is complex enough, as e.g. the Internet, we can not enforce everything.

While closed environments are quite static, open environments tend to be constantly changing in large parts, regardless of our actions. Interaction partners appear, disappear, are prevented, or something else happens that we have to take into account for our business to run.

Furthermore, the number of interaction partners that can be invoked to perform a certain task is rising fast as the environment opens to the world. So our decision making process of whom we incorporate into our business is getting more complex.

BPM Shift III:

BPM shifts from closed to open environments as the application area is extended from internal office workflows to agile collaborations in open networks like the Internet.

New Requirement III:

A formalism taking the third shift into account should support change.

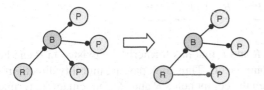

Fig. 5. Link passing mobility in π-calculus

5.3 Arising Theory: The Pi-Calculus

After having gathered the requirements for next generation BPM systems, we focus on the π-calculus. In particular, we're going to show how the different requirements can be fulfilled by applying it. We will not stuck on technical details of the calculus but focus on the key concepts it provides. For a technical discussion of how the π-calculus actually works, the interested reader is referred to [2, 20].

The most interesting concept of the π-calculus is called *link passing mobility*. Link passing mobility directly resembles dynamic binding as depicted in figure 5. The left hand side shows the three different roles, denoted as circles. A business process requesting a service (R) knows a service broker (B), denoted by the line (channel) between, where the dot denotes the target. The service broker, in turn, has knowledge about a number of service providers (P). The service broker evaluates the request of the service requester and returns the corresponding channel. The service requester then uses this channel to dynamically bind to the service provider. Hence, the link structure of the example changes over time as shown at the right hand side of the figure. By using link passing mobility, the first requirement can be directly fulfilled by the π-calculus without producing any formal overhead. To highlight the simplicity of the formal representation we give an example:

$$\underbrace{x(y).\bar{y}\langle req \rangle.R'}_{R} \mid \underbrace{\bar{x}\langle ch \rangle.B'}_{B} \mid \underbrace{ch(req).P'}_{P} .$$

The equation shows the different roles from figure 5 in the π-calculus. We use underbraces to denote which part corresponds to which role. Basically, each π-calculus system is made up of concurrent *components*, divided by a vertical bar. Thus, R, B, and P are defined concurrently. Concurrent components may interact using directed channels. A transmission via a channel is represented by a lowercase letter or name with a bar above, such as in component B. A reception via a channel is represented by a lowercase letter or name matching to a transmission channel, such as in component R. According to this concept, initially the components B and R can interact, leading to the transmission of the channel to P from B to R via x. Inside component R, the placeholder y is then replaced by the received channel, i.e. ch. The updated description of the system looks then like this:

$$\underbrace{\overline{ch}\langle req\rangle.R'}_{R} \mid \underbrace{B'}_{B} \mid \underbrace{ch(req).P'}_{P} \ .$$

Now the new channel ch between R and P that has formerly not existed in R can be used for direct interaction of the components. Thus, link passing mobility directly resembles a dynamic binding between the components R and P. The remaining formal description of B has become B' that will not be further refined here.

Besides introducing link passing mobility, the π-calculus also inherits concepts from its predecessor, the calculus of communicating systems (CCS). Regarding the second requirement, the scoping of channels is of specific interest. By extending the formal representation from above to

$$\underbrace{x(y).\overline{y}\langle req\rangle.R'}_{R} \mid \mathbf{v}ch \underbrace{(\overline{x}\langle ch\rangle.B'}_{B} \mid \underbrace{ch(req).P')}_{P} \ ,$$
$$\underbrace{}_{\text{Scope of } ch}$$

we can *restrict* the scope of the channel ch initially to the components B and P. The restriction of the channel ch is formally denoted as $\mathbf{v}ch$. The channel ch can not be used outside of its scope. If there exists another channel named ch outside the defined scope, it is actually different. Thus, in the example given no other component is able to interact with P initially. However, by interacting via the unrestricted channel x with component B, other components can acquire the channel ch:

$$\mathbf{v}ch \underbrace{(\overline{ch}\langle req\rangle.R'}_{R} \mid \underbrace{B'}_{B} \mid \underbrace{ch(req).P')}_{P} \ .$$
$$\underbrace{}_{\text{Scope of } ch}$$

By using the concepts of scopes and *scope extrusions* in combination with link passing mobility, the π-calculus directly supports advanced composition and visibility. Business processes can be encapsulated as services by representing them as concurrent components of a π-calculus system with restricted channels. Only precisely defined channels can then be used for interaction. Furthermore, it is possible to provide restricted names for specific other components, e.g. channels dynamically created for specific customers.

The structure of a π-calculus system, that is made up of concurrent components, is also sufficient to fulfill the third requirement. Components of a π-calculus system can easily be replaced, dropped, or added. If, for instance, we would like to add a second service provider to our example, that listens to the same channel for the sake of simplicity, this can be done as follows:

$$\underbrace{x(y).\overline{y}\langle req\rangle.R'}_{R} \mid \mathbf{v}ch \underbrace{(\overline{x}\langle ch\rangle.B'}_{B} \mid \underbrace{ch(req).P'}_{P} \mid \underbrace{ch(req).Q')}_{Q} \ .$$
$$\underbrace{}_{\text{Scope of } ch}$$

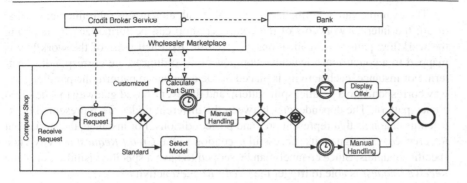

Fig. 6. A sample Workflow/Collaboration in BPMN notation [21]

The second service providers is called Q and can be accessed non-deterministically via ch by R. A more advanced setting would allow a dynamic registration of clients at the service broker. Recapitulating, the π-calculus is appropriate to fulfill the three arising requirements of BPM. The next section introduces a practical example.

5.4 Example

Figure 6 shows an internal workflow of a computer shop as well as its interaction with the (digital) environment. The computer shop offers the advantage of financing a computer purchase with the lowest possible interest for a certain customer as well as calculating realtime prices for the components. For the first advantage, the shop incorporates an external credit broker service. The services mediates loans up to €5000 based on the personal data of the customer. After finding the lowest customer specific interest, the offering bank is informed to send a binding credit offer to the computer shop. The second advantage is given by incorporating a wholesaler marketplace that searches for the lowest available component prices.

The example in figure 6 contains the internal workflow for processing a request from a customer. This results in an offer containing a loan offer with the specific conditions. As the credit processing takes some time and is independent of a specific sum up to €5000, it is the first task in the internal workflow. Technically, it is an asynchronous service invocation, containing a correlation to the workflow instance for the callback action of the bank. Afterwards, the customer request is further evaluated. If the customer selects a standard, pre-configured computer, the price is taken from an internal database. If the computer should be customized, the wholesaler marketplace is searched for the lowest available prices. Technically, this is implemented by a synchronous service invocation. If this task did not finish within a given timeframe, the offer has to be handled manually. Afterward the workflow consists of a deferred choice pattern, modeled using an event-based BPMN gateway. If a response from a bank is received, the offer is displayed. Otherwise a manual handling is required.

The example can be formalized using the π-calculus in several refinements. First of all, the internal workflow of the computer shop can be formalized by applying the workflow pattern formalizations as given in [8]. Each node of the workflow is mapped to a concurrent π-calculus component according to the corresponding pattern. For instance, each activity is placed inside a sequence pattern, the parallel gateway corresponds to a parallel split pattern, and the event-based gateway to a deferred choice pattern. The dependencies between the different nodes are represented by π-calculus channels that represent pre- and postconditions. For instance, the start event *Receive Request* signals its successful execution to the *Credit Request* activity via a specific channels. Since channels can be scoped to have a specific visibility, only the *Receive Request* is able to trigger the *Credit Request* activity.

The interesting questions arise in formalizing the interactions between the computer shop and its environment. In the activity *Credit Request*, a *Credit Broker Service* is triggered. While there exists a static binding between both of them, the broker in turn communicates a call-back channel of the computer shop's workflow to a *Bank* dynamically bound. Furthermore, the *Wholesaler Marketplace* can be bound static as in the example but also easily adapted to support dynamic binding if more then one marketplace is available. Technically, link passing mobility and addition of components is used to formalize the interactions. In [9], a catalogue of service interaction pattern formalizations is provided. These formalization can be applied to different interaction scenarios. A complete π-calculus formalization of the example can be found in [22].

5.5 Conclusion

This chapter investigated shifting requirements in the area of business process management, that supersede static, centralized, and closed systems by agile and distributed solutions enacted in open environments. We argued that a formalism able to represent BPM systems should support at least three requirements. The first one is dynamic binding that allows run time integration of new partners into the business processes. The second one is the support for advanced composition and visibility, allowing the representation of business processes as compositions of distributed services. The last requirement is about supporting change of business processes by allowing the addition, change, and removal of activities.

As we have investigated in this chapter, the π-calculus is able to fulfill all three requirements. At the heart of the calculus is the capability for link passing mobility, that directly resembles dynamic binding. The compositional capabilities together with scoping of channels furthermore provide a direct support for the remaining requirements.

Recent results [8, 22] have shown that the π-calculus is well suited for modeling classical workflows, nowadays known as service orchestrations, as well as service choreographies, that together form a core foundation of future BPM based on the shifting requirements. While recent standards like BPEL4WS [23], BPMN [21], or WS-CDL [24] tackle the problem from a practical side, a formal foundation for BPM is still missing. This chapter revealed the strengths of the π-calculus as a formal foundation for business process management.

References

1. Puhlmann, F.: Why do we actually need the Pi-Calculus for Business Process Management? In Abramowicz, W., Mayr, H., eds.: 9th International Conference on Business Information Systems (BIS 2006), volume P-85 of LNI, Bonn, Gesellschaft für Informatik (2006) 77–89

2. Milner, R., Parrow, J., Walker, D.: A Calculus of Mobile Processes, Part I/II. Information and Computation **100** (1992) 1–77

3. van der Aalst, W.M.P., ter Hofstede, A.H., Weske, M.: Business Process Management: A Survey. In van der Aalst, W.M.P., ter Hofstede, A.H., Weske, M., eds.: Proceedings of the 1st International Conference on Business Process Management, volume 2678 of LNCS, Berlin, Springer-Verlag (2003) 1–12

4. Smith, H., Fingar, P.: Business Process Management – The Third Wave. Meghan-Kiffer Press, Tampa (2002)

5. Smith, H., Fingar, P.: Workflow is just a pi process. BPTrends (2004) http://www.bpmi.org/downloads/LIB-2004-01-4.pdf (September 23, 2005).

6. van der Aalst, W.M.P., ter Hofstede, A.H.M., Kiepuszewski, B., Barros, A.: Workflow Patterns. Distributed and Parallel Databases **14**(1) (2003) 5–51

7. Havey, M.: Essential Business Process Modeling. O'Reilly, Cambridge (2005)

8. Puhlmann, F., Weske, M.: Using the Pi-Calculus for Formalizing Workflow Patterns. In van der Aalst, W., Benatallah, B., Casati, F., eds.: Proceedings of the 3rd International Conference on Business Process Management, volume 3649 of LNCS, Berlin, Springer-Verlag (2005) 153–168

9. Decker, G., Puhlmann, F., Weske, M.: Formalizing Service Interactions. In Dustdar, S., Fiadeiro, J., Sheth, A., eds.: Proceedings of the 4th International Conference on Business Process Management (BPM 2006), volume 4102 of LNCS, Berlin, Springer Verlag (2006) 414–419

10. van der Aalst, W., van Hee, K.: Workflow Management. MIT Press (2002)

11. van der Aalst, W.M.P.: Exterminating the Dynamic Change Bug: A Concrete Approach to Support Workflow Change. Information System Frontiers **3**(3) (2001) 297–317

12. van der Aalst, W.M.P., ter Hofstede, A.H.M.: YAWL: Yet Another Workflow Language (Revised version. Technical Report FIT-TR-2003-04, Queensland University of Technology, Brisbane (2003)

13. Martens, A.: Analyzing Web Service based Business Processes. In Cerioli, M., ed.: Proceedings of Intl. Conference on Fundamental Approaches to Software Engineering (FASE'05). Volume 3442 of Lecture Notes in Computer Science., Springer-Verlag (2005)

14. Leymann, F., Roller, D.: Production Workflow: Concepts and Techniques. Prentice Hall PTR, New Jersey (2000)

15. Petri, C.A.: Kommunikation mit Automaten. PhD thesis, Institut für Instrumentelle Mathematik, Bonn (1962)

16. Dehnert, J., Rittgen, P.: Relaxed Soundness of Business Processes. In Dittrich, K., Geppert, A., Norrie, M.C., eds.: CAiSE 2001, volume 2068 of LNCS, Berlin, Springer-Verlag (2001) 157–170

17. van der Aalst, W.M.P.: Verification of Workflow Nets. In Azéma, P., Balbo, G., eds.: Application and Theory of Petri Nets, volume 1248 of LNCS, Berlin, Springer-Verlag (1997) 407–426

18. Burbeck, S.: The Tao of E-Business Services. Available at: `http://www-128.ibm.com/developerworks/library/ws-tao/` (2000)

19. Dayal, U., Hsu, M., Ladin, R.: Organizing Long-Running Activities with Triggers and Transactions. In: Proceedings of the 1990 ACM SIGMOD international conference on Management of data, New York, ACM Press (1990) 204–214

20. Sangiorgi, D., Walker, D.: The π-calculus: A Theory of Mobile Processes. Paperback edn. Cambridge University Press, Cambridge (2003)

21. BPMI.org: Business Process Modeling Notation. 1.0 edn. (2004)

22. Overdick, H., Puhlmann, F., Weske, M.: Towards a Formal Model for Agile Service Discovery and Integration. In Verma, K., Sheth, A., Zaremba, M., Bussler, C., eds.: Proceedings of the International Workshop on Dynamic Web Processes (DWP 2005). IBM technical report RC23822, Amsterdam (2005)

23. BEA Systems, IBM, Microsoft, SAP, Siebel Systems: Business Process Execution Language for Web Services Version 1.1 (BPEL4WS). (2003)

24. W3C.org: Web Service Choreography Description Language (WS-CDL). 1.0 edn. (2004)

6 Variability Modeling and Product Derivation in E-Business Process Families

Arnd Schnieders, Frank Puhlmann

Business Process Technology Group
Hasso-Plattner-Institute for IT Systems Engineering at the University of Potsdam
D-14482 Potsdam, Germany
{arnd.schnieders,frank.puhlmann}@hpi.uni-potsdam.de

6.1 Introduction

Nowadays, process oriented software systems, like many business information systems, don't exist only in one single version, which covers the whole target market. Instead, many different variants of the system exist, which are specialized according to diverging customer needs. Until now, the corresponding customization has to be done manually, being a time-consuming and error-prone task. However, the ability to rapidly and cost-effectively develop and deploy customer tailored system variants is crucial to the competitiveness of companies developing business software. In order to cope with these challenges, techniques for the efficient production of similar software systems have been developed. These techniques, known as software product family engineering [1], have already been applied successfully in several enterprises [2]. However, up to now the investigation of product family engineering techniques for families of process oriented software, in short process family engineering, has been widely neglected. In this chapter we therefore present our findings in the area of process family architectures for e-business systems, described as variant-rich process models in the Business Process Modeling Notation (BPMN) [3] as well as product derivation issues regarding the particularities in process family engineering.

This chapter is structured as follows: In section 6.2 we give a brief introduction to some basic concepts and describe in section 6.3 their application to an e-business process family. Section 6.4 introduces an approach for variability modeling in e-business process family architectures and for the automization and consistency maintenance during the derivation of process family members. In section 6.5 we

W. Abramowicz and H.C. Mayr (eds.), Technologies for Business Information Systems, 63–74.
© 2007 *Springer.*

illustrate our findings based on an exemplary process family of e-business shops. In section 6.6 we summarize the contents of this chapter.

6.2 Preliminaries

In this section we give a brief introduction to Process Family Engineering and Process Family Architectures.

6.2.1 Process Family Engineering

Product family engineering is a paradigm to develop software applications using a set of software subsystems and interfaces that form a common structure based on which derivative products tailored to individual customer needs can be efficiently developed [4]. Another important aspect is that within a software product family reuse isn't restricted to the reuse of implementation artifacts but is expanded to any development artifact (like e.g. requirement or design models).

Product family engineering is characterized by a so called dual lifecycle [5] as indicated in figure 1 [6]. In order to emphasize that our work focuses on the development of process-oriented software, we use the term process family engineering instead of product family engineering and process family infrastructure instead of product family infrastructure. However, the basic development process is the same for product family engineering as for process family engineering. In the first section of the process family development process (called process family engineering) generic development artifacts (called the process family infrastructure) are developed based on which process family members are derived efficiently in the corresponding phase within the second section (called application engineering) of the process family engineering process. During the derivation of process family members variation points containted in the generic artifacts of the process family infrastructure have to be configured according to the customer requirements. Thereby, dependencies between the variation points within the same as well as between different development artifacts have to be regarded. In our approach, we use an additional model, called variability management model, to control the dependencies between the variabilities within the process family. A specialty of process family engineering in contrast to product family engineering is that the process family architecture can act as a requirements artifact in addition to its role as design artifact. So, the customer can select a product not only based on the typical requirements artifact, like e.g. a feature model, but also based on the process family architecture. This has to be taken into consideration during product derivation.

6.2.2 Process Family Architectures

During the design of a process family a process family architecture (PFA) is developed based on the process family requirements. The PFA acts as reference

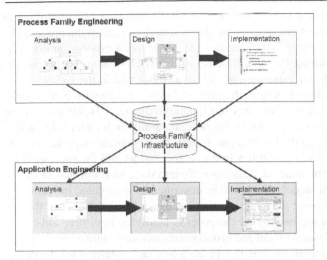

Fig. 1. Process Family Engineering Process

architecture for the members of the process family and describes the basic structure for the applications of the process family. It defines the reusable system parts with their interfaces and covers both, the functional as well as the non-functional requirements on the process family. Moreover, the PFA describes which techniques shall be applied for realizing the variability (i.e. the variability mechanisms) and on which variation points they shall be applied. The selection of appropriate variability mechanisms is crucial for the design of the process family since they can have a substantial impact on the functional and non-functional properties of the system. Additionally, the proper selection of a variability mechanism guarantees for an easy generation of process family members based on the process family infrastructure.

Thus, for supporting process family engineering, concepts and a notation for process family architecture variability mechanisms (PFA variability mechanisms) are required, which allow for modeling architecturally relevant decisions concerning the realization of the system's variability. Later, during implementation, the process family architecture variability mechanisms are realized in the code by implementing variability mechanisms, which are both application domain as well as programming language dependent. Additionally, a binding time can be specified in the process family architecture for the variability, which is also application domain dependent.

6.3 E-Business Process Family

In this section we describe how the concepts described in section 6.2 apply to the development of an e-business process family. We thereby follow the process family engineering reference model shown in figure 1.

Concerning the development of the process family infrastructure we follow the FODA feature diagram notation [7] to describe the requirements on the process family during the analysis phase. Based on these requirements a process family architecture is developed during the design phase using BPMN enhanced by the PFA variability mechanisms for variability modeling as described in the following section. Most of the variabilities within the process family architecture can be linked to an arbitrary combination of features in the feature diagram. However, there are also variabilities, which are specific to the process family architecture. In order to allow for an automatic product derivation as well as for maintenance reasons, the dependencies between the variabilities in the feature model and the process family architecture have to be maintained. Therefore, we introduce an additional model, the variability management model, which will be described in more detail in section 6.4. The variability management model also maintains the constraints between the variabilities within the feature model and the process family architecture. This makes sure that a consistent feature model and process architecture is derived during application engineering. In the implementation phase a program generator for the process family is implemented based on the process family architecture. However, here we won't go into detail concerning the generator implementation. More information can be found in [8]. Concerning the variability implementation, since we assume the e-business application to be written in Java, Java specific variability mechanisms are used to implement the PFA variability mechanisms applied in the BPMN based process family architecture. However, variability implementation issues will not be regarded in this chapter. More information about variability implementation can be found in [8].

In the analysis phase of application engineering the specific requirements on the e-business system to be developed are captured based on the feature model and the variant-rich BPMN model. During product derivation, the dependencies and constraints within the variability management model have to be regarded. The resulting application specific BPMN model is used as configuration model for the program generator. Based on the BPMN model the generator derives application specific Java components from the variant rich Java components and assembles them to the desired e-business system.

6.4 Modeling and Configuring Process Family Architectures in E-Business Process Families

In this section we introduce an approach for modeling variability within BPMN models. Moreover, we deal with the problem of describing and maintaining the dependencies between the variabilities within the variant-rich BPMN model as well as between the feature model and the variant-rich BPMN model using a variability management model.

6.4.1 Modeling Variability in BPMN

According to the requirements for a process family architecture stated in section 6.2.2, a variant-rich business process diagram needs to contain three additions to standard business process diagrams. The first addition is a marking of the places where variability occurs (variation point). Second, the possible resolutions (variants) should be shown in the diagram. Third, the variability mechanism for realizing the variability should be represented. For providing the required additions to model variability within variant-rich BPMN models, we propose to adapt the concept of a stereotype from the UML2 specification to BPMN. Each BPMN activity, association, and artifact can have a stereotype attached.

The stereotype *"VarPoint"* is introduced to highlight variation points. The stereotype *"VarPoint"* can be further specialized. A *"Abstract"* variation point represents alternative behavior; it has to be resolved with a specific variant. A *"Null"* variation point represents optional behavior; it can be resolved with a specific variant. *"Alternative"* is a short representation of an abstract variation point with a specific variant which is the default resolution to this variation point. A *"Optional"* variation point is a short representation of a *"Null"* variation point and a specific variant.

Variants are denoted using the stereotype *"Variant"*. The *"Variant"* stereotype can also be expressed graphically as a puzzle-piece as a marker at the bottom of an activity. The stereotype *"Variant"* can have the tagged value *Preconditions* which provides information about the dependency of the subprocess variant from a certain feature and variant configuration. Since these dependencies can become arbitrarily complex, we provide only a simplified version in the process family architecture. If the selection of a subprocess variant requires the selection of a number of features and variants, the *Preconditions* tagged value will contain these features and variants as a list of comma-separated names. However, if the dependency is more complex, e.g. if a certain subprocess variant shall only be selected if feature 1 and 2, and moreover variant 2 have been selected, but not feature 5 or 6, the *Preconditions* tagged value would contain the following expression: *F(feature 1, feature 2, variant 2, feature 5, feature 6)*. This indicates that the dependency is a more complex one depending on the selection of the features and variants given as parameter values. The concrete dependency information is maintained within the variability management model. Additionally, the stereotype *"Variant"* can have the tagged value *Effects* providing information about the effects resulting from the selection of the variant. These are represented like the preconditions with the difference that no features, but only variants can be affected.

Variants are connected to their variation points by means of associations. The variability mechanism realizing the variability is assigned to the association as a third kind of stereotype. In general, variability mechanisms can be categorized into basic variability mechanisms and variability mechanisms, which are derived from the basic variability mechanisms. As the name indicates, basic variability mechanisms are stand-alone mechanisms, which don't require any other variability mechanisms. We

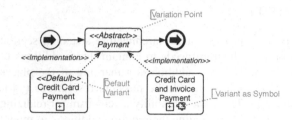

Fig. 2. Encapsulation in BPMN

have identified four types of basic variability mechanisms: *encapsulation of varying sub-processes, parameterization, addition/omission/replacement of single elements*, and *data type variability*. Since data flow is not supported directly in BPMN. Moreover, we support *addition/omission/replacement of single elements* only in a restricted form by *BPMN inheritance*. Concerning the second category of derived variability mechanisms we can further divide this category into variability mechanisms derived by restriction and by combination of other variability mechanisms. *BPMN inheritance* and *extension* are two examples for variability mechanisms derived by restriction and *design patterns* an example for a variability mechanism derived by combination. More details about BPMN variability mechanisms can be found in [8].

For a more convenient illustration, the stereotype *"Variable"* can be used to denote variability below the level of detail currently shown. Figure 2 gives an example for modeling a variation point and two associated variants using the variability mechanisms *encapsulation of varying subprocesses* in this case.

6.4.2 Variability Management for Automatic and Consistent Product Derivation

The variability management model allows for a consistent and partly automatic configuration of the feature model and the variant-rich BPMN model. In this chapter, we will focus on the dependencies related to the feature model and variant-rich process model, while we do not consider implementation artifacts.

The variability management model contains of a set of links to the variation points of every variant-rich process family artifact. Moreover, for every variation point the variability model maintains references to the corresponding variants. For every variant an internal identifier as well as the preconditions and effects for the selection of the variant are stored. The preconditions and effects of a variant are represented in propositional logic. The internal identifier of a variant is used as literal for representing the variant in precondition and effect expressions. The precondition and effect expressions of the feature variants only contain literals that represent feature variants. The precondition expressions of the process model variants can contain literals representing both, feature as well as process model variants, while the effect expression can only contain literals representing process model variants.

The entirety of precondition and effect expressions within the variability model result in the process family constraints, which have to be fulfilled by any valid product configuration. So any product configuration, being represented as a set of selected feature model and process model variants has to fulfill the process family constraints. This has to be proved during product derivation. For verification, the selected and de-selected feature and process model variants are represented as a set of expressions in propositional logic of the form *variant* = *true* (in case the variant has been selected) and *variant* = *false* (in case the variant has been deselected), while *variant* is the name of the literal representing the selected variant. So in order to verify that a configuration fulfills the process family constraints it has to be proved if the configuration fulfills the process family constraints. This can be accomplished by a SAT-checker for example.

Moreover, if a variant has been selected a SAT-checker can calculate resulting configurations based on the process family constraints. The SAT-checker therefore checks whether new expressions of the form *variant* = *false* or *variant* = *true* can be deduced from the process family constraints and the current configuration.

6.5 Example

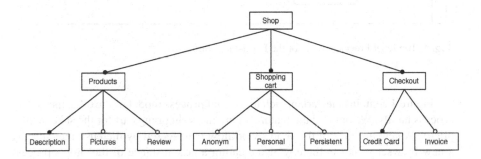

Fig. 3. Features of the E-Business Shop

This section presents a variant-rich process model for a process family of e-business shops also demonstrating some variability implementation details. A feature model is given in figure 3. An e-business shop consists of three mandatory features: products, shopping carts, and checkout. A product has a description as mandatory sub-feature, as well as optionally pictures and reviews. A shopping cart has three optional sub-features. It can either be anonymous (e.g. accessed by a proxy) or per-sonalized. A personalized shopping cart allows for customer dependent discounts and for payment on invoice. Furthermore, a shopping cart can be made persistent, meaning that each time the customer returns, the shopping cart is loaded. The checkout has one mandatory sub-feature, offering a credit card checkout and an optional sub-feature invoice checkout.

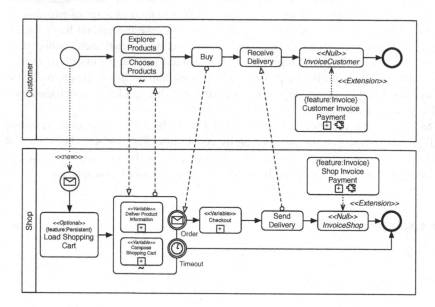

Fig. 4. Top-level Process Model of the E-Business Shop

Figure 4 contains the variant-rich high-level process model of the e-business shop process family. We omitted the feature anonymous shopping cart for the sake of simplicity. A new instance of the shop's workflow is triggered by the customer starting a new browser instance, thereby also creating a new instance of the shop's process (denoted with *"New"*). The customer then explores and chooses products in interaction with the shop, where the shop delivers product information and composes the shopping cart. If the customer decides to buy, she triggers the checkout sub-process of the shop. The shop then sends the delivery and both parties additionally handle invoice payment if the feature is included in this particular shop configuration.

The variant elements have been realized by different variability mechanisms. The customer's pool contains the optional behavior *InvoiceCustomer*, which is represented by a null activity. If the feature *Invoice* is selected, the sub-process *Customer Invoice Payment* is included at the extension point. The shop's pool has the optional task *Load Shopping Cart*, which is included if the feature *Persistent* (shopping cart) is selected. The null activity *InvoiceShop* is filled with *Shop Invoice Payment* if the invoice feature is selected. The task *Shop Invoice Payment* corresponds to the *Customer Invoice Payment*. The tasks *Shop Invoice Payment* and *Customer Invoice Payment* always appear together. The sub-processes *Deliver Product Information*, *Compose Shopping Cart*, and *Checkout* contain variability at a lower level, denoted with the *"Variable"* stereotype. For a lack of space we only consider the *Checkout* sub-process in detail.

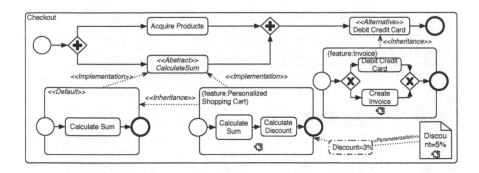

Fig. 5. Checkout Sub-Process of the E-Business Shop

Figure 5 expands the sub-process *Checkout*. It uses the concept of design patterns to describe the possible resolutions to the alternative variation point *CalculateSum*. The first resolution implements the default behavior, i.e. it only calculates the sum. The second, alternative resolution, specializes the default one by using inheritance to add the additional calculation of a discount. The percentage of the discount is parameterized with a default value of 3. The task *Debit Credit Card* also has an alternative implementation derived by using inheritance.

Figure 6 shows an extract from the corresponding variability management model for the feature model and variant-rich process model. Optional features are represented by two variant identifiers. One represents the selected feature while the other one represents the deselected feature. In general all variants of the same variation point are mutually exclusive. This constraint hasn't been represented in the variability management model for the sake of readability. The constraints within the variability management model are formalized using propositional logic. Take for example variation point 3 (*PM_VP3*) of the variant-rich process model. The corresponding constraint expression in propositional logic (*CExpr(PM_VP3)*) looks as follows:

$((ShopInvoicePayment \wedge \neg Null\_VP3) \vee (\neg ShopInvoicePayment \wedge Null\_VP3))$
$\wedge (ShopInvoicePayment \rightarrow Invoice) \wedge (ShopInvoicePayment \rightarrow CreateInvoice) \wedge$
$(ShopInvoicePayment \rightarrow CustomerInvoicePayment) \wedge (Null\_VP3 \rightarrow \neg Invoice) \wedge$
$(Null\_VP3 \rightarrow \neg CreateInvoice) \wedge (Null\_VP3 \rightarrow \neg CustomerInvoicePayment)$

The first part $((ShopInvoicePayment \wedge \neg Null\_VP3) \vee (\neg ShopInvoicePayment \wedge Null\_VP3))$ makes sure that only one variant is selected for the variation point.

The remaining expression reflects the preconditions and effects of the variant selection. Now, for getting a valid configuration of the process family the constraints for all variants have to be true. Thus the process family constraints look as follows:
$CExpr(FM\_VP1) \wedge ... \wedge CExpr(FM\_VP6) \wedge CExpr(PM\_VP1) \wedge ... \wedge CExpr(PM\_VP6)$

Variation Point Reference	Variant Identifier	Preconditions	Effects
Feature Model			
FM_VP4	Personal		¬Anonym
FM_VP6	Invoice		Personal
		•	
		•	
		•	
Variant-Rich Process Model			
PM_VP1	CustomerInvoicePayment	Invoice	CreateInvoice ∧ ShopInvoicePayment ∧
	Null_VP1	¬Invoice	¬CreateInvoice ∧ ¬ShopInvoicePayment ∧
PM_VP3	ShopInvoicePayment	Invoice	CreateInvoice ∧ CustomerInvoicePayment
	Null_VP3	¬Invoice	¬CreateInvoice ∧ ¬CustomerInvoicePayment
PM_VP4	CalculateSum		
	CalculateSumPersonalized	Personal	
PM_VP6	CreateInvoice	Invoice	ShopInvoicePayment ∧ CustomerInvoicePayment
	DebitCreditCard		¬ShopInvoicePayment ∧ ¬CustomerInvoicePayment

Fig. 6. Extract from Variability Management Model

Now let's assume that the customer wants an invoice to be created. Thus, in the variant-rich process model shown in figure 5 she selects the corresponding variant (the one derived from the *Debit Credit Card* activity using inheritance). This corresponds to the selection of the variant *Create Invoice* of the variation point *PM_VP3* in the variability management model. Hence, *CreateInvoice = true*. Now, the following follow-up configurations can be derived automatically based on the process family constraints:

Variant-rich process model:

- *Invoice = true*, since *CreateInvoice → Invoice* (see *CExpr(PM_VP6)*)
- *ShopInvoicePayment = true*, since
  CreateInvoice → ShopInvoicePayment (see *CExpr(PM_VP6)*)
- *CustomerInvoicePayment = true*, since
  CreateInvoice → CustomerInvoicePayment (see *CExpr(PM_VP6)*)
- *DebitCreditCard = false*, since *CreateInvoice XOR DebitCreditCard*
  (see *CExpr(PM_VP6)*)

- $Null\_VP1 = false$, since $CustomerInvoicePayment \rightarrow Null\_VP1$
  (see $CExpr(PM\_VP1)$)
- $Null\_VP3 = false$, since $ShopInvoicePayment\ XOR\ Null\_VP3$
  (see $CExpr(PM\_VP3)$)

Feature model:

- $Personal = true$, since $Invoice \rightarrow Personal$ (see $CExpr(FM\_VP6)$)
- $Anonym = false$, since $Personal \rightarrow \neg Anonym$ (see $CExpr(FM\_VP4)$)

In one of the last follow-up configuration steps $Personal = true$ has been derived. Therefore, the precondition of the variant $CalculateSumPersonalized$ of the process model variation point PM_VP4 has been fulfilled. A tool could now notify the user and ask him, whether $CalculateSumPersonalized$ shall be selected.

6.6 Conclusions

Process Family Engineering hasn't been considered adequately in research so far. Therefore, in this chapter we have introduced an approach for process family architecture modeling and implementation, which contributes to a rapid and cost-effective development and deployment of customer tailored process-oriented business information system variants.

We have shown how a process family architecture for a family of e-business systems can be modeled in BPMN following a variability mechanism centric approach. We have also introduced an approach for the support of automated derivation of follow-up configurations during product derivation using a variability management model, which can economize the configuration work and assures the consistency of the resulting configuration. An algorithm for the automatic configuration would also prove user configurations before accepting them. Therefore, the satisfiability of the process family constraints with the current configuration has to be checked.

References

1. Becker, M.: Adaptation Support in Software Product Families (in German). PhD thesis, Technical University of Kaiserslautern (2004)
2. Reuys, A., Pohl, K., Gacek, C., Bermejo, J., Martínez, J.M., van der Sterren, W., Känsälä, K., Vehkomäki, T., Lerchundi, R., Martínez, R.A.C., Dueñas, J.C., Mittrach, S., Waeber, F., Berde, B., Sophie, V.: System Family Process Frameworks. ESAPS deliverable ESI-WP2-0002-04, University of Essen, Fraunhofer IESE, Sainco, Philips, Nokia, European Software Institute, Universidad Politécnica de Madrid, Siemens, Thomson-CSF/Alcatel LCAT (2000)
3. White, S.A.: Business Process Modeling Notation. BPMN 1.0, Business Process Modeling Initiative (2004)

4. Pohl, K., Böckle, G., van der Linden, F.: Software Product Line Engineering: Foundations, Principles, and Techniques. Springer (2005)

5. Weiss, D.M., Lai, C.T.R.: Software Product-Line Engineering: A Family-Based Software Development Process. Addison-Wesley Longman Publishing Co., Inc., Boston, MA, USA (1999)

6. European ESAPS Consortium: ITEA-ESAPS Full Project Proposal (1999)

7. Kang, K., Cohen, S., Hess, J.A., Novak, W.E., Peterson, A.S.: Feature-oriented domain analysis (foda) feasibility study. Technical Report CMU/SEI-90-TR-21 (1990)

8. Schnieders, A., Puhlmann, F.: Variability Mechanisms in E-Business Process Families. In Abramowicz, W., Mayr, H., eds.: Proceedings of the 9th International Conference on Business Information Systems (BIS 2006). Volume P-85, pp. 583-601 of LNI., Bonn, Gesellschaft für Informatik (2006)

7 Investigation of Reporting Tools for Cadastre Information Systems

Dariusz Król[1], Jacek Oleksy[2], Małgorzata Podyma[3], Michał Szymański[1], Bogdan Trawiński[1]

[1] Wrocław University of Technology, Institute of Applied Informatics, Poland
{dariusz.krol,trawinski}@pwr.wroc.pl
[2] Siemens, Software Development Center, Poland
[3] Computer Association of Information Bogart Ltd., Poland

7.1 Introduction

The speed of Internet grows and brings more and more information to our homes what amazing not only it's users, but also experts. Computers have more power than we could imagine few years ago, the amount of disk space we have is even more than we need. And then comes the problem of technologies used, the problem of technologies with which web applications are built. This work focuses on investigations which are to show the best reporting tools in case of cadastre information systems. To conduct this research two environments are built. Local for the desktop system and open-wide for Internet version. The research is not conducted on artificial systems, but on real life implementations which is very important for the final result.

Cadastre systems are systems designed for the registration of parcels, buildings and apartments as well as their owners and users. The majority of cadastre systems in Poland are developed in two-layer client-server architecture and deployed on Microsoft SQL Server or Oracle database management systems running on Intel servers. The desktop system has been deployed in above 100 local governments throughout Poland while the internet system providing an internet access to cadastral databases is used in about 50 intranets and extranets. The module structure of the cadastre system and cooperating complementary systems is shown in Fig. 1, where three main registers of the cadastre system are land register, building register and apartment register.

W. Abramowicz and H.C. Mayr (eds.), Technologies for Business Information Systems, 75–85.
© 2007 *Springer.*

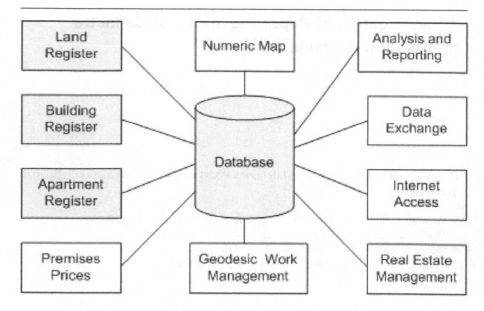

Fig. 1. Architecture of the cadastral system

The investigation process of selecting reporting tools in both internet and desktop cadastre systems is described in the chapter. During last five years several versions of reporting mechanisms were designed and programmed, i.e. mechanisms based on Crystal Reports [1, 3, 11], Free PDF library [10], Microsoft Reporting Services [2, 6] and XML technology [4, 5, 9]. The study has been carried out by the Department of Information Systems at Wrocław University of Technology in cooperation with a commercial software company.

The rest of chapter is organized as follows. The testing of Crystal Reports, Free PDF Library and XML implemented using PHP, ASP and Java in the internet cadastre system is given in Sec. 7.2. In Sec. 7.3, we present the testing of Crystal Reports, Microsoft Reporting Services and XML implemented using Visual C++ in the desktop cadastre system. We conclude in Sec. 7.4.

7.2 Testing of Reporting Mechanisms Implemented in the Internet Cadastre System

The analysis of the prices of reporting tools and the results of benchmark tests shows that these tools are rather designed for large scale internet applications. Their performance exceeds considerably the requirements of our cadastre system and the prices could not be accepted by Polish local governments. So that the authors of the system were forced to look for less expensive solutions. Three versions of reporting mechanisms were chosen and implemented in the EGB2000-INT system, i.e. mechanisms based on Crystal Reports [7], Free PDF library [10] and XML technology [8]. Each solution was tested using Web Application Stress Tool in order to determine what limits in scalability and efficiency could be observed and finally to decide whether the system could be deployed and exploited by information centres in Poland. The most frequently used report i.e. an extract from land register unit (LRUextract) was the main subject of all tests. The Web Application Stress Tool is a Microsoft's product which allows to test the performance of internet services due to simulating a great number of users. The tool enables the tester to record all requests and server responses during a session in form of a test script. The scenario can also be created and edited manually or using IIS log files. Having recorded the script the tester can determine test parameters including the number of iteration, the number of users (threads), connection bandwidth, time of a test. During testing the heaviest load of the server is simulated. The Web Application Stress loads the server continuously, that means the tool sends a request, the server processes it and sends a result back to the tool and having received the response it starts immediately to generate next request. Such operation does not occur during normal work of the system. More probably, when a user receives the page with retrieved data, he starts to browse the result and only after some time he formulates next query. After a test is completed the Web Application Stress generates a report comprising besides general information as time, number of users and requests also detailed figures of e.g. how many times each page was demanded, what was the server response time, how many errors were generated by server.

7.2.1 Testing of Reporting Mechanism using Crystal Reports and Free PDF Library

The architecture of reporting mechanism using Crystal Enterprise 8.5 implemented is shown in Fig. 2. The configuration of the experiment was as follows. Intel PC with 600 MHz clock and 256 MB RAM was used as the server. Two versions of an internet system cooperating with SQL Server and Oracle database management systems were tested. Windows 2000 Server operating system with IIS web server were installed in the same computer as Oracle 8.1.6 and MS SQL Server 2000 DBMS. Both databases contained the same data. In order to be closer to the real activity of users the test scenario comprised calls for three reports using different system options. The tests simulated continuous work of 1, 3, 6 or 12 users and lasted 1 minute. Each test was repeated three times and the mean value of each result was calculated. The results presented in Fig. 4a allowed us to state that reporting solutions were efficient enough to cope with assumed system load in both cases of Oracle and SQL Server databases.

In Fig. 3 the architecture of reporting mechanism using Free PDF library implemented is presented. The server used in the experiment was Intel Pentium PC with 1433 MHz clock and 512 MB RAM. Two configurations of operating system, application technology, web server and DBMS were tested: (1) Linux, PHP, Apache and

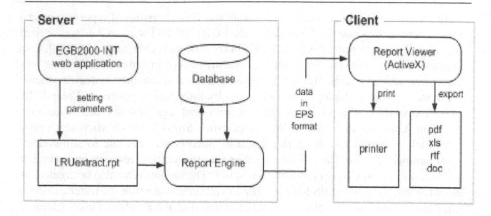

Fig. 2. Architecture of reporting mechanism using Crystal Reports

MySQL - an open source solution, (2) Windows 2000 Server, ASP, IIS, SQL Server 2000 and Crystal Reports as reporting tool. In each case database contained the same data. The Web Application Stress simulated continuous work of 1, 5, 10, 15 or 30 users and the test scenario comprised several steps of data retrieval and generation of reports using 12 different system options. The tests lasted 3 minutes for 1, 2, 5, 10 and 15 threads, and 5 minutes for 30 threads. The results presented in Fig. 4b indicated that an open source reporting solution managed to serve the system load easily while the configuration with Crystal Report did not cope with 15 and more users.

7.2.2 Testing of Reporting Mechanism using XML Technology

Two versions of an internet system using XML technology were tested. First was programmed in PHP language and the second in Java. The architecture of the first one is presented in Fig. 5. All steps of generating XML document were programmed within the application, therefore for each type of the report required a separate code to be developed. The following hardware was used in the experiment: Intel Pentium PC with 2.8 GHz clock and 2 GB RAM was used as the server. Windows 2000 Professional operating system with Apache web server were installed in the same computer as MS SQL Server 2000 DBMS. Test results of reports retrieving 1, 10, 100 and 500 parcels were shown in Fig. 7a. In this experiment growing load of the system from normal to excessive was simulated. As it can be seen in Fig. 7a system malfunctions when the number of users is bigger than 15. The capabilities of the system seemed to be overridden when the number of records was equal to 500 and the number of users was greater than 5. When the number of users was bigger than

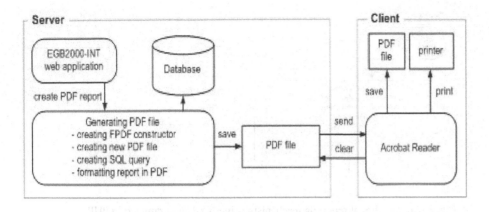

Fig. 3. Architecture of reporting mechanism using Free PDF library

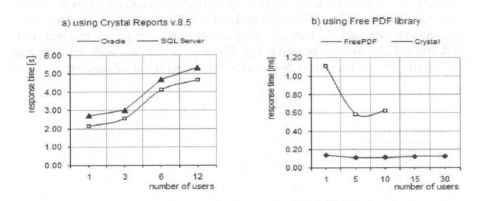

Fig. 4. Test results for a) Crystal Reports and b) Free PDF library

15 the Windows operating system could not remove all threads from memory and therefore the results of the tests were undetermined.

The architecture of the Java version one is presented in Fig. 6. In order to make the code simpler and more readable, XML document pattern and predefined SQL queries were used. The computer system used in the tests was Intel Pentium IV 3.2 GHz with hyper-threading technology and 2 GB RAM. The operating system was Windows Server 2003 SP1 with Microsoft SQL Server 2000. As the application server Apache Tomcat 5 was used. This time AppPerfect's WebTest Load Tester was applied. All tests were carried out with the same database and using the same

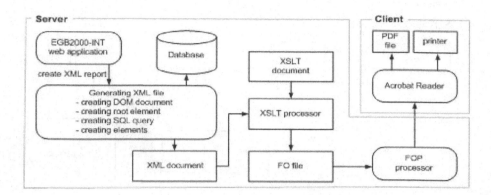

Fig. 5. Architecture of reporting mechanism using XML programmed in PHP

scenario. Continuous work of 1, 2, 10, 15 and 30 users was simulated to reflect small, medium and heavier load of the system. Each test simulated five loops through the scenario by each user. The tests covered different numbers of parcels reported i.e. 1, 10, 100 and 250. As it can be seen in Fig. 7b the better code was achieved at the cost of the efficiency of the system. Nevertheless the results remained acceptable.

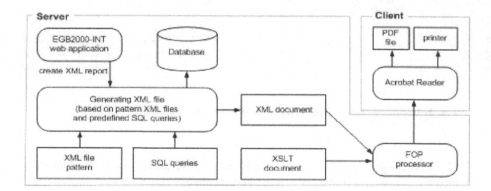

Fig. 6. Architecture of reporting mechanism using XML programmed in Java

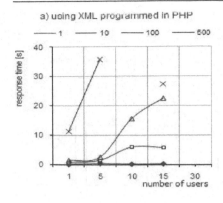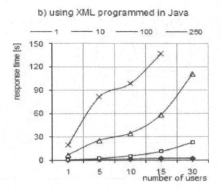

Fig. 7. Test results of reporting mechanism using XML technology

7.3 Testing of Reporting Mechanisms implemented in the Desktop Cadastre System

Three versions of reporting mechanisms were implemented in the desktop cadastre system, i.e. mechanisms based on Crystal Reports 10 (CR10), Microsoft Reporting Services (MRS) and XML technology (XML). Each solution was tested with the most frequently used report i.e. an extract from land register unit. The following hardware was used in the experiment: Intel Pentium PC with 2.8 GHz clock and 2 GB RAM as the server. Windows 2000 Professional and Microsoft SQL Server 2000 were installed in the computer. The configuration is common for smaller information centres where the cadastre system is exploited.

7.3.1 Testing of Reporting Mechanism using Crystal Reports and Microsoft Reporting Services

The architecture of reporting mechanism using Crystal Reports 10 implemented in the desktop system is shown in Fig. 8. The LRUextract.rpt report containing SQL queries selecting data from database is called with a set of parameters. Report Engine sends formatted data in EPS format to Report Viewer which enables to print or export the report. The tests simulated continuous work of 1, 2, 5 or 10 users which generated about 20 the same reports containing 1, 10, 100 or 500 parcels. Mean time of generating individual reports was calculated. The results presented in Fig. 10a allowed us to state that the performance of the reporting solution was acceptable, taking into account the results of users' expectations research and the analysis of report usage.

In Fig. 9 the architecture of reporting mechanism using Microsoft Reporting Services implemented in the desktop system is presented. The application calls a report

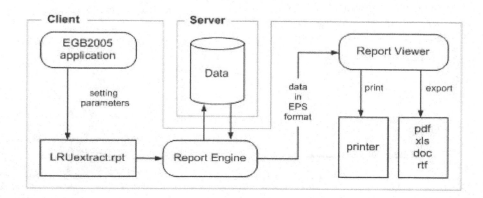

Fig. 8. Architecture of reporting using Crystal Reports 10

using a browser. Report Server uses a report definition retrieved from the Report Server Database and data taken from the data source to create a report. Then the report is transformed into the HTML format and sends to the browser. The tests simulated continuous work of 1, 2, 5 or 10 users which generated above 20 the same reports containing 1, 10, 100 or 500 parcels. Mean time of generating individual reports was calculated. The Microsoft Reporting Services mechanism gave the best results (see Fig. 10b).

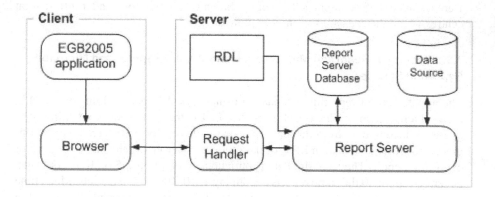

Fig. 9. Architecture of reporting using Microsoft Reporting Services [3]

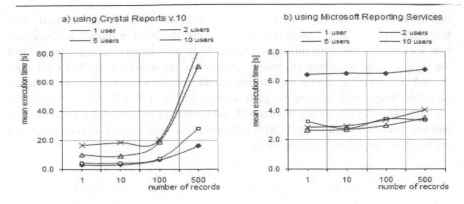

Fig. 10. Test results for a) Crystal Reports and b) MS Reporting Services

7.3.2 Testing of Reporting Mechanism using XML Technology

In Fig. 11 the architecture of reporting mechanism using XML technology implemented in the desktop system is presented. The application formulates a SQL query and sends it to the DBMS and saves retrieved data in a XML file. Processor XSLT sends formatted report to a browser or enables to create the report in the PDF using XSLT FO.

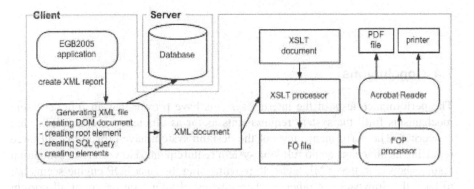

Fig. 11. Architecture of reporting using XML technology [3]

The tests simulated continuous work of 1, 2, 5 or 10 users which generated about 20 the same reports containing 1, 10, 100 or 500 parcels. Mean time of generating individual reports was calculated. These tests gave the better results than previous tests especially as far as bigger number of records included in reports is concerned (see Fig. 12a). This mechanism also seems to be satisfactory taking into account the results of the questionnaire and the analysis of report usage. Further tests were carried out using the reports with different data in order to investigate what impact report caching could have on the performance. In Fig. 12b 1/S and 2/S also mean one and two users generating reports with the same data and 1/D and 2/D denote one and two users executing reports with different data. Almost no difference between the results of both tests could be observed.

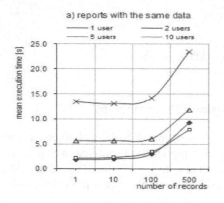 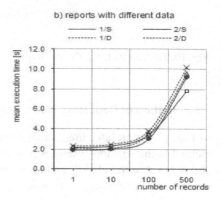

Fig. 12. Test results of XML mechanism

7.4 Conclusions

The performance tests of the internet systems have proven that all four reporting mechanisms fulfil the system requirements as far as efficiency and scalability are concerned. The performance tests of the desktop system have proven that all three reporting mechanisms could fulfil the system requirements. However, our evaluation results show also that XML technology with using the Java FOP engine seems not to have the drawbacks of other mechanisms tested taking into account all present aspects of the cadastre system. However, in the current implementation there is a problem with a productivity. The only chance lies in the continuous development of XML technology and the FOP engine. Behind practicing this technology an easiness of designing reports and their transparency are big advantage over others. In addition, a fact is important that XML is a format at present more and more often taken into practice.

References

1. Crystal Enterprise 9.0 Baseline Benchmark (2003) Windows Server 2003 on IBM@server xSeries 16-way, Crystal Decisions
2. Feature comparison. Microsoft SQL Server 2000 Reporting Services vs. Business objects Crystal Reports (2004) Certia Business Intelligence Team
3. Król D, Oleksy J, Podyma M, Trawiński B (2006) The analysis of reporting tools for a cadastre information system. In: Abramowicz W, Mayr H C (eds) Business Information Systems. Klagenfurt 150-163
4. Król D, Oleksy J, Podyma M, Trawiński B (2006) Comparative analysis of reporting mechanisms based on XML technology. Annales Universitatis Mariae Curie-Skłodowska. Sectio AI, Informatica 5:145-151
5. Król D, Podyma M, Trawiński B (2005) Selection and testing of reporting tools for an Internet Cadastre Information System. Frontiers in Artificial Intelligence and Applications. IOS Press 130:305-316
6. Microsoft SQL Server 2000 Reporting Services (2004) Product Evaluation Guide. Microsoft
7. Pawson D (2002) XSL-FO. O'Reilly
8. Peck K G (2004) Crystal Reports 10: The Complete Reference, McGraw-Hill
9. Podyma M (2005) Review and comparative analysis of reporting tools for internet information systems. M.Sc. Thesis (in Polish), Wrocław University of Technology
10. Skupień M (2003) An Internet Information System of Parcels and Buildings in Linux. M.Sc. Thesis (in Polish), Wrocław University of Technology
11. Włochowicz S (2002) An Internet Information System of Parcels, Buildings and Apartments using Oracle and Ms SQL Server Databases. M.Sc. Thesis (in Polish), Wrocław University of Technology

8 Internet Supported Mass Enrollment to High Schools

Andrzej P. Urbański

Institute of Computer Science
Department of Computer Science and Management
Poznań University of Technology, ul.Piotrowo 3a, 60-965 Poznań, Poland
andrzej.urbanski@cs.put.poznan.pl

8.1 Introduction

Fairness in educational enrollment means that a student with better previous educational results is preferred to a worse student in every school they apply to.

However, in this chapter we show that in the case of mass enrollment it is difficult to make it entirely fair. This observation made in practice in 2002 (see section 8.3.1) has lead us to the design and implementation of a client-server enrollment system working over the Internet (see section 8.3.2). In this chapter we make an attempt to formally prove that computer support is necessary to achieve fair mass enrollment (see section 8.3.3). In section 8.4 we formally define enrollment and its fairness. In section 8.5 we formally criticize mass enrollment performed with the use of traditional methods, while in section 8.6 we introduce algorithms devoted to computerized mass enrollment coordination and prove their correctness.

8.2 Basic Background

In Poland we have the following types of schools:

- primary school (6 years)
- junior high school (3 years) – called "gimnazjum"
- high school or vocational school (usually 3 years).

W. Abramowicz and H.C. Mayr (eds.), Technologies for Business Information Systems, 87–95.
© 2007 *Springer.*

In this chapter we focus on high school or vocational school enrollment, which in Poland has a unified framework. For this reason, we will use the term "schools" to denote both high schools and vocational schools.

Moreover, we will use the term "students" to denote schoolchildren who graduated from junior high school and apply to a high school or a vocational school.

8.3 Motivation for This Work

8.3.1 Dramatic Event as a Motivation

Since the early seventies of the previous century, Polish schools have been enrolling new students on the basis of their school certificates only. Each school can have slightly different rules to compute the number of points from the grades on the certificates. From among all applying candidates each school admits no more students than the number of free places and chooses the candidates who have the highest number of points.

In 2002 the Polish Department of Education changed the rules of school enrollment by allowing the candidates to apply to an unlimited number of schools at the same time (before that the applicant could choose just one school). In that year it led to total chaos in the enrollment process in many schools in Poland, especially in big cities, where thousands of students applied to hundreds of schools and many of them tried to enroll to as many as ten schools simultaneously. The best students were admitted to every school they applied to and consequently blocked places, which prevented the rest from being accepted at all. It took long weeks full of frustration before they finally found a school while better students gradually unblocked places by deciding which school to choose.

8.3.2 Our First Solution at a Glance

This event has made us realize that a centralized information processing system for all enrolling schools (or at least all the schools from the whole metropolitan area) would solve the problem.

Contrary to the chaos in 2002, the subsequent enrollment in Poznań in 2003 was a great organizational success. Students could submit their certificates and preferences until Friday afternoon and received the final results the following week – on Tuesday morning. On Sunday before the Tuesday a super-committee of all school principals worked together and modified their school's offers in order to improve compliance with students' preferences.

As a result, each student was admitted to one school at most. More than 90% of students found schools in this stage of enrollment. The rest did not because they had provided too short preference lists.

8.3.3 Need for a Theoretical Justification

Our enrollment coordination algorithms and systems are mostly viewed as a solution to a specialized problem in a case-specific organizational environment. However, we believe that it can have several more global applications.

For this reason we decided to focus on objective formal methods, criticize traditional methods used in mass enrollment and prove that computer-oriented algorithms overcome the difficulties which arise while using the traditional methods.

8.4 The Enrollment Problem and Its Fairness

In order to define the enrollment problem, we assume that each candidate provides an ordered list of schools starting from the most desired one.

Definition 1. The enrollment problem

<u>**Input**</u>
p – preferences; $pi,j=k$ means that k-th school was ranked j-th by candidate i
q – quality of a student; $q_{i,k}=v$ means that student i in the opinion of school number k is valued at v (in this chapter we assume that a different quality value is assigned to each student); if the value does not depend on the school (each school has the same opinion) we omit k
s – maximum school capacity; $sk=l$ means that school k can take in not more than l new students
n – number of students
m – number of schools

<u>**Output**</u>
r – enrollment result; $ri=j$ means that student i is assigned to a school number j on his preference list; 0 means that there is no school for student i

<u>**Problem**</u>
Find integer ri for $i=1,2,...n$ such that:

1. $$\forall_{i \in <1,n>} 0 \leq r_i \leq m$$

2. $$\forall_{k \in <1,m>} s_k \geq \left| \left\{ p_{i,r_i} = k \mid i \in <1,n> \right\} \right|$$

3. If student i is admitted to school r_i and student j is not, despite his or her preferences, student i should have a higher value of the quality function than j.

$$\forall_{i,j \in <1,n>} \exists_{k<r_j} \left(p_{j,k} = p_{i,r_i} \Rightarrow q_i > q_j \right)$$

Point (3) in **Definition 1** describes a fairness rule, which is intuitive and could be easily checked on publicly available lists of admitted candidates.

8.5 Traditional Distributed Enrollment

Traditionally, each school performs the enrollment independently from the others, and the process is not coordinated by anyone. We distinguish two variants of such enrollment: with strongly limited and unlimited number of schools the student can apply to at the same time.

8.5.1 Limited Registrations

The most common limit set by different countries throughout the years is between one and three.

ALGORITHM 1

Each school performs its individual enrollment process at the same time. No school can recruit more students than the number of available places.

THEOREM 1

ALGORITHM 1 is not fair.

PROOF

We can easily imagine a situation in which a student with fairly good educational results applies to very popular schools and is not admitted anywhere in the first stage of the enrollment process because of too many better candidates. Had he or she chosen a less besieged school, he or she would have been admitted straight away. The algorithm is not fair because the results of enrollment depend on the student's ability to predict school's popularity in a given year.

8.5.2 Unlimited Registrations

The great inconvenience and disadvantage of this method lies in the fact that the organizers of enrollment have to force students to make hasty decisions. Moreover, in practice the process appears to be very long and inefficient. However, in this chapter we discuss its fairness only.

ALGORITHM 2

Each school starts its enrollment at the same time.
After the applications' submission deadline, students who are potentially admitted are required to confirm their enrollment within a few days or else they are deleted from the list. Candidates who were rejected at first are now added to the list of admitted students to fill in the vacancies but again they are given some time to confirm their enrollment. The process continues until the lists contain confirmed enrollments only. What is more, each student can confirm his or her enrollment in one school only, which means that the decision has to be final.

THEOREM 2

ALGORITHM 2 is not fair.

PROOF

Not fair, because it requires students to make risky decisions in a short period of time. Good but nervous students will probably confirm the first offer, although they had a chance to get to a better school, provided that they waited patiently until better students confirmed their enrollments elsewhere and unblocked places.

8.6 Centralized Coordination of Mass Enrollment

In the previous section we have proved that traditional distributed mass enrollment is not fair. When we discovered this in practice (see section 8.3) we introduced computerized central mass enrollment coordination, the fairness of which we will prove in this section. We will separately discuss several variants applied in different circumstances.

8.6.1 Coordination Algorithm for the Unified Criteria Problem

The unified criteria problem is the simplest one, but still useful in practice (see [3] for examples). It assumes that all schools use the same student ranking methods and therefore it is enough to compute one quality value for each student.

ALGORITHM 3

Sort the student records by their educational results starting from the best student. Take the first student from the list and let him choose any school which still has vacancies. Remove the student from the list, and repeat the procedure for the next student.

THEOREM 3

The sorting algorithm is fair for the unified criteria problem.

PROOF

Fairness rule from **Definition 1** will be fulfilled, because only a candidate with better results can steal another candidate's dream place in a given school.

8.6.2 Cloned Applications Algorithm for Different Ranking Criteria in Every School

The following algorithm was first implemented on a notebook in 2002 and used to build the first enrollment system in 2003 (see section 8.3). It is almost the same as the traditional **ALGORITHM 2**, but all decisions are made "inside the computer" (student preference lists are used instead of asking students for confirmation in the course of the enrollment process), which makes work much faster, and the results– fair because it does not require risky and hasty decisions from students.

ALGORITHM 4

Step 1: For each school there is a queue of candidates:

$$\underset{k \in <1,m>}{\forall} C_k = \left\{ i \in <1,n> | \; p_{i,j} = k \right\}$$

$$\underset{k \in <1,m>, i, j \in <1,n>}{\forall} |C_k| \geq i > j \Rightarrow q_{c_k^i, k} < q_{c_k^j, k}$$

Each student is cloned to appear in the queue of every school he included in his or her preference list.

Step 2: Queue L of potentially admitted students is created and initially assigned:

$$L := \left\{ i \in <1,n> | \; \underset{l \in <1,s_k>}{\exists} \; c_k^l = i \right\}$$

Step 3: Subsequent student number "i" is taken from L and removed from it.

Step 4: We are looking for a minimum value of "mj" where

$$p_{i,mj} = k \wedge \underset{l \in <1,|C_k|>}{\exists} (c_k^l = i \wedge l \leq s_k)$$

Step 5: For all j greater than mj we remove "i" from a corresponding C_k

Step 6: Add to L students who moved above the admittance border in any C_k

Step 7: If L is not empty then go to Step3.

Step 8: All C_k contain a list of admitted students (on positions from 1 to s_k).

THEOREM 4

Cloned applications algorithm is fair.

PROOF

1. The property of fairness is guaranteed in Step1, which enforces the right order of students in each school. This order is not changed in subsequent steps and only superfluous entities are removed in Step5.
2. Algorithm finds a solution in a finite number of steps, because each entry from C is added to and removed from L only once.

However, it was found that this algorithm behaves strangely in some cases and thus is not entirely fair [3].

Definition 2.

For at least two students i and j of which one has $p_{i,1}=1$ and another $p_{j,1}=2$. If a given algorithm assigns them in a reversed order i.e. $r_i=2$ and $r_j=1$ we call it a paradox of crossed preferences.

THEOREM 5

ALGORITHM 4 allows for the occurrence of the paradox of crossed preferences.

PROOF

Assume we have only two students and two schools with only one free place in each one. Preferences are as follows: $p_{i,1}=1$, $p_{j,1}=2$, $p_{i,2}=2$, $p_{j,2}=1$; and quality factors: $q_{i,1}=100$, $q_{j,1}=200$, $q_{i,2}=200$, $q_{j,2}=100$. It is easy to notice that **ALGORITHM 4** will find result $r_i=2$ and $r_j=1$.

8.6.3 Moving Applications Algorithm for Different Ranking Criteria in Every School

When one thinks about a new generation of enrollment systems one thinks about something extremely flexible. When we analyzed the enrollment problem for the first time, we thought of agent-based systems [1,2]. However, existing environments are not ready to be used in such responsible applications. Today's agent-based environments do not implement persistent systems [2]. Nevertheless, our experiments on agent-based systems resulted in creating a simple and lucid algorithm, which could also be implemented traditionally:

ALGORITHM 5

proc AddToSchool(t:Student,k:School);

For a school k queue of candidates is updated:

$$C'_k = \{i \in C_k \cup \{t\}\}$$

$$\forall_{k \in <1,m>, i,j \in <1,n>} |C'_k| \ge i > j \Rightarrow q_{c'^i_k,k} < q_{c'^j_k,k}$$

if $|C'_k| > S_k$

then begin

AddToSchool("last student from C_k", "next school on his/her preference list");

RemoveLastFrom C'$_k$;

end;

end (* AddToSchool *);

begin

    for all t **from** all students

      AddToSchool(t,$p_{t,1}$);

end;

Of course, this algorithm is fair:

THEOREM 6

Moving applications algorithm is fair.

PROOF

ALGORITHM 5 works on the basis of a rule "better removes worse". Each student tries to apply to the first school on their preference list. If there are already no free places there, the student is moved to their next preference, but even if the algorithm initially assigns a student to the first or next school on their preference list, the place is not guaranteed and can change in subsequent steps. This is a direct application of the fair enrollment rule (**Definition 1**).

What is more interesting is that it does not allow for the paradox of crossed preferences:

THEOREM 7

ALGORITHM 5 does not allow for the paradox of crossed preferences.

PROOF

Let us assume we have only two students and two schools with only one free place in every school. Preferences are as follows: $p_{i,1}=1$, $p_{j,1}=2$, $p_{i,2}=2$, $p_{j,2}=1$; and quality factors: $q_{i,1}=100$, $q_{j,1}=200$, $q_{i,2}=200$, $q_{j,2}=100$. It is easy to notice that **ALGORITHM 5** will find the correct result: $r_i=1$ and $r_j=2$.

8.7 Conclusions

In our first paper [3] we have sketched a much wider area of applications for enrollment systems including internal (already implemented and used in practice at Poznań University of Technology since 1998) and external enrollment at Universities. Out next step should be to refine our algorithms or even find more sophisticated ones, all to make the enrollment process as efficient and fair as possible.

Acknowledgements

This work was partially supported by grant DS-91-425 from Poznań University of Technology.
The author wishes to thank Aleksandra Wojnowska for her comments on an earlier version of this chapter, which allowed for significant improvements.

References

1. Mazurek C., Stroiński M., Urbański A.P., "A Client-Server System for Mass Recruitment to Secondary Schools in a Metropolitan Area", eAdoption and Knowledge Economy(eds. P.Cunningham and M.Cunningham), Vienna, IOS Press, 2004, pp.1801-1808.
2. Płóciennik M., "Solving recruitment problems in agent-based environment", M.Sc. Thesis, Dept. of Computer Science and Management, Poznań University of technology, September, 2004(in Polish).
3. Urbański A.P., Nawrocki J., "Algorithms for fair and efficient educational recruitment", Conference on EDI-EC, Łódź, Acta Universitas Lodziensis, FOLIA OECONOMICA 167, 2003, pp.429-442 (in Polish).

9 Dealing with Administrative Discretions in E-Government: The Citizen Consultation Model

Wanchai Varavithya, Vatcharaporn Esichaikul

School of Engineering and Technology
Asian Institute of Technology, Thailand
{Wanchai.Varavithya, vatchara}@ait.ac.th

9.1 An Overview of Administrative Discretions

Public administrative discretion refers to the degree of latitude or flexibility exercised by public administrators when making decisions or conducting any agency business [1]. As such, discretions can be viewed as a source for arbitrariness, unfairness, corruption or irrational outcomes and need to be eradicated. However, this chapter argues that taking away discretions from the government might cause an official to ignore citizen-individualized circumstances and thereby overlook special needs of citizens. This chapter suggests the open government concept coined by Nelson [2] to bring about transparency and openness in discretionary decision-making. Nelson defines the concept of 'open government as "Participation contributes to open government, open government contributes to the need to justify official actions in terms of morally acceptable principles, and the need to justify contributes to better decisions."

With the goal of eliminating the discretionary decision-making by whim, caprice, chance, or ritual, Galligan [3] introduces the concept of "consultation" as a mode of participation that connotes the presentation of arguments and proof in order to influence the way issue is to be settled. The decision-maker has a duty to hear and consider, but may decide for reasons which go beyond the submissions of the parties, and may act according to standards which are defined only broadly or settled only in the course of the decision.

With the aim of promoting the concept of open government, this chapter presents the e-government discretionary framework [4] as a point of departure (Table 1). The framework describes collaboration activities based on two dimensions: the citizen consultation process and the administrative decisions as classified by Galligan [3]. The level of discretions emphasizes that the use of discretions is low

97

W. Abramowicz and H.C. Mayr (eds.), Technologies for Business Information Systems, 97–108.
© 2007 *Springer*.

in the adjudication decisions where the rules are clear and explicit. However, discretions play a partial role in the modified adjudication, as it has to deal with how person or situations are to be treated. In the policy issue decisions, discretion is vital in the decision-making processes, not only to an official but also to citizens who must exercise discretions through voting, public hearing, etc. The e-government discretionary framework is an excellence tool to be used as a lens to analyze and design coordination and collaborative activities in the discretionary e-government problem domains.

Table 1. The e-government discretionary framework

| | | Classification of discretionary decisions[a] | Citizen Consultation Process | | |
			Phase 1) Disclosure of facts and evidence before decision	Phase 2) Formulate or apply existing standards, and make decisions	Phase 3) Issue legal decision and appealing procedures
Level of Discretion	Low	Adjudication	Inform of applicable rules, evidences, fact of the case.	Apply existing standards to the fact of the case.	Issue a statement of reasons
	Medium	Modified Adjudication	Propose, argue, debate on reasons, facts, evidence and 'open-texture' language.	Formulate a new set of standards or apply existing standards based on merit of the case.	Collaborative writing and issuing a statement of reasons
	High	Policy Issue	Notify or educate public of rights and obligations under the laws.	Make decision through voting or signing petition.	View, verify, or track results of a decision-making

[a]Adapted from Galligan [3]

9.2 Design of the Citizen Consultation Model

As modified adjudication decisions represent a large portion of decisions entrusted to an official [3], this chapter intends to design the Citizen Consultation Model (CICO) to support every step of the citizen consultation process under the modified adjudication decision shown in Table 1. Samples in this type of decisions can be found in business registration services, social welfare, immigration, police, deportation, etc. The special requirements are:

- An official is a person who is held accountable for decision outcomes.
- Decision-making is aimed at a citizen-individualized problem in relation to his or her situation, not at a general public issue.
- In certain cases, a decision-maker is required to formulate a new set of standards, which could be unpredictable and difficult to model.

Based on the above special requirements, CICO has three prime objectives: first, to provide a platform in order to facilitate discussions and argumentations amongst participants; second, to assist a discretionary decision-maker in formulating a new set of standard; and third, to advise the best alternative to a decision-maker. The CICO conceptual model is depicted in Fig. 1.

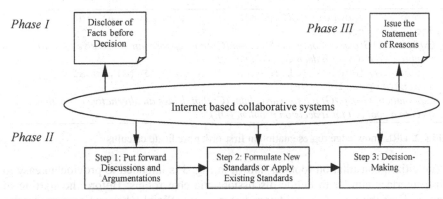

Fig. 1. CICO conceptual model

This chapter presents the participation platform of Step 1 with the aim to facilitate participants who take part in the consultation processes and to assist a decision maker in the formulation of new standards in Step 2.

9.2.1 The Citizen Participation Platform

In Step 1 of Fig. 1, instead of using a normal web forum, i.e. chat-room, web board that are simple but often lead to chaos, the semi-formal approach is applied with an intend to let participants thinks and discuss the issue within a certain knowledge representation framework. A semi-formal vocabulary of Decision Representation Language (DRL) developed by Lee and Lai [4] is selected as a language for representing discussions and argumentations. DRL was implemented in SIBYL, a tool for managing group decision rationale similar to a knowledge-based system which provides services for the management of dependency, uncertainty, view points, and precedents [5]. The strength of DRL is the tendency to instigate people to be aware of the decision objectives against which alternatives in relation to explicit goals and be able to evaluate each alternative in order to make decisions. It also allows the user to formulate arguments to support or deny claims. The basic elements of decision-making in DRL are:

- *A decision problem* represents a decision issue or a problem of choosing the alternative that best satisfies the goals.
- *Alternatives* represent options from which to choose or a possible solution to a decision problem.
- *Goals* represent properties that an ideal option should have.
- *Claims* represent the means of argumentation, which puts forward in the relation to alternatives and goals (i.e. supports or denies).

In order to keep the whole discussions and arguments in a knowledge base, argumentations in DRL knowledge representation will be transformed into the first-order predicate calculus as shown in Fig. 2.

```
Group (G) (supports (claim(C), (alternative (A), goal (G),
decision_problem DP)))
```
Explanation: Group (G) put forward claim (C) that supports an alternative (A) with respect to a goal (G) for a decision problem (DP)
```
Group (G) (denies (claim(C), (alternative (A), goal (G),
decision_problem (DP)))
```
Explanation: Group (G) put forward claim (C) that denies an alternative (A) with respect to a goal (G) for a decision problem (DP)

Fig. 2. DRL knowledge representation in first-order predicate calculus

The citizen consultation room as shown in Fig. 3 is intended to provide an easy to use interface similar to public discussions via chat rooms. Before the starting of phase II of the citizen consultation process, an official who acts as a moderator must designate an instance of promulgation, case identification, groups and names of participants, and start date and due date, an instance for a decision problem, alternatives, and goals. Participants can always use a mouse to point at a DRL argumentation element and use the right-mouse button to initiate the corresponded elements, i.e. a new decision problem, sub-alternatives, sub-goals, questions & answers and can enter text statement or upload file down the root node of the hierarchical structure graph. This way, participants can influence the nature of decision problem, alternatives, and goals, and decide whether it should include more or cross out any unnecessary alternatives or goals.

The next step is shown in Fig. 4 where participants can solicit their opinions or put forward discussions and argumentations by appraising an alternative with respect to a goal in the decision matrix room. A participant expresses their claim arguments as 'supports' or 'denies' and can initiate a discussion by posting questions or answers instance. CICO facilitates the argument polarize feature for participants by clicking a tap control and viewing the whole set of arguments in three different views: alternatives, goals, and participant point of views. This feature helps participants gain a full understanding of the case and thereby enhances the openness principal. Participants may put before the decision-maker an argument that may compete or rebut each other in an equal of opportunity mode of participation.

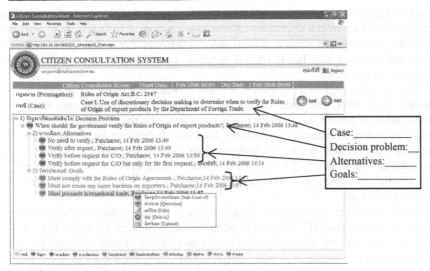

Fig. 3. Sample screen of the citizen consultation room

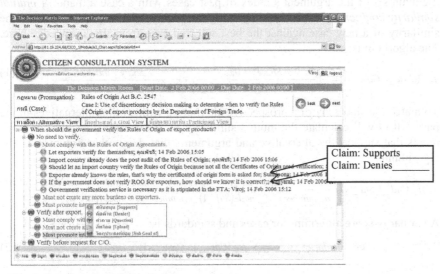

Fig. 4. Sample screen of the decision matrix room

9.2.2 The Formulation of Standards

To help formulate a new set of standard for a decision making in Fig. 2, instead of using argumentation-based reasoning [7] or resorting to formal approaches, such as probability reasoning and fuzzy logic, this chapter suggests CBR technique [8] to support a decision making by learning form past experiences. CBR is a very useful technique in representing specific knowledge tied to a case and providing useful lessons that help a decision-maker achieve a goal. CICO intents to provide a decision maker with knowledge from past experiences that consist of case arguments and its outcomes. The CBR role in CICO consists of two major functions: *indexing and matching*.

Indexing DRL elements must represent the context of a descriptive argumentation statement. Therefore, indexing should be carried out using concepts that a decision-maker understands and normally uses to describe the frame of reference of arguments, such as education, psychological, etc. Index can be suggested automatically by matching a concept pertaining to the knowledge-base with a word contained in the instance of DRL. If an existing index concept is not relevant, a decision-maker can create a new index concept and add it to the knowledge-base for future matching.

Matching is the process of comparing two cases to one another and determining the degree of matching [8]. The CICO adopted the reminding approach [8], which looks for relevant similarities between new cases whose arguments were put forward and the cases in which they are reminded of. This chapter adopted *a similarity-scoring mechanism* [9] to calculate the relevant similarity by the matching of the main set of the argument's index of past cases with a case at hand. *A mutual similarity coefficient* is calculated by using the binary relationship to measure the similarity of a new case against the best selected case from the knowledge-base. The algorithm is:

$$\mu_{sim}\left(Case\_1, Case\_n\right) = \frac{1}{n}\left(\frac{Share\_index}{number\_of\_node\left(Case\_1\right)} + \frac{Share\_index}{number\_of\_node\left(Case\_n\right)}\right) \quad (1)$$

To match the similarity of a prospective alternative with similar alternatives in the past, CICO will calculate the mutual similarity of the coefficient value for arguments that support the alternative and arguments that deny other arguments. The algorithm is:

$$\mu_{sim}\left(Std\_1, Std\_n\right) = \frac{1}{n}\left(\frac{Share\_index}{number\_of\_node\left(Std\_1\right)} + \frac{Share\_index}{number\_of\_node\left(Std\_n\right)}\right) \quad (2)$$

A similarity score algorithm for cases and standards is:

$$Case\_similarity\_score = \sum \mu_{sim}\left(Case\_1...Case\_n\right) / \sum (n) \quad (3)$$

$$Standard\_similarity\_score = \sum \mu_{sim}\left(Std\_1...Std\_n\right) / \sum (n) \quad (4)$$

The CICO advises the best alternative based on the *argument contribution score*, which is calculated from the total weights of argument in relation to the past outcomes. The basic idea derives from the nature of a discretionary decision-making in which a decision-maker is inclined to subscribe to arguments that had brought about success outcomes in the past. The higher the argument contribution score, the outcome is more likely to be satisfactory. The argument contribution score are calculated as follows:

- The outcomes of the past cases are designated as *satisfactory or unsatisfactory*.
- In the case of a *satisfactory outcome*, an argument that supports the selected alternative and an argument that denies unselected alternatives are scored as a *positive* contributor; therefore, the contribution score shall be increased by one point.

```
If Case_n: 'satisfied' (Alt_1: selected, Alt_n: rejected)
Then    Group_n, Claim_n <Supports> [Alt_1, Goal_n,
        DP_n][value +1],
        Group_n, Claim_n <denies> [Alt_n, Goal_n,
        DP_n][value +1]
```

- In the case of an *unsatisfactory outcome*, an argument that supports a selected alternative and an argument that denies unselected alternatives are scored as a *negative* contributor; therefore, the contribution score shall be decreased by one point.

```
If Case_n: 'unsatisfied' (Alt_1: selected, Alt_n: rejected)
Then    Group_n, Claim_n <Supports> [Alt_1,  Goal_n,
        DP_n][value -1],
        Group_n, Claim_n <Denies> [Alt_n, Goal_n,
        DP_n][value -1]
```

- The argument contribution score of each arguments is calculated as:

$$Score_{arg\_n} = \sum \left[Value_{satisfied} + Value_{unsatisfied} \right] \tag{5}$$

- The total argument contribution score of a set of standards is calculated as:

$$Total\_Score_{Std\_n} = \sum \left[Score_{arg\_n} \right] \tag{6}$$

The case similarity score and the argument contribution score calculated from the matching of problem statements, goals, alternatives, and claims of the cases together with outcomes (if any) will assist a decision maker to use discretions in a more intelligence and reasonable manner.

9.3 System Evaluation and Limitation

The experiment focuses on the impact of CICO in the use of discretions by public authorities towards the good governance. The experiment task was to make discretionary decisions on the setting up policy under the Ministry of Commerce that effect citizens (or exporters). The experiments participants were nine exporters who are affected by government decisions, three authorities who make decisions, and two experts. Exporters who involved the experiment already familiarize with the department's policy and work details. The experiment was conducted in three weeks time period in February 2006 and completed under the direction of the facilitator by the following procedures.

- After the training, an officer generated a problem statement, goals, and alternatives.
- Each exporter took half an hour to review and generate questions or arguments according to goals and alternatives.
- Approximately one week later, exporters were asked to review the whole arguments again and generated more arguments if they wished to.
- Three officers separately reviewed the whole arguments and selected an alternative as a final decision.
- All exporters scrutinized the final decisions and filled in the questionnaires.

The objective of the questionnaire was to get exporter's assessments about the good governance principle from the discretionary decision-making processes and outcomes. To fill the questionnaire in, citizens had to give an answer from the strongly agree, agree, neutral, disagree, strongly disagree scale. Citizens had to evaluate the level of good governance criteria [10], i.e. openness and transparency. The excerpted results from twenty question items are depicted in Fig. 5.

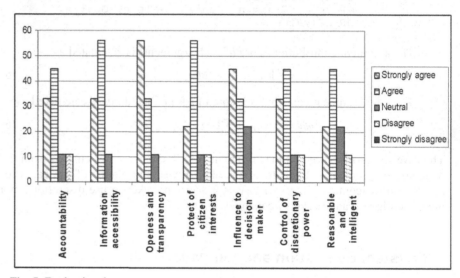

Fig. 5. Evaluation data

The feedback was certainly encouraging. There was an average of 3.5 arguments per person. In all issues arising from the questionnaires, the percentage of the positive answers (the sum of the 'strongly agree' and 'agree' percentages) was over 70 %. It is clear that by involving citizens in the discretionary decision-making processes, the majority of citizens were convinced that by using CICO, they could influence a decision-maker to think more thoroughly and make decisions in a reasonable and intelligent manner. Furthermore, the openness and transparency principle is achieved as the actions of citizens can be seen for the purpose of scrutiny and supervision, which can prevent any elements of arbitrariness and ensure that people interests are taken into account. However, the consistency of decision-making from the points of views of citizens is not very satisfying, as the experiment cases were limited to two rounds within a short period of time.

Based on the experimental experience, it should be noted that CICO is not well support for:

- A case where decision makers consider merely supportive arguments for approval and allow a junior officer to filter and dismiss the case if any negative argument is found before final decision.
- Non-routine discretionary decision-making as it cannot fully benefit from past experiences.
- An environment with low trust and security between citizens and authorities
- Citizens who are not comfortable with arguing with authorities.

9.4 Related Works

Based on the implementation of DRL in CICO, an argumentation-based reasoning seems to be a prime candidate technique for our future works. The basic question is to determine how far the reasoning technique can provide in an attempt to automate the CICO in the discretionary context. An argumentation theory has greatly contributed to the development of artificial intelligence application in law, which aims at structuring knowledge representation and modeling dialectical reasoning. Stranieri et al. [11] used the generic/actual argument model to predict judicial decisions regarding a property split following divorce under Australia law. The argumentation theory of Toulmin [12] was applied in the development of the Split-Up systems [13]. The argumentation based representation is central to the Split-Up system, which is used to structure Australian family law to be generated and enables the task of determining the percentage split of assets to award each party of a failed marriage by integrating rule-based reasoning and neural networks into one seamless system.

EMBRACE is a legal knowledge based systems that deal directly with discretion issues in the Australia Refugee Law [14]. EMBRACE is constructed based on the argument structure of Toulmin as in the Split-Up system. Its framework is intended to capture arguments within the Australia Refugee Law and facilitates the integration of information gathering and retrieval for the purpose of argument construction and drafting. However, the system does not attempt to automatically interpret information retrieved related to any specific argument, but facilitates the validation and substantiation of data, claims and their values by users.

Issue-Based Information Systems [15] is a vital argumentation-based model. IBIS elements consist of an issue (decisions to be made or goals to be achieved), positions (data that have been brought up to declare alternative option), and constraints (preference relations between two positions). SIBYL [6], which is an extension of gIBIS, is a tool for managing group decision rationale and implements using DRL as a representation language. SIBYL allows users to evaluate alternatives with respect to the goals specified in order to make the final decision.

Zeno argumentation framework invented by Gordon and Karacapilidis [16] focuses on the multiple participants who put forward arguments in order to contest and defeat other arguments. GeoMed is a sample of group decision support system for Geographical Mediation on the World Wide Web using Zeno argumentation framework [17]. It supports the collaborative environment planning which is performed through debates, negotiations and argumentation amongst various agents. Mediation services within GeoMed provide an issue based conferencing and group decision support systems. GeoMed's task is not intended to play the role of a cop or judge but acts as an assistant and advisor and leave the final decisions and actions to users to decide.

HERMES system uses similar argumentation elements as GeoMed [18]. In HERMES, the constraint is a key element which represents preference relations that are critical to the argumentation-based reasoning. The primary task of HERMES system is to provide direct computer support for the argumentation, negotiation and mediation process in a group decision-making. It was implemented in Java (applets) and runs on the Web; therefore, it facilitates distributed collaborative discussions. In HERMES, constraint is an important element that provides a qualitative way to weight reasons, which are more (or less) important than or are equally important. Karacapilidis and Papadias emphasize that the mix of human and computer reasoning is still necessary to assist and advise decision makers in HERMES.

Other argumentation-based approach is demonstrated by Zhang et al. [19] who developed the frame-based argumentation information structure and implement in a group argumentation support system prototype (FBA-GASS). The proposed frame-based information structured is applied in electronic brainstorming and argumentation to support group decision task generation and identification in organization. Decision can be reached via a consensus or voting.

From the reviews of the argumentation-based reasoning systems, the technique is very useful in facilitating and structuring citizen discussions and argumentations. It is also practical in the transformation of arguments into a FOB to be kept in a knowledge-base. Argumentation techniques encourage a decision-maker to think thoroughly and make decisions in a reasonable and intelligent manner. Furthermore, citizen can see through the whole set of arguments for the purpose of scrutiny and supervision, which can efficaciously prevent the elements of arbitrariness and ensure that people interests are taken into account.

However, in the discretionary decision-making context, there are still several problems to be solved. First, despite the fact that the argumentation technique is an effective tool to structure argumentation knowledge, it is still difficult to model a reasoning mechanism for unfettered discretionary domains [20]. Second, discussions and argumentations proposed by citizens may not always be logically valid, and therefore cannot automatically transform premises to reach the conclusion using logic calculations. Third, argumentation-based reasoning does not take past experiences into consideration; hence, the principle of transparency and fairness cannot be fully achieved.

Karacapilidis et al. [21] have demonstrated the integrated framework of a case-based reasoning and an argumentation-based reasoning technique for group decision processes. The framework addresses the presence of various selection criteria, preferences, goals, etc. as viewpoints that can evolve over time. The integration of CBR techniques aims at supporting agents involved in group decision-making processes to retrieve, adapt, and re-use old cases at a part of a discussion episode. However, the Karacapilidis's framework is not intended to use CBR to directly support the decision-making.

9.5 Conclusion

The e-government discretionary framework is presented in this chapter as a point of departure to analyze and design the coordination and collaboration of discretionary decision-making in modified adjudication decisions. CICO contributes to the instrumental rationality of discretionary decision-making and follows the commitment to a democratic government. By providing the participation platform via the Internet, an official, citizens, and affected parties can put forward discussions and argumentations relevant to the cases, which is an effective way to enforce caution on the decision-maker and reflect more on the issue. The experiment and evaluation of CICO in a real digital government setting is proved that majority of citizens are convinced of the good governance outcomes from an administrative discretionary decision-making. An extension of CICO with the focus on a large-scale citizen involvement and use of discretions in setting up a public policy is a challenging issue for future researches.

References

1. Warren KF (2003) Encyclopaedia of Public Administration and Public Policy. ISBN: 0-8247-4240-0: 35-38
2. Nelson WN (1990) Justifying Democracy. In: Galligan D.J. Discretionary Powers A Legal Study of Official Discretion, Clarendon Press Oxford
3. Galligan DJ (1990) Discretionary Powers A Legal Study of Official Discretion. Clarendon Press Oxford
4. Varavithya W, Esichaikul V (2006) Dealing with discretionary decision-making in e-government: an open government approach. Electronic Government: International Journal 3 (4): 356-372
5. Lee J, Lai K (1991) What's in design rationale. Human-Computer Interaction 6 (3-4): 251-280
6. Lee J (1990) SIBYL: A tool for managing group decision rationale. Artificial Intelligence at MIT: Expanding Frontiers the MIT press: 104-133
7. Hua, HG, Kimbrough SO (1998) On hypermedia-based argumentation decision support systems. Decision Support Systems 22: 259-275
8. Kolodner J (1993) Case-Based Reasoning. Morgan Kaufmann Publishers

9. Pai K, Campbell JA (1997) An application of rule-based and case-based reasoning within a single legal knowledge based system. In: Proceeding of the data base for advances in information systems, fall, 28 (4)

10. SIGMA (1999) European Principles for Public Administration. SIGMA PAPERS: No. 27, CCNM/SIGMA/PUMA (99) 44/REV1

11. Stranieri A, Zeleznikow J, Gawler M, Lewis B (1999) A hybrid rule-neural approach for the automation of legal reasoning in the discretionary domain law in Australia. Artificial Intelligence and Law 7 (2-3): 153-183

12. Toulmin S (1958) The Users of Arguments. Cambridge, University Press

13. Zeleznikow J, Stranieri S (1995) The Split-up Systems: integrating neural networks and rule-based reasoning in the legal domain. In: Proceedings of the 5th International Conference on Artificial Intelligence and Law: 185-194

14. Yearwood JL, Stranieri A (1999) The integration of retrieval, reasoning and drafting for refugee law: a third generation legal knowledge based system. In: Proceeding of ICAIL, Oslo, Norway, ACM

15. Kunz W, Rittel HWJ (1970) Issues as elements of information systems. In: Working paper, No. 0131, University Stuttgart

16. Gordon T. and Karacapilidis N. (1997) The Zeno argumentation framework. In: Proceedings of the Sixth International Conference on Artificial Intelligence and Law, ACM Press: 10-18

17. Karacapilidis N, Papadias D, Gordon T, Voss H (1997) Collaborative environmental planning with GeoMed. European Journal of Operational Research 102 (2): 335-346

18. Karacapilidis N, Papadias D (2001) Computer supported argumentation and collaborative decision making: the HERMES system. Information System 26: 259-277

19. Zhang P, Sun J, Chen H (2005) Frame-based argumentation for group decision task generation and identification. Decision Support Systems 39: 643-659

20. Zeleznikow J (2000) Building Decision Support Systems in Discretionary Legal Domains. International Reviews of Law Computers & Technology 14 (3): 341–356

21. Karacapilidis NI, Trousse B, Papadias D (1997) Using Case-Based Reasoning for Argumentation with Multiple Viewpoints. In: Proceedings of the 2nd International Conference on Case-Based Reasoning (ICCBR' 97), Providence, Rhode Island, Springer-Verlag, Berlin

10 Examples of Situation Spaces in Context-aware Business Solutions

Jerzy Bartoszek, Grażyna Brzykcy

Technical University of Poznań, Institute of Control and Information Engineering, Pl. M. Skłodowskiej-Curie 5, 60-965 Poznań, Poland
{Jerzy.Bartoszek,Grazyna.Brzykcy}@put.poznan.pl

10.1 Introduction

An interaction of at least two constituents influences a final form of information system. On the one hand, the result is justified by our desire for data processing, and on the other – by a current state of the hardware and software technologies and the available computing infrastructures. Accordingly, methods of system designing and implementation but also concepts, models and architectures used in these processes, are continuously adopted and improved for better reflection of the characteristics of real problems (represented by data) and the ways of solving them (data processing).

For today's enterprises information is of primary value and one of the essential problems is being able to access the right information at the right time and to achieve this goal in a useful and user-friendly manner. For decision-makers the real problem is not a lack of information, but rather efficient extraction of required information from a great number of information sources.

Current business solutions for SMEs (medium-sized enterprises), particularly search tools, are inadequate for global information structure mainly because of their syntax-orientation. Moreover, the way in which the information is stored and the way in which it can be accessed have not been designed to be interoperable. As the amount of information one has available to make economic decisions keeps growing, the advanced search engines enabling intelligent access to heterogeneous information sources ought to be provided. Designing the new business solutions that are semantic-oriented and context-aware is the main challenge for software engineers. It is also evident that we need new abstractions in information system to cope with explicit representation of divers aspects of (meta)knowledge, context and reasoning.

W. Abramowicz and H.C. Mayr (eds.), Technologies for Business Information Systems, 109–119.

The SEWASIE system (SEmantic Webs and AgentS in Integrated Economics) [5], result of the European IST (Information Society Technologies) project, is a good example of the new generation solutions. This system is a collection of information nodes and specialized agents that are mediators between information sources and users. Information nodes provide a virtual view of information sources via some metadata (e.g. ontologies and indexes). The semantic enrichment of data stores is the basis of structured and efficient (reduction of the overall transaction costs) communication in the system.

By means of this paper we attempt to involve in the efforts of research community and present a partial solution of content-oriented processing. We propose to use a general concept of situation and high-level abstraction of communication and synchronization at the information source level. Our solution combines ideas of tuple spaces, the theory of situations and logic programming into one coherent mechanism. This mechanism can be used to build knowledge-based multi-agent systems, which are distributed, XML-oriented, and equipped with reasoning machinery. It is particularly suited for context-aware business solutions, such as enhanced workflow systems, semantic search engines and integrated intelligent user environments that ought to satisfy all the above mentioned features.

For today's complex information systems situatedness, openness and locality in control and interactions are distinctive characteristics. Situation theory [4, 9] faces these requirements and seems to be a suitable theoretical foundation of software systems. Moreover, with its orientation on meaning and information content, situation theory accurately matches the basic principles of global semantic networks. The basic concepts of this theory are recalled in section 4.

Partiality and relevance of information together with context-dependence and extensive reification are other essential hypotheses of situation semantics. All these properties make situation theory particularly convenient for using with open systems that are not fixed and possibly not completely available.

Other interesting model originates from tuple spaces and the Linda coordination language [15]. A short description of Linda and some examples of systems with tuple spaces are contained in section 3. An evolution of tuple space computing to the form of Semantic Web middleware [25] is also related there.

In this work we indicate possibility of building a bridge between well-founded theory and efficient implementation of tuple space computation model. We make a suggestion to use tuple spaces to represent situations. In our solution we assume that tuple spaces are enhanced with Prolog-like deduction.

The rest of the paper is organized as follows. In section 2 we outline concepts of data meaning and context. In section 3 an overview of tuple space computing is presented. Section 4 introduces Situation Spaces. Examples of Situation Spaces are presented in section 5.

10.2 Meaning and Context in Information Systems

Information is universally used in different sciences and seems to be a way of conceiving various aspects of the world. An exciting study of the information-based way of analyzing actions performed by an agent (also human being) one can find in [10]. In this paper the utilization of information stance in a broad area of different sciences, particularly social sciences, is also suggested. Problems of human interaction, considered in this draft, are similar to those found in the contemporary information systems. In accordance with commonly accepted characteristics (e.g. [7, 12, 27]), today's software systems should be built of autonomous components (named agents) that can perceive and affect the environment (may be partially). An agent with locally defined flow of control and with some form of context-awareness (e.g. locality in interactions) can cooperate with other agents in an open system.

Problems (data) may have a different form and a choice of data representation can affect the way data are computed. However, information content (meaning of data) should not depend, at any rate, on an assumed shape of data. On the other hand, agents may perform many actions more efficiently provided that sense (meaning of data) is known. This is a very basic requirement of Semantic Web [6], which is a vision of a distributed network of data (knowledge) resources that can be automatically and effectively processed with respect to their semantics. The intensive efforts undertaken in order to realize this vision bear witness to the significant value that is put down to information meaning. We appear to be on the way of a radical shift in programming paradigm to the attitude that is oriented at information content (content-oriented processing).

Meaning is defined as the function of an item in the world that is perceived by an agent. But perception is merely partial because of restricted cognitive resources of an agent, its limited knowledge and the world dynamics. Therefore interpretation of data and knowledge is always partial and sensitive about context. So, explicit representation of context and contextual knowledge maintenance is an alternative, which is difficult to avoid in information systems. To equip a system with these abilities a reification mechanism need to be extensively used.

The content-oriented approach to information retrieval and routing is also clearly visible in practical works. We can see the partial specification of the Semantic Web vision that takes a form of various standards (e.g. for resources – URI, RDF, mark-up languages – XML, ontologies – OWL). Software engineers and scientists are making a great effort elaborating subsequent standards.

Another important task in the Web is to realize global resources, where information is published and persistently stored. To properly solve the problem, the model of tuple spaces is proposed. Information is there represented as a shared space in which data can be placed and retrieved by agents. Access to the space is realized by means of some straightforward operations oriented at information content (tuple space computing). These systems take advantage of the Linda model [15] that is a simple abstraction of synchronization and communication mechanisms. Linda is a suitable solution to heterogeneity of agents, protocols and processes in distributed open environments.

In modern applications the primary importance of explicit representation of context is already recognized and yet various context models have been published [20]. Different attempts to formalize context are also undertaken (e.g. [16, 2, 3, 14]). In business applications Giunchiglia's approach to context may be particularly suitable for software agents because the main focus is on context reasoning. A context consists of all the knowledge that is used by an agent for deliberation about its goals (making effective decisions in current situation).

It is worth noticing that all the above mentioned features of information are captured and formally described in situation theory.

10.3 Tuple Space Computing

All the activities undertaken in the tuple space system consist in flow of tuples. Agents can exchange data by writing and reading information (tuples) and synchronize with each other using a built-in mechanism of pattern matching over a shared memory of tuples (a space or a blackboard). An agent can insert a tuple t using the out(t) operation. Another agent can retrieve a tuple that matches a given template T (and remove it from the tuple space) using the rd(T) (in(T)) operation, which are blocked. Linda combines synchronization and communication in an extremely simple and abstract manner. It is superior to client-server model, since it uncouples interacting processes both in space and in time.

Tuples, operations and distributed tuple spaces have been implemented in Prolog-D-Linda [22, 23]. In this system tuples are expressed as Prolog facts, and tuple spaces are Prolog databases. Additionally, tuple spaces can contain rules (i.e. Prolog clauses).

The XMLSpaces conception [24] is an extension to the Linda systems. In XMLSpaces the main role is played by XML documents. A pattern matching of ordinary tuples in the Linda systems is replaced by extended matching flexibility on nested tuples and on various data types for fields of tuples.

In Semantic Web Spaces [25] the original model of tuple space computing is extended in different ways to meet requirements of nowadays information systems (multiagent, XML-oriented, applied to open distributed environments). All the tuples are represented as XML documents. With a set of resources descriptions and new operations (introduced, due to a truth assignment to RDF-tuples) and matching relations we obtain so called RDFSpaces. In OWLSpaces, the further extension of the Semantic Web Spaces, it is permitted to use ontologies specified in OWL and reasoning capabilities. These metadescriptions are treated as XML documents and are contained in a space. An agent is now able to read different aspects of data semantics from a given space (may be previously unknown to him). Taking advantage of this additional contextual knowledge agent can improve efficiency of searching, reasoning or other activities. Finally, a context concept comes into force. It supports the semantic partitioning of the Semantic Web Spaces (analog of views or perspectives in databases) and plays a key role in definitions of context-aware solutions.

Similar functionality is also supported by other semantic tuple space systems (e.g. sTuples [18] based on JavaSpaces [21] and Triple Spaces [13]).

It should be noted that another powerful theory is known – the situation theory – where concepts like (meta)information, context and constraints (a form of rules) play a crucial role.

10.4 Situations in Tuple Space Computing

The situation theory gives a small number of concepts with individuals, relations and situations, which are suitable for world modeling. The most basic concept is infon. If R is an n-place relation and a1, ..., an are objects appropriate for the respective argument places of R, then a tuple <<R, r1→a1, ..., rn→an, 1>> denotes the informational item that a1, ..., an are standing in the relation R, and a tuple <<R, r1→a1, ..., rn→an, 0>> denotes the informational item that a1, ..., an are not standing in the relation R. r1, ..., rn describe roles of objects a1, ..., an and they are also called the names of arguments of R. Objects like <<R, r1→a1, ..., rn→an, p>> are called infons (p is called its polarity and is equal to 0 or 1).

Some arguments of R may be missing. In this way infons can represent partial information. Minimality conditions for R indicate which groups of argument roles of R need to be filled in order to produce a well-formed (well-defined) infon. If σ1 and σ2 are two infons with the same relation R, and σ2 has at least the same arguments as σ1, then σ1 subsumes σ2 (in σ1 there is less information than in σ2).

A situation is a part of reality, which can be picked out by a cognitive agent. Situations make certain infons factual. Taking into consideration a situation s and an infon σ, it is written s ⊨ σ when s supports σ (σ is true in s). If I is a finite set of infons and s is a situation, we write s ⊨ I, if s ⊨ σ for every σ in I.

Given a real situation s, the set {σ | s ⊨ σ} is taken to be the corresponding abstract situation. The form of situation is more amenable to symbolic manipulation.

If all infons of the situation s1 are also supported by the situation s2, we say that s1 is a part of s2. The part-of relation is antisymetric, reflexive and transitive. It provides a partial ordering of the situations.

Sometimes a special situation, called world, need to be considered, while all other situations are parts of it.

Objects used in situations are classified into different types. The basic types include temporal locations, spatial locations, individuals, relations, situations, infons, parameters and polarity. But one of the most valuable aspects of situation theory is flexibility of the agent's scheme of individuation – a way of carving the world into uniformities (i.e. types).

If s is a situation, p is a parameter and I is a finite set of infons (involving p), then there is a type [p | s ⊨ I] of those objects to which p may be anchored in s, so that all conditions in I are satisfied. It is written o:T to indicate that object o is of type T.

Taking into account a situation parameter S and a set I of infons, there may be a corresponding type [S | S ⊨ I] of situations in which the conditions in I obtain. This process of defining a type from parameter S and a set I is known as situation type abstraction.

In the situation theory, the "flow of information" (or information processing) is realized via constraints. A constraint [S1 => S2], where S1 and S2 are situation types, corresponds in essence to the infon <<involves, S1, S2, 1>> of some (meta)situation. Cognitively it means that, if there is a situation s1 of type S1, then there is a situation s2 of type S2. It should be noted that, although the types S1 and S2 may involve parameters, the constraint is parameter-free infon that links two specific situation types. In general, any constraint may be dependent on a set B of background conditions under which it will convey information. This is written as [S1 => S2] / B.

It was shown in [2] that situation theory can be used both as a knowledge representation scheme and to support contextual reasoning. They proposed an extended situation theory where contexts are modeled with situation types and constraints.

The infrastructure for semantic network, suggested in the paper, consists of situation spaces (which are situations themselves). By analogy to terms previously used for sets of spaces we name it Situation Spaces.

In our solution the situation theory plays a role of formal, well-founded base for tasks of knowledge processing and representation. This theory gives a small set of concepts with individuals, relations and situations, which are suitable for world modeling. Another value of this theory is a possibility of homogenous representation of data, metadata, inference rules and other constraints by means of situations and reification mechanism. As a consequence, using the same concept of situation one can express various aspects of context, that are ontologies applied by the agents, accessible resources, their localization (place and time), knowledge shared by the agents, agents' mental states etc. Context may be easily modified as situations are modeled by means of sets of infons. One more crucial feature of situation theory is ability of expressing partial knowledge. As situation theory has been devised to create a theory of meaning and information content it is particularly suitable for agents' communication and knowledge exchange. Moreover, situation semantics is regarded as one of the best tools of analyzing the meaning. Situation theory has been adopted in many fields. It was used in applications related to context, discourse theory and even to form scenario descriptions supporting the process of requirement analyses in system design [19]. It is also worth noticing the presence of some implementations of situation theory (see [11]).

We assume that all the data in Situation Spaces take a form of XML documents. This representation of data has al least two advantages: standardization and realizability in distributed environments, for instance, on .NET platform. XMLSpaces are originally implemented on this platform.

The decision of including logical inferences into the Situation Spaces appears to have a minor value because any inference engine may be placed instead. However, we decided to choose verified Prolog solutions.

Let us outline the key implementation decisions and assumptions expressing our solution. As it was shown in [11], situation theory can be adopted in Prolog-like systems. In our opinion especially useful are Prolog systems with types. We prefer systems like LIFE [1] where:

- types are treated in the same manner as constants (which are 1-element types) and may be used in terms,

- we can represent partial information because this system uses feature structures [8],
- inference engine is built upon the hierarchy of types.

In our approach, any infon <<R, a1, ..., an, p>> can be expressed as Prolog-like fact R(a1, ..., an, p), where R is a predicate name, a1, ..., an are terms and p is 0 or1.

In similar manner expression s ⊨ σ may be represented as supports(s, σ, 1). We can also represent Prolog-like rules as infons. For example, the rule H:-B. defined in the program C can be treated as infon <<is_a_rule, C, H, B, 1>>.

We assume that situations can contain infons, which are metadescriptions. In this manner the idea of self-described situations can be realized. The essential types of metadescriptions are ontologies, which describe terms and concepts of the given situation. Situations can be treated as XMLSpaces. They have names and URIs.

Mental states of agents are also represented by situations, whereas constraints from situation theory provide the mechanism that captures the way agents make inferences and act. Agent actions can be defined by Prolog-like rules.

10.5 Examples of Context-aware Solutions

Let us assume that we adopt the Situation Spaces in a traffic-control system (compare to [26]). Let us imagine that in this system there are two locations (separate areas) l1:LOC1 and l2:LOC2. In every location there is a space, called respectively desc1 and decs2. The first one is a situation of type DESC1 and the second one is a situation of type DESC2. These spaces contain descriptions of such objects like cars, petrol stations, car services and other points of interest. These descriptions form small ontologies.

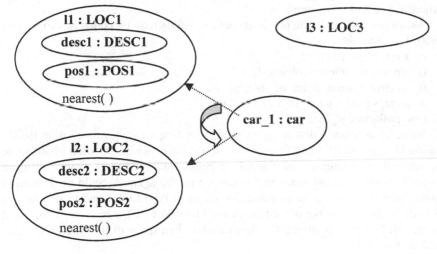

Fig.1. The scheme of Situation Spaces

In terms of the situation theory these ontologies can be presented as follows:

desc1 |= <<is_a, car, object, 1>>
desc1 |= <<is_a, point_of_interest, object, 1>>
desc1 |= <<is_a, petrol_station, point_of_interest, 1>>
desc2 |= <<is_a, car, object, 1>>
desc2 |= <<is_a, point_of_interest, object, 1>>
desc2 |= <<is_a, car_service, point_of_interest, 1>>

Of course, we can describe in similar manner some individuals:

desc1 |= <<is_a, car_1, car, 1>>
desc2 |= <<is_a, car_1, car, 1>>
desc1 |= <<is_a, petrol_station_1, petrol_station, 1>>
desc1 |= <<is_a, petrol_station_2, petrol_station, 1>>
desc2 |= <<is_a, petrol_station_1, petrol_station, 1>>
desc2 |= <<is_a, petrol_station_2, petrol_station, 1>>
desc2 |= <<is_a, car_service_1, car_service, 1>>

To express facts that some of petrol stations are also car services while others are not, we use infons with positive and negative polarity:

desc2 |= <<is_a, petrol_station_1, car_service, 1>>
desc2 |= <<is_a, petrol_station_2, car_service, 0>>

So, in the space desc1 we have two petrol stations and in the space desc2 we have two petrol stations and one car service. In desc2 the petrol station number 1 is also a car service.

Each object has the property gps_position described by an infon. For example

<<gps_position, car_1, lon_value, lat_value>>

In localization l1 and l2 there is an additional space, called pos1 and pos2. Infons of these spaces describe actual positions of all considered objects, for example:

pos1 |= <<gps_position, petrol_station_1, x , y, 1>>
pos2 |= <<gps_position, car_service_1, z, w, 1>>

where x, y, z and w are numbers.

As we pointed out in the previous section, infons may be coded as Prolog-like facts. For example:

is_a(car, object, 1).
is_a(point_of_interest, object, 1).
is_a(petrol_station, point_of_interest, 1).
is_a(car_service, point_of_interest, 1).
gps_position(car_1, x, y, 1).

Now, let us assume that an agent A, representing a car_1, moves from the location l1 to the location l2. In each location it needs an information about some nearest points of interest (for example, a petrol station or a car service). But, in every location, the knowledge that is needed by the agent A could be defined in quite different manner. For example, in spaces of type LOC1 and LOC2 we can find different Prolog-like procedures, called nearest(C, P), which show the point of interest P nearest to the car C. The procedure in a space of the type LOC1 may look as follows:

LOC1 : nearest (C, P):- find_all(P1, (DESC1 : is_a (P1, point_of_interest,1),
        POS1 : dist(C, P1, D), D=<Radius), L), min(L, C, P).

In this definition find_all creates a list L of all these points of interest, which are located not far than Radius from the object C and the procedure min finds the nearest point on this list. In the reasoning process we take into account the ontological knowledge from the space of the type DESC1and the domain-oriented knowledge from the space of type POS1.

In any space of the type LOC2, the agent A uses a procedure nearest, which may look like the following one:

LOC2 : nearest (C, P):- find_all(P1, (DESC2 : is_a (P1, car_service,1),
        POS2 : dist(C, P1, D), D=<Radius), L), min(L, C, P).

So, in the first case the procedure find_all finds all points of interest (i.e. petrol stations and car services) while in the second case, only car services. Moreover, if the agent A "knows" the constraint [LOC3 => LOC2], where LOC3 is another location type, then in any location l3 of type LOC3 it uses the same version of the procedure nearest as in the location l2. It is worth to notice that dependencies between types LOC3 and LOC2 needn't be so rigorous as in the case of object modeling. Particularly, there is no necessity for LOC3 to be a subtype of LOC2. Also, let us remark that in situation theory we have sophisticated mechanism of types defining. It allows us to organize information and properly elaborate comprehensive contexts of agent's actions.

In [17] is described an interesting example of a context model based on multilevel situation theory and ontology. There is considered a contact center. If someone, who has a mobile phone, calls to this center, some simple situations are created which contain "said" (explicitly in the call) and "unsaid" (obtained from sensor and reasoning mechanisms) information about this call. Following [17] let us assume that we have the situation s1, which characterizes type of the call, and the situation s2, which characterizes the calling customer. They represent the "said" information. Infons involved by s1 describe a call and are as follows:

   <<call_type, call, inbound, 1>>
   <<inbound_type, inbound, technical,1>>
   <<technical_type, technical, complaint,1>>
   <<complaint_reason, complaint, prod_funct, 1>>

The situation s2 involves only one infon

   <<customer_id, customer, cust_id, 1>>

The "unsaid" information is contained in the situation s3, which describes, for example, the customer location. Thus, the situation s3 involves infon:

   <<location, cust_id, cust_location, 1>>

All the above situations are parts of a bigger situation s, which describes the present call. Let us assume that s is of the type S1.

There is another situation, say h:H, which includes the relevant historical information about the customer. It may contain infons about other products of the company, which owns the customer, infons about similar calls made by him to the contact center and so on. Situation s:S1 and h:H determine (via the constrain [S1=>S2] / H) some situation, of the type S2, which may be used to solve problems signaled by the user in the call. The programming agent that is attended to the call may automatically deduce this situation and help the calling customer.

Searching on the space for tuples that can match a given template takes in situation theory a form of querying which situation is of a given type. To answer the query one can inspect only the relevant part of a space – an adequate context (situations of a given type and constraints with this type).

10.6 Conclusions

The above examples convince us that Situation Spaces may be used in practical applications. This approach encourages us to utilize a high-level of abstractions for knowledge representing and context-dependent reasoning.

Situation Spaces could be implemented as advanced search and deduction engine. It provides intelligent access to heterogeneous information sources on the Web. There are many benefits of using this engine: a reduction of transaction costs, efficient deduction and search, context-dependent communication facilities. Within the business solutions Situation Spaces can support integrated, context-aware and personalized data acquisition. We hope that because of efficient implementation of tuple spaces Situation Spaces may be exploited effectively.

References

1. Ait-Kaci H, et all (1994) The Wild LIFE Handbook. Paris Research Lab
2. Akman V, Surav M (1996) The Use of Situation Theory in Context Modeling. Computational Intelligence 12 (4).
3. Baclawski K, Kokar M, Matheus C, Letkowski J, Malczewski M (2003) Formalization of Situation Awareness. In: Kilov H (ed) Behavioral Specifications of Businesses and Systems. Kluwer Academic Publishers
4. Barwise J, Perry J (1983) Situations and attitudes. MIT
5. Bergamaschi S, Quix C, Jarke M (2005) The SEWASIE EU IST Project. SIG SEMIS Bulletin vol 2
6. Berners-Lee T, Hendler J, Lassila O (2001) The Semantic Web. Scientific American 284:34-43
7. Bradshaw J (ed) (1997) Software agents. The MIT Press
8. Carpenter B (1990) The logic of typed feature structures: inheritance, (in)equations and extensionality. 2nd European Summer School in Language, Logic and Information
9. Devlin K (1991) Logic and information. Cambridge University Press
10. Devlin K, Rosenberg D (2005) Information in the Social Sciences. Draft www.stanford.edu/~kdevlin/HPI_SocialSciences.pdf

11. Erkan T, Akman V (1995) Situations and Computation: An Overview of Recent Research. In: Griffith J, Hinrichs E, Nakazawa T (eds) Proceedings of the Topics in Constraint Grammar Formalism for CL, pp 77-104

12. Estrin D, Culler D, Pister K, Sukjatme G (2002) Connecting the Physical World with Pervasive Networks. IEEE Pervasive Computing 1(1), pp 59–69

13. Fensel D (2004) Triple Space Computing. Techical Report. Digital Enterprise Research Institute (DERI)

14. Gangemi A, Mika P (2003) Understanding the Semantic Web through Descriptions and Situations. In: Meersman R, Zahir Tari et al (eds) Proceedings of the International Conference on Ontologies, Databases and Applications of SEmantics, Springer

15. Gelernte D, Carriero N (1992) Coordination Languages and their Significance. Communication of the ACM 35(2):97–107

16. Giunchiglia F (1993) Contextual Reasoning. Epistemologica 16:345-364.

17. Kalyan A, Gopalan S, Sridhar V (2005) Hybrid Context Model based on Multilevel Situation Theory and Ontology for Contact Centers. In: Proceeding of the 3rd International Conference on Pervasive Computing and Communications Workshops, pp 3-7

18. Khushraj D, Lassila O, Finin T (2004) sTuples: Semantic Tuple Spaces. Proceedings of the 1st Annual Conference on Mobile and Ubiquitous Systems

19. Pinheiro F (2002) Preliminary thoughts on using situation theory for scenario modelling. In: V Workshop Iberoamericano de Ingenieria de Requisitos y Ambientes de Software, pp 272-280

20. Strang T, Linhoff-Popien C (2004) A Context Modeling Survey. The 6th International Conference on Ubiquitous Computing, Nottingham

21. Sun Microsystems (1998) JavaSpace Specification

22. Sutcliffe G, Pinakis J (1990) Prolog-Linda – An Embedding of Linda in muProlog. In: Tsang C (ed) Proceedings of the 4th Austrialian Conference on AI, p 331–340

23. Sutcliffe G, Pinakis J (1991) Prolog-D-Linda: An Embedding of Linda in SICStus Prolog. Technical Report 91/7, The University of Western Australia, Department of CS

24. Tolksdorf R, Liedsch F, Nguyen D (2004) XMLSpaces.NET: An Extensible Tuplespace as XML Middleware. In: Proceedings of the 2nd International Workshop on .NET Technologies

25. R. Tolksdorf R, Nixon L, Liebsch F (2004) Semantic Web Spaces. Technical Report B-04-11, Freie Universität Berlin

26. Tolksdorf R, Nixon L, Paslaru-Bontas E, Nguyen D, Liebsch F (2005) Enabling real world Semantic Web applications through a coordination middleware. In: Gómez-Pérez A, Euzenat J (eds) The Semantic Web: Research and Applications, Springer, pp 679-693

27. Zambonelli F, Van Dyke Parunak H (2003) Towards a Paradigm Change in Computer Science and Software Engineering: A Synthesis. The Knowledge Engineering Review 18

11 ERP Implementation Effort Estimation Using Data Envelopment Analysis

Stefan Koch

Institute for Information Business, Vienna University of Economics and BA

11.1 Introduction

In the last years an increasing number of enterprise resource planning (ERP) systems like SAP R/3, BaaN or Oracle Applications have been implemented. This implementation of the selected solution is risky and complex for individual companies, since on the one hand the software and especially the necessary manpower is relatively expensive and on the other hand in this process possibly the internal business processes need to be adapted as well. These results in the desire to compare the efficiency of implementation projects in order to identify best practices, and especially to estimate effort and costs associated with new projects. This information would be beneficial for project managers involved in such projects, but also for consulting companies and ERP vendors. However, this proves to be difficult, since ERP implementation differs from the development and implementation of individual software solutions in some important points. It actually changes the enterprise and the business processes in many cases, and a majority of the necessary expenditure flows not into the production of new program code, but into adjustment work (so-called customizing). Thus traditional metrics for the size of software products as for instance function points [1] or lines-of-code [2] are not easily applicable which leads in further consequence to problems in computing productivity and efficiency. The data envelopment analysis (DEA) [3] on the other hand allows for such a comparison in particular even if several input and output factors are present. Furthermore, the results of a DEA can also be used to arrive at effort and cost estimates for future projects. In this paper, we will describe the application of DEA in this context of ERP implementation projects.

W. Abramowicz and H.C. Mayr (eds.), Technologies for Business Information Systems, 121–132.
© 2007 *Springer.*

11.2 ERP Implementation Effort Estimation

ERP systems are application programs which are used for the enactment and support of all business functions as well as for the administration of all information necessary for these tasks. The main characteristics of ERP are further process orientation by execution of function chains, implementation of all business processes, the internal integration of all parts of the software with a single database, the applicability in many industries as well as the adaptability to national characteristics, a uniform GUI and the possibility of adapting the software within pre-defined limits to the requirements of a given enterprise.

The implementation of an ERP system in an enterprise represents a special topic of high concern. This area entails among other things the customizing, the adjustment of the enterprise-neutrally delivered standard software to the specific business requirements of an enterprise. In [4], a fine-grained understanding and classification of these tailoring activities is developed, resulting in a typology of 9 different types. Due to the high integration of the underlying software and possible changes to the organisation resulting from implementation, the resulting projects are characterised by high complexity (and most often also high costs and long running times) [5,6,7,8,9]. In some cases such projects can lead also to major problems up to the bankruptcy of the enterprise [10,11]. Therefore the literature (and also suppliers of ERP systems as for example SAP [12]) offers diverse suggestions and guidelines for performing and managing such projects [6,8,9], critical success factors [13,14] as well as for the interplay of adjustment of the organization and to the software by customizing or even programming [11].

These challenges and the data on cost and schedule overruns result in the need for assessing and comparing the efficiency of ERP implementation projects, and in a second step for estimating costs and effort for future projects. For both tasks, the relevant inputs and outputs of such a project need to be defined. While in the simple (and idealised) case of software development, input can be given by the developer effort, and the output characterised by some software product metric, the situation in this case is more complex. While inputs are not much more difficult to capture, outputs seem problematic. Due to the fact that often no new code is produced, but customizing within the software takes place, together with possible changes to the business processes, a set of output metrics needs to be defined in order to completely assess the output produced. Traditional software product metrics can, for the case of programming effort, have a place in it. For the resulting case of several outputs (and possibly several inputs), in addition most often measured on completely different scales, traditional approaches for computing the productivity and efficiency can not be used. DEA on the other hand has been developed to deal with this problem. Also Kitchenham and Mendes [16] agree that productivity measures need to be based on multiple size measures.

Besides comparing productivity, estimating the effort for future projects has a high priority. Naturally, it follows from the reasons given above that estimation approaches developed for new software development, like most notably

COCOMO [17] or others, relying on standard software product metrics, are not applicable. Literature currently does not yield any approaches specifically targeted at ERP implementation projects. Given a large and diverse enough database, machine-learning approaches like for example regression trees [18] or analogy-based estimation [19] might prove helpful. Myrtveit and Stensrud [20] have detailed the usage of analogy-based estimation and multiple regression in this context, but could not prove the first one to generally outperform the latter. In this paper, we will describe how DEA can be applied to this problem.

11.3 Data Envelopment Analysis

The principle of the border production function was introduced by Farell [21] and enhanced by Charnes, Cooper and Rhodes into the first DEA model [22,3]. The object of analysis is generally the Decision Making Unit (DMU [3]). This term includes relatively flexibly each unit responsible for the transformation of inputs into outputs, for example hospitals, supermarkets, schools or bank branches. The basic principle of DEA can be understood as a generalization of the normal efficiency evaluation by means of the relationship from an output to an input into the general case of a multi-output, multi-input system without a any given conversion rates or same units for all factors. In contrast to other approaches, which require the parametric specification of a production function, DEA measures production behavior directly and uses this data for evaluation, deriving a production function from mean relations between inputs and outputs by determining the outside cover of all production relations, and identifying "best practicing" DMUs. A DMU is understood as being efficient if none of the outputs can be increased without either inputs increasing or other outputs being reduced, as well as vice versa.

For each DMU an individual weighting procedure is used over all inputs and outputs. These form a weighted positive linear combination, whereby the weights are set such that they maximize the production relationship of the examined unit. The efficiency of an examined unit is limited with 1. That means that no a-priori weightings are made by the user, and that the weights between the DMUs can be different. For each evaluation object the DEA supplies a solution vector of weighting factors and a DEA efficiency score with a value of 1 denoting DEA-efficiency. This means that within the selected model variant no weighting vector could be found which would have led to a higher efficiency value. For each inefficient DMU the DEA returns a set of efficient DMUs exhibiting a similar input/output structure to give ideas for efficiency increases (reference set or DEA benchmark).

The first model of the DEA was introduced by Charnes, Cooper and Rhodes [3] and is designated as CCR model. The different models of the DEA can be divided on the basis of two criteria: the orientation of the model and the underlying assumption regarding the returns to scale. With input-oriented models the reduction of the input vector maximally possible is determined, whereas with output-oriented models the maximally possible proportional increase of the output vector is determined. With constant returns to scale size-induced productivity differences are considered into the efficiency evaluation, with variable returns to scale the differences are neutralized by the model. The most common example of such a model is the BCC model by Banker, Charnes and Cooper, [23].

In the area of software development, Banker and Kemerer use this approach in order to prove the existence of both rising and falling returns to scale [24]. Banker and Slaughter use the DEA in the area of maintenance and enhancement projects [25], proving rising returns to scale. Mayrhauser et al. [26] also report applying DEA on a data set of 46 software projects to analyze impacts on efficiency. An investigation of 30 SAP R/3-projects was done by Myrtveit and Stensrud [27]. As inputs the costs, as outputs the number of the users, EDI and conversions are used. The authors point out large differences in productivity between projects, as well as the presence of variable returns to scale. Kitchenham [28] gives an in-depth discussion on the application of DEA in software development.

11.4 Data Set

11.4.1 Description

For the empirical validation, data on a number of ERP implementation projects was necessary. Therefore a questionnaire was developed, which was after a pretest sent to Austrian companies which had already introduced an ERP system. Altogether 300 enterprises of different industries were addressed, using customer lists of several different suppliers including SAP and BaaN which had already been used in a preceding study on ERP system selection processes [15]. Out of 43 questionnaires returned, 39 could be included into the analysis.

For each enterprise, data characterising the organisation itself, and the implementation project were asked. In the first group, industry and number of employees were collected. For industries, a considerable number of enterprises is present only from trade (8) and production (14). Results regarding the business size show that the sample contains relevant numbers from different groups: Both smaller enterprises (less than 250 employees) are represented with 38.5%, but also large organisations with more than 2000 employees (20.5%), with the rest in-between.

Next it was explored which modules (or parts) of the software were implemented. The area of finance and accounting was most strongly represented: 87% of the regarded enterprises introduced the financial module , controlling 79%. Furthermore 64% implemented distribution, 44% manufacturing, 28% project, 13% transport, 15% service and 51% others. In the mean, an enterprise implemented 3.82 different modules (standard deviation 1.48). In order to more exactly specify the ERP solution resulting from the implementation project, four additional variables were explored (see Table 1). These are based the number of employees in the enterprise who use the standard software after final implementation, the extent of the modifications to the software in lines-of-code (which according to the typology developed in [4] constitutes a form of ERP tailoring), the number of interfaces to other software systems (another form of ERP tailoring according to [4]), and the number of locations in which the solution was introduced.

Table 1. Characteristics of implemented ERP solutions (N=39)

	Max	Mean	St.Dev.
Number of Modules	7.00	3.82	1.48
Users	1,500.00	217.46	364.23
Modifications (in LOC)	5,000.00	227.95	841.70
Interfaces	100.00	12.10	20.39
Locations	62.00	4.26	9.98

The last group of variables are concerned with costs and duration of the ERP implementation project (see Table 2), with the costs both taken in total and several sub-components, including cost of the software, acquisition of any necessary hardware, as well as any costs associated with employing external consultants (with only 3 enterprises not using consultants).

Table 2. Effort and costs of ERP implementation projects (N=39)

	Max	Mean	St.Dev.
Duration of Implementation (in Weeks)	156.00	43.05	29.45
Effort (in Person-Years)	1200.00	65.68	245.58
Total Costs (in EUR)	14,535K	1,477K	2,718K
Costs for Software (in EUR)	5,814K	361K	977K
Costs for Hardware (in EUR)	4,360K	267K	743K
Costs for Consultants (in EUR)	5,814K	519K	997K

As a first preliminary analysis preceding DEA, correlations between the described variables are evaluated. All variables used for characterising effort and costs are positively correlated, with coefficients of 0.67 between total costs and effort up to 0.95 (significance level in all cases 0.01). The duration of the project is however only correlated with the total costs at 0.44, but not with the effort in person-years. Regarding the characteristics of the project, the number of the users and interfaces show an influence on total costs, duration and effort, the extent of modifications and number of locations however no statistically provable one. In particular a high correlation to the costs exists, for the number of the users at 0.91 and interfaces at 0.81. For the effort in person-years the correlation-coefficients are 0.5 (for users) and 0.54 (for interfaces), for the duration 0.52 respectively 0.33. Also the number of modules implemented has a significant positive correlation to the total costs (coefficient of 0.42 with $p<0.01$). If a non-parametric correlation coefficient is applied due to the skewness of the data, results do not change.

11.4.2 Application of DEA

First, the available projects were subjected to a DEA, in order to compare their productivity and efficiency. Several software products are available for this, some of which are freeware. In this case, the program accompanying the book by Cooper, Seiford and Tone [29] was used, which can compute different DEA models, input or output-oriented, as well as with constant or variable returns to scale.

The first choices to be taken concern the definition of input and output factors, as well as the model to be applied. Banker and Kemerer have demonstrated the existence of both increasing and decreasing returns to scale in software projects [24], also Myrtveit and Stensrud recommend to use a model with variable returns to scale [27]. Using a data set of maintenance and extension projects Banker and Slaughter have found increasing returns to scale [25]. Kitchenham [28] gives an overview of research result and reasons for differences on economies and diseconomies of scale in software development. In addition, the size of an ERP implementation project can under most circumstances not be chosen by the decision makers, which would also point to using a variable return to scale model. In order to confirm this, efficiency scores for all projects are computed using both different assumption and the results are compared. Regarding the orientation of the model an input orientation is selected, since the ERP system necessary for an organization, hence the output, is determined by the requirements, and this is to be reached with minimal input factors. Thus BCC-I is applied with variable returns to scale, and CCR-I for constant returns to scale.

Regarding the definition which factors are to be used as inputs and outputs, it is to be considered that with an increase in the number of factors more DMUs are estimated to be efficient. In the available case the total costs offer themselves as inputs as well as the effort in person-years. As outputs the duration of the introduction, the number of users, the number of interfaces and the implemented modules are used. The duration of the project is for many organisations of high interest and further is characteristic for how efficiently and fast the effort could be applied. The extent of modifications and the number of locations do not exhibit significant influence on costs and effort, and therefore are not included.

The results for the application of the selected models are summarized in Table 3. It can clearly be seen that with the model BCC-I with variable returns to scale the efficiency scores are higher both in average and median as well as minimum. Likewise the number of DEA efficient projects rises strongly from 6 to 22, which corresponds to 56% of all projects. This increase in the efficiency evaluation can be explained by the fact that size-induced productivity differences are balanced by the model, and thus some small projects are no longer dominant. But even in the BCC-I model an average saving potential of nearly 25% is shown. Compared with the results of Myrtveit and Stensrud a higher average efficiency is found, since they found a value of 0.56 using a model with variable returns to scale [27].

Table 3. Results from applying CCR-I and BCC-I models (N=39)

	CCR-I	BCC-I
Average Efficiency Score	0.4472	0.7552
Std. Dev.	0.3219	0.3239
Median	0.3726	1
Minimum	0.0039	0.0267
Number of Efficient Projects	6	22

To check whether variable or constant returns to scale are present, a statistical test on equality of the distributions of the efficiency scores from both models is applied. Since the efficiency scores are not normal distributed, a non-parametric test for dependent samples (e.g. Wilcoxon rank) can be used, showing a significant difference between the efficiency scores (level of significance 0.01). As a BCC-I model could also apply constant returns to scale if these would best fit the data, this shows that variable returns to scale are present and the BCC-I model is to be used. This result is identical with those of Myrtveit and Stensrud [27], as well as results from software development [24,25].

11.5 Effort Estimation with DEA

11.5.1 Approach

We propose to use DEA in effort and cost estimation in a similar way to the application for productivity comparison, in which the input and output factors are known, and the efficiency is to be computed. For effort estimation, the outputs are determined, and a certain efficiency level is set. Determining the outputs will, depending on the different measures included, be possible in advance. In our example, the number of users, modules and interfaces will be relatively clearly defined at the beginning. The duration will be set by management, or depend on other restrictions. Of higher interest is the efficiency level. There are several possibilities for setting a value: One would be to optimistically hope for DEA-efficiency to be reached, thus implying a project on the current production frontier, another would be to set a lower value (e.g. 0.5) in order to be on the safe side. The last possible value would be an orientation on the current status, and use the mean (or median) efficiency achieved by all other projects, or of constructing a confidence interval using mean and standard deviation. Exploring several of these alternatives shows one of the advantages of this method, in that several scenarios can easily be computed. In addition, while the computation itself is complex and not easily communicated, the notion of efficiency score and associated scenarios with resulting estimations will be easily comprehended by decision-makers. If all of these values have been determined, the resulting set of equations is solved for both the weights associated with the input and output factors, given the usual condition that the same set of weights may not result in an efficiency value of more than one for any project, and in addition setting the efficiency score for the current project at the determined value, and also the input factors themselves. It should be noted that a single solution will most certainly not be possible given multiple input factors, but a certain trade-off between the input factors is resulting. Exploring this trade-off, e.g. between costs for consultants and in-house costs, might be of interest.

11.5.2 Validation

For validation, we use the data set presented above. In order to decrease complexity, and also to make comparisons to other approaches easier, we limit the analysis to the single-input case, thus resulting in a single solution for a set efficiency level. This allows to calculate standard measures for estimation quality. To this end, we compute a new BCC-I model in a first step, this time using only effort as input, while keeping all output factors. The decreases the sample size to 35, as 4 projects did not contain effort data. The results are not very different from those above, and give an average efficiency of 0.718 (median 0.885) and 16 efficient projects.

Then we proceeded to estimate the effort for each single project, using all other projects as data set. This jack-knifing technique offers two distinct advantages compared to partitioning the data set into a training set and a holdout sample, in that more cases can be estimated thus giving a better indication of predictive quality, and that each case can be estimated using a larger sample, thus increasing quality. As a first step, each case was eliminated from the total set, and the BCC-I model as above was computed using the remaining projects in order to determine the respective mean efficiency. In Table 4, the resulting value for each case can be seen, with the very low bandwidth (between 0.710 and 0.739) underlining the stability of the results. Then, effort for each single project was estimated as described. The output factors were taken from the data, as they are supposed to be easily determined by the organisation. We then used three different scenarios for the efficiency to be achieved by the project: An optimistic scenario with the efficiency on the production border, i.e. DEA-efficiency of 1, a pessimistic scenario with efficiency of 0.5 and a realistic scenario assuming the mean efficiency within the set. For all three possibilities, estimated effort was computed, and compared to the real value. Table 4 gives the relevant data, including magnitude of relative error (MRE) for each case under each scenario. For three projects an estimation was not possible, as they lie on the production frontier due to their high output in a factor, no matter what the input. These cases are discarded from further analysis.

As can be seen, the mean magnitude of relative error (MMRE) is between 154.81 and 315.94, with the optimistic scenario performing best, the median magnitude of relative error (MdMRE) is 48.36 in the realistic and 48.23 respective 70.05 in the optimistic and pessimistic case. Using a Wilcoxon rank test, it can be shown that the differences in MRE between the others and the pessimistic scenario are statistically significant (at level 0.01), while the realistic and optimistic ones are not significantly different. A different quality indicator, pred(0.2), is for the optimistic scenario 31.25%, for the pessimistic and the realistic 15.63%. Using this quality measure, again the optimistic scenario performs best. This performance results from the data set studied, which sports a high number of efficient projects and is not normal distributed. Therefore using the mean efficiency score did not prove to be the best strategy in the realistic scenario, the median would have performed better. It should also be noted that the pessimistic scenario underestimates effort in 9 cases, and the optimistic scenario overestimates in also 9 cases.

Compared to the results of Myrtveit and Stensrud [20], who have used analogy-based and multiple regression for estimating their dataset of ERP projects, the results are comparable but do not point to DEA as a generally better performing estimation methodology. They report an MMRE of 126 for practitioners using a multiple regression model (MdMRE of 43), of 136 for practitioners using the analogy tool (MdMRE of 51), and for the tools alone of 127 (MdMRE 35) for multiple regression respective 154 (MdMRE 52) for the analogy tool. These numbers are quite near to the results of the optimistic scenario.

Table 4. Results from effort estimation (N=32)

Case	Eff. (act.)	Mean Eff.	Est. (opt.)	MRE (opt.)	Est. (pess.)	MRE (pess.)	Est. (real.)	MRE (real.)
1	6.00	0.715	5.00	16.67	10.00	66.67	7.00	16.67
2	2.00	0.725	1.00	50.00	2.00	0.00	1.38	31.00
3	1.00	0.710	1.00	0.00	2.00	100.00	1.41	41.00
4	3.00	0.724	1.53	49.00	3.06	2.00	2.12	29.33
5	5.00	0.733	1.08	78.40	2.16	56.80	1.49	70.20
6	3.00	0.723	1.65	45.00	3.30	10.00	2.28	24.00
7	15.00	0.735	2.36	84.27	4.72	68.53	3.22	78.53
8	5.00	0.714	4.24	15.20	8.48	69.60	5.95	19.00
9	3.00	0.710	3.00	0.00	6.00	100.00	4.22	40.67
10	1.00	0.710	1.00	0.00	2.00	100.00	1.41	41.00
11	6.00	0.729	2.10	65.00	4.20	30.00	2.95	50.83
12	3.00	0.718	2.16	28.00	4.32	44.00	3.00	0.00
13	13.00	0.716	19.17	47.46	38.34	194.92	26.77	105.89
14	1.00	0.710	1.00	0.00	2.00	100.00	1.41	40.86
15	5.00	0.723	12.10	142.00	24.20	384.00	16.74	234.87
16	4.00	0.731	1.05	73.75	2.10	47.50	1.44	64.11
17	10.00	0.727	4.28	57.20	8.56	14.40	5.89	41.11
18	1.00	0.721	1.79	79.00	3.58	258.00	2.48	148.28
19	13.00	0.716	10.20	21.54	20.40	56.92	14.24	9.54
20	2.00	0.715	1.62	19.00	3.24	62.00	2.26	13.22
22	20.00	0.730	6.36	68.20	12.72	36.40	8.71	56.44
24	5.00	0.724	145.60	2812.00	291.20	5724.00	201.03	3920.58
25	8.00	0.735	1.18	85.25	2.36	70.50	1.61	79.93

(Cont.)

Table 4. (Cont.)

26	3.00	0.710	3.20	6.67	6.40	113.33	4.51	50.22
27	4.00	0.717	5.62	40.50	11.24	181.00	7.84	96.09
28	12.00	0.723	6.79	43.42	13.58	13.17	9.40	21.70
29	3.00	0.710	22.72	657.33	45.44	1414.67	32.00	966.77
30	1.00	0.729	2.76	176.00	5.52	452.00	3.79	278.71
31	1000.00	0.739	4.15	99.59	8.30	99.17	5.61	99.44
32	20.00	0.733	4.43	77.85	8.86	55.70	6.05	69.77
34	1.00	0.710	1.04	4.00	2.08	108.00	1.46	46.49
35	5.00	0.713	4.42	11.60	8.84	76.80	6.20	23.93
MMRE	-	-	-	154.81	-	315.94	-	212.82
MdMRE	-	-	-	48.23	-	70.05	-	48.36

11.6 Conclusion

In this paper, we have argued to apply DEA for ERP implementation project effort and cost estimation. This type of projects differs from traditional software development in a significant way, making it an ideal case for applying this non-parametrical method allowing for multi-input and multi-output relations with different units of measurement. Using a data set of 39 projects from a questionnaire, we have shown that their efficiency can indeed be compared, and DEA has been applied for the first time for effort estimation. From a first validation we can draw the following insights: DEA can achieve estimation results comparable in predicitve quality to other approaches like analogy-based methods, if properly set up. Using a measure of central tendency suitable to the data set will yield best predictive results. One main advantage is that different scenarios can easily be set up and explored. Another point in comparison with other approaches is that multi-input situations can be analysed, although then a single solution will in most cases not be found, which on the other hand leaves possibilities for exploring trade-offs between different input factors. Further restrictions of this method lie in the need to set an efficiency level, which leads to multiple possibly solutions, the chance that a new project might expand the production frontier and thus be more efficient than those previously encountered, and the need for a diverse data set of projects. Future research will be necessary to develop a set of metrics and measures for quantifying ERP implementations, for example using different ERP tailoring types [4].

References

1. Albrecht, A.J., & J.E. Gaffney, "Software Function, Source Lines of Code, and Development Effort Prediction: A Software Science Validation", IEEE Transactions on Software Engineering, 9(6), pp. 639-648, 1983.

2. Park, R.E., "Software Size Measurement: A Framework for Counting Source Statements". Technical Report CMU/SEI-92-TR-20, Software Engineering Institute, Carnegie Mellon University 1992.
3. Charnes, A., W. Cooper, & E. Rhodes, "Measuring the Efficiency of Decision Making Units", Europ. Journal of Operational Research, 2, pp. 429-444, 1978.
4. Brehm, L., A. Heinzl, & M.L. Markus, "Tailoring ERP Systems: A Spectrum of Choices and their Implications", Proc. 34th Hawaii Int. Conf. on System Sciences, Hawaii, 2001.
5. Davenport, T.H., "Putting the enterprise in the enterprise system", Harvard Business Review, July-August, pp. 121-131, 1998.
6. Kirchmer, M., Business Process Oriented Implementation of Standard Software, Springer-Verlag, Berlin, 1998.
7. Scheer, A.-W., ARIS – Business Process Frameworks, 3rd edition, Springer-Verlag, Berlin, 2000.
8. Wallace, T.F., & M.H. Kremzar, ERP: Making It Happen: The Implementers' Guide to Success with Enterprise Resource Planning, Wiley, New York, 2001.
9. Welti, N., Successful SAP R/3 Implementation: Practical Management of ERP Projects, Addison-Wesley, Reading, MA, 1999.
10. Scott, J.E., "The FoxMeyer Drugs' bankruptcy: Was it a failure of ERP?", Proc. 5th Americas Conf. on Information Systems (AMCIS 1999), Milwaukee, pp. 223-225, 1999.
11. Scott, J.E., & I. Vessey "Managing Risks in Enterprise Systems Implementations", Communications of the ACM, 45(4), pp. 74-81, 2002.
12. Brand, H., SAP R/3 Implementation With ASAP, Sybex, Alameda, CA, 1999.
13. Holland, C.P., & B. Light, "A Critical Success Factors Model for ERP Implementation", IEEE Software, 16(3), pp. 30-36, 1999.
14. Bingi, P., M.K. Sharma, & J.K. Godla, "Critical Issues affecting an ERP implementation", Information Systems Management, 16(3), pp. 7-14, 1999.
15. Bernroider, E., & S. Koch, "ERP Selection Process in Midsize and Large Organizations", Business Process Management Journal, 7(3), pp. 251-257, 2001.
16. Kitchenham, B., & E. Mendes, "Software Productivity Measurement Using Multiple Size Measures", IEEE Transactions on Software Engineering, 30(12), pp. 1023-1035, 2004.
17. Boehm, B.W., Software Engineering Economics, Prentice Hall, Englewood Cliffs, NJ, 1981.
18. Selby, R.W., & A.A. Porter, "Learning from Examples: Generation and Evaluation of Decision Trees for Software Resource Analysis", IEEE Transactions on Software Engineering, 14(12), pp. 1743-1756, 1988.
19. Shepperd, M., C. Schofield, & B. Kitchenham, "Effort Estimation Using Analogy", Proc. 18th Int. Conf. on Software Engineering (ICSE 1996), pp. 170-178, Berlin, 1996.
20. Myrtveit, I., & E. Stensrud, "A Controlled Experiment to Assess the Benefits of Estimating with Analogy and Regression Models", IEEE Transactions on Software Engineering, 25(4), pp. 510-525, 1999.
21. Farell, M.J., "The Measurement of Productive Efficiency", Journal of the Royal Statistical Society, Series A 120(3), pp. 250-290, 1957.
22. Charnes, A., W. Cooper, & E. Rhodes, "A Data Envelopment Analysis Approch to Evaluation of the Program Follow Through Experiments in U.S. Public School Education". Management Science Research Report No. 432, Carnegie-Mellon University, Pittsburgh, PA, 1978.

23. Banker, R.D., A. Charnes, & W. Cooper, "Some Models for Estimating Technical and Scale Inefficiencies in Data Envelopment Analysis", Management Science, 30, pp. 1078-1092, 1984.

24. Banker, R.D., & C. Kemerer, "Scale Economies in New Software Development", IEEE Transactions on Software Engineering, 15(10), pp. 416-429, 1989.

25. Banker, R.D., & S.A. Slaughter, "A Field Study of Scale Economies in Software Maintenance", Management Science, 43(12), pp. 1709-1725, 1997.

26. Mayrhauser, A., C. Wohlin, & M. Ohlsson, "Assessing and Understanding Efficiency and Success of Software Production", Empirical Software Engineering, 5(2), pp. 125-154, 2000.

27. Myrtveit, I., & E. Stensrud, "Benchmarking COTS Projects Using Data Envelopment Analysis", Proc. 6th Int. Software-Metrics-Symposium, Boca-Raton, pp. 269-278, 1999.

28. Kitchenham, B., "The question of scale economies in software - why cannot researchers agree?", Information & Software Technology, 44(1), pp. 13-24, 2002.

29. Cooper, W., L. Seiford, & K. Tone, Data Envelopment Analysis, Kluwer Academic Publishers, Boston, MA, 2000.

12 Contrasting Rankings from Social Choice Aggregation Methods for Business Information System Selection in Multiple Case Studies

Edward Bernroider, Johann Mitlöhner

Institute for Information Business
Vienna University of Economics and Business Administration
Augasse 2–6, A-1090 Vienna, Austria
{edward.bernroider,mitloehn}@wu-wien.ac.at

12.1 Introduction

This article focuses on decision making for Information System (IS) selection, in particular in the context of business applications. The complexity of business IS is increasing continuously, covering a wide range of different aspects. These aspects can be adequately covered by multiple criteria in decision making methods, which have been developed for the last decades to support the evaluation, selection, and follow-up controlling of IS. The area of multiple attribute decision making (MADM), where problems are represented by several (conflicting) attributes or criteria, was described as the most well known branch of decision making [11]. These methods appeal to management due to their intuitive, simple and cost effective application. They are relatively transparent, allowing others to see the logic of the results and enabling the inclusion of the full range of intangible consequences in terms of considered attributes. Nevertheless, many difficulties in MADM exist that lead to application errors in business practice. Model extensions proposed to avoid these errors are in general coupled with increased complexity that in turn hinders their acceptance. In this article, we seek to increase the awareness and analyze the applicability of well researched selection rules originating from social choice theory in the context of business IS decisions. In particular, we seek to contrast rankings from various social choice aggregation methods and compare the outcomes with results from traditional utility ranking methods applied in practice considering two ex-post case studies.

W. Abramowicz and H.C. Mayr (eds.), Technologies for Business Information Systems, 133–144.

The remainder of this article is structured as follows. Firstly, the research background and objectives are clarified. Next, social choice methods are summarized and thereafter applied in two case studies showing the selection of enterprise wide IS in Austrian companies. The results are compared with the outcomes of traditional MADM based on simple additive weighting as utility aggregation method. Finally, conclusions are given.

12.2 Research Background and Objectives

MADM refers to making preference decisions over a finite number of alternatives that are characterized by multiple, usually conflicting, attributes. A MADM problem can be expressed by a matrix, where columns indicate the attributes considered and rows denote the competing alternatives. Each MADM problem needs to be solved by one of the numerous MADM methods available. It is essential for many compensatory MADM methods to obtain comparable scales by normalization of attribute ratings. Solving the MADM problem can imply the aggregation of utilities into an overall evaluation for each alternative leading to a final ranking. In many applications a weight vector describing the relative importance values of each attribute is used to aggregate the alternative evaluations.

In this paper we focus on MADM in a finite IS selection problem, where usually the number of alternatives is limited and a wide choice of selection attributes are considered. In the field of IS evaluation the MADM approach 'Information Economics' received considerable attention [7]. The model gives the decision makers the means to identify and assess a comprehensive set of evaluation attributes in the IS evaluation problem setting, therefore it primarily assists in the important generation of attributes. Other more general concepts provide assistance to identify places where important criteria, especially benefits, might be found, e.g. [4].

The common frameworks used in systematic IS selection for MADM are based on additive value models, usually either the Analytic Hierarchic Process [9] (AHP) or some kind of utility ranking models (based on the so-called "Nutzwertanalyse" - NWA) [13]. In both cases the decision maker tries to maximize a quantity called utility or value. This postulates that all alternatives may be evaluated on a single scale that reflects the value system and the preferences of the decision maker. To generate this super scale, multiple single-attribute value functions are consolidated, most regularly by a simple additive procedure. In the mentioned methodologies (AHP and NWA) the assessment of attribute weights and single-attribute value functions is supported. The value aggregation per alternative is in the case of AHP, undertaken by a weighted sum of those single-attribute value functions. In terms of NWA, the decision maker is allowed to choose among a set of methods and typically relies on the standard recommendation, again formally a weighted sum approach. In the weighted sum method, the overall suitability of each alternative is thereby calculated by averaging the score of each alternative with respect to every attribute with the corresponding importance weighting. In business practice, important pre-conditions of the NWA (and the AHP) are violated. Regularly, scale types are mis-used or scale transformations made are invalid, e.g., ordinally scaled values are used as if they were cardinally scaled. Another major problem lies in the necessity of defining attribute weights, which is known as a major challenge for decision makers.

Another, more general, nevertheless major criticism of MADM is that different methods may yield different results when applied to the same problem. This phenomenon is known as the inconsistent ranking problem caused by the use of different MADM methods [12]. The availability of a wide selection of methods for solving IS decision problems generates the paradox that the selection of a MADM method for a given problem leads to a MADM problem itself [11].

In this article we turn to popular social choice methods for solving MADM problems in the IS selection process. These methods should appeal to business practices since they demand less rigorous information from the decision maker. No single-attribute value functions need to be derived and no weighting of attributes is needed. The analogy between voting and multiple criteria decision support is easily found. If attributes are replaced by voters, and alternatives by candidates, a social choice problem is designed. In other words, the preferences of an individual in social choice problems play the same role as the preferences gained along a single dimension or attribute in MADM [3]. A major motivation for this analogy lies in the fact that voting theory has developed since the original works by Borda, Condorcet and Arrow [1] to a large amount of results at disposal for use in MADM.

This article explores popular social choice selection rules in two ex-post case studies. We refer to selecting business IS alternatives with many different goals. The first case study describes an Enterprise Resource Planning (ERP) Software selection, which can be seen as a well suited example for a complex Business Information System selection problem. The second case study refers to a decision problem where enterprise application integration software is evaluated for a large Austrian Bank (Erste Bank).

12.3 Overview of Social Choice Aggregation Rules

A preference is a statement on a set of alternatives. We use $a \succ b$ to denote that a is strictly preferred to b, or $a \succeq b$ for weak preference, i.e. b is not preferred to a.

The problem of preference aggregation in social choice consists of finding an aggregate ranking such that the preferences stated by the individual voters are expressed in a meaninful way; e.g., an alternative that is bottom-ranked by all individuals should not receive first place in the aggregate ranking. A profile is a set of n rankings on m alternatives, e.g., $a \succ b \succ c, b \succ c \succ a, c \succ a \succ b, b \succ c \succ a$ for $n = 4$, $m = 3$, and alternatives a, b, c. We assume that profiles do not contain indifferences, i.e. the voters are not allowed to state $a = b$ but must decide on $a \succ b$ or $b \succ a$; however, the resulting aggregation may contain indifferences, and the winner set may contain more than one alternative.

As already stated, in the MADM context the voters are replaced by the dimensions or attributes considered. In contrast to the scoring methods typically used in MADM the evaluation of the alternatives is now reduced to finding the n rankings of alternatives for the m dimensions or attributes, instead of defining n single-attribute value functions. It is usually much easier for experts to provide rankings such as $b \succ c \succ a$ for each category instead of numeric values such as $a : 18, b : 25, c : 22$, which are usually questionable yet fundamental for the NWA analysis.

While there are various approaches to preference aggregation, each algorithm results in an aggregate relation which we denote as a set of pairwise comparisons of the m alternatives stated in $m \times m$ matrix notation. We use boolean values (written as 1 for true and 0 for false) to encode weak preference, such that $x \succeq y$ is encoded as 1 and $x \prec y$ as 0. Encoding weak preference instead of strict preference has the advantage that indifference can be encoded as well, by stating 1 both for $x \succeq y$ and $y \succeq x$. A plausible aggregation of the rankings stated above is the relation $[[1,0,0],[1,1,1],[1,0,1]]$, a matrix with three rows stating that $a \succeq a, a \prec b, a \prec c$ (first row), $b \succeq a, b \succeq b, b \succeq c$ (second row), and $c \succeq a, c \prec b, c \succeq c$ (third row), which is equivalent to the aggregate ranking $b \succ c \succ a$.

While the social choice aggregation rules are aimed at generating an ordering over all alternatives, special emphasis is on selecting the winner. If an alternative x exists that beats all other alternatives in pairwise comparisons, x is a Condorcet winner [6]. An obvious demand on an aggregation rule is that it select x as a winner, if x is the Condorcet winner. Another demand on an aggregation rule is that it result in an aggregate relation that can be interpreted as a preference relation, i.e., that does not contain intransitivities or cycles. In the following we give a short overview of popular methods of rank aggregation from social choice theory, which will be used in the case studies. Detailed definitions are available in the literature, such as [6, 8].

Simple Majority (SM): A well-known voting procedure is the simple majority rule which counts the number of rankings where alternative x is preferred to y versus the number of rankings where y is preferred to x; a positive margin means that x wins against y in pairwise comparison and results in $x \succ y$ in the aggregate relation, a negative margins leads to $x \prec y$, and a zero margin means indifference. This rule is simple and intuitively apealing; unfortunately, it can easily result in cycles, such that $x \succ y, y \succ z, z \succ x$ (drop the fourth voter from the example given above to arrive at a cycle). In addition, transitivity is not guaranteed, i.e. $x \succ y$ and $y \succ z$ does not necessarily entail $x \succ z$. These disadvantages limit the use of the simple majority rule in practical applications.

Transitive Closure (TC) The transitive closure removes intransitivities from the SM relation by applying repeated matrix multiplication with itself until no more change occurs. This approach can result in a large winner set, limiting the practical use of this rule.

Maximin (MM): The Maximin rule scores the alternatives with the worst majority margin they each achieve and ranks them according to those scores.

Copeland (CO): The Copeland rule scores the alternatives with the sum over the signs of the majority margins they achieve and ranks them according to these scores.

Plurality (PL): The plurality rule ranks the alternatives according to the number of times they received top place. While easily understood and commonly applied, especially in political elections, this rule often fails the put the Condorcet winner in the winning set, if one exists. This is not surprising considering the fact that this rule ignores all the preference information stated by the voters except for the top-ranked alternative.

Antiplurality (AP): A similar rule known as the Antiplurality rule ranks the alternatives according to the number of times they did not receive last place. This rule also often fails to elect the Condorcet winner if it exists.

Borda (BO): The Borda rule assigns points decreasing by a fixed amount to consecutive positions, e.g. in the case of three alternatives it assigns 2 points for first place, 1 point for second and zero for last place. The alternatives are then ranked according to their total score.

Nanson (NA): The Nanson rule repeatedly calculates the Borda scores and drops the alternatives with the minimal scores, using the iteration number for the final ranking, i.e. alternatives which survive the dropping process longer are ranked higher.

Kemeny (KE): The Kemeny rule chooses the ordering with minimal distance to all rankings in the profile, where distance is defined as the number of different pairwise relations.

Slater (SL): The Slater rule chooses the ordering with minimal distance to the outcome of the simple majority rule, where distance is defined as the number of different entries in the aggregate relations.

Young (YO): The Young rule ranks alternative x by the minimum number of voters which must be dropped to make x a simple majority winner.

Dodgson (DO): The Dodgson rule ranks alternative x by the minimum number of switches of adjacent alternatives in the voters' rankings it takes to make x a simple majority winner.

While the first eight rules can be computed in time polynomial in n and m, the last four rules in the list (KE, SL, YO and DO) are computationally more costly and become impractical with larger numbers of alternatives and voters. However, in the typical IS selection the number of alternatives is not very large, and with typical values of $m \leq 3$ and $n \leq 25$ the computational complexity does not pose a problem. In the following section we will take a look at such IS selection problems and apply the rules discussed to these situations.

12.4 Case Studies

In this section two case studies are presented to show the viability of applying social choice voting rules to information system selection in typical realistic settings. The first case study provides are rather clear-cut result, while the second hints at problems with this approach.

12.4.1 Case 1

The first case refers to Primagaz Austria, an international wholesaler of liquid and gaseous fuels and related products (SHV Holdings N.V.). It needed to replace their legacy IT environment for Enterprise Resources Planning (ERP) applications through standard software. Their independent decision making process was based on multiple attributes and alternatives. Thus, it provided an ideal grounding for ERP/IS investment appraisal analysis with multiple criteria.

The applied ERP decision making methodology was based on the NWA complemented with vendor related perceptions and a separate financial analysis. The NWA yielded an ERP utility score for each alternative (we will refer to them as A, B and C) through simple additive weighting based on a number of pre-selected attributes reflecting their specific range of targeted software specific functionalities and benefits. Table 1 denotes the defined categories with the scores of the three alternatives.

Table 1. Scores from individual categories in the Primagaz case study

Category	Alternative A	Alternative B	Alternative C
Controlling and Reporting	13	15	14
Accounting	14	21	16
Logistics	9	6	6
Purchasing	8	7	5
Local Divisions	12	13	9
Services and Engineering	15	18	18
Sales	24	25	27
Management	13	16	14
Weighted Utility Scores	**253**	**288**	**252**

The weighted utility scores for the three alternatives A, B, and C were 253, 288 and 252 respectively. Alternative B outranks its opponents whereas A and C seem to have a tie, i.e. they can be considered as equally good. This situation demonstrates shortcomings of the NWA: The resulting utility scores are hardly interpretable and do not provide a clear-cut ranking. Furthermore, the common mistake of using ordinally scaled utility values in a simple additive weighting model was observed.

The application of social choice rules would limit the demands placed on the data considerably. No value judgments and no weighting of attributes would be needed.

Removing weights from the analysis has the implicit assumption that every attribute is of equal importance. Therefore, analyzing the robustness of the winner becomes even more important. Preference information must be gathered in terms of the alternatives for each dimension/attribute, which were derived for our ex-post analysis from the supplied case study data. The aggregation rules described above were applied to the preferences resulting from the application of 8 criteria to 3 alternatives in the case study. For this purpose, the values from Table 1 were translated into rankings for each category, such as $B \succ C \succ A$ for Controlling, $B \succ A \succ C$ for Purchasing, and so on. The ties in Logistics and Services were broken lexicographically, i.e. $A \succ B \succ C$ for Logistics, and $B \succ C \succ A$ for Services. The result is shown in Table 2.

In terms of alternative B, the application of all methods validates B as the winner, i.e. as the best alternative. This remains unchanged even if the ties in Logistics and Services are resolved differently. Table 3 gives an overview of the results for all four combinations of tie resolves. In terms of the remaining alternatives, C seems to be slightly preferable in comparison to A. The results suggest further investigating the ratings of A compared to C in order to achieve a more stable ranking outcome. Similar interpretations were achieved in the NWA, where A was valued higher by one value unit in comparison with C.

Applying different voting rules (and, when necessary, tie resolves) to the same input data provides a simple way of judging the robustness of the results. In this example alternative B was always selected as the winner. This is an obvious indicator towards the reliability of the winner set. Furthermore, in some situations the Maximin, Young, and Plurality rules identified the almost identical utility values in the MADM analysis of alternatives A and C by stating an explicit indifference $A = C$.

Table 2. Application of the voting rules to the Primagaz data, ties resolved lexicographically

Rule	Relation	Ranking
SM	$[[1,0,0],[1,1,1],[1,0,1]]$	$B \succ C \succ A$
BO	$[[1,0,0],[1,1,1],[1,0,1]]$	$B \succ C \succ A$
CO	$[[1,0,0],[1,1,1],[1,0,1]]$	$B \succ C \succ A$
TC	$[[1,0,0],[1,1,1],[1,0,1]]$	$B \succ C \succ A$
NA	$[[1,0,0],[1,1,1],[1,0,1]]$	$B \succ C \succ A$
MM	$[[1,0,1],[1,1,1],[0,0,1]]$	$B \succ A \succ C$
KE	$[[1,0,0],[1,1,1],[1,0,1]]$	$B \succ C \succ A$
SL	$[[1,0,0],[1,1,1],[1,0,1]]$	$B \succ C \succ A$
YO	$[[1,0,1],[1,1,1],[0,0,1]]$	$B \succ A \succ C$
DO	$[[1,0,0],[1,1,1],[1,0,1]]$	$B \succ C \succ A$
PL	$[[1,0,1],[1,1,1],[0,0,1]]$	$B \succ A \succ C$
AP	$[[1,0,0],[1,1,1],[1,0,1]]$	$B \succ C \succ A$

Table 3. Results for all four different ways of resolving the ties in Services and Logistics

Rule	Ranking 1	Ranking 2	Ranking 3	Ranking 4
SM	$B \succ C \succ A$	$B \succ C \succ A$	$B \succ C \succ A$	$B \succ C \succ A$
BO	$B \succ C \succ A$	$B \succ C \succ A$	$B \succ C \succ A$	$B \succ C \succ A$
CO	$B \succ C \succ A$	$B \succ C \succ A$	$B \succ C \succ A$	$B \succ C \succ A$
TC	$B \succ C \succ A$	$B \succ C \succ A$	$B \succ C \succ A$	$B \succ C \succ A$
NA	$B \succ C \succ A$	$B \succ C \succ A$	$B \succ C \succ A$	$B \succ C \succ A$
MM	$B \succ A \succ C$	$B \succ A = C$	$B \succ A = C$	$B \succ C \succ A$
KE	$B \succ C \succ A$	$B \succ C \succ A$	$B \succ C \succ A$	$B \succ C \succ A$
SL	$B \succ C \succ A$	$B \succ C \succ A$	$B \succ C \succ A$	$B \succ C \succ A$
YO	$B \succ A \succ C$	$B \succ A = C$	$B \succ A = C$	$B \succ C \succ A$
DO	$B \succ C \succ A$	$B \succ C \succ A$	$B \succ C \succ A$	$B \succ C \succ A$
PL	$B \succ A \succ C$	$B \succ A = C$	$B \succ A \succ C$	$B \succ A = C$
AP	$B \succ C \succ A$	$B \succ C \succ A$	$B \succ C \succ A$	$B \succ C \succ A$

12.4.2 Case 2

In the second case study the investment decision refers to an enterprise application integration software in a large Austrian Bank (Erste Bank). There were three alternatives, and the number of attributes was 14. The utility values listed in Table 4 resulted from weighted sums over degrees of satisfaction for a large number of goals (0: none, 1: partial, 2: full, 3: excess). Again, the company relied on ordinal scales which were falsely treated as metric scales in the applied NWA with a simple additive weighting aggregation technique. The values were propagated through two additional layers with the weights stated in the table to arrive at the final utility values given in the bottom line. The level of difference between the alternatives can hardly be interpreted. Nevertheless, the traditional MADM resulted in a final ranking $A \succ B \succ C$. The simple sum of scores showed the applying weights helped alternative A to outrank B, whereas C again remains as being ranked last.

The social choice rules were applied in the same manner as in the previous case study by using the second level utility values, i.e. before any weighting as indicated in the table. Unfortunately, in this ex-post case there are seven ties observable in the utility values. We present two ways of resolving the ties are presented here: lexicographical order, and inverse lexicographical order.

The results are presented in Tables 5 and 6. Alternative C is almost unequivocally ranked bottom, which corresponds to the outcome of the traditional weighted utility ranking analysis as indicated by the total utility values. However, different tie resolving almost totally reverses the relation of A and B, identifying these alternatives as nearly indifferent. This seems to contrast with the weighted utility scores which seem to indicate a clear preference for alternative A. This limitation is due to the ex-post character of this case study. In a live ex-ante approach, the social choice rules would require rankings in terms of single attributes instead of single point estimates of utility

Table 4. Utility values for the three investment alternatives in the Erste Bank case study

Criteria	W1	W2	A	B	C
Common	10		**1.090**	**1.180**	**1.360**
General Information		40	1.450	1.300	1.750
Future Strategy		60	0.850	1.100	1.100
Business related	40		**1.870**	**1.810**	**1.638**
Workflow		23	1.750	1.750	1.550
Data representation		12	1.650	1.950	1.450
Deployment		6	0.800	2.000	2.450
Data transmission		17	1.900	2.000	1.900
Operations		12	2.150	1.950	1.950
Monitoring		23	2.250	1.550	1.250
Application Integration		7	1.750	1.750	1.650
Architecture and Security	25		**0.391**	**0.243**	**0.458**
IT Architecture		45	0.350	0.000	0.560
Security		35	0.333	0.403	0.333
System requirements		20	0.585	0.510	0.450
Commercial and procurement	25		**1.450**	**1.270**	**1.040**
Delivery concept		40	1.450	1.000	0.800
Project Support		60	1.450	1.450	1.200
Weighted Utility Scores			**1.317**	**1.220**	**1.166**
Sum of Scores			18.718	18.713	18.393

scores. Nevertheless, the sum of scores shows that when the bias of the weights is removed the results correspond closely to those of the social choice rules.

Table 5. Application of the voting rules to the Erste Bank data, ties resolved lexicographically

Rule	Relation	Ranking
SM	$[[1,1,1],[0,1,1],[0,0,1]]$	$A \succ B \succ C$
BO	$[[1,1,1],[0,1,1],[0,0,1]]$	$A \succ B \succ C$
CO	$[[1,1,1],[0,1,1],[0,0,1]]$	$A \succ B \succ C$
TC	$[[1,1,1],[0,1,1],[0,0,1]]$	$A \succ B \succ C$
NA	$[[1,1,1],[0,1,1],[0,0,1]]$	$A \succ B \succ C$
MM	$[[1,1,1],[0,1,1],[0,0,1]]$	$A \succ B \succ C$
KE	$[[1,1,1],[0,1,1],[0,0,1]]$	$A \succ B \succ C$
SL	$[[1,1,1],[0,1,1],[0,0,1]]$	$A \succ B \succ C$
YO	$[[1,1,1],[0,1,1],[0,0,1]]$	$A \succ B \succ C$
DO	$[[1,1,1],[0,1,1],[0,0,1]]$	$A \succ B \succ C$
PL	$[[1,1,1],[0,1,1],[0,0,1]]$	$A \succ B \succ C$
AP	$[[1,1,1],[1,1,1],[0,0,1]]$	$A = B \succ C$

Table 6. Application of the voting rules to the Erste Bank data, ties resolved in inverse lexicographical order

Rule	Relation	Ranking
SM	$[[1,0,1],[1,1,1],[0,0,1]]$	$B \succ A \succ C$
BO	$[[1,0,1],[1,1,1],[0,0,1]]$	$B \succ A \succ C$
CO	$[[1,0,1],[1,1,1],[0,0,1]]$	$B \succ A \succ C$
TC	$[[1,0,1],[1,1,1],[0,0,1]]$	$B \succ A \succ C$
NA	$[[1,0,1],[1,1,1],[0,0,1]]$	$B \succ A \succ C$
MM	$[[1,0,1],[1,1,1],[0,0,1]]$	$B \succ A \succ C$
KE	$[[1,0,1],[1,1,1],[0,0,1]]$	$B \succ A \succ C$
SL	$[[1,0,1],[1,1,1],[0,0,1]]$	$B \succ A \succ C$
YO	$[[1,0,1],[1,1,1],[0,0,1]]$	$B \succ A \succ C$
DO	$[[1,0,1],[1,1,1],[0,0,1]]$	$B \succ A \succ C$
PL	$[[1,0,1],[1,1,1],[1,0,1]]$	$B \succ A = C$
AP	$[[1,0,1],[1,1,1],[0,0,1]]$	$B \succ A \succ C$

12.4.3 Distances of Voting Rules

The outcomes of the various voting rules in each case largely overlap, although certain rules, esp. PL and AP, can be identified as outliers even in this small sample. In a related work we showed that the Plurality and Antiplurality rules tend to produce relations that are removed from the core defined by the remaining aggregation rules [2]. Figure 1 shows the results from a simulation with 1000 random profiles with $m = 3$ alternatives and $n = 25$ attributes; the distances of the relations resulting from the various aggregation rules as defined by the number of different bits in the aggregate relations is plotted using a method from phylogenetics, the nearest neighbor tree [10]. The tree shows that rules like DO and NA produce identical relations in almost all cases, while PL and AP show the maximum difference, which makes them ideal candidates for robustness analyses.

A possible application of this figure is to determine a choice of methods based on their disparity in these result, which can be used for decision making or validating purposes. If strongly differential rules produce the same ranking outcomes, then the validity of the results is supported, otherwise questioned.

12.5 Conclusions

The main motivation for social choice rules are the demands on the input data. In contrast to the traditional NWA, no single-attribute value functions need to be derived and no weighting of attributes is needed. Instead rankings for each dimension reflected through the attributes for each alternative are needed. This approach avoids the many problems known in quantifying weights and criteria values as well as errors

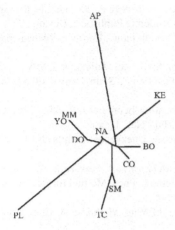

Fig. 1. Distances of voting rules

in method application, e.g. wrong scale definitions and transformations (as observed in the article).

In the first case study, the outcome of traditional multiple attribute decision making methods (NWA) and of the applied social choice rules are largely identical. In the second case study, the results differ in terms of a sub-ranking of two alternatives resulting from the greater number of ties between alternatives from the perspective of individual attributes. Thus, the social choice methods are content with a set of simple preference relations, yet in the case studies presented they arrived at largely the same results (with limitations in case 2). To increase validity of results, a set of social choice methods to compare ranking outcomes can be used.

Future work will further analyze characteristics of voting rules and consequence for MADM in IS selection, such as manipulability, Condorcet criterion, and computational feasibility. Based on the achieved results, a modified NWA based procedural model will be developed to supply business practice with the possibility of selecting a suitable aggregation rule portfolio including diverse social choice selection rules. The main goal is to apply less information demanding MADM selection approaches and also to support validation, since this requirement is often neglected in practice.

References

1. Arrow KJ (1963) Social Choice and Individual Values, Wiley, New York, 2nd Edition
2. Bernroider E, Mitlöhner J (2006), "Social Choice Aggregation Methods for Multiple Attribute Business Information System Selection", In: Abramowicz W, Mayr HC, Business Information Systems, GI Lecture Notes in Informatics, Vol. P-85

3. Bouyssou D, Marchant T, Pirlot M, Perny P, Tsoukias A, Vincke P (2000) Evaluation and Decision Models - A critical Perspective, Kluwer Academic Publishers, Boston
4. Farbey B, Targett D, Land F (1994) "The great IT benefit hunt", European Management Journal, 12(3):270-279
5. Felsenstein J (2004) Inferring Phylogenies, Sinauer Associates, Sunderland, MA
6. Fishburn PC (1977) "Condorcet Social Choice Functions", Siam Journal of Applied Mathematics, 33:469-489
7. Parker MM, Benson RJ, Trainor HE (1988) Information Economics, Linking Business Performance to Information Technology, Prentice-Hall, New Jersey
8. Saari D (2001) Decisions and Elections Explaining the Unexpected, Cambridge University Press
9. Saaty TL (1980) The Analytic Hierarchy Process, McGraw Hill, New York
10. Saitou N, Nei M (1987) "The Neighbor-Joining Method: a new Method for Reconstruction of Phylogenetic Trees", Mol. Biol. Evol., 4:406-425
11. Triantaphyllou E (2000) Multi-Criteria Decision Making Methods: A Comparative Study, Kluwer Academic Publishers, London
12. Yeh CH (2003) "The selection of multiattribute decision making methods for scholarship student selection", International Journal of Selection and Assessment 11(4):289-296
13. Zangemeister C (1976) Nutzwertanalyse in der Systemtechnik, Wittemann, Munich

13 Managing Adaptive Information Projects in the Context of a Software Developer Organizational Structure

Pawel Cichon, Zbigniew Huzar, Zygmunt Mazur, Adam Mrozowski

Wrocław Institute of Technology
{Adam.Mrozowski, Pawel.Cichon, Zbigniew.Huzar, Zygmunt.Mazur}@pwr.wroc.pl

13.1 Notation

The presentation of the research described in this article is based on the Software Process Engineering Metamodel (SPEM), which is used to describe a concrete software development process or a family of related software development processes. An object-oriented approach has been chosen to model a family of related software processes and the UML profile has been used as a notation. This introduction covers only a minimal set of process modeling elements necessary to describe the presented processes. More details can be found in SPEM specification delivered by OMG

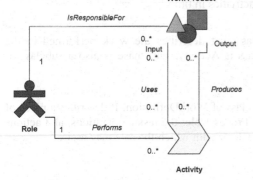

Fig. 1. The SPEM Conceptual Model: Roles, Work Products, and Activities

W. Abramowicz and H.C. Mayr (eds.), Technologies for Business Information Systems, 145–157.
© 2007 Springer.

[OMG 2005]. At the core of SPEM is an idea that a software development process is a collaboration of abstract active entities called process roles that perform operations called activities on concrete, tangible entities called work products. The overall goal of the process is to bring a set of work products to a well-defined state. The fragment of SPEM conceptual model is presented in the Figure 1.

The notation used in the article for the presented conceptual model includes the following elements:

 This symbol indicates a stand alone, complete, end-to-end process class - Process. It is distinguished from normal ProcessComponents[1] by the fact that it is not intended to be composed with other components. The class Process can also represent a family of processes, which is a process component out of which multiple overlapping processes can be defined.

 ProcessRole is a subclass of ProcessPerformer described below.

 ProcessPerformer defines a performer for a set of WorkDefinitions in a process. ProcessPerformer has a subclass ProcessRole. ProcessPerformer represents the "whole process" or one of its components in an abstraction, and is used to own WorkDefinitions that do not have a more specified owner.

 Phase is a specialized subclass of WorkDefinition thus its prerequisite defines the phase entry criteria and its goal (often called a "milestone") defines the phase exit criteria. Phases are defined with the additional constraint of sequentially; that is, their enactments are executed with a series of milestone dates spread over time and often assume minimal (or no) overlap of their activities in time.

 WorkDefinition is a class that describes the work performed in the process. Its main subclass is Activity, but Phase is also a subclass of WorkDefinition.

 Activity is the main subclass of WorkDefinition. It describes a piece of work performed by one ProcessRole: the tasks, operations, and actions that are performed by a role or with which the role may assist.

---

[1] ProcessComponent constitutes a chunk of process descriptions that are internally consistent and may be re-used with other ProcessComponents to assemble a complete process.

WorkProduct is anything produced, consumed, or modified by a process. It may be a piece of information, a document, a model, source code, and so on. WorkProduct describes one class of work product produced in a process.

 Document is a category of WorkProduct.

 UMLModel is a category of WorkProduct.

13.2 Introduction

The complex information projects are difficult to estimate because of multi-resource fullness and a short life cycle, which indicates a short period between next modifications or extensible development of application functionalities [Boehm 1981]. Therefore complex systems are often adapted to budget during process of execution, even though in a canonical model of the project management a business contract is entered into, on the base of a cost of subsystems and tasks, the project is decomposed. Most important is to create an information system that makes business run as efficient as a client wants, and fit in the time frames and the client's budget. Contract is signed mostly on the base of non-functional requirements with most important elements that expose main priorities: scope[2], cost and time. This type of contract is called adaptive contract[3], and information projects thus based are called adaptive projects. These projects, as other information projects types[4] such as waterfall, agile, optional scope etc., are successful, when they meet functional and non-functional requirements, which determine the quality of the final product. The difference is that adaptive projects emphasize extensively non-functional requirements. The non-functional requirements

[2] Scope defines specification of business processes that should be covered by the entire project.

[3] Terms adaptive contracts and adaptive projects used by the authors, are also called fixed price contracts and fixed price projects for the sake of stable non-functional requirements (the price set by the client covers resource function, project complexity and its time duration). Adaptive projects are fixed price projects, which allow specifying functional requirements during entire project life cycle (adapting functional to non-functional requirements), this is the reason for "adaptive" adjective usage. Adaptive contracts are fixed price contracts in view of adaptive projects (term adaptive contract is used mainly for syntactic coherence with adaptive project term).

[4] Projects are named mainly for the sake of the most important characteristic, which is the basis for non-formal project typization.

constitute the basis for functional specification, which is postponed to further phases of the adaptive project (Figure 2, Figure 3, Figure 5).

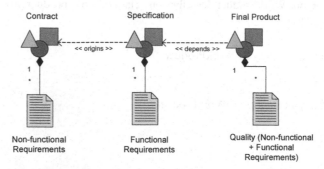

Fig. 2. Requirements in the context of adaptive project life cycle

Specification of functional requirements during project execution poses the main difficulty for software developer because continuous changes of requirements cause that it is difficult to foresee entire project realization cycle at the beginning. Therefore a software developer has to respond as quickly as possible to changes at the project execution and functional requirements must meet the actual client's needs with reference to production capabilities, cost and time limits.

The article presents description of adaptive type of an information project, unique execution process of an adaptive project and company organizational structure for remote adaptive project execution with the use of SPEM language [OMG 2005, Sas 2003]. Originality of the described approach relies in parallelism of implementation and design of productive process sub-phases (Figure 5) in the context of evolving functional requirements and in setting consultants and project data set in a standard matrix organization structure of an information company. The presented solution allows quicker reaction to the functional changes that may appear during the development process.

13.3 Adaptive Process and Project Realization Method

The traditional approach to an information project execution presupposes that the phases of design, implementation, testing and migration occur sequentially. The next phase starts upon completion of the preceding phase ends, therefore the first versions of the working system are delivered to the client relatively late because in the last phases of the project life cycle. Adaptive process is guided by a different approach to the traditional one mainly because it delivers the working application to the client as soon as possible, through making design sub-phase parallel to implementation sub-phase, making them iterative and taking advantage of phase interdependency (Figure 2,

Figure 4). This leads to the creation of a sub-process oriented to the delivery of the project development results to the client in the form of functional subsystems.

An adaptive project allows for functional requirement extension during the project execution. When an adaptive contract is signed, mainly its range is specified, in terms of business processes that will be covered by the entire project. There was proved that a realization of just 20 percent of the functionality makes 80 percent of client's satisfaction [Popendieck 2004], it means quality and business value of the final product. An adaptive project promotes this point of view first of all by emphasizing quick delivery of the most important 20 percent of functionality and the project guidance by the customer. The client verifies and specifies functionality of the system and in such a way affects the whole informational system execution process. Continuous process adaptation to the customer requirements to obtain the highest possible business value of the final product describes the adaptive process, which is fundamental for adaptive projects.

The analysis of project management methods (RUP, USDP) leads to conclusion that most of them have no strict marginal conditions[5]. Such an instance brings about solutions that are oriented to predictability[6] in unpredictable processes which increase the project failure risk. A method dedicated to the case of an adaptive project, preceded by signing a fixed price type contract is presented below. The adaptive projects are partially unpredictable, because of defining functional requirements during process realization and that couldn't signify unpredictable and uncontrolled process (called realization chaos). Therefore a repetitive realization process and right organizational structure has to be created that assures control over unpredictability and let react efficiently to changes of functional requirements and processes while realization of the project. Reaction to functional requirements changes needs tight collaboration between the team members and domain experts (consultants) [McConnell 1998]. This collaboration goes beyond standard business roles (every worker should be regarded as an expert and consultations should constitute a preferred solution of problems) and preparation of an evolving process to meet continuous functional requirement realization needs regular audits (evaluation of milestone progress).

The project execution process starts with the vision phase. In that stage consultants and customer representatives focuses, among other things, on defining of a document describing non-functional requirements that are a part of the contract (Figure 3). The consultants, working together with domain experts, create a list of business processes that have to be covered by a system. It is important to describe points of integration of the new system, existing infrastructure and external processes. The goal of the vision phase is to define the project scope in the context of non-functional requirements and point out the most important threats. Furthermore, there is a coordinator and domain experts (on the customer's side) selected, responsible for functional requirements of the system specification. They decide about supplementation or

---

[5] For safe application of the methodology values of environment parameters must be met.

[6] Predictable solutions are the solutions that have all functional and non-functional requirements set before the project starts. This allows for creating of an entire project at the very begin.

removal of a specified functionality proposed by the consultants. After contract signing the project team commences work.

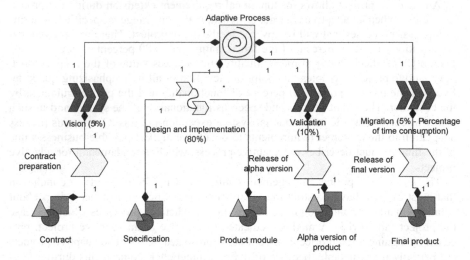

Fig. 3. The execution process of adaptive projects with marked phases and artifacts

The method presented here assumes an iterative approach as regards the risk[7] in the design and implementation phases. Extensive and narrow[8] implementation[9] of many components[10] [Kasprzyk 2004] parallel comes true. The objective is a quick stabilization which entails partial implementation of base software and hardware components, associated with functionality that has high business priorities and definition of interfaces , the cooperation rules and environment. From the customer's viewpoint the approach above has a psychological value because early implementation of key functionalities helps to stabilize the high level of customer's involvement in the project and that facilitates smooth project execution [Cockburn 2003]. It is very important because in iterative designing directed to the client, customer decides about elements introduced in successive iterations, demanding implementation of the most important modules from his point of view. A single iteration[11] consists of sub phases, presented on Figure 4.

---

[7] For the early iterations the most risky elements are chosen.

[8] Implementation that contains the most important elements of the system from the customer and supplier's perspective.

[9] Programming activities that include only frames of functionalities. These frames may be extended in further iterations.

[10] Subsystem that contains one or several coherent use cases.

[11] Set of activities that lead to creation of a functional system module.

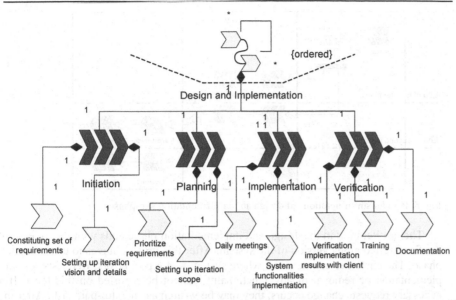

Fig. 4. Decomposition of a design and implementation phase into sub phases and activities

The most important activities in specified sub phases are as follows:

Initiation. The team members create a list of use cases and their extensions. More-over, all the possible risks should be identified. The sub-phases' goal is to specify the functional elements of a system that should be implemented in a coming iteration.

Planning. Choice of the functionalities (their verification) that must be implemented in the context of a business value for a client. Setting the iteration scope by removing less important functional requirements from the planning phase.

Implementation. Putting into practice those functionalities which are consistent with the verified requirements list. The sub-phase ends with a release of the tested inter-nal[12] version of a sub system.

Verification. Representatives of the developer and the client organize a meeting to discuss the implemented functionality. They point to weakness and strengths parts of a solution, identify potential problems and indicate possible extensions. The goal is to show the best possible way to develop the existing application.

---

[12] Internal testing means verification of partially finished product and is made during production process (Verification sub-phase of design and implementation phase).

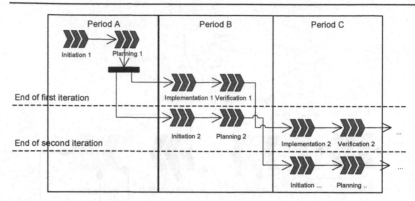

Fig. 5. Parallelism of iterations of design and implementation sub-phases

The last iteration in the design and implementation phase ends with the release of the final, tested alpha version of the system. After this project moves to the validation phase. The customer can now test whole system and report errors. Requests for supplementation or removal of any functionality cannot be reported on this level. If a necessary requests change occurs, they may be written as an extra-paid task. After the external[13] testing has been completed and the errors corrected the system is transferred from a test environment to production servers. This stage is called the migration. As the result of analyze of the projects that had not been completed successfully [Jonson 2001] the presented process contains the following key points:

– Self-organizing teams that cannot exceed 10 persons. During the iteration project the managers and the team leaders do not plan tasks for the team members. The teams are self-organized. Members share the tasks among themselves and decide about time frames necessary for each task execution. Only the disputes are solved by team leaders. Strong task orientation is preferred and the whole team should responsible for meeting the deadline [Highsmith 2002].
– Project executed with the use of iterations (Figure 5). Additionally, for projects realized by many distributed teams it's suggested to do two first iterations in a centralized structure at one site (Figure 6). A leaders' team should be created for these iterations. A common team should contain one or two most experienced programmers from the future remote teams. During these two iterations the greatest emphasis is put on requirement specification, which includes the most important components and their interfaces. The components related with the most important for the customer business runs are created more efficiently due to direct communication and cooperation of the best programmers. When the basis are ready, the main programmers are coming back to their teams and acting as team leaders. Further work can be done remotely. This way every team has it's leader but also a person who

---

[13] External testing is synonym to validation and means tests performed by customer after final product release by software developer.

has created fundaments of a system. Moreover, thanks to the team leaders' direct cooperation in the first two iterations further communication between teams has also improved during the whole project.

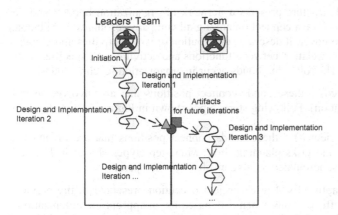

Fig. 6. Iterative implementation based on distributed teams

- Adaptive planning guided by the customer. The client takes a part in building functional requirements after each iteration and may make decisions in cooperation with developers' consultants. Customer has direct influence to order of use case implementation and may choose these of the highest business value.
- Adding a new functionality to an on going iteration has to be locked. Consultants, team members or the customer's representatives are not allowed to add new functionalities to the running iteration. Team leaders together with the project managers are acting as a firewall that isolates the team members from customer's change requests. If changes appear, the project managers negotiates their implementation in the future iterations (putting into tasks queue) [MacCormack 2001].
- Daily meetings of the entire team. Decisions are made in maximum one hour.. This method promotes the approach that wrong decisions are better than no decisions. Wrong decision can be corrected in the future iterations but no decision leads to the project stagnation [MacCormack 2001]. The tasks set for one day must be completed during that day. If any problems appear their are discussed at a next day meeting.
- An internal version release at the end of each iteration and a demo version for the client at least every two iterations.

13.4 Software Developer Organizational Structure as Regards of Adaptive Projects Execution

The organizational structure presents a network of organization bonds[14] and dependencies, which constitute a connection among all company resources, both human as well as material. Moreover, it describes distribution of work activities and employees' hierarchy, shows correlation between functions and activities and specifies a responsibility allocation. The following bonds occur in organization [Cichon 2004]:

Technical (task oriented) – these bonds connect positions that are involved in task execution (implementation). Following stereotypes shown in Figure 7 <<produces>>, <<elaborates>>.
Functional (function oriented) – these bonds connect positions that are involved in decision management and tasks planning. Following stereotypes shown in Figure 7 <<supervises>>, <<is subordinated>>, <<consults>>, <<cooperates>>.

The method of adaptive fixed price project execution presented in the previous chapter realization is efficient only when it is based on an appropriate organizational model. Organizational models the best for the presented process are task-oriented structures like the matrix model [Cichon 2004]. The matrix model, depends on managers' and team leaders' competences, can be divided to: weak - when a manager allows the team leader to allocate tasks to the team members, strong - when the manager assigns the tasks and neutral – when the manager together with team members perform task allocation. Whatever the model the manager's role should always be focused on planning, scheduling and budgeting and the team leaders' role on technical supervision. Figure 7 presents an organizational model drafted for remote run of process presented in the previous chapters and is based on neutral matrix model.

A team member is directly subordinated to the team leader, who verifies the work progress and is responsible for implementation quality. Moreover, leaders are responsible for implementation coherency, repository data update and team members' training. Teams should be grouped by specialization. In this way the team leaders and project managers can be certain that their teams have the necessary knowledge to carry out the assigned tasks. Project managers are responsible for scheduling, budget verification, changes and risk management. They may also with cooperation of team leaders allocate tasks packages to teams. The executed assignment is based on functional requirements and system decomposition delivered by the consultants working at customers' site, who are responsible for the system analysis and decomposition into modules[15]. Project managers, consultants and team leaders are obliged to report work progress at weekly project meetings.

---

[14] Information exchange channel.
[15] A functional part of the system.

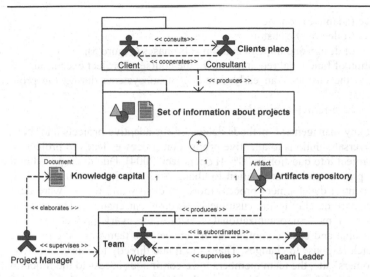

Fig. 7. A neutral matrix model for presented process of fixed price projects execution

The set of information about projects includes knowledge capital and remote repository, which is extremely important for remote cooperating teams and consultants. Firstly, it allows keeping project big picture[16]; secondly, it's essential for future projects and maintenance of already-designed systems. Thirdly, it's an integral part of intellectual capital of a organization. It contains the knowledge about previous projects that could be used for result comparison, drawing conclusions and risk minimization. The knowledge capital covers project documentation – schedule, budget, cost tables, risk calculations, teams and resources lists and other data important from the managing perspective. The remote repository is a set of artifacts - product source codes with descriptions, managed by a versioning system with changes annotations. Every worker must have uninterrupted access to the set of information about the projects, as presented in Figure 7. This is the only way in which the workers may understand their role in the project while working remotely and localize assigned tasks in whole project perspective.

13.5 Summary

The article is the cooperation result of IMG consultants with scientists from Wroclaw University of Technology. The developer as well as the customer take the risk of adaptive contracts execution which makes the specialized method of leading unpredictable projects is necessary. This method presupposes the consideration of characteristic elements of adaptive projects such as:

---

[16] Big picture means complete information data set, which describes the project execution.

- Fixed price (adaptive) contract,
- Process controlled by the customer,
- Parallelism of design and implementation sub-phases (Figure 5),
- Specification of functional requirements in the course of project execution,
- Delivery to the customer an early versions of subsystems during the project development,
- Absence of long-term planning[17].

There aren't any management methods dedicated for adaptive projects and the application of universal solutions to adaptive production processes leads to project failure or calling project into question in 70% [Popendieck 2004]. Due to proposed in the paper adaptive process and its orientation to changes of functional requirements the customer may control development process more efficiently and the software developer may react more quickly to the customer's requirement changes. The presented solution proposes a modern organizational structure for every project execution, which ensures stable and clear communication between the teams and the customer, essential for quick response to changes. Thanks to it and directly to consultants working on the customers' site, the team members have continuous access to the functional requirements and domain experts. Moreover, the presented structure is opened for telecommuting [Cichon 2004] and actually put into practice by Swiss consulting group IMG. The first fixed price projects with the use of described method were completed successfully, what constitutes great potential of project execution in the future.

References

[Boehm 1981] Boehm, B., *Software Engineering Economics*, Prentice-Hall, 1981

[Cichon 2004] Cichon, P., Huzar, Z., *Remote project management using modern organizational forms*, ISAT Proceedings, Wroclaw University of Technology Publishing House, 2004, pp.39-47

[Dubielewicz 2003] Dubielewicz, I., Sas, J., *SPEM/UML Profile in business processes of project management*, WNT, 2003, pp. 479-495

[Cockburn 2003] Cockburn, Alistair., *Characterizing People as Non-Linear*, First-Order Components in Software Development, http://alistair.cockburn.us/crystal/articles/cpanfocisd/characterizingpeopleasnonlinear.html, 2003

[Highsmith 2002] Highsmith, J., *Agile Project Management: Principles and Tools*, Cutter Consortium Executive Report, 2002

[Jonson 2001] Jonson, J., *Standish Group Chaos Report*, 2001

[Kasprzyk 2003] Kasprzyk, A., *SelectPerspective™ Methodology, Components in practice*, WNT, 2003, pp.121-126

[MacCormack 2001] MacCormack, A., *Product-Development Practices That Work*, MIT Sloan Management Review, 2001

---

[17] Short term planning concentrates only on planning coming iteration instead of planning of whole project.

[MacCormack 2001] MacCormack, A., Verganti, R., and Iansiti, M., *Developing Products on Internet Time: The Anatomy of a Flexible Development Process*, Management Science, 2001

[McConnell 1998] McConnell, S.: *Software Project Survival Guide*, Microsoft Press, 1998

[OMG 2005] OMG, *Software Process Engineering Metamodel Specification*, OMG Press, 2005

[Poppendieck 2004] Poppendieck, M., *Website: www.poppendieck.com*, 2004

14 Requirements for Establishing a Conceptual Knowledge Framework in Virtual Enterprises

Reyes Grangel, Ricardo Chalmeta, Cristina Campos

Grupo de Investigación en Integración y Re-Ingeniería de Sistemas (IRIS), Dept. de Llenguatges i Sistemes Informàtics, Universitat Jaume I, Campus del Riu Sec s/n, 12071 Castelló, Spain
{grangel, rchalmet, camposc}@uji.es

14.1 Introduction

The global economy, customer orientation and the swift evolution of Information and Communication Technologies (ICT) are some of the factors that have produced a new economic scenario, where information and knowledge have became strategic resources for enterprises [1]. The virtual enterprise arises in this context as a new organisational paradigm in which valuable cooperation can be established among partners in order to exploit competitive advantages by sharing resources, skills and costs, and by establishing a new model of interoperability [2].

A virtual enterprise is a network of independent enterprises, often competitors, that form a temporary alliance with the aim of developing a product or service so as to be able to take advantage of new market opportunities and to make it easier to achieve their objectives by sharing resources and costs [3].

To reach this goal the partners in a virtual enterprise need a real, continuous communication by means of ICT. The success of this kind of enterprises is based on interoperability, which is accomplished using different ICT with the objective of efficiently managing data, information and knowledge. Different database technologies (data warehouses, data mining, OLAP, peer-to-peer architectures, and so forth) have been used to manage the vast amount of data and information produced in this kind of enterprises in an efficient way. However, a key issue for virtual enterprises is sharing information, but more especially knowledge. Therefore, they need to implement efficient knowledge management systems in order to deal with the complexity of sharing and distributing information and knowledge among the partners in a virtual enterprise.

159

W. Abramowicz and H.C. Mayr (eds.), Technologies for Business Information Systems, 159–171.
© 2007 *Springer.*

Traditional knowledge management systems have been introduced by enterprises as a good solution to enable them to share and distribute knowledge among their employees. Nevertheless, in the context of virtual enterprises, where several partners with different procedures, methods, rules, culture and so on are integrated within a single virtual enterprise, the implementation of a knowledge management system is a far more complex task and it cannot be developed only by applying technological issues. Thus, a common conceptual framework that enables partners in a virtual enterprise to share data, information, and knowledge is needed before establishing a knowledge management system.

Therefore, the development of knowledge management systems in the context of virtual enterprises demands new, more specific requirements to establish this common framework. Such a framework should be focused on a holistic point of view of the enterprise and it is the basis for providing a common understanding about business for the partners that make up a virtual enterprise. In this paper, we present a set of knowledge requirements that are needed to develop this kind of systems. The requirements presented here are related to the explicit dimension of the conceptual blocks of knowledge defined in the KM-IRIS methodology [4] , which has been developed by the IRIS Group in order to establish knowledge management systems in virtual enterprises.

The chapter is organised as follows. Section 2 shows a review of the concepts related to knowledge framework and states the problems related to knowledge management systems within the context of the virtual enterprise. The KM-IRIS methodology developed by the IRIS Group to establish knowledge management systems in virtual enterprises is presented in section 3, as the context in which the requirements are proposed. Section 4 describes the knowledge requirements gathered for explicit dimension within the context of the KM-IRIS methodology, and then they are classified and analysed. Finally, section 5 outlines the conclusions.

14.2 Knowledge Perspective

The concept of knowledge has been defined from very different points of view, but in the context of enterprise information systems it has been usually linked to the concepts of data and information. In this section, we present some definitions of knowledge in order to provide a characterisation of enterprise knowledge as the basis for defining the requirements needed to establish knowledge management systems in the context of virtual enterprises. Moreover, a brief review of knowledge management systems, as well as the problems concerning the virtual enterprise are also detailed.

14.2.1 The Concept of Enterprise Knowledge

Data become information when they add value to the enterprise, and information becomes knowledge when insight, abstraction and a better understanding are added to it. Thus, knowledge can be defined as the capacity for effective action in a domain of human actions [5].

Nonaka [6] defines knowledge as the justified belief that increases the capacity of an entity for effective action. Polanyi, on the other hand, describes knowledge by means of a three-level model based on the concept of personal knowledge [5]:

1. Skill: capacity to act according to rules.
2. Know-how: skill plus capacity to act in a social context.
3. Experience: know-how plus skill to influence rules and knowledge domain.

Therefore, the paradox of knowledge is that it is inside of people's minds, but at the same time we need to capture, to store, and to distribute it for its effective use within enterprises. The conventional creation of knowledge is usually performed following the model in which data are transformed into information, and information is transformed into knowledge, but it can also follow the reverse model in which knowledge precedes information and data [5]. As a result, knowledge can be represented by means of links among data, information and knowledge inside a system, but other data, information and knowledge can also come from outside the system through other connections (see Fig. 1). Indeed, the structure of knowledge is a complex network of connections of data and information, which is also part of a feedback process with existing knowledge, both inside and outside of the system.

The process of converting this knowledge from the sources available to an organisation and then connecting people with that knowledge is one of the definitions provided to explain knowledge management [7, 8]. Furthermore, knowledge management facilitates creation, access and reuse of knowledge, typically by using advanced technology, such as the World Wide Web, Lotus Notes, the Internet and intranets [9]. In general, two kinds of knowledge are accepted within the field of knowledge management [5]:

- Explicit Knowledge: implicit, mental models and individual experiences.
- Tacit Knowledge: formal models, rules and procedures.

Taking into account the definition provided by [10] enterprise knowledge can been seen as information made actionable in a way that adds value to the enterprise. We defined enterprise knowledge as the network of connections among data and information that enables people involved in the enterprise to act and to make decisions that add value to the enterprise. Moreover, two dimensions can be defined in enterprise knowledge, explicit and tacit, following the current interpretation [11] that defines a fuzzy borderline between explicit and tacit knowledge.

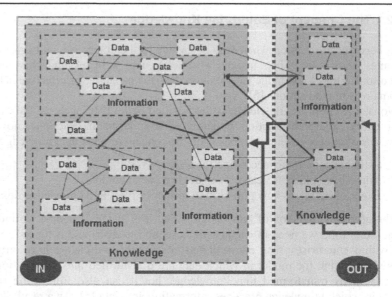

Fig. 1. Complex relationship among data, information and knowledge

14.2.2 Knowledge Management Systems

Both types of knowledge, explicit and tacit, can be represented as models and therefore managed. Knowledge management has been used in different kinds of enterprises with the aim of improving profits, being competitively innovative, or simply surviving [12] by implementing diverse kinds of knowledge management systems. A knowledge management system is a specialised system that interacts with the organisation's systems to facilitate all aspects of knowledge engineering [12].

Different generations of knowledge management systems are described in [11], where it is also explained why they did not live up to the expectations they had aroused:

- First generation, from 1990 to 1995: Despite the fact that the term 'knowledge worker' was defined by Peter Ducker in the 1960s, knowledge management was not introduced into the management field until the 1990's. At that time two main factors gave rise to a real, deep need for new processes of knowledge exchange: the first one was that 'Business Process Reengineering' was becoming rather outdated, and the second one was the increasingly common use of laptops in consulting businesses. Therefore, having a strategy based on knowledge management became 'fashionable' and the role of Chief Knowledge Officer (CKO) was defined. However, early adopters did not achieve their prospects.

- Second generation, from 1996 to 2000: Based on the erroneous belief that knowledge could be codified and supported by the well-known model 'SECI' (which was presented in a paper by Nonaka in 1991, but really started to have an impact in 1995 with the publication of the book [6]). This work was based on a previous one made by Polayni, who had proposed two types of knowledge, explicit and tacit. In 1997, Tsoukas pointed out that explicit and tacit knowledge were not two separate forms of knowledge, but rather, inseparable and necessary components of all knowledge. Nonaka later introduced his new model 'Ba' without achieving the success of the previous one. Within this framework, the most common approach was to implement a knowledge management system in the form of an empty database, which has to be filled by employees. The results, even after adding bonus systems, showed that this strategy was not really good and people did not utilise this kind of systems. The main reason provided by consultants to justify this situation was that enterprises need a cultural change, but this is a contradiction since the success of an enterprise is also due to the current cultural situation in that enterprise.

- Second generation 2, a variant in central Europe: Built on systems theory and based on a following process proposed to manage knowledge that involved the following phases: identification, acquisition, development, distribution, use and retention of knowledge.

- Third generation, from 2001 onwards: Snowden divided knowledge into five components: artefacts, skills, heuristics, experiences and natural talents (ASHEN). And, three knowledge categories were proposed in [11]: (1) processes, (2) organisation and culture, and (3) information technology. This means that knowledge can be managed better if we consider its components rather than knowledge as a whole.

Nevertheless, the benefits of Knowledge Management Systems are well-described in a great number of papers [13], many of which also deal with the context of virtual enterprises. This kind of enterprises needs to establish a real cooperation among partners in order to generate a product or service. ICT are used to create or assemble productive resources, including research, manufacturing, design, business, learning and training, for example [9]. Thus, the architecture of information systems in a virtual enterprise should provide a set of tools for supporting the smart integration of the virtual enterprise [14]. This technological infrastructure, also applied to knowledge management, can improve interoperability among the partners of in virtual enterprise.

However, and in spite of the fact that ICT is extremely important to communicate and distribute knowledge among the partners in a virtual enterprise, the definition of a common conceptual framework that enables partners to gain a common understanding about the business and goals of the virtual enterprise is also needed. This framework had been achieved by means of implementing a knowledge management system, but the main problems in establishing this kind of systems in virtual enterprises are:

- The partners that make up a virtual enterprise implement different processes with distinct rules and procedures to perform the main activity of their businesses.

- The partners in a virtual enterprise usually have different types of infrastructure, organisational structure, decisional units, and so forth.
- The success of each of the partners that make up a virtual enterprise is due to several factors, such as know-how, the use of resources, core skills, and so on.
- The data, notations, documents, and so forth managed by each partner are diverse and sometimes the same documents are used for different purposes.

14.3 Proposed Approach to Knowledge Management in Virtual Enterprises

The IRIS Research Group at the Universitat Jaume I in Castelló (Spain) has been working on several projects related to the Virtual Enterprise in different sectors (transport, tile industry, textile, and so forth) since 1999 [14–17]. The main aim of these projects has been to define and apply an architecture capable of supporting the design and creation of a Virtual Enterprise in an integrated way. This architecture has been called ARDIN.

Taking into account the problems mentioned above, the research group is currently participating in a Spanish Research Project entitled: 'Knowledge Management in the context of Virtual Enterprises'. Its objective is to add a new dimension to the ARDIN architecture that enables knowledge to be compiled, managed, and applied within a virtual enterprise. The new dimension has been formally organised according to the following issues:

1. A methodology for directing the process of development and implementation of a knowledge management system in a virtual enterprise.
2. A set of models to allow the identification, representation, and communication of the knowledge inherent to a virtual enterprise.
3. The design of a technological infrastructure that allows knowledge to be stored, processed, and distributed inside a virtual enterprise.

The chapter is related to the point 1, the methodology, called KM-IRIS. The aim of this methodology is to provide appropriate steps and techniques to guide the implementation of a knowledge management system in a virtual enterprise. The methodology is divided into five phases: identification, extraction, representation, processing and exploitation [4].

The results shown in this paper are concerned with the first of these phases, the aim of which is to identify what knowledge is useful to an enterprise in general. Each enterprise has its own vision, mission, and strategies and thus the knowledge that adds value to its business is different in each particular case. However, and bearing in mind that some common concepts are to be found in any enterprise, the methodology provides several conceptual blocks of knowledge defined according to the dimensions of the enterprise in order to help them identify the most useful knowledge for them, that is to say, their target knowledge.

The set of requirements presented in this paper are related to explicit knowledge, and, despite the fact that each enterprise should identify its own target knowledge, they can be useful for enterprises in order to define target with regard to each conceptual block of knowledge. The main conceptual blocks of knowledge defined in this methodology are:

- Explicit knowledge: organisation, process, product, and resource.
- Tacit knowledge: owner, supplier and customer, employee, and administration and trade union.

The last activity in the first phase of the methodology has consisted in describing and classifying the requirements in different categories so as to be able to perform a better analysis. The method used to gather these requirements was based on experiences gained from several projects carried out by the IRIS Group concerning virtual enterprises in diverse sectors. Finally, the requirements were validated in a real case study of a virtual textile enterprise with the implementation of its knowledge management system.

14.4 Requirements for Explicit Knowledge

In section 2, we have defined enterprise knowledge as actions that allow people to act and to make decisions with the result of adding value to the company. Moreover, knowledge management systems were described as a good solution to acquire, distribute and exploit this knowledge. However, some negative issues were also pointed out and a number of problems for virtual enterprises were described. In this section, we present a set of requirements for establishing a conceptual knowledge framework that allows for common understanding among the partners in a virtual enterprise -something that is needed before the implementation of its knowledge management system.

The requirements were collected from the user's point of view, taking into account, for each conceptual block of explicit knowledge defined in the KM-IRIS methodology, the knowledge that partners need to improve the performance and interoperability of the virtual enterprise. In the first phase of the methodology, the first grouping of distinct kinds of knowledge is called a conceptual block of knowledge. This first classification is made by identifying the big items related to the enterprise on which it wishes to develop its knowledge management system, since these are the most interesting subjects that the enterprise needs to know in order to gain a deeper knowledge of its businesses and the capacity to improve them. Furthermore, the aim of improving knowledge management in the virtual enterprise by establishing a common conceptual knowledge framework is also considered.

Then, the four conceptual blocks of explicit knowledge defined in this methodology are described. However, despite the use of the adjective 'explicit' it must be pointed out that in these blocks we can find both explicit and tacit knowledge requirements, since explicit and tacit knowledge are not two separate forms of knowledge, but instead inseparable, necessary components of all knowledge [18].

- Organisation: this details the knowledge about the structure of the organisation, providing different visions: administrative, systemic, and from the human resources point of view. Moreover, it captures the target structure, decisional structure and rules structure of the enterprise.
- Process: this provides knowledge on general issues about processes in enterprises such as ICOMs (Input, Control, Output, and Mechanisms), documents, rules, know-how, and so forth; and on flows (of work, documents, of material, and so on). Different levels of processes are then defined including decisional and collaborative processes.
- Product: this describes the main knowledge about the products and/or services provided by the enterprise, taking into account the process of achievement and marketing, the composition options, the quality, the cost and so forth.
- Resource: this classifies knowledge about human resources and material resources into three main categories: location of these resources, potential use of them, and finally, the cost associated.

The requirements collected for the conceptual blocks of Organisation and Process, for example, are presented in tables A1 and A2 in Appendix A. In these tables, besides a brief description of each requirement, they are also classified into several categories, which are defined from two points of views:

1. First, the Enterprise Modelling context, in which the intention is to analyse the enterprise from a holistic point of view and therefore several dimensions related to the enterprise, such as organisation, process, product, and so forth, are defined.
2. Second, Knowledge Learning theory, in which the way to learn is based on three issues: concepts, procedures, and attitudes.

The relationship between these two points of view used to classify requirements in this work can be seen in Table 1.

14.5 Conclusion

Knowledge management systems can be used in virtual enterprises in a similar way how they are used in an individual enterprise. However, the specific features of this new organisational paradigm requires the introduction of a conceptual framework of knowledge, which enables the partners that make up a virtual enterprise to share the same concepts and to be more familiar with the other partners' procedures and attitudes, in order to implement an efficient knowledge management system.

Table 1. Framework to classify explicit knowledge requirements

	Organisation	Process	Product	Resource
Concepts	Target structure Organisational structure Human resources vision System vision Control and decisional structure	General Process level	Composition Quality	Location Potential
Procedures	Business rules	Flows	Generation process Cost	Cost
Attitudes	Business rules		Markering	

In this paper, we have shown some of the requirements to establish this framework in a virtual enterprise, while considering each conceptual block of explicit knowledge defined in the methodology KM-IRIS, that is to say, organisation, process, product, and resource. The requirements are classified taking into account two points of view, first, several enterprise dimensions defined in the context of Enterprise Modelling and, second, the three dimensions defined in Knowledge Learning theory. This set of requirements can be used as a reference for virtual enterprises that need to implement a knowledge management system.

Acknowledgements

This work was funded by CICYT DPI2003-02515. Also, it is partially supported by the European Commission within the 6th Framework Programme (INTEROP Network of Excellence, (IST2003508011), [19]). The authors are indebted to TG1 and TG2.

References

1. Kalpic B, Bernus P: Business process modelling in industry–the powerful tool in enterprise management. Computers in Industry 47 (2002) 299–318 2.
2. Kosanke, K.: Enterprise Inter-and Intraorganizational Integration, Building International Consensus. In: Proceedings of the ICEIMT'02 Conference. (2002)
3. Browne, J., Zhang, J. : Extended and virtual enterprises -similarities and differences. International Journal of Agile Management Systems 1/1 (1999) 30–36
4. Chalmeta, R., Grangel, R., Fernandez, V. (Methodology for knowledge management systems implementation) in evaluation.
5. Splieger, I.: Technology and Knowledge: bridging a 'generating' gap. Infomation and Management 40 (2003) 533–539

6. Nonaka, I., Takeuchi, H.: The Knowledge Creating Company: How Japanese Companies Create the Dynamics of Innovation. Oxford University Press (1995)
7. O'Leary, D.E., Kuokka, D., Plant, R.: Artificial Intelligence and Virtual Organizations. Communications of the ACM 40 (1997) 52–59
8. O'Leary, D.E.: Guest Editor's Introduction: Knowledge Management Systems: Converting and Connecting. IEEE Intelligent Systems 13 (1998) 30–33
9. Devedzic, V.: A survey of modern knowledge modeling techniques. Expert systems with applications 17 (1999) 275–294
10. Vail, E.F.: Knowledge mapping: getting started with knowledge management. Information Systems Management Fall (1999) 16–23
11. Schutt, P.: The post-Nonaka Knowledge Management. In: Proceedings of I-KNOW'03. (2003)
12. Abdullah, M.S., Benest, I., Kimble, C., Evans, A.: Techniques For Developing Knowledge Management Systems. http://citeseer.ist.psu.edu/abdullah02techniques.html (2005)
13. Liao, S.: Knowledge management technologies and applications -literature review from 1995 to 2002. Expert Systems with Applications 25 (2003) 155–164 Elsevier.
14. Chalmeta, R., Grangel, R.: ARDIN extension for virtual enterprise integration. The Journal of Systems and Software 67 (2003) 141–152 Elsevier.
15. Chalmeta, R., Campos, C., Grangel, R.: References architectures for enterprises integration. The Journal of Systems and Software 57 (2001) 175–191 Elsevier.
16. Chalmeta, R., Grangel, R., Ortiz, A., Poler, R.: Virtual Integration of the Tile Industry (VITI). In Jeusfeld, M., Pastor, O., eds.: Conceptual Modeling for Novel Application Domains. Volume 2814/2003 of Lecture Notes in Computer Science., Springer-Verlag (2003) 65–76
17. Chalmeta, R., Grangel, R.: Performance measurement systems for virtual enterprise integration. International Journal of Computer Integrated Manufacturing 18 (2005) 73–84 Taylor & Francis.
18. Tsoukas, H.: The tyranny of light. Futures 29 (1997) 827–843
19. INTEROP: Interoperability Research for Networked Enterprises Applications and Software NoE (IST-2003-508011). http://www.interop-noe.org (2005)

Appendix A. Requirements for conceptual blocks of explicit knowledge

Table A1. Conceptual block: organisation

Ontological category	Target knowledge	Description
Target structure	Strategic level	To know which is the enterprise's vision and mission, and also to identify clearly which are the strategic objectives and strategy established in the enterprise in the long term to reach its mission.
	Tactic level	To know what decisions are taken and how resources are assigned in the medium term

		to follow the strategy defined at the strategic level.
	Operative level	To know how the enterprise's daily activities and operations are planned, coordinated and executed in the short term and who is in charge of these activities.
Organisational structure	Administrative view	To know first which is the structure from administrative and executive point of view taking into account the different kinds of virtual enterprises: in star, in network, ans so forth and, second, which is the organisation chart for individual enterprise as well as virtual enterprise.
	Human Resources	To know which is the hierarchic organisation established in enterview prise, defining the different levels that exist, that is to say, departmental units, departments, sections, and so on.
	System view	To know from a system point of view which are the systems identified in enterprise and which are its main functions and relationships.
Decisonal structure	Decisional centres	To know which is the structure of enterprise taking into account the decision taken by employees at distinct levels.
	Cost centres	To know enterprise's costs associated a each element that exists in enterprise to analyse them considering different clusters performed according to the strategy adopted.
Business rules	Lines of action	To know which are the main guidelines and directives of behaviour established in enterprise to achieve a good functioning of all elements involved in it.
	Rules	To know which are strict rules provided by the company in order to perform all the enterprise activities.

Table A2. Conceptual block: process

Ontological category	Target knowledge	Description
General	ICOMs	To know for each process which are the elements needed to perform a process, that is to say, the inputs needed and output obtained as well as the constraints and the mechanisms to carry out the process.
	Splitting of processes	To identify the main macroprocesses performed in enterprise and how they are divided into microprocesses, activities, tasks, and so on.
	Documents	To identify the primary documents that are used for each process, such as orders, delivery notes, invoices, and so forth.
	AI-IS and TO-BE views	To understand which is the current situation of enterprise processes and which should be the desired situation.
	Procedures	To know for each process the specific procedures that it is needed to perform in enterprise.
	Know-how	To identify specific, special skills and capabilities that enterprise has in each process.
	Cost	To analyse which are the costs linked to processes, and their profitability and added value for customers.
Flow	Of materials	To know the different ways in which the materials are transformed in enterprise and in which processes are involved these materials.
	Of data / information / knowledge	To know which are the main track that data run in enterprise to be transformed into information and knowledge, in order to identify the main mechanisms, techniques, and methods to obtain information and knowledge.
	Of decision / control	To understand step by step how decisions are taken in enterprise and they control the enterprise performance.
	Workflow	To know which is the sequence of the different tasks that make up one activity, and how they are carried out and by who.
	Of documents	To know which is the sequence and possibilities of transforming documents involved in processes and by means of what rules this transformation is performed.

(Cont.)

Table A2. (Cont.)

Process level	Operative processes	To know which are the processes developed by enterprise at the operative level, realizing which are the core processes, in which enterprise is the leadership; which are the added value processes that add value to enterprise and to its products/services; and which are the supporting processes.
	Decisional processes	To know how the processes related to decision-making at the strategic, tactic and operational level are implemented.
	Collaborative	To know what are the processes that involve other partprocesses ners of virtual enterprise and how they are carried out.

15 Two Methods for Schema Design for Intelligent XML Documents in Organizations

Anne Honkaranta, Eliisa Jauhiainen

University of Jyväskylä, Finland
anne.honkaranta@it.jyu.fi, raelurja@cc.jyu.fi

XML markup language provides means for incorporating semantics, i.e. "meaning" of logical content parts residing within documents. Therefore it has become the *lingua franca* for Semantic Web, e-Business applications and for enterprise application integration. In order to realize novel, intelligent XML-based document applications in organizations, schemas defining the domain-oriented semantics are needed. So far, the potential of XML has not bee fully utilized in organizational documents, due to the lack of XML support in common and inexpensive office software. Due to the arrival of XML support on common software such as Microsoft Office 2007 and Open Office 2.0 organizations need knowledge about schema languages and their design methods for designing intelligend XML document applications for document content reuse, content integration across documents, and document content retrieval from Web Services and other source. This paper introduces three schema languages and compares the features of two potential methods for document-oriented schema design.

15.1 Introduction

XML (Bray et al. 2006) was initially developed as a markup language for documents for electronic publishing and technical documentation – for managing the reuse, management and publishing of broad and complex collections of documents and publications. XML is becoming a standard to represent any kind of content in any application domain, because it is able to represent any kind of structured or semi-structured documents (Psaila 2000). XML has been widely adapted to enterprise system integration, as e-Business format, and for Web Services. XML is becoming increasingly used for storing and exchanging all kinds of data on the Internet as well (Elmasri 2002).

The use of XML for common organizational documents has been limited due to the fact that XML-capable software has until now been quite specialized and

173

W. Abramowicz and H.C. Mayr (eds.), Technologies for Business Information Systems, 173–182.
© 2007 *Springer.*

expensive. Introduction of new XML software for office use also requires training, and may be resisted by users who are used to their common-purpose, sophisticated office tools. Along with the introduction of XML into common-purpose office software such as Microsoft Office 2007 (Microsoft 2006) and OpenOffice 2.0 (Open Office Org 2006) the office documents shall already be stored as XML documents, providing a base for developing intelligent XML document applications based on organizational requirements.

Realization of intelligent, domain-oriented document applications relies on the possibility to develop and utilize domain-oriented schemas for XML documents.

This chapter is focused on the XML schema languages and schema design for organizational documents. It presents updated and revised findings based on the paper presented at the BIS 2006 conference (Jauhiainen and Honkaranta 2006). Section 2 of the chapter introduces three commonly known schema languages – DTD (Maler and El Andaloussi 1996), XMLSchema (Fallside and Walmsley 2004) and RelaxNG (Clark 2001).   Section 3 introduces two schema design methods; the Maler and El Andaloussi method (1996), and the Kennedy (2003) method. The Maler and El Andaloussi method (1996) is generally recognized as the "best practice" for the DTD design (Thompson 2000). It has also been incorporated into the RASKE document management methodology (Salminen 2003) and it has clearly influenced the schema design methods developed for the Document Engineering (Glushko and McGrath 2002) and the Unified Method for Content Management (Rockley et al. 2003) approaches. Section 4 discusses the findings and sums up the chapter.

15.2 Schema Languages

A schema, such as DTD (Maler and El Andaloussi 1996) or XML Schema schema (Fallside and Walmsley 2004) describes the names of elements and their order for a document type, and attributes adding incremental information about the elements (Boukottaya et al. 2004).

Following subsections introduce the two most popular schema languages, the DTD (Bray et al. 2006), and the XML Schema (Fallside and Walmsley 2004) schema for intelligent XML documents. A possible schema language replacing DTD's in future – RelaxNG – is also described. The three aforementioned schema languages are grammar-based languages providing context-free grammar according to top-down production rules in a specified form.

15.2.1 DTD

DTD (Document Type Definition) is a part of XML language definition itself, and perhaps the most commonly known schema language at the time (Marinelli et al. 2004). Figure 1 illustrates the DTD syntax by giving an example of a XML document considering Addressbook and the DTD schema defining markup rules for it.

XML Document (Addressbook)	A DTD for Addressbook document type

`<Addressbook>`
  `<Card>`
    `<Name>`Jane Doe`</Name>`
     Email> jane.doe@company.org
     `</Email>`
  `</Card>`
 	
`<Card>`
    `<Name>`Tom Smith`</Name>`
  `<Email>`tom.smith@company.com
  `</Email>`
  `<Phone>`+358 14 123456`</Phone>`
  `</Card>`
`</Addressbook>`
	`<!ELEMENT Addressbook (Card+)>`
	`<!ELEMENT Card (Name, Email,`
	`Phonenumber?)>`
	`<!ELEMENT Name (#PCDATA)>`
	`<!ELEMENT Email (#PCDATA)>`
	`<!ELEMENT Phone (#PCDATA)>`

Fig. 1. An Addressbook XML document and a DTD schema for it

DTDs provide a sophisticated regular expression language for defining elements, their ordering and attributes for a document type. It has its own syntax for declaring content models. DTD schema was designed for textual documents and is therefore rather limited by its capabilities to control the values of attributes and elements (Marinelli et al. 2004). In other words, the built-in set of data types for elements in DTD are limitied in practice to three: an element contains either parseable data (PCDATA), non-parseable data (NDATA) or no content at all, i.e. element is EMPTY. DTD provides 7 data types for restricting the attribute content. All together DTD supports 10 data types.

15.2.2 RelaxNG

RelagNG (Clark 2001) schema language is built on two preceding schema languages; TREX (Tree regular expression for XML) and RELAX (Regular language of description for XML).

While the DTD's content model is an expression over elements, the RelaxNG schema defines patterns as expressions over elements, text nodes and attributes. RelaxNG schemas may be declared by XML syntax or by using compact non-XML syntax (Clark and Murata 2001).

The RelaxNG schema defines patterns that a document must match. Patterns may appear as components of the main schema or reside separate from the content model declarations (Clark and Murata 2001). In RelaxNG attribute lists are declared apart from element an pattern which enables the specification of dependencies between elements and attributes and between their values. This feature is a significant difference between RelaxNG and any other schema language. (DuCharme 2004) One of the limitations of the RelaxNG is its inability to define default values for element and attributes (Marinelli et al. 2004). RelaxNG is considered to be simpler and even as technically superior to the XML Schema language discussed on the next subsection.

15.2.3 XML Schema

XML Schema (Bray et al. 2006) schemas are themselves XML documents, which improves the programmatic processability of the XML Schema schemas. The use of XML syntax for a schema language is not totally a positive feature for a schema: the XML syntax is rather verbose and makes the schemas long and rather difficult to read on their textual form (Marinelli et al. 2004).

XML Schema language is superior to DTDs by its capability of restricting the content types of element and attribute content. It supports even 44 different data types such as date, integer, string, and so on, and also allows regular expression patterns to be used for posing even more stricter requirements for element content (Bray et al. 2006). For example, our address book "Mail" element could be restricted by XML schema in a way that the content of the element must contain the "@"-sign. XML Schema language has other additional features over DTD schemas, like support for namespaces and possibility to define elements as global or local, or as reusable data types.

In practice only small amount of schemas use the advenced features provided by XML Schema language. This means that majority of the schemas found in the Web may be expressible by DTD schemas, even though the modelling power of the XML Schema is notably higher. (Bex et al. 2005) Figure 2 illustrates the XML Schema schema and its counterpart as RelaxNG schema for the Addressbook XML document.

XML Schema	RelaxNG
<?xml version=1.0" encoding="ISO-8859-1" ?>	<?xml version=1.0" encoding="ISO-8859-1" ?>
<xs:schema xmlns:xs="http://www.w3.org/2001/XMLSchema">	<element name="addressBook" xmlns="http://relaxng.org/ns/structure/1.0">
<xs:element name="Addressbook">	
<xs:complexType>	<oneOrMore>
<xs:sequence>	<element name="Card">
<xs:element name="Card" maxOccurs="unbounded">	<element name="name">
<xs:complexType>	<text/>
<xs:sequence>	</element>
<xs:element name="Name" type="xs:string"/>	<element name="Email">
<xs:element name="Email" type="xs:string"/>	<text/>
	</element>

```
<xs:element name="Phonenumber"
type="xs:string" minOccurs="0"/>          <optional>
</xs:sequence>                            <element name="Phonenumber>
</xs:complexType>                         <text/>
</xs:element>                             </element>
</xs:sequence>                            </optional>
</xs:complexType>                         </element>
</xs:element></xs:schema>                 </oneOrMore>
                                          </element>
```

Fig. 2. Examples of XML Schema and RelaxNG schemas for the Addressbook document type

XML Schema is generally considered as complex (van der Vlist 2002). However, XML Schema is the most widely used among all the schema languages. Possible reason for the popularity of XML Schema language is that it is supported by a number of popular software. Microsoft, for example, relies on XML Schema schemas for custom schema use on its Office 2007 software. Also a number of XML development environments provide support for XML Schema schema design (f.ex., Altova XML Spy; www.altova.com). More profound comparisons on schema languages may be found in Lee and Chu (2000) and Jauhiainen and Honkaranta (2006).

15.3 Methods for Schema Design

This section describes the two potential schema design methods; the Maler and El Andaloussi (1996) method and the Kennedy (2003) method.

15.3.1 The Maler & El Andaloussi Method

Maler and El Andaloussi (1996) method has been considered as a best practice on the field (Maler & El Andaloussi 1996, Thompson 2000). The methodology (Maler and El Andaloussi 1996) can be divided in three phases, which are:

- Document analysis,
- Document type modelling, and
- Producing a document analysis report

The document analysis phase consists of the three steps that are: 1.) Identifying potential document components, 2.) Classifying the components identified, and 3.) Validating the requirements.

Document component is broader by its content than an individual element consisting of text. For example, in our Addressbook a possible document component is a Card-element. Document component should be a logical unit of document content which may, for example, be reused from elsewhere or need to be presented to a human reader as a unit. For example, a "list of attendees" is a potential component for a memo document type rather than an "attendee_name".

Step 2 considers classifying the *potential components* with respect to their content-based and structural similarities. For example, "list-of-attendees" and "list-of-items" may be broadly classified as list component types. The third step considers studying the available schemas for similar kinds of document types and deciding if a domain-oriented schema is needed, or if a related, existing schema or its components may be tailored for the purpose at hand.

The document type modeling phase consists of seven steps, which are: 4.) Selecting semantic components, 5.) Building the document hierarchy, 6.) Building the information units, 7.) Building the data-level elements, 8.) Populating the branches of the document hierarchy, 9.) Declaring connections between elements, and 10.) Validating the design.

In step 4 the component lists are revisited for dropping out all but necessary components. Step 5 considers modelling the components into *document hierarchy* model which represents main components for the document type. Figure 3 illustrates a document hierarchy model as Elme-diagram for the Addressbook document type. In the figure the components are depicted by rectangles. Three dots underneath a component depict that that the content model is represented in another diagram. The document hierarchy ends to "cloud" symbols depicting the portions of more-detailed level content models. "+", "?" and "*" are occurrence symbols indicating that a component may repeat from one to many, zero to one, or from zero to many times.

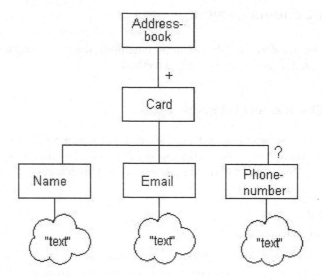

Fig. 3. An Example of document hierarchy model for an addressbook

Steps 6 and 7 concern the design of Information units and data-level components. Information units are groups of logically related elements that should be modelled as a whole; such as a list heading and list item, or a figure and its caption. Data-level elements consider markup within text, such as if concepts need to be separated from other text in order to specify differing layout for them. Information units and data-level elements are revisited on step 8 for populating the branches of the tree diagrams with information units and data-level elements defined. Step 9 considers the identification of requirements for cross-references and links within the document type and across documents and other content sources.

Finally in step 10 the whole design is revisited. This step ends the second phase of the Maler & El Andaloussi method (1996). The last phase of the method considers producing the document analysis report.

After the schema design the actual schema instance is declared by using the schema language selected for the purpose.

15.3.2 The Kennedy Method

Kennedy (2003, 92-94) lists nine rules for defining XML schemas. The rules consider:

1. Data analysis
2. Coding the data
3. Use of container elements
4. Use of group or block elements
5. Use of subelements for multi-value data
6. Avoiding mixed content
7. Use of meaningful names
8. Correct use attributes and elements, and
9. Reviewing the desing.

The first rule, data analysis, follows the Maler & El Andaloussi method. It consists of a) identifying the document components and b) classifying them into logical groups. The data analysis in the Kennedy method covers additional tasks with regard to the Malar and El Andaloussi method. These consider deciding upon the recurrence or optionality of a document component, and about its importance.

The second rule is about coding the data. This rule considers if a component is actually a locical content component or whether it is merely a presentation kind of component, in which case the component should be considered on the style sheet design rather than on content design.

Third rule is about using "collection" elements. By the collection element Kennedy refers to elements that may occur multiple times at the same level, such as list items. If the aforementioned elements are identified, one should create a container element for them. For example, we may define a "list" element as a container for list items. Kennedy declares that use of collection elements makes the XML more human readable and easiler to process by recursive loops, such as the "for-each" element use in the XSLT transformation language. Another example or a collection element is the "author" element; if it repeats multiple times within a document type, one should define container element "authors" to group the "author" elements.

Kennedy's fourth rule is about remembering that XML markup forms commonly a tree structure within documents. The tree should be wide instead of tall. The fifth rule states that the best way to represent multi-valued data is via subelements.

Sixth rule exhorts that one should avoid mixed element content and the seventh one that the element names should be meaningful. The eight rule emphasizes the correct use of elements and attributes. According to Kennedy, XML document schmas commonly contain lots of elements and   fewer attributes than elements whereas schemas for data-oriented XML documents and data transfer may consist even greater amount of attributes than elements. Therefore the application domain and document type may affect the schema design considerations.

The final rule is about recognizing that defining the schemas is similar to database desing in respect that the design process is commonly iterative one by its nature. As database schemas are defined by inserting test data into table structure defined, the XML document schemas are tested by writing example documents, and testing the design against style sheet definitions and content manipulation needs.

Kennedy's method is similar to Maler and El Andaloussi method also by its modelling notation; both of the methods use the so called "Elm" models for visual schema design. Figure 3, the document hierarchy model provides an example of the Elm modelling notation.

15.4 Discussion and Conclusion

Although XML is currently used as a standard for any kind of content, its use on common organizational documents has been limited by the lack of inexpensive software with XML support. However, along the introduction of novel office software such as OpenOffice 2.0 and becoming Microsoft 2007 the situation changes in a radical way. Organizations may start benefiting from the use of intelligent XML documents, which provide means for content integration, retrieval and reuse across document collections and external content sources such as databases or WebServices. Realization of the intelligent XML document applications rely on the domain- and application-oriented markup. Schema provides a base for XML processing, content filtering, and content organization. Therefore schema design is a base for document-oriented XML document management and its importance should not be overlooked.

There are several schema languages for XML document schemas. Perhaps the most common one is W3C's XML Schema - a rich schema language with multiple features and datatypes. However, XML Schema definition is considered as complex. Even though many applications support the use of XML Schema, the expressive power of DTD may be quite enough for defining narrative, document-oriented document types. XML Schema language features and the capability to define strict rules for XML content on a data-type level may be needed for example for technical documentations consisting lots of measures and measure units, or for document types that exchange content with databases or applications with stricter requirements for data typing.

Even if an organization would not need the sophisticated features of XML Schema schema language, many organizations may use it due to its broad support on software tools. It remains to be seen if the RelaxNG as an "improved version" of the DTD schema is capable to challenge the XML Schema language as it seems to be gaining more software support. The technical capabilities of the RelaxNG and the XML Schema language in terms of expressiveness and the ability data typing are sligthly differing, yet sufficient for document schemas.

This chapter reviewed the Maler and El Andaloussi (1996) method that was originally defined for DTD design and the Kennedy (2003) method targeted for RelaxNG schema design. There are many similarities between the Kennedy and the Maler & El Andaloussi method. The Kennedy method adopts the first two steps of the Maler and El Andaloussi method. The Kennedy's method also applies the Maler and El Andaloussi method for defining container elements which are typical for document-oriented XML document types. Both Kennedy and Maler and El Andaloussi emphasize the importance of domain-oriented, meaningful element names. Both methods also remind DTD or schema designers that schema design is usually an iterative process and the document structures should be tested before implementation.

It may be concluded that both the Kennedy and the Maler and El Andaloussi method may be adoptable for organizational XML document type schema design. More recent schema design methods, such as the one included in the Document Engineering approach (Glushko and McGrath 2005) and the one utilized in the Unified Content Strategy (Rockley et al. 2003) are influenced by the Maler and El Andaloussi method. Even though the DTDs are nowadays often replaced by XML Schema schemas the Maler & El Andaloussi method may provide a solid starting point for organizational schema design, or one for developing methods for novel design requirements.

References

1. Bex G.J, Martens M., Neven F. & Schwentick T. (2005) Expressiveness of XSDs: From Practice to Theory, There and Back Again. In Proceedings of the Fourteenth International World Wide Web Conference, Chiba, Japan, May 2005, pp-.712–721.
2. Boukottaya A., Vanoirbeek C., Paganelli F. & Abou Khaled O. (2004) Automating XML Documents Transformations: a Conceptual Modelling Based Approach. In the Proceedings of the 1st Asia-Pacific Conference on Conceptual Modelling, ACSW 2004, Dunedin, New Zealand.
3. Bray, T., Paoli, J., Sperberg-McQueen, C., Maler, E., Yeargeau, F., & Cowan, J. (2006). Extensible Markup Language (XML) 1.1 (2nd ed.). W3C Recommendation 16 Aug 2006. Available at http://www.w3.org/TR/2006/REC-xml11-20060816/ [1.9.2006]
4. Clark J. (2001) The Design of RELAX NG. [Online]Available at http://www.thaiopensource.com/relaxng/design.html [16.1.2006]

5.   Clark J. & Murata M. (2001) RELAX NG Specification.
6.   DuCharme B.(2004) Documents vs. Data, Schemas vs. Schemas. XML 2004 Conference, Washington D.C.
7.   Elmasri R., Wu Y-C., Hojabri B., Li C. & Fu J. (2002) Conceptual Modeling for Customized XML Schemas. In the Proceedinsg of the 21st International Conference on Conceptual Modeling (ER). Vol 2503 of Springer LNCS. Springer, pp. 429–443.
8.   Fallside, D, & Walmsley, P. (2004). XML Schema Part 0: Primer. 2nd Edition. W3C Recommendation, 28 Oct. 2004. Available at http://www.w3.org/TR/xmlschema-0/ [16.6.2005]
9.   Glushko, R. J. & McGrath T. (2005) Document Engineering: Analyzing and Designing Documents for Business Informatics and Web Services. MIT Press.
10.   Jauhiainen, E. & Honkaranta, A. (2006). A Review on XML Document Schemas and Methods for Schema Design. In The Abramovicz, W. & Mayr, H. (Eds.). Proceendings of the 9th International Conference on Business Information Systems. Series of the Gesellschaft für Informatik.Bonn. Vol P-85. 201-210.
11.   Kennedy D. Relax NG with XML Data Structures. (2003) National Advisory Committee on Computing Qualifications, Palmerston Nth.
12.   Lee D. & Chu W. (2000) Comparative Analysis of Six XML schema Languages. SIGMOD Record, 29(3). 76–87.
13.   Maler E., El Andaloussi J. (1996) Developing SGML DTDs. From Text to Model to Markup. Upper Saddle River NJ: Prentice Hall.
14.   Marinelli P., Sacerdoti Coen C. & Vitali F. (2004). SchemaPath, a Minimal Extension to XML Schema for Conditional Constraints. In the Proceedings of the 13th International Conference on the World Wide Web (WWW13), New York City, U.S.A. ACM, 2004.
15.   Mircosoft.   (2006).   Microsoft   Office   2007.   Available   at http://www.microsoft.com/office/preview/default.mspx [14 .9.2006]
16.   OpenOffice Org. (2006). Open Office Organization Home Page. Available at http://www.openoffice.org/ [20.7.2006]
17.   Psaila G. ERX: A Conceptual Model for XML Documents. (2000) In the Proceedings of ACM Symposium on Applied Computing (SAC), Villa Olmo, Italy. 898-903.
18.   Rockley, A., Kostur, P., & Manning, S. (2003). Managing Enterprise Content: A Unified Content Strategy. U.S.A.: New Riders.
19.   Salminen A. Document Analysis Methods. (2003) In Bernie C.L. (Ed.) Encyclopedia of Library and Information Science, Second Edition, Revised and Expanded. New York: Marcel Dekker. 916-927.
20.   Thompson H. S. (2000) XML Schema Types and Equivalence Classes. Reconstructing DTD Best Practice. In the Proceedings of the XML Europe 2000 conference.
21.   van der Vlist E. XML Schema Languages .(2002) In the Proceedings of XML Europe 2002, Barcelona, Spain.

16 IS Evolution Benefit Assessment – Challenges with Economic Investment Criteria

Irja Kankaanpää[1], Jussi Koskinen[1], Tero Tilus[1], Henna Sivula[1], Heikki Lintinen[1], Jarmo J. Ahonen[2]

[1] Information Technology Research Institute, University of Jyväskylä, P.O. Box 35, 40014 Jyväskylä, Finland
[2] Department of Computer Science, University of Kuopio, P.O. Box 1627, 70211 Kuopio, Finland

16.1 Introduction

Maintenance and system evolution activities have a significant role in the information system (IS) life cycle. It has been estimated that approximately 80% of the total IT expenses are allocated for maintenance activities [20]. According to Lehman's first law, maintenance is necessary, because software needs to be continuously improved or it will get out of date and cannot respond to the requirements of its environment [19]. Despite the importance of IS evolution investments, there is a gap between the IT related costs and company profitability [27]. Brynjolfssen [10] described this as a productivity paradox: information technology utilization has increased since the 70's but simultaneously productivity has slowed down.

The work effort of maintenance is generally proportional to the life time of a system. Therefore, it is more dominant in legacy information systems [7]. Besides being old, a legacy system is typically large at size and contains vital information for the user organization, uses out-of-date technology, and is laborious to maintain [3] [4]. There are three strategies to deal with a legacy system: 1) maintaining and using the system as it is, 2) developing or purchasing a new system to replace it, or 3) radically improve, i.e. modernize, the legacy system in order to meet the new business needs [4] [25, p 8-10].

IT investments can be roughly classified in two categories, acquisition projects and development projects [24]. In the context of IS evolution, acquisition project includes purchasing off-the-self software in order to replace the existing legacy system. Development investment refers to a project that aims at developing new or modernizing the existing system. Therefore, replacement can be either an

183

W. Abramowicz and H.C. Mayr (eds.), Technologies for Business Information Systems, 183–191.

acquisition or development project, while modernization is always a result of development activity. The major difference between acquisition and development projects, in terms of investment evaluation, is the length of time that is required for the benefits to start to appear [24]. In the first, an organization starts to benefit from the investment as soon as the acquisition has been made. In the latter, the benefits start to accumulate only after the project has been completed [24].

Evolution investments are economically significant and, consequently, their justification in financial terms is important. Because a legacy system is closely tied to an organization, a careful consideration of operational environment and organizational context is a prerequisite for its successful migration [5], and should be incorporated in the evaluation process. However, in reality the management often expects plainly financial evidence to support evolution decisions. In this paper, the goal is to study the advantages and disadvantages of financial investment criteria and their suitability in IS evolution benefit assessment. Additionally, a framework for evaluation method selection is presented.

This is a work-in-progress paper that summarizes the preliminary work on IS evolution benefit assessment within an industry co-operation project called ELTIS (Extending the Lifetime of Information Systems) during 2003-2005. The project was carried out in the Information Technology Research Institute (ITRI), University of Jyväskylä, Finland. It focused on prolonging the lifetime of IS in an economically viable manner.

16.2 Investment Criteria

Dehning and Richardson [12] conducted a literature review on studies covering the impacts of IT on firms' performance in 1997-2001. In most of these studies, IT investments had been evaluated with the means of direct performance or accounting measures. That is where the business owner, by tradition, is expecting to see the implications of investments. In case of IS evolution investments, however, the benefits are not necessarily reflected on the firm's performance or accounting figures. The financial investment criteria can only detect tangible benefits while ignoring the intangibles. In the past, several benefit assessment methods have been developed in order to address this problem [15]. In this paper, the focus is on the so called classical financial investment evaluation methods. On the basis of a literature review, the advantages and disadvantages of eight financial investment criteria are presented and their suitability on IS evolution assessment is evaluated.

Classical financial investment criteria can be divided in three categories: 1) discounted cash flow criteria, 2) payback criteria, and 3) accounting criteria. Discounted cash flow criteria include *net present value* (NPV), *internal rate of return* (IRR), and *profitability index*. Payback criteria consist of *payback period* and *discounted payback* period. Accounting criteria consists of *average accounting return* (AAR). [23, p 256]. Other investment criteria include *return on investment* (ROI) method and *real options* approach (option pricing models)

[11, p 139]. Investment criteria, their advantages and disadvantages are described in Table 1.

In general, discounted cash flow criteria are considered the most preferred option when evaluating investment proposals [23, p 256]. NPV is in most cases the recommended approach [23, p 256]. On the contrary, investment criteria based on accounting figures are not as useful with respect to investment planning is because they are aggregated and past-oriented [23, p 245]. They can be used, however, as complementary criteria together with other investment criteria.

Table 1. Investment criteria

Criteria and definition	Advantages	Disadvantages
NPV The difference between investment's market value and cost [23, p 233].	Includes time value of money [11, p 73]. No serious flaws [23, p 256].	Unsuitable for analyzing acquisitions because of short-term and user-oriented focus [13]. Unable to deal with uncertainty [24].
IRR The discount rate that makes the NPV of an investment zero [23, p 245].	Includes time value of money [11, p 73]. Results are easy to communicate and understand [23, p 253].	May lead to incorrect decisions if project cash flows are unpredictable, investment options are mutually exclusive, [23, p 253] or level of uncertainty is high [24].
Profitability Index The present value of an investment's future cash flows divided by its initial cost [23, p 253].	Results are easy to communicate and understand. Useful if investment funds are scarce. [23, p 253-254].	May give misleading results when investments options are mutually exclusive [23, p 254].
Payback period A time period from the moment when an investment is made to the moment when the cash flow from the investment equals the original investment cost [23, p 240].	Simple and easy to under-stand. Adjusts for uncertainty of later cash flows. [23, p 240]	Requires an arbitrary cut-off point. Ignores time value of money and cash flows beyond cut-off date. Biased against long-term or new projects, and liquidity. [23, p 240]
Discounted payback period The length of time required for an investment's discounted cash flows to equal its initial cost [23, p 240].	Includes time value of money [23, p 242].	Ignores cash flows beyond cut-off date [23, p 256]. Biased towards liquidity [23, p 242].
AAR An investment's average net income divided by its average book value [23, p 243].	Easy to calculate. Needed information is often available. [23, p 245]	Ignores the opportunity cost [9] and time value of money [23, p 245]. Does not compare to real market returns [9].
ROI The ratio of net benefits plus the	One of the most significant calculation methods for	Ignores the scale of the investment and timing of cash

(Cont.)

Table 1. (Cont.)

original investment divided by the initial investment [11, p 70].	evaluating managerial performance [6, p 207]. Simple and clear [11, p 70].	flows. Not useful for planning. [6, p 207]. Insufficient if used alone [11, p 72-73].
Real options An approach used to evaluate alternative management strategies using traditional option pricing theory [2].	Able to deal with uncertainty [24]. Provides managerial flexibility [11, p 146] [24]. Includes timing and risk [11, p 142].	Complex to communicate. Input values are difficult to estimate. Reliance on assumptions. [16]

Traditionally, the financial analysis of IT acquisition projects has been conducted with NPV or discounted cash flow analysis [13]. During the last few decades, also options pricing models have been applied in IT evaluation [24]. ROI has been used to evaluate the benefits of software reuse [20]. However, there are no reports on the use of these investment criteria in IS evolution decision making particularly.

In the context of IS evolution, the best suited financial evaluation methods are simple and require minimum use of resources. After comparing the characteristics of investment criteria, it can be concluded that discounted cash flow criteria and ROI would be appropriate considering those requirements. IRR and profitability index, however, may lead to incorrect results in the case of mutually exclusive investments, i.e. when accepting one investment prevents taking another [23, pp 253-254]. Therefore, they may not be suitable method for IS evolution options evaluation, since they in most cases are mutually exclusive. For instance, acquisition of a new system and modernization of the existing system most likely are investments from which only one is chosen. NPV has been criticized of its inability to deal with project uncertainty [24]. Because of that it may not be a preferred criterion in system modernisation evaluation. Real options approach seems to provide with the most holistic tool to compare (replacement) and development (modernization, replacement) projects. It can cope with the risks and uncertainty related to modernization and provides future oriented results. Also, it provides managerial flexibility allowing decisions about the investment to be changed as new information becomes available [11, p 146] [24]. However, it is mathematically demanding, which sets certain limitations to its use [16]. Also, it requires relatively detailed input data [16] which may cause the estimation method itself become heavy and uneconomical to use. Due to its past-oriented nature, accounting criterion is not useful with respect to IS evolution options evaluation.

In order to avoid one-dimensional view of an IT investment, use of more than one financial criteria is suggested [11, p 73] [23, p 254]. For instance, payback and AAR can be used to reinforce the results of NPV calculation [11, p 73]. The recommended methods for IT investment assessment, in general, are NPV, IRR and payback period [11, p 73]. Additionally, calculation should be conducted before and after the project [11, p 76].

16.3 Challenges

The main challenge in evaluating IT investments with financial criteria is the selection of a suitable benefit assessment method. As presented above, classical investment criteria are not uniformly suitable for every situation. If a method is selected carelessly, the results may recommend a refusal of a potential investment proposal simply because the selected method ignores a relevant factor [23]. Respectively, an unprofitable investment may seem potential if improper analysis methods are used.

The second challenge is related to existing and available data. In order to conduct a benefit assessment for investment options, a company has to gather IT-related data concerning its own activities to support management decision making [27]. This presumes the existence of a proper metrics program and follow-up. Without systematic data collection there is no accumulated history data on which the investment estimation could be based on. A related risk is that selected metrics do not capture the value of IT [27], i.e. insignificant or false metrics are being monitored.

The third challenge with economic criteria is that the benefits often appear in non-financial form [22, p 7] and the collected data is to be conversed in a commensurable format before benefit assessment can be carried out [14]. Data conversion may be problematic if benefits appear as soft issues, which are difficult to express in terms of money. In order to avoid confusion with data conversion, the expected benefits should be identified before data acquisition.

The fourth challenge, concerning particularly IS evolution evaluation, is in the comparison of different types of investment options. For instance, if all three evolution strategies are possible, there are minimum of three evolution options to be compared. Those can be for instance:

1. replace the existing system with system X (vendor X)
2. replace the existing system with system Y (in-house development)
3. modernize the existing system (in-house modernization)

Or, alternatively, the investment options can be:

1. replace the existing system with system X (vendor X)
2. replace the existing system with system Y (vendor Y)
3. modernize the existing system (vendor Y)

The successful comparison of investment option combinations necessitates that the selected evaluation method(s) are in compliance with the investment options and that the organization has the ability to use them accordingly.

As a conclusion, it can be suggested that it is unattainable to predefine the appropriate evaluation method for IS evolution options assessment. Some of the investment criteria fit better than the others but in the end the selection should be made on the basis of the investment situation at hand combined with the available resources, skills, and data.

16.4 ISEBA Framework

In the past research, various methods and approaches have been presented in order to merge IT evaluation with financial investment criteria. In 1987, Parker and Benson et al. [21] introduced information economics that seeks to unify financial justification, value, and innovation valuation with decision making. In 1992, Farbey et al. presented a model for matching an IT investment with a suitable evaluation method [15]. More resent models include a manager friendly roadmap for IT investment evaluation [28] and an evaluation method's matrix as a solution for customized IT investment evaluation [18]. A point of consensus for these methodologies is that their focus is on financial benefits of IT in general. Also, there are methods for software modernization cost and work effort estimation, i.e. COCOMO II [8], FPA [1] and Softcalc [26], but it seems that availability of methods for IS evolution evaluation is currently minimal. For this reason, a new framework for this particular purpose was outlined.

ISEBA (Information System Evolution Benefit Assessment) is a framework to support comparison of IS evolution options. Its goal is to provide assistance in the selection of a benefit evaluation method for investment situation at hand. It is based on empirical research consisting of interview study of industrial decision making and industrial co-operation projects, and a comprehensive literature survey. It obliges instructions about the required metrics and follow-up data for both intangible and financial evaluation methods. ISEBA consists of eight phases: 1) identifying the characteristics of investment situation, 2) identifying investment type, 3) defining investment assessment emphasis, 4) estimating organizational capabilities and comparing them to the requirements and labour intensity of potential benefit estimation methods, 5) selecting suitable method(s) and identifying related risks, 6) gathering required follow-up and metrics data for benefit assessment, 7) performing benefit assessment for investment proposals, and 8) interpreting and valuating results.

The implementation of ISEBA follows the form of a decision-tree. Phases 1 to 4 rule out the improper methods and provide a list of potentially suitable methods. In Phase 2, the investment type (acquisition or development project) of investment proposals is defined. This defines the post-investment measurement timing. The assessment emphasis in Phase 3 refers to financial or non-monetary benefits. It can be decided that either financial or intangible benefits or both are assessed depending on the investment characteristics. In phase 4, it is important to evaluate the resources and skills the organisation is able to allocate for evaluation. Also, the existing metrics and follow-up data are assessed. The final selection of suitable methods is based on the comparison on of the potentially suitable methods and organisation's resources, skills and available data (phase 5). ISEBA supports method selection by providing a description of each method and the required input data per method. In Phase 6, data acquisition (if needed) is carried out. The execution of benefit assessment takes place in phase 7. Finally, in phase 8 the results are examined and valuated in compliance with organization's strategies.

If more than one investment proposal is to be evaluated, it is defined in Phase 1. A more detailed description of ISEBA is given in [17].

16.5 Summary

On the basis of the literature survey, it can be concluded, that the overall benefits of IS evolution have not been studied comprehensively so far. The comparison of the characteristics of investment criteria shows that the best suited criteria for IS evolution evaluation are NPV and ROI. IRR, payback, and AAR can be used as additional criteria in order to verify their results. Accounting criteria tend to be too general and past-oriented while real options rely strongly on assumptions and option prizing methods are demanding to apply. As a summary of the literature survey it can be concluded that there is no straightforward rule for defining the appropriate evaluation method for IS evolution options assessment. The selection should be made on the basis of the investment situation at hand combined with the available resources, skills, and data. Also, it is suggested that none of the investment criteria should be used alone but together with supporting criteria.

Potential challenges related to evolution investment assessment are selecting a proper analysis method, collecting suitable metrics data, data conversion, and comparison of different types of evolution options. Inspired by these challenges ISEBA framework was created. ISEBA has been further developed and validated empirically in real life cases which incorporate evolution benefit assessment. Report of the validated framework and completed two software industry related projects that ELTIS promoted has been published [17]. Report of the further developed framework, named ISEBA+, will be forthcoming.

References

1. Albrecht A, Gaffney J (1983) Software function, source lines of code, and development effort prediction: a software science validation. IEEE Transactions on Software Engineering 9 (6) pp 639-648
2. Alleman J, Hirofumi S, Rappoport P (2004) An Investment Criterion Incorporating Real Options. In: Real Options – Theory Meets Practice, The 8th Annual International Conference, www.realoptions.org (on-line; read 23.8.2004)
3. Bennett K (1995) Legacy Systems: Coping with Stress. *IEEE Software* 12 (1), pp 19-23
4. Bennett K, Ramage M, Munro M (1999) Decision Model for Legacy Systems. *IEE Proceedings – Software* 146 (3) pp 153-159
5. Bergey JK, Northrop LM, Smith DB (1997) *Enterprise Framework for the Disciplined Evolution of Legacy Systems*. Technical report, CMU/SEI-97
6. Bierman H Jr, Drebin AR (1968) *Managerial Accounting: An Introduction.* The Macmillan Company, New York

7. Bisbal J, Lawless D, Wu B, Grimson J (1999) Legacy Information Systems: Issues and Directions. *IEEE Software* 16 (5) pp 103-111

8. Boehm B, Horowitz E, Madachy R, Reifer R, Clark B, Steece B, Brown A, Chulani S, Abts C (2000) Software Cost Estimation with COCOMO II. Prentice Hall

9. Brealey R, Myers SC (1996) Principles of Corporate Finance. 5th edn, McGraw-Hill, USA

10. Brynjolfssen E (1993) The Productivity Paradox of Information Technology. Communications of the ACM 36 (12) pp 67-77

11. Curley C (2004) Managing Information Technology for Business Value. Intel Press, Hillsboro, OR

12. Dehning B, Richardson VJ (2002) Returns on Investment in Information Technology: A Research Synthesis. Journal of Information Systems 16 (1) pp 7-30

13. Dos Santos BL (1991) Justifying Investments in New Information Technologies. Journal of Management Information Systems 7 (4) pp 71-89

14. Erdogmus H, Favaro J, Strigel W (2004) Return on Investment. IEEE Software 21 (3) pp 18-22

15. Farbey B, Land F, Targett D (1992) Evaluating Investments in IT. Journal of Information Technology 7 pp 109-122

16. de Jong B, Ribbers PMA, van der Zee HTM (1999) Option pricing for IT valuation: a dead end. EJISE Electronic Journal of Information Systems Evaluation, http://www.ejise.com/volume-2/volume2-issue1/issue1-art1.htm

17. Kankaanpää I, Sivula H, Ahonen JJ, Tilus T, Koskinen J, Juutilainen P (2005) ISEBA - A Framework for IS Evolution Benefit Assessment. In: Remenyi D (ed) Proceedings of the 12th European Conference on Information Technology Evaluation, Academic Conferences Ltd, UK, pp 255-264

18. Lech P (2005) Evaluation methods' matrix – A Tool for customized IT investment evaluation. In: Remenyi D (ed) Proceedings of the 12th European Conference on Information Technology Evaluation, Academic Conferences Ltd, UK, pp 297-306

19. Lehman MM, Perry DE, Ramil JF (1998) Implications of Evolution Metrics on Software Maintenance. In: Khoshgoftaar TM, Bennett K (eds) Proceedings of the International Conference on Software Maintenance, IEEE Computer Society, Los Alamitos, California, pp 208-217

20. Lim WC (1996) Reuse Economics: A Comparison of Seventeen Models and Direction for Future Research. In Proceedings of the 4th International Conference on Software Reuse, IEEE Computer Society, pp 41-50

21. Parker MM, Benson RJ, Trainor HE (1988) Information Economics – Linking Business Performance to Information Technology. Prentice-Hall, Singapore

22. Remenyi D, Money A, Sherwood-Smith M with Irani Z (2000) The Effective Measurement and Management of IT Costs and Benefits. 2nd edn, Butterworth-Heinemann, Oxford

23. Ross SA, Westerfield RW, Jordan BD (1998) Fundamentals of Corporate Finance. 4th edn, McGraw-Hill, USA

24. Schwartz ES, Zozoya-Gorostiza C (2000) Valuation of Information Technology Investments as Real Options. In: The 4th Annual Real Options Conference, www.realoptions.org (on-line, read 23.8.2004)

25. Seacord RC, Plakosh D, Lewis GA (2003) Modernizing Legacy Systems – Software Technologies, Engineering Processes, and Business Practices. Addison-Wesley, Boston, MA

26. Sneed HM (1995) Estimating the Costs of Software Maintenance Tasks. In: Proceedings of the 11th International Conference on Software Maintenance, IEEE Computer Society, pp 168-181
27. Verhoef C (2002) Quantitative IT Portfolio Management. Science of Computer Programming 45 pp 1-96
28. Videira A, da Cunha PR (2005) Evaluating IT Investments: A Managerial Friendly Roadmap. In: Remenyi D (ed) Proceedings of the 12th European Conference on Information Technology Evaluation, Academic Conferences Ltd, UK, pp 501-510

17 Adaptive Human-to-Human Collaboration via Negotiations of Social Protocols

Willy Picard

The Poznań University of Economics
ul. Mansfelda 4,
60-854 Poznań, Poland
picard@kti.ae.poznan.pl

17.1 Introduction

Enterprises are increasing constantly their efforts in order to improve their business processes. A main reason for this may be the fact that enterprises are exposed to a highly competitive global market. As a consequence, enterprises improve their business processes to become more competitive and to increase their performances. Among the most visible actions associated with this effort towards better support for better business processes, one may distinguish the current research work concerning Web services and associated standards: high-level languages such as BPEL or WS-Coordination take the service concept one step further by providing a method of defining and supporting workflows and business processes.

However, it should be notice that most of these actions are directed towards interoperable machine-to-machine interactions over a network. Support for *human-to-human interactions* over a network is still insufficient and much research has to been done to provide both theoretical and practical knowledge to this field.

Among various reasons for the weak support for human-to-human interactions, one may distinguish the following two reasons: first, many *social elements* are involved in the interaction among humans. An example of such a social element may be the roles played by humans during their interactions. Social elements are usually difficult to model, i.e. integrating non-verbal communication to collaboration models. Therefore, their integration to a model of interaction between humans is not easy. A second reason is the *adaptation capabilities* of humans which are not only far more advanced than adaptation capabilities of software entities, but also not taken into account in existing models for collaboration processes.

W. Abramowicz and H.C. Mayr (eds.), Technologies for Business Information Systems, 193–203.

This paper is a try to provide a model for human-to-human interactions which addresses, at least to some extend, the two characteristics of the interactions between humans. It should however been kept in mind that the results presented here are a work in progress and therefore they are not claimed to be sufficient.

The rest of this paper is organized as follows. In section 2, the concept of *social protocol*, used to model collaboration processes, is presented. Section 3 then expands on the use of *negotiation* as a mean for *adaptation* of social protocols. Next, related work is reviewed. Finally, section 5 concludes this paper.

17.2 Modeling Collaboration Processes as Social Protocols

A social protocol aims at modeling a set of collaboration processes, in the same way as a class models a set of objects in object-oriented programming. In other words, a social protocol may be seen as a model which instances are collaboration processes (Picard 2005b).

Social protocols model collaboration at a group level. The interactions of collaborators are captured by social protocols. Interactions are strongly related with social aspects, such as the role played by collaborators. The proposed model integrates some of these social aspects, which may explain the choice of the term "social protocols".

17.2.1 Formal Model of Social Protocols

Before social protocols may be formally defined, others concepts must first be defined, as well as the related notation.

Role. A role r is a label. Let's denote R the set of roles.

In a given group, a set of roles is played by the collaborators, which means that collaborators are labeled, are associated with given roles. The set of roles R_g played in a given group g is a subset of R, i.e. $R_g \subset R$. Collaborators usually play different roles. Roles may be associated with collaborators to specify the way they should interact with the rest of the group. Interactions among collaborators are modeled with the concept of *action*.

Action. An action a is an execution of a software entity. Let's denote A the set of actions.

An action may be for instance the execution of a web service, a commit to a CVS repository, the sending of an email. Within a group, collaborators are interacting by executing actions. The execution of actions is a part of the common knowledge of the group, i.e. all collaborators are aware of the execution of an action by one of the members of the group.

Behavioral Unit. A behavioral unit bu is a pair *(role, action)*. Let's denote BU the set of potential behavioral units. Formally, $BU=R\times A$.

The concept of behavioral unit comes from the idea that the behavior of a collaborator is to a large extend determined by the role he/she plays. Therefore, roles and actions have to be associated to determine the behavior, i.e. the set of actions that a collaborator playing a given role should expose.

By extension, one may say that a behavioral unit is executed. A behavioral unit $bu=(r,a)$ is said to be executed iff a collaborator labeled with role r executes action a. It should be noticed that only collaborators labeled with role r can execute the behavioral $bu=(r,a)$.

State. A state s is a label associated with a given situation in a collaborative process. Let's denote S the set of states.

In a given collaborative process p, the set of states that may occur S_p is a subset of S, i.e. $S_p \subset S$.

Transition. A transition t is a triplet *(bu, s_{source}, $s_{destination}$)*. Let's denote T the set of transitions. Formally, $T=BU\times S\times S$.

Now that all concepts underlying social protocols have been formally presented, the concept of social protocol may be defined.

Social Protocol. A social protocol p is a finite state machine consisting of $\left\{ S_p, S_p^{start}, S_p^{end}, R_p, A_p, \Delta_p \right\}$ where $S_p^{start} \subset S_p$ is the set of starting states, $S_p^{end} \subset S_p$ is the set of ending states, $S_p^{start} \cap S_p^{end} = \varnothing$ and Δ_p: $T_p \rightarrow [0,1]$. Let's denote P the set of social protocols.

In a social protocol, collaborators are moving from state to state via the execution of behavioral units. In other words, the executions of behavioral units are transition conditions. As mentioned before, a behavioral unit may be executed only by a collaborator labeled with the appropriate role.

In the context of social protocols, the Δ_p function puts an additional constraint on the execution of behavioral units. The Δ_p function defines the "desirability" of a transition within the given protocol for the whole group. The highest the value of the Δ_p function for a transition t, the highest the desirability of this transition for the group. If the value of the Δ_p function for a transition t is zero, then the group does not desire this transition to be executed.

The conditions that protocols have to fulfill to be valid, both structurally and semantically have already been presented in (Picard 2005a).

17.2.2 Social Protocol Example

The example of social protocol which is presented in this section is oversimplified for readability reasons. It is obvious that social protocols modeling real-world collaboration processes are usually much more complex.

The chosen collaboration process to be modeled as a social protocol may be described as follows: a set of users are collaborating on the establishment of a "FAQ" document. Some users only ask questions, while others, referred as "experts" may answer the questions. Other users, referred as "managers", are may interrupt the work on the FAQ document. The work on the document may terminate either by a success (the document has been written and the manager estimates that its quality is good enough to be published) or by a failure (the users did not find any way to collaborate and the manager has estimated that the work on the FAQ should be interrupted).

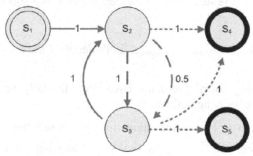

Fig. 1. Example of social protocol

A possible model of this collaboration process as a social protocol is presented in Figure 1. In Figure 1, five states $s_1,...,s_5$ are represented as circles. State s_1 is a starting state, states s_4 and s_5 are ending states. States are named as follows:

- state s_1: *waiting for first question*
- state s_2: *waiting for answer*
- state s_3: *waiting for next question*
- state s_4: *failed termination*
- state s_5: *successful termination*

Transitions are represented as arrows, and the line style is associated with the role of the users that may execute a given transition. Continuous line style is used to represent transitions that may be executed by "normal users", fine-dashed style for transitions that may be executed by "experts", and fine-dotted style for transitions that may be executed by "managers".

The figures closed to the arrows represented the value of the desirability function for the associated transition. Transitions are summarized in Table 1.

Table 1. Transitions for the example of social protocol and their associated desirability values

Source state	Destination state	Role	Action	φ
S_1	S_2	Normal	Ask question	1
S_2	S_3	Expert	Answer question	1
S_2	S_3	Expert	Suppress question	0.5
S_2	S_4	Manager	Failure ending	1
S_3	S_2	Normal	Ask question	1
S_3	S_4	Manager	Failure ending	1
S_3	S_5	Manager	Successful ending	1

17.2.3 Social Protocol Filtering

The introduction of the Δ_p function is one of the main innovations presented in this paper. It allows collaborators for presenting various granularity levels of a given social protocol with regards to a *desirability threshold*.

Binary Social Protocol. A social protocol p is a binary social protocol iff its desirability function takes only the values 0 and 1, i.e. Δ_p: $T_p \rightarrow \{0,1\}$. Let's denote P_{01} the set of binary social protocols.

Let's assume that the desirability threshold equals θ, with $0 < \theta \leq 1$. Social protocol filtering consists in transforming a social protocol into a binary social protocol, by "suppressing" all transitions whose desirability is inferior to the desirability threshold. Formally, social protocol filtering may be defined as follows:

Social Protocol Filtering. Given a desirability threshold θ, with $0 < \theta \leq 1$, social protocol filtering is a function $\varphi : P \times [0,1] \rightarrow P_{01}$ such that $\varphi(p,\theta) = p'$ with

$$S_p = S_{p'}, S_p^{start} = S_{p'}^{start}, S_p^{end} = S_{p'}^{end}, R_p = R_{p'}, A_p = A_{p'} \qquad \text{and}$$

$$\Delta_{p'}(t) = \begin{cases} 0, & \text{if } \Delta_p(t) < \theta \\ 1, & \text{if } \Delta_p(t) \geq \theta \end{cases}$$

An example of social protocol filtering is presented on Figure 2. In this example, the result of the filtering of the protocol presented in section 2.2 for the value of the desirability threshold $\theta = 0.6$. All transitions with a desirability value lowest than the desirability threshold, i.e. the transition allowing experts to suppress a question, have been suppressed.

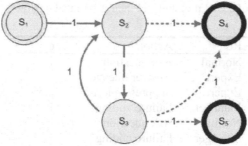

Fig. 2. Filtered social protocol presented in section 2.2 for the value of the desirability threshold $\theta = 0.6$

17.2.4 Social Protocol Design

The proposed model for collaboration processes may be used to design protocol-based collaboration support systems in which social aspects are taken into account. Following the model, specification of a protocol-based collaboration support system involves four areas: action specification, role specifications, states specifications, and, desirability.

The specification of actions focuses on the definition of the functionalities that the collaborators need to achieve their common goal. All software entities needed to achieve this goal should be inventoried and documented.

The specification of roles focuses not only on the identification of the roles that may be played in the related collaboration processes, but also on the definition of behavioral units which are required.

When needed behavioral units have been identified, states may be specified. To do so, all situations that may occur during related collaborative processes should be identified and documented. These situations may then be mapped to states.

Having states and behavioral units, the only missing element for a complete description of a social protocol is the definition of the desirability function. During the design of the desirability function, one should start by identifying transitions which are mandatory (resp. are forbidden or make no sense) and assign them with the value 1 (resp. 0).

17.3 Adaptation of Social Protocols via Negotiation

While social protocols support, at least to some extend, the integration of some social elements (such as roles) to models of interactions among humans, the adaptation capabilities of humans are not taken into account into social protocols. There is however the need to provide adaptation mechanisms to social protocols. Indeed, interactions among humans are often a context-aware activity. In this paper, context-awareness refers to the capabilities of applications to provide relevant services to their users by sensing and exploring the users' context (Dey et al. 2001; Dockhorn Costa et al. 2005). Context is defined as a "collection of interrelated conditions in which something exists or occurs" (Dockhorn Costa et al. 2005). The users' context often consists of a collection of conditions, such as, e.g., the users' location, environmental aspects (temperature, light intensity, etc.) and activities (Chen et al. 2003). The users' context may change dynamically, and, therefore, a basic requirement for a context-aware system is its ability to sense context and to react to context changes.

Adaptive mechanisms are therefore required as complements to the formerly proposed model for human collaboration processes. The mechanism proposed in this paper is based the idea that social protocols may be negotiated. Two aspects of social protocols may be negotiated independently: first, the desirability function may be negotiated; second, states/behavioral units sets may be negotiated.

17.3.1 Desirability Negotiation

The first element of social elements that could be the object of adaptation may be the desirability function. The values taken by desirability function for various transitions define the desirability of the whole group with regards to single transitions. By modifying the value of the desirability function, the whole group may adapt the social protocol to the situation in which the group is.

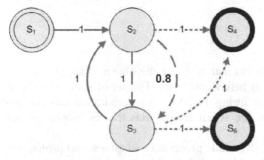

Fig. 3. Filtered social protocol presented in section 2.2 after the desirability value of transition "suppress question" has been increased by 0.3 (desirability threshold $\theta = 0.6$)

By increasing the desirability value of a given transition, a group may decide that a transition is "desirable" for a given desirability threshold, and therefore the transition associated with the modified value will become available. By decreasing the desirability value of a given transition, a group may decide that a transition is not "desirable" any more, and therefore the transition associated with the modified value will become unavailable for a given desirability threshold.

Table 2. Transitions for the example of social protocol and their associated desirability values

Source state	Destination state	Role	Action	Φ
s_1	S_2	Normal	Ask question	1
s_2	S_3	Expert	Answer question	1
s_2	s_3	**Expert**	**Suppress question**	**0.8**
s_2	s_4	Manager	Failure ending	1
s_3	s_2	Normal	Ask question	1
s_3	s_4	Manager	Failure ending	1
s_3	s_5	Manager	Successful ending	1

Effects of a potential modification of the desirability function of social protocol presented in Section 2.2 are presented in Figure 3. In the presented example, the original social protocol presented in Section 2.2 has been adapted by the whole group via negotiations. The result of the negotiation is the group agreement stating that the desirability value for the transition "suppress question" has to be increased by 0.3. The modified desirability values associated with transitions are presented in Table 2.

After filtering, the adapted version of the social protocol is presented in Figure 3. Comparing with Figure 2, one may notice that the transition "suppress question" is now a desirable transition, at the desirability threshold of 0.5, which was not true before adaptation.

17.3.2 Structural Negotiation

The second element of social elements that could be the object of adaptation may be the set of states and/or the set of behavioral units. The set of states consists of the set of situations that may occur during the life of a collaboration process. The set of behavioral units consists of the set of interactions that collaborators may perform.

By adding/suppressing state(s), the whole group may adapt a social protocol by providing/suppressing situation(s) to the collaboration process. It should be noticed that the addition/suppression of state(s) is related with the addition/suppression of transitions leading and originating from the modified state(s).

By adding/suppressing transition(s), the whole group may adapt a social protocol by providing/suppressing interaction(s) to the collaboration process. It should be noticed that the addition/suppression of transition(s) is usually not related with the addition/suppression of state(s) to/from which the added/suppressed transition(s) lead(s)/originate(s).

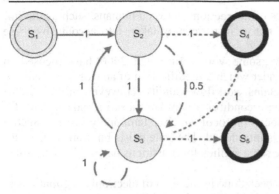

Fig. 4. Social protocol presented in section 2.2 after a transition related with the action "comment a question" has been added from s_3 to s_3

Effects of the addition of a transition in the social protocol presented in Section 2.2 are presented in Figure 4. In the presented example, the original social protocol presented in Section 2.2 has been adapted by the whole group via negotiations. The result of the negotiation is the group agreement stating that a new transition is needed so that an expert may comment a question many times before answering it. The modified set of transitions is presented in Table 3.

Table 3. Transitions for the example of social protocol and their associated desirability values

Source state	Destination state	Role	Action	φ
s_1	s_2	Normal	Ask question	1
s_3	s_3	**Expert**	**Comment question**	**1**
s_2	s_3	Expert	Answer question	1
s_2	s_3	Expert	Suppress question	0.5
s_2	s_4	Manager	Failure ending	1
s_3	s_2	Normal	Ask question	1
s_3	s_4	Manager	Failure ending	1
s_3	s_5	Manager	Successful ending	1

17.4 Related Work

As process modeling is concerned, many works have already been conduced in the research field of workflow modeling and workflow management systems. Paul Buhler and Jose M. Vidal (Buhler and Vidal 2005) proposed a mechanism allowing for enacting workflows in an adaptive way using multi-agent systems (MAS). Robert Müller and al. presented in (Müller et al. 2004) various mechanisms for adaptation of workflows to deal with exception occurrences in running workflow instances, with an application to medical treatments. However, to our best knowledge, current works concerning workflow adaptation focus on interactions among software entities. Characteristics of interactions between humans, such as the importance of social aspects, are not or insufficiently taken into account by these works.

Still in the field of workflows, some works (Aalst et al. 2000) have focused on formal models and conditions under which a modification of an existing – and potentially running – workflow retains workflow validity. However, in the case of human interactions, some of these conditions may be relaxed as adaptation of a social protocol may lead to a social protocol which is temporally invalid. Such a case appears when a new state is introduced. The state exists but transitions leading to it have to be defined. The same applies for transitions having the brand-new state as a source.

Some interesting works have been done in the field of electronic negotiations to model electronic negotiations with the help of negotiation protocols. In (Kersten et al. 2004), it is stated in that, in the field of electronic negotiations, "the protocol is a formal model, often represented by a set of rules, which govern software processing, decision-making and communication tasks, and imposes restrictions on activities through the specification of permissible inputs and actions". One may notice the similarity with the concept of social protocol. The reason for this fact is that the model presented in this paper was originally coming from a work on protocols for electronic negotiations (Picard and Huriaux 2006). However, to our knowledge, none of the works concerning negotiation protocols provides mechanisms for protocol adaptation. Moreover, these works are by nature limited to the field of electronic negotiations which is just a subset of the field of human collaboration.

17.5 Conclusions

While many works are currently done on modeling collaboration processes in which software entities (agents, web services) are involved, modeling collaboration processes in which mainly humans are involved is an area that still requires much attention from the research community. Some of the main issues to be addressed are the social aspects of collaboration and the adaptation capabilities of humans. In this paper both issues are addressed. The concept of social protocol aims at being a start of answer to the question of computer support for social collaboration. The idea of negotiation of social protocol is a try to weaken constraints usually limiting the interaction between collaborators, so that the adaptation capabilities of humans may be integrate in the life of a social protocol.

The main innovations presented in this paper are 1) the introduction of the desirability function as a way to provide filtering functions to social protocols, 2) the idea of negotiation of social protocols, based either on negotiation of the desirability function or on the negotiation of the structure of the protocol. The proposed concepts are currently under implementation as extensions to the *DynG* protocol (Huriaux and Picard 2005), a social protocol-based platform. The next steps will include a refinement of the concept of role, so that relationships between roles, e.g. specialization, compositions, may be integrate to the presented model. Automated support for social negotiation would be an interesting feature for a social adaptive protocol-based framework, but negotiation models supporting contextual and social elements are still to be built.

References

1.   van der Aalst WMP, Basten T, Verbeek HMW, Verkoulen PAC, Voorhoeve M (2000) Adaptive Workflow: On the Interplay between Flexibility and Support. In: Filipe J (ed) Enterprise Information Systems, Kluwer Academic Publishers, Norwell, pp. 63–70
2.   Buhler P, Vidal JM (2005) Towards Adaptive Workflow Enactment Using Multiagent Systems. Information Technology and Management Journal, Special Issue on Universal Enterprise Integration, 6(1):61–87
3.   Chen H, Finin T, Joshi A (2003) An Ontology for Context-Aware Pervasive Computing Environments. Knowledge Engineering Review, Special Issue on Ontologies for Distributed Systems, 18(3):197–207
4.   Dey AK, Salber D, Abowd GD, (2001) A Conceptual Framework and a Toolkit for Supporting the Rapid Prototyping of Context-Aware Applications. Human-Computer Interaction, 16(2-4):97–166
5.   Dockhorn Costa P, Ferreira Pires L, van Sinderen M (2005) Designing a Configurable Services Platform for Mobile Context-Aware Applications. International Journal of Pervasive Computing and Communications (JPCC), 1(1):27–37
6.   Huriaux T, Picard W (2005) DynG: a Multi-protocol Collaborative System. In: Funabashi M, Grzech A. (eds) Challenges of Expanding Internet: e-Commerce, e-Business and e-Government, Proceedings of the 5th IFIP International Conference on e-Commerce, e-Business, and e-Government (I3E 2005), Poznan, Poland, Springer, pp. 591–605
7.   Kersten GE, Strecker SE, Lawi KP (2004) Protocols for Electronic Negotiation Systems: Theoretical Foundations and Design Issue. In: Bauknecht K, Bichler M, Pröll B (eds) Proceedings of the 5th Conference on Electronic Commerce and Web Technologies (EC-Web04), Sarragoza, Spain, IEEE Computer Society, pp 106–115
8.   Müller R, Greiner U, Rahm E (2004) AGENTWORK: A Workflow-System Supporting Rule-Based Workflow Adaptation. Data and Knowledge Engineering, Elsevier, 51(2):223–256
9.   Picard W (2005a) Towards Support Systems for Non-Monolithic Electronic Negotiations. The Contract-Group-Message Model". Journal of Decision Systems, Special Issue on Electronic Negotiations - Models, Systems and Agents, 13(4): 423–439
10. Picard W (2005b) Modeling Structured Non-monolithic Collaboration Processes. In: Camarinha-Matos L, Afsarmanesh H, Ortiz A (eds) Collaborative Networks and their Breeding Environments: Proceedings of the 6th IFIP Working Conference on Virtual Enterprises (PRO-VE 2005), Valencia, Spain, Springer, pp. 379–386
11. Picard W, Huriaux T (2006) DynG: A Protocol-Based Prototype for Non-monolithic Electronic Collaboration. In: Shen W, Chao KM, Lin Z, Barthès JPA, James A, (eds) CSCW in Design 2005, LNCS 3865, pp. 41–50

18 Is E-learning More Suitable for Full-time or for Part-time Students?

Viktorija Sulčič

UP Faculty of Management Koper, Slovenia

18.1 Information and Communication Technology in Education

E-learning was first introduced at the Faculty of Management (FM) in the academic year 2002/2003. Until now the same course has been carried out for full-time and part-time students. The course was supported by a virtual learning environment. The blended learning approach was used as the e-learning model. The teacher's assessments were based on students' weekly activities and achievements. Differences between groups of students and the differences caused by using a different blended learning approach will be presented bellow. Apart from the differences that were found, some common characteristics arose; namely students appreciating the introduction of innovative learning methods and the tutor's support in the e-classroom. Considering the students' appreciation of the introduction of e-learning, further development of e-learning practices is recommended. Online training courses for teachers and tutors are being organized at the faculty and further research regarding the impact of e-classroom usage on all participants of e-learning are being carried out at this moment.

The increasing usage of information and communication technology (ICT) in education brings numerous important changes for students and teachers as well as for institutions. On one hand, the development of the ICT improves the accessibility of education, while on the other hand it also brings about tectonic shifts in the process of teaching/learning as well as changes in administration and management of education. Until recently, ICT in education was mainly used as a support tool for administrative processes [RIS, SITES 2000, 60], which means that - in spite of numerous activities on the national as well as on the local level - key education processes are still relatively seldom supported by ICT in Slovenia. Obviously, the introduction of ICT in educational institutions is similar to the introduction of ICT in companies, where processes in accounting, finance and human resources are normally supported first [Turban et al. 1999, 48].

W. Abramowicz and H.C. Mayr (eds.), Technologies for Business Information Systems, 205–215.
© 2007 *Springer.*

With the development of distance education (DE), different teaching methods have been developed, which is mainly due to temporal and spatial separation between teachers and students [Saba 1999, Holmberg 1995]. Correspondence education, tele-education, on-line and Internet study gives the learner/student a more active role as compared to the role known in traditional education (where education is carried out in a physical classroom). A more active role of the learner/student is also stressed in contemporary pedagogy and didactics, and is in accord with the educational changes as stimulated with the onset and progress of the information society [SITES 2000, 3].

Taking into account the fact that education can be carried out over the Internet or the intranet on institution premises, it is much better to speak about electronic or e-learning rather than about DE, i.e. about the education, during which study materials are transmitted to learners/students through electronic media (the Internet, intranet, extranet, satellites, audio/video equipment, CD-ROMs [InternetTime Group 2002]. The key characteristic therefore is not the spatial/temporal separation of participants in education (which was the main reason for introducing DE at the beginning) but an elementary change in the method of work, caused by the intensive use of ICT in everyday and in professional life.

E-learning is becoming increasingly interesting for different educational and other public institutions as well as businesses, because the wide-scale introduction of lifelong learning concepts [Trunk Širca and Sulčič 2003] and the growing importance of knowledge is increasing the demand for different educational forms [Vasquez Bronfman 2000, 1405]. Private and public educational institutions worldwide provide for the increasing demand with a variety of educational programs, offering new forms of education increasingly supported by ICT (especially by the Internet). Therefore the fact that the market of e-learning has been one of the fastest growing markets in North America is no surprise [HKGCC 2002].

18.2 Research Results and Practical Implications

18.2.1 Introduction of the E-classroom at the FM

We started with the introduction of web technologies in our courses in the academic year 2002/2003, when the courses were supported by simple web pages. There, students could find all the information needed, study materials, assignments, etc. related to a certain course, but all the communication between students and teachers was based on e-mails, phone calls or personal communications.

During the academic year 2003/2004 we introduced a virtual learning environment (e-classroom). We have chosen an open source virtual learning environment called Moodle (www.moodle.org) and the blended learning approach – face-to-face meetings were combined with the activities performed in the e-classroom.

The same course - "Digital Economy and e-Business" (DEeB) has been carried out in the e-classroom (www.eucilnica.si) in the last three years for full-time and for part-time students (Table 1). The DEeB course was previously taught in the traditional classroom in 55 hours per semester. Topics of the course are very suitable for the blended learning approach, because e-learning is actually a form of e-business. So students could gain the knowledge of e-business from their own e-learning experience.

Table 1. Students in DEeB through years

Academic year	Students	#
2003/2004	Full-time (FT)	37
2004/2005	Part-time (PT)	105
2005/2006	Full-time (FT)	43
	Part-time (PT)	66

In the academic year 2005/2006 we carried out a combined course for both part-time and full-time students. The course is valued with 6 ECTS for both study options, so there was no need to carry out two separate courses. Joining both groups became a challenge for us, as we had not yet attempted a joined delivery of the course for the two study options.

The teacher prepared the curriculum and study materials in advance. Several tutor helped the teacher organizing the work in the e-classroom, motivated students, monitored and assessed their work.

The course was divided into weekly activities, which held students' weekly obligations. Students worked individually or in small groups and had to post their written assignments in thematic forums within the e-classroom on a weekly basis. The communication among students and between students and their tutors was took place in the e-classroom (discussion groups).

A different blended learning approach was used for full-time and for part-time students. While seven face-to-face meetings were organized in 14 weeks for full-time students in the academic year 2003/2004, only two face-to-face meetings were organized for part-time students in the year 2004/2005 and for the joined group of part-time and full-time students in the year 2005/2006 in the span of 8 weeks. In this case students got together in a real classroom at the beginning of the course, when the whole learning process was presented to them, and at the end of the course, when students presented their final projects. In between the two meetings students performed their study activities exclusively in the e-classroom.

During the duration of the course we assessed the impact of e-learning on students and students' ICT acceptance. Based on the flexibility offered by e-learning, we predicted that e-learning should be better accepted by part-time students than by full-time students and among employed students with families. We predicted that full-time students would prefer face-to-face meetings because they like being in classrooms with their classmates more than being in the virtual environment without any physical contact. Also, our prediction was that the tutor should have important impacts on students' success and that working in small groups of students would yield better results than working in bigger groups.

In the following parts of the paper, based on the data analysis, we try to confirm or to reject our expectations. Our research is based on the observation of the differences between full-time and part-time students in the joined group and the differences between students from the two different generations. The blended learning approach is also observed.

18.2.2 Empirical results

Questionnaire and respondents data

Students were polled by means of e-questionnaires when they enrolled in the e-course and by conventional questionnaires at the end of the term. In the academic year 2005/2006 only e-questionnaires were used.

In the first (entrance) questionnaire we primary wished to inquire about their computer and Internet literacy, their personal characteristics and other abilities important for e-learning. Questions about students' equipment and access to the Internet were also included into the entrance questionnaire.

With the final questionnaire at the end of the course, we wished to assess the impact on students' characteristics and abilities, etc.. In the paper only data from the final questionnaire are presented.

The statistically significant differences between sample averages were tested with independent t-test or with the nonparametric Man-Whitney U test, depending on the normal data distribution.

The part-time students are commonly employed and they are approximately twelve years older than full-time students (average age for PT: 34.2; for FT: 22.1).

Students gave their answers on a five-degree scale, where 1 represented the lowest grade or their disagreement with the statement, and 5 represented the highest grade or absolute agreement with the statement.

As mentioned before, working with the joined group of full-time and part-time students in the year 2005/2006 was a challenge for us. 60 % of the enrolled students were full-time students. We organized two face-to-face meetings for all 109 students enrolled in the course. The part-time study at our faculty is organized in four centers. The introduction meetings were organized in two centers. We joined the majority of full-time and part-time students who came from the surroundings (78% students of the course) in one center and students from the other two centers at one of the two centers. Because of the number of students enrolled in the course the first group was further divided in two equally large groups. The teacher also played a tutor role in one group of students; while she also monitored the whole work of the students and the work of the others two tutors. The teacher assessed most of the students' assignments as well.

In the first two years there were more male students in the course (53% among full-time students and 56% among full-time students) than in the last year (32% among full-time and 36% among part time students).

Implementing the e-classroom in the course

A tutor, who organized the work in the e-classroom, motivated the students, facilitated communication among them and reported to the teacher about his/her work on a weekly basis, supported each group of students.

The comparison of means of all four researched groups regarding the attitude towards the teacher and the tutor is presented in Table 2.

Table 2. Students' opinion about tutor/teacher

Statements	FT 03/04	PT 04/05	FT 05/06	PT 05/06
It was much easier to approach the teacher/tutor in the e-classroom than in conventional courses.	4.6	3.9	3.8	4.6
The tutor can replace the teacher.	4.4	3.2	3.6	4.0
he presence of the tutor in the e-classroom can improve my study success in a course.	3.9	3.5	4.0	4.6

From Table 2 some differences are visible, but we need to stress that there were same major differences in the execution of the course among different generations. The course for full-time students in 2003/2004 was organized in one group supported by an assistant. Part-time students in 2004/2005 were divided in four groups that were supported by tutors, who were mostly students of DEeB from the previous academic year. As mentioned before, the blended learning approach also differs. There was more physical contact with full-time students in 2003/2004 than with part-time students in the following year. For this reason we will compare part-time and full-time students in the joined group and than part-time/full-time students among them.

The statistical significance was tested with the Man-Whitney U test hence the data were not properly normally distributed. Comparing the means in the joined group showed statistically significant differences. The e-learning offered to the part-time students gave them more opportunities to contact their teachers then the classical study (P=0.00), even if the contacts were mostly virtual. The part-time students are more convinced that the tutor could easily replace the teacher (P–0.02). We should stress that in the last academic year the students were supported by more qualified tutors than in the previous years (39 % students were supported by the teacher who taught the course in the classical course too). According to the opinion of part-time students the tutor's role is also very important for their study success (P=0.00).

The tutor, who supports the students in the e-classroom, should be a subject expert and he/she should develop good pedagogical skills. Part-time students in 2005/2006 are more in agreement with the statement that it was easier to approach the teacher/tutor in the e-learning course than it is in classical courses than part-time students in 2003/2004 (P=0.00). They were also more supportive of the idea that a tutor can replace the teacher in virtual environment (P=0.00). There are no statistically significant differences between the tutor's impacts on full-time student's success (P=0.43). The part-time students differ from full-time students statistically at all variables (P=0.00).

If we compare all generations, we do not find any statistically significant differences between full-time and part-time students at all. But as mentioned before, there are many other variables that influence differences between students (tutor support, group size etc.).

E-classroom usage and personal characteristics of students

In addition, students' personal characteristics (creativity; study, organizational, managerial and interpersonal skills) were monitored and compared. In Table 3 means are presented.

Table 3. Students' opinion about changes in their abilities due to the participation in the e-classroom

At the completion of studies I...	FT 03/04	PT 04/05	FT 05/06	PT 05/06
...was a more experienced user of computer and programs.	3.9	3.5	3.9	3.6
...was more motivated for studying.	3.7	2.9	3.6	4.1
...displayed more self-initiative.	3.7	3.2	3.6	4.0
...became more creative.	3.7	3.4	3.7	4.1
...developed better organizational skills.	3.7	3.4	3.6	4.0
...improved my communication skills.	3.5	3.3	3.6	4.0
...improved my team-work skills.	3.4	3.7	3.7	3.9
...improved my managerial skills.	3.3	3.3	3.6	3.6
...became more determined.	3.3	3.4	3.6	4.1
Average	3.6	3.3	3.7	3.9

As can be seen from Table 3. the values for full-time and part time students are different – the ratio between the first two generations is right opposite to the ratio of the groups in the third generation of DEeB students. We already explained the reason for this difference.

The data were normally distributed and the t-test was used to establish the statically significant differences between the means of the groups. Among the joined group statistically significant differences were found only in three cases: part-time students become more motivated (P=0.01), more self-initiative (P=0.02) and more determined (P=0.01) after the completion the e-learning course. Among the groups of full-time students there were no significant differences found. It is interesting that significant differences were found among part-time students enrolled in 2004/2005 and in 2005/2006. Part-time students from the previous generation became more motivated, more self-initiative, more creative, had developed better organizational and team work skills and became more determined (all P are 0.00) after the completion the e-learning course. This finding is interesting because of the fact that part-time students of the previous generation did not study together with full-time students as this year's part-time students did.

As we can see, the ICT has impacts mostly on students' motivation, self-initiative and their willingness to end the things they have started.

Students' opinion about the e-classroom and study materials

We used an open source e-classroom Moodle, which is used in 163 countries around the world. For the time being there are 49 registered sites in Slovenia. [Moodle 2006].

In the academic year 2003/2004 we used an older version of Moodle (1.1.1), whereas in the academic year 2004/2005 we used the version 1.4.3, which was translated into Slovenian (the old version used English user interface). The version 1.5.2 was used in 2005/2006. Every new version offers many useful features that help managing e-learning.

At the end of both courses students were asked to express their opinion about the e-classroom (Table 4).

Table 4. Students' opinion about the e-classroom

The e-classroom was...	FT 03/04	PT 04/05	FT 05/06	PT 05/06
...a user-friendly environment.	4.4	4.0	4.1	4.6
...easy to use.	4.6	4.2	4.3	4.4
...clearly organized.	3.9	4.1	4.2	4.5
Average	4.3	4.1	4.2	4.5

Data were not properly normally distributed so Mann-Whitney U test was used to identify statistically significant differences between means presented in Table 4. For part-time students in 2005/2006 the e-classroom was user-friendlier (P=0.00) and more clearly organized (P=0.01) than for their mates, who studied full-time in the same course. The same results were found in the comparison of the means for part-time students. Among groups of full-time students there were no statistically significant differences found.

All study materials were delivered through the e-classroom. In Table 5 we show students' opinions about study materials.

Table 5. Students' opinion about study materials

Statements	FT 03/04	PT 04/05	FT 05/06	PT 05/06
Materials were understandable.	4.2	4.1	3.7	4.4
Materials were clearly presented.	4.3	4.2	3.4	4.3
I wished for more interactive materials.	3.0	2.6	2.7	3.0

Study materials were well accepted by both full-time and part-time students. They did not have any problems with using and understanding them. Interactive materials were not strongly preferred by researched students.

Part-time students in 2005/2006 had fewer problems with understanding the materials than their mates, who were enrolled as full-time students (P=0.00). For part-time students the materials were clearly presented (P=0.00). Similar results were found in the comparison of the group of full-time students. The generation 2005/2006 significantly differs from the generation 2004/2005. Among part-time students in different academic years there were no statistically significant differences found. The preferences to interactive materials were not statistically significant for any of the compared groups mentioned before.

In our previous research preferences for printing study materials among our students were found [Sulčič et. al. 2006]. We performed a nonparametric Mann-Whitney Test that showed that part-time students in 2005/2006 printed study materials more often than full-time students in the same generation.

Students' opinions about course implementation

At the end of the term, students were asked about their opinions on the implementation of the course (Table 6).

Table 6. Students' opinions about the course

Statement	FT 03/04	PT 04/05	FT 05/06	PT 05/06	P for FT/PT
Online study is more interesting than conventional study.	4.6	3.9	4.0	4.5	0.01
Online study is easier than conventional study.	4.2	2.6	3.4	3.7	
More knowledge is acquired through online than conventional study.	4.0	3.7	3.6	4.2	0.00
If I had the opportunity I would study this way (again).	4.0	3.0	3.6	4.2	0.00
The implementation of the course was in accordance with my expectations.	3.7	3.3	3.6	4.2	0.00
For me, online learning is less expensive than conventional learning.	3.7	3.2	3.5	4.0	0.00
The course forced me to work harder than I normally work for other courses.	3.3	4.5	4.0	4.0	
There was more cooperation between fellow students than in conventional study.	3.3	3.9	3.5	4.0	0.00

In 2005/2006 the part-time students' opinions statistically significantly differ from the full-time students' opinions. For part-time students the online study was more interesting, they acquired more knowledge, they cooperated more with their fellow students and they wish to study in such a way. Probably the cost of the study stimulates them to prefer online to classical study.

Our blended learning approach is based on weekly activities carried out in the e-classroom and face-to-face meetings. The weekly activities were well accepted, especially among part-time students (Table 7).

Table 7. Opinions about e-learning activities

Statement	FT 05/06	PT 05/06	P
I had no difficulties to accept the activities.	3.8	4.1	
The activities were not difficult.	2.9	3.4	0.01
The activities were clearly explained.	3.4	4.1	
The activity-based study suited me well.	3.9	4.3	0.03
The activities made the course more practical.	3.7	4.4	0.00

In Table 7 the averages of opinions related to study activities are presented.

75% of full-time students and 82% of part-time students respondents assessed their acceptances of weekly activities with 4 or 5 on a 5-degree scales. Taking into account the success rate of students at the final exam (91,7 %) and their satisfaction with the study methods, weekly activities should be introduced in other courses as well. Students enjoyed the study flexibility and the relaxed atmosphere, but did not like the burden of obligations and the time limits of the tests.

18.3 Conclusions

The first attempt to introduce the blended learning approach – a combination of the e-classroom and face-to-face meetings - is rather encouraging. Activity based study encourages more evenly distributed student workload throughout the semester, which supports efficient preparation throughout the study period. Therefore the success rate is greater than in classically organized courses. The e-classroom also helps teachers to monitor students' activities and their workload better.

During the course students became increasingly motivated, showed more self-initiative, and improved other skills, which speaks in favor of a bright future of e-learning as one of the means for the implementation of life-long learning, through which individuals can constantly improve their employment opportunities.

The research also showed that e-learning can be performed without the usage of complicated technologies, because students involved in our study preferred paper based materials to computer based interactive materials. We focused our efforts on defining student activities through which students developed competences defined in the curriculum. It is obvious that in e-learning learning methods should also gradually change.

The survey results indicate that the selection of tutors is very important. Therefore additional efforts and resources are being invested into the appropriate selection and good training of tutors. In this academic year, two groups of teachers and assistants completed online training courses for teachers and tutors. The course was developed and performed by the Center for e-learning at the Faculty of Management.

We found out that courses for full-time and part-time students can be carried out together without major difficulties. In the paper we tried to compare part-time and full-time students of different generations, but the results hardly hold significant findings because the teaching methods differ from year to year. Based on the data from 2005/2006 we can conclude that e-learning is very suitable for part-time students because we found out that they became more motivated and more self-initiative, which is very important for continuing learning. They also acquired more knowledge in this way. We did not find out that full-time students prefer classical courses to e-learning courses. Obviously, the lack of physical contact in the virtual environment is not as important as we predicted at the beginning of the paper.

The tutor's role in the e-learning courses is very important, especially for part-time students. They appreciated the opportunity to have more contact with the academic staff – teacher or tutor - because during classical courses they only meet with the teacher a few times and then have no organized contact until the final exam. In the e-learning courses fellow students and the tutor are always at hand for communication, for an exchange of opinions, and for help when needed.

References

[InternetTime Group 2002] InternetTime Group. Available: http://www.internettime.com/ [2. 6.2002].

[HKGCC 2002] HKGCC – Hong Kong General Chamber of Commerce. Edport.com. Available: http://www.chamber.org.hk/info/member_a_week/edport.asp [2. 6. 2002].

[Holmberg 1995] B. Holmberg, The Evolution of the Character and Practise of Distance Education. In *Open Learning, vol. 10*, No. 2, pp. 47-53.

[Moodle 2006] Moodle Sites. Available: http://moodle.org/sites/ [14. 9. 2006].

[RIS] RIS – Raba interneta v Sloveniji. (Use of Internet in Slovenia) *Uporaba interneta: Gospodinjstva 2003/2*. (Use of Internet: Households). Available: http://www.ris.org/ [20. 8. 2004].

[RIS] RIS – Raba interneta v Sloveniji. (Use of Internet in Slovenia). *E-izobraževanje.* (E-learning) Available: http://www.ris.org/ [20. 6. 2005].

[Saba 1999] F. Saba, Distance Education: An Introduction. Available: http://www.distance-educator/portals/research_deintro.html [2. 10. 2000].

[SITES 2000] SITES – *Druga mednarodna raziskava uporabe informacijskih in komunikacijskih tehnologij v izobraževanju*. Ljubljana: Oddelek za IEA raziskave – Pedagoški inštitut, 2000.

[Sulčič 2005] V. Sulčič, *Digitalna ekonomija in e-poslovanje - Zaključno poročilo o izvedbi predmeta v študijskem letu 2004/2005 (izredni študij)*. Gradivo za delovni zvezek v postopku recenzije. Fakulteta za management Koper, Koper, 2005.

[Sulčič et.atl. 2006]. V. Sulčič, D. Lesjak and N. Trunk Širca. E-classroom in Higher Education. In *Lecture Notes in Informatics (LNI) – Proceedings, Vol. P-85*. Bonn: Gesellschaft für Informatik, 2006.

[Trunk Širca and Sulčič 2003] N. Trunk Širca and V. Sulčič, Lifelong Learning and Higher Education Institutions; from Strategic Principle through Implemented Example to

Systematic Solution? In *Knowledge Society – Challenges to Management; Globalisation, Regionalism and EU Enlargement Process*. 4th International Conference of the Faculty of Management Koper, University of Primorska, Fakulteta za management, Koper, 2003.

[Turban et. al. 1999] Turban, E. and E. McLean and J. Wetherbe, *Information Technology for Management – Making Connections for Strategic Advantage*. John Wiley & Sons, Inc., New York, 1999.

[Vasquee Bronfman 2000] S. Vasquez Bronfman, Linking Information Technology and Pedagogical Innovation To Enchance Management Education. In *ECIS 2000 – A Cyberspace Odyssey, vol.2*. Wirtschaftsuniversität, Vienna, 2000.

19 Automated Acquisition of Semantic Relations for Information Retrieval Systems

Dariusz Ceglarek, Wojciech Rutkowski

Poznan University of Economics, Poland
Department of Management Information Systems

19.1 Introduction

Considering a continuous rise of world's information resources, it is necessary for companies and other organizations to obtain, aggregate, process and utilize them in an appropriate manner in order to maximize the effectiveness of activities that are being conducted.

Since the document libraries (or a number of sources to filter from) are becoming bigger and bigger, it is crucial to provide a trusted system which would be able to find the resources relevant to user's needs. This is a main goal of information retrieval (IR) systems. (Daconta et al. 2003)

Traditionally, the effectiveness of IR systems is measured by two basic factors: *recall* and *precision*. Both are quantified by a percentage or a value between 0 and 1. Suppose we have a set of documents. A user has specific information needs, represented by a *query*. Task of IR system is to provide the user with *relevant* documents from the set. Recall equals a relation of relevant documents returned by IR system to the number of all relevant documents, and precision is a relation of returned relevant documents to all returned documents.

Were everything perfect, the recall and precision of IR system would reach 100%. This is a goal of developing and improving retrieval systems.

19.1.1 Economic Significance of Recall and Precision

In business effectiveness of retrieval systems reflects on profitability. The higher recall the system achieves, the more relevant and, therefore, valuable documents

W. Abramowicz and H.C. Mayr (eds.), Technologies for Business Information Systems, 217–228.

are delivered. In other words, full recall means the widest access to all useful information.

The second indicator, precision, affects the time resources needed to browse and utilize the results. In case of low precision of retrieval systems, lots of manual work is required to determine which of the results are useful (relevant to the needs) and reject inessential (irrelevant) resources. The higher precision, the more time is spared on such process, what directly reflects on work efficiency and costs.

Concluding, improving the effectiveness of retrieval systems is beneficial for organizations whose activities are based on information and knowledge.

19.1.2 Topic of Interest

Information searching and exploring takes place in a domain dependent semantic context. A given context is described through its vocabulary organized along hierarchies that structure the information space. These hierarchies are simplified views on a more complex domain specific semantic network, that form a shared and coherent background knowledge representation. The exploration of documents is more effective. Hierarchies (extracted from the semantic networks) provide with a language and synthetic representation to be explored by the users to express their information need.

This paper shows that improving the effectivity of information retrieval by utilizing more and more sophisticated models grooves on inclusion of mechanisms reflecting and using information of semantic relations between concepts of language.

Text documents are most often a subject of retrieval, the complexity of human natural language, however, negatively affects the results of classic algorithms implemented in IR system. Retrieval methods are getting accommodated to identify semantic relations between word (i.e. relations between the meanings of words or the concepts they represent) and use this knowledge to compare and match documents with user's needs more accurately. Such knowledge is represented in structures like thesauri or semantic networks.

Thesauri or semantic networks can be created manually Unfortunately, it is a very time-consuming task and needs an involvement of expert knowledge. This paper reviews methods which allows to automatically extract mentioned knowledge – semantic relations between words – from a corpus of documents.

The above approach is supported by following arguments. Utilizing semantic relations improves the effectiveness of IR systems: they allow to increase the recall of retrieval by identifying potentially more relevant documents, and refining ranking functions has an impact on higher retrieval precision. Economic significance of such improvement has been described in previous subsection.

In turn, automated acquisition of semantic relations means a huge facilitation in creating structures representing language knowledge (as for example thesauri) which can be used in retrieval systems.

Special emphasis has been put on usefulness of presented methods in retrieval systems for flexile languages, especially Polish. High flexibility of such languages, meaning a multiplicity of word forms, is an additional difficulty for methods or algorithms which performance is satisfactory when working with less flexible languages.

19.1.3 Methodology

This paper is based on review of recent research and publications concerning especially the last five years. Within the author's research, some experiments were conducted including implementation of proposed methods and evaluation of results.

Evaluation was done on a corpus of 4 thousand documents, articles gathered from a news portal. Every document had its structure analyzed, the text was tokenized and the resulting words lemmatized. The procedure is described in detail in section 4.2.

19.2 Evolution of Information Retrieval Systems

Information retrieval may be characterized as systems which provide the user with documents that will best satisfy their need for information. Different approaches have been proposed in the literature to enhance system effectiveness, specifically methods to improve the document representation or matching documents with a query, for instance by query reformulation.

With regard to document representation which is a key point in IR a common solution is to choose significant sets of weighted terms. Several works have investigated a richer representation in order to get better query matching. Natural Language Processing (NLP) is one of the means that have been tested. An alternative way to go beyond "bags of words" could be to organize indexing terms into a more complex structure such as a hierarchy or an ontology. Texts would be indexed by concepts that reflect their meaning rather than words considered as chart lists with all the ambiguity that they convey.

In this section some information retrieval models have been presented with an aim to understand their evolution and emphasise a tendency of incorporating word semantics into retrieval algorithms. (Baeza-Yates and Ribeiro-Neto 1999)

A *Boolean model* is the most basic retrieval model. It is operated on set theory: set of documents returned by retrieval system is a conjunction of sets representing respective query words. Semantic knowledge, thus, cannot be used in Boolean model at all. Documents from library can either match the query or not – returned documents are not ranked or sorted in any way. Therefore, the Boolean model is the simplest, and on the other hand, the most primitive one.

A *ranking function* which orders a collection of documents by their probable relevance to a user query is introduced in *algebraic models* such as *vector space model* (VSM). Vector models are very common and create a base for further development.

Advantage of the VSM is the continuous ranking function which allows to fluent affection on precision and recall of IR system. Depending on assumed threshold, retrieval system can return more documents (what lifts up the recall but lowers the precision) or less documents (what means lower recall but higher precision). Therefore, recall and precision indicators, as well as the number of returned documents, can be easily controlled.

The main disadvantage of vector models is the presumption that the dimensions are orthogonal, that is the words are fully independent. Obviously, this is not the case when natural language is concerned.

The above restriction induces further evolution of IR. The main tendency observed in the alternative models involves possible interdependencies between terms and register them as semantic relations between concepts. That was not a case in basic models.

Fuzzy logic model operates on fuzzy sets theory, which rejects the restriction that an element must either belong to a given set or not. Fuzzy set theory permits the gradual assessment of the membership of elements: every element has a *membership function* which determines its degree of membership to a given set (Zadeh 1965). Fuzzy logic IR model rejects the constraint of Boolean logic model where term frequency in a documents has no influence on ranking function.

Another alternative retrieval model is *neural network* model. It uses a neural network with three layers: query layer, dictionary layer and document corpus layer. There are links between the second and third layer with weights. The weight represents frequency of the word occurring in the document. Signal from query terms is sent to second layer neurons, and then passes to document where it accumulates.

The backward propagation emulates hidden semantics which is not represented by simple term to document frequency. Especially the terms activated as a result of backward propagation can be semantically similar to query terms but are not explicitly included in the query. This effect causes a rise in retrieval recall and, providing good weighting, more precise result ranking.

Another retrieval model concerning hidden semantics is *Latent Semantic Indexing* (LSI). It is based on the VSM but reduces the number of dimensions in order to improve speed and effectivity. Its main task is to limit the number of dimensions by representing the documents as good as possible. In LSI term frequencies and co-occurrences are analyzed and the most similar words are merged into synthetic concepts. (Letsche and Berry 1996)

In the above short preview of retrieval models we can observe two different trends. The first is a tendency to improve a ranking function – it needs to be continuous and allow to control the effectivity of IR system fluently by exchanging recall and precision.

In the above evolution of IR it can be seen that the more sophisticated and effective model is, the more semantic knowledge it utilizes (Hotho et al. 2003). Particular models entertain relations between words, their co-occurrences and similarity. User queries can be expanded by lexically related words (Mandala et al. 1999).

That is why an idea of including semantic knowledge represented by such structures as thesauri or semantic networks is suggested. In the next section we will describe semantic knowledge representation. In section 5, on the other hand, several methods allowing to create these structures in an automated way are reviewed.

19.3 Representation of Semantic Knowledge

According to the introductory statement, natural language is a very complex system which needs to be represented in a way that would be understandable for computer systems. In this section some structures that can represent a part of semantic knowledge have been described.

From data processing point of view, words are strings of characters. These strings can be compared, and as a result – equal or different. There are some metrics characterizing the similarity between the strings of characters, like the Levenshtein distance which says how many characters have to be deleted, inserted or substituted to transform one string into another. But such indicators do not say about the similarity of concepts represented by words and do not, thus, reflect the complexity of language.

Some of main relations identified in natural language are described in the following subsection.

19.3.1 Word Relations

Two groups of word relations can be distinguished: collocations and lexical relations. The former is based on word co-occurrences and connection with their common meaning while the latter affects the concepts represented by words.

Collocation is a pair of words often occurring together in a text. The meaning of the word pair results from a sum of meanings or can be totally different as in the case of idiomatic expression. Collocations are statistical phenomenon which can be observed using statistical methods, and is tightly connected with word meanings.

Lexical relations between words reflect the interdependences between the concepts – meanings of the words. The most important lexical relations are described below.

Synonymy and *similarity* are the relations occurring between words with corresponding concepts that are equal or close near, respectively. Similarity can be graded as discrete or continuous value.

Antonymy is a relation occuring when word meanings are opposite.

Meronymy and *holonymy* occurs between words when concept represented by the first word is a part of a concept represented by the second word. *Meronym* is the word that represents a part of *holonym* – word that possesses the part.

Hypernymy and *hyponymy* express hierarchical relations between concepts. Hypernym is a word with broader meaning than a narrower hyponym. In other words, a concept of the hypernym is a superordinate of a hyponym's concept.

As in the case of similarity, the above relations can be weighted – their strength can be graded as a value, either discrete or continuous.

Identifying semantic relations, assembling information about the relations, and utilizing it to refine retrieval systems, streamlines the results of IR system, as stated before, has a rational impact on effectivity of activities based on appropriate information set.

19.3.2 Structures

Semantic knowledge, as identified semantic relations between words, should be stored in an appropriate data structure in order to be utilized to refine retrieval systems and their results.

Dictionary is a structure to start with. It does not contain the information about semantic relations but is only a vast set of words that serves as a base for further processing. Dictionary is a representation of words occurring in considered collection of text documents (document corpus). Depending on application, we can distinguish several types of dictionaries:

- dictionary of all words occurring in document corpus,
- dictionary of words typical for a given topic,
- dictionary of words of specific part of speech,
- defining dictionary (one-language dictionary),
- two-language dictionary (or multi-language),
- stoplist.

A particular dictionary is a frequency dictionary, which is a structure containing information about number or frequency of given words in document corpora. All kinds of dictionaries previously mentioned can be useful in text processing or acquiring semantic relations, what is described in section 4.

Structures described below include information of semantic relations in addition to the set of words. Some concepts from graph theory are used to characterize these structures: concepts are represented by graph nodes and arcs are semantic relations between concepts.

Taxonomy is a structure representing hierarchical relations between concepts or corresponding words. Taxonomies are common in sciences, used to organize domain terminology. Semantic relations included in taxonomy are hypernymy and hyponymy. In case of two concepts linked with such relations, the higher one in the hierarchy is a superordinate term for the second one (subordinate term).

Using graph theory terminology, a taxonomy is a rooted tree with distinguished root concept. The further from the root words are, the more specific concepts they represent. Analogically, the shorter path from root concept to a word is, the more general the word is.

A structure containing word similarity relations is called a *thesaurus*. Thesauri incorporate such lexical relations as synonymy and antonymy – as particular, opposite sorts of word similarity (identity in case of synonymy, reverse in case of antonymy). Thesauri are included into IRS mechanisms while they are getting more advanced and efficient, mainly to expand user queries, match and compare documents in a better way (Jing and Croft 1994).

Finally, a *semantic network* is a structure incorporating knowledge about all possible semantic relations between words. Semantic networks store information about similarity relations (like a thesaurus): word similarity, synonymy, antonymy; hierarchical relations (like a taxonomy): hypernymy or hyponymy and meronymy or holonymy relations. Semantic network can incorporate connotations as well – these are any other word associations.

Using the graph theory terminology, semantic networks can be represented as directed graphs. Direction is crucial in case of hierarchical relations. Edges between concepts can be weighted as well – in order to reflect strength of a relation.

Semantic networks are the most advanced structures representing semantic knowledge. That is why their utilization in information retrieval systems should bring the biggest improvement in their effectivity. The information included in semantic network can be used in order to limit the number of keywords to describe a document, expand user queries or identify concepts if a word represents more than one meaning.

19.4 Automated Acquisition of Semantic Relations

Use of information on semantic relations leads to an improvement of IR effectivity. The more relations in a structure the better usefulness for retrieval system. Building an extensive semantic network (or other structure) is, however, a complex and time consuming task.

Dictionary of domain keywords contains usually hundreds thousand words (biggest one – few millions of words). Then, relations are to be added: several links for each word resulting with thousands, or even millions relations.

Creating such a huge structure needs a lot of work and is nearly impossible. That is why automated methods can help – by acquiring semantic relations in textual documents and incorporating them into a structure as, for instance, semantic network.

In this section several methods allowing to automatically acquire semantic relations betweens words in a corpus of documents are being presented.

Some preconditions have been assumed. First, all documents are written in one language. Originally, most of methods were developed and evaluated for the English language. For purpose of this work presented methods were implemented and evaluated for the Polish language exemplifying one of highly flexible languages and generating some additional morphological problems. Second, the corpus of textual documents consists of documents concerning one domain. This condition limits the effect of homonymy – different meaning of one word. It is quite helpful and realistic since document corpora in business concern mainly one domain. On the other hand, there are methods allowing to specify a meaning of a word representing multiple concepts (Schuetze and Pedersen 1995).

19.4.1 Flexible Languages

Problems emerge when documents are written in highly flexible language. They are characterized by a multiplicity of forms of one word and complicated syntax.

In languages with simple word inflection (such as English) multiple forms of one word can be reduced to one term using *stemming algorithms*. The idea of such algorithms in mainly cropping word suffix, following defined rules. Stemming is relatively simple when the returned string is not necessarily a right word, only an unique identifier. A task of providing a word in basic form for a given word in any form is lemmatization.

Let's look at the inflection of the verb "lock" in order to compare the complexity of lemmatization task for English and highly flexible languages. In English, it has four forms: *lock, locks, locking, locked*. In Polish, the same word is "blokować", and the inflection of this word has 37 forms.

There are two ways of constructing a lemmatizing tool: dictionary or rule approach. The former is to build a dictionary of all word forms with links to their basic forms (*lemmas*). The latter is to define a set of rules by which word forms are reduced to their lemmas. The first approach is accurate providing that all words are present in the directory. The second approach finds lemma for every word, nevertheless, there is a possibility that the returned lemma is not a correct word.

The solution which joins the benefits of dictionary and algorithmic lemmatizer is a *hybrid lemmatizer* (Weiss 2005). Every given word is checked in a dictionary and, if any appropriate entry exists, lemma is returned. If there is no such word, rule methods are executed and lemma is derived.

Hybrid lemmatizer can find a lemma for every given word with small chance of returning wrong word.

19.4.2 Methods

In this subsection several methods allowing building a structure representing semantic knowledge are being described. As stated before, first step is to gather an appropriate set of words from document corpus representing a given domain.

Every document has its structure analyzed. Chapters, sections, and paragraphs are being detected at this point. Then, lexical analysis is executed – processing the text and splitting it into particular words. Words are split by detecting word separators – that is spaces, punctuation. Words are subject to lemmatization, to limit the effect of inflection, and *stopwords* (very frequent words without or with very small semantic importance – such as conjunctions) are removed from further analysis. After removing multiple word occurrences the result is a set of unique words in the whole corpus. (Frakes and Baeza-Yates 1992)

In algorithmic lemmatization tests (using two sets of words, counting over 70,000 and 130,000 words) the number of unique words (in many forms) was reduced by 65-75%, and most of the unrecognized words (about 15%) were in foreign language, erroneous or proper names.

At the phase of lexical analysis *collocations* can be detected. Collocation is a relationship between words that often occur together forming an expression and common concept. Automated acquisition of collocation is processed with statistical methods – every pair (or group) of words is counted and the resulting number is compared with frequencies of single words' occurrences. Is the relation of pair frequency to single words frequencies high, the pair is considered as a collocation. (Evert and Krenn 2001)

If a user query contains a collocation it should trigger searching the same collocation (with respect to word order) in documents in retrieval process as if the collocation were a single concept.

In a corpus of documents of a 2 million words size as an effect of computing frequencies of every pair of words, there were nearly 3,000 collocations occurring more than 10 times. The effectivity of finding a correct collocation was estimated 85%.

At this phase the set of words can be reduced to domain dictionary. This can be achieved by comparing word frequencies in two document corpora: one general and one domain. Words with higher frequency in domain corpus than in general corpus can be considered to be typical for the domain while words with similar frequencies are words used commonly in everyday language.

Main advantage of the above method is limiting the size of base dictionary and – in case of VSM – reducing the number of dimensions, which improves the algorithm speed.

Building domain dictionary by comparing word frequencies is very effective. In evaluation, an input dictionary (20,000 lemmas) was reduced close to 3,000 words typical to the domain given (and, therefore, most valuable for retrieval purposes) thanks to selecting words which relative frequency in domain document corpus (in comparison to frequency in general corpus) was higher than average.

Having a domain dictionary we can start acquiring semantic relations. First method, allowing to automatically acquire similarity relations, depends on word co-occurrences. The idea of this method, is to compute the correlation between occurrences of two words in one block of text (paragraph, section, sentence – provided by structure analysis).

A simple solution is used in LSI model which depends on computation of Pearson's correlation coefficient. More sophisticated approach assumes building a vector for every word. Here the dimensions represent documents and the weights correspond to importance of a respective word in a document (Qiu and Frei 1995). Comparing word vectors can be conducted with the same measures as in VSM, that is, for instance, cosine measure.

Another method uses conditional co-occurrence. Correlation coefficients are calculated for a pair of words by measuring frequency of the first word only in documents with the second word present. High conditional co-occurrence for a given pair of words can mean that the first word occurs nearly always when the second word is present. If the measure calculated for the same pair of words with reversed order (that is frequency of the second word in documents containing the first word) is low we can assume that the first word is a broader term than the second. That is, some kind of hierarchical relation between these words, particularly, the first word is a hypernym of the second word which is a hyponym. (Sanderson and Croft 1999)

In evaluation, 700 nouns from a given domain were selected and then conditional co-occurrence computed for every pair. Making two additional assumptions, that the probability of conditional co-occurrence must be above 70% and the pair of words must co-occur in minimum 0.5% of documents, over 400 relations were returned as a result. In this group 45% relations were correct pairs of hypernym-hyponym. Another 25% represent other semantic relations. Other relations were erroneous but contained a variety of proper names. It was estimated that by automated identification of proper names the effectivity of hierarchic relation acquisition method could reach 60-70%.

In order to automatically acquire synonymy relations the method based on a two-language directory has been proposed. It uses a feature of such dictionary to propose more than one translation to a given meaning. As a result, there are few words – synonyms – collected around one concept.

OpenThesaurus project is an implementation of the method (Naber 2004), and according to the developers, its accuracy reaches 90% while the rest is being corrected manually.

There is one more method allowing to automatically derive hierarchic relations. Similarly to the previous method, it uses dictionary (a one language, definitional dictionary in this case). This method builds *definitional sequences* – starting from any word (usually noun) it gets a definition of the word. The definition is then parsed and lexically analyzed to find the first noun in the definition. The method is based on an observation that the first noun in a definition of word is usually its hypernym (Hammerl and Sambor 1993).

Basing on the above property and making use of definitional dictionary, several semantic relations can be acquired in an automated way. As an evaluation, 700 words were used to determine their hypernyms automatically. The assumption that in case of multiple definitions only the first will be used, appeared. The accuracy of this method was estimated to 85%, which is a good result taking the assumption into account.

Acquiring semantic relations of virtually every type is possible using a method of detecting key phrases. It is based on an assumption that two words linked with a semantic relation in the text often occurs in proximity, are separated by a characteristic terms. For example, such phrases as "…, and other …", "… including …", "… such as …", "… is a part of …" indicate that the word before and the word after are semantically related (Hearst 1992; Koo et al. 2003).

The above method was developed and tested for the English language. However, when evaluated on highly flexible language, it performs poor. Search for 20 key phrases in document corpus resulted in about a hundred pairs of words. Three best phrases were found 60 times, showing correct relations in 50%.

In order to acquire hierarchic relations between terms, *formal concept analysis* was proposed (Cimiano et al. 2003). It utilizes an observation that most of verbs can be used together with objects having some specified features (for example "flyable", "fluid", "edible", "drivable"). Considering sets of such features, it is possible to build a hierarchy of objects: these, having more features, are broader terms (hypernyms) while the objects with less attributes are narrower terms (hyponyms).

In evaluation of all presented methods a polysemy effect was omitted. The methods, thus, could show higher effectivity than estimated. There is research on identifying concepts represented by homonyms and some methods allowing to determine which of the meanings is represented in a given document have been developed. The methods base mainly on context analysis – identifying characteristic, typical to respective meaning terms (Sanderson 1994).

19.5 Summary

Described methods of automated semantic relations acquisition have various performance. In the case of highly effective methods, such as: building a domain dictionary, finding collocations, identifying synonym groups or building definitional sequences, it is possible to gather relatively numerous semantic relations and incorporate them into semantic network or other structure.

Some methods, for instance conditional co-occurrence or key phrases method, perform not so well. They can, however, be still enhanced by improving their mechanisms, especially by taking such omitted effect like homonymy into account. Word sense ambiguity is important reason of IR performance decrease and is subject to further research.

Semantic knowledge, represented in a structure such as semantic network can be utilized to improve the effectivity of information retrieval systems as, for instance, by expanding user queries in order to refine the results, and, as shown in the introduction, the improvement of retrieval recall and precision, positively reflects on the profitability of information systems.

References

1. R. Baeza-Yates, B. Ribeiro-Neto, *Modern Information Retrieval*, ACM Press, Addison-Wesley Longman Publishing Co., New York 1999
2. P. Cimiano, S. Staab, J. Tane, *Deriving Concept Hierarchies from text by Smooth Formal Concept Analysis*, Karlsruhe 2003
3. M. C. Daconta, L. J. Obrst, K. T. Smith, *The Semantic Web: A Guide to the Future of XML, Web Services, and Knowledge Management*, John Wiley & Sons, 2003
4. S. Evert, B. Krenn, "Methods for the qualitative evaluation of lexical association measures", *39th Annual Meeting of the Association for Computational Linguistics*, Toulouse, 2001, http://www.collocations.de/AM/

5.   W. B. Frakes, R. Baeza-Yates, *Information Retrieval: Data Structures and Algorithms*, Prentice Hall, 1992

6.   M. A. Hearst, "Automatic Acquisition of Hyponyms from Large Text Corpora", *Proceedings of the Fourteenth International Conference on Computational Linguistics*, Nantes 1992

7.   R. Hammerl, J. Sambor, *O statystycznych prawach językowych*, Polskie Towarzystwo Semiotyczne, Warszawa 1993

8.   A. Hotho, A. Maedche, S. Staab, "Ontology-based Text Document Clustering", *Proceedings of the Conference on Intelligent Information Systems*, Zakopane, Physica/Springer, 2003

9.   Y. Jing, W. B. Croft, *An Association Thesaurus for Information Retrieval*, Amherst 1994

10.   S. O. Koo, S. Y. Lim, S. J. Lee, "Building an Ontology based on Hub Words for Information Retrieval", *IEEE/WIC International Conference on Web Intelligence*, Halifax 2003

11.   T. A. Letsche, M. W. Berry, „Large-Scale Information Retrieval with Latent Semantic Indexing", *Information Sciences – Applications*, 1996, http://www.cs.utk.edu/~berry/lsi++/

12.   R. Mandala, T. Toukunaga, H. Tanaka, "Combining Multiple Evidence from Different Types of Thesaurus for Query Expansion", *SIGIR'99*, ACM, Berkley 1999

13.   D. Naber, "OpenThesaurus: Building a Thesaurus with a Web Community", *OpenThesaurus*, 2004, http:// www.openthesaurus.de/

14.   Y. Qiu, H. Frei, *Improving the Retrieval Effectiveness by a Similarity Thesaurus*, Technical Report 225, Departament Informatik ETH Zürich, 1995

15.   M. Sanderson, "Word Sense Disambiguation and Information Retrieval", *Proceedings of the 17th International ACM SIGIR*, Dublin 1994

16.   M. Sanderson, B. Croft, "Deriving concept hierarchies from text", *SIGIR'99*, ACM, Berkley 1999

17.   H. Schütze, J. O. Pedersen, "Information Retrieval Based on Word Senses", *Proceedings of the 4th Annual Symposium on Document Analysis and Information Retrieval*, Las Vegas 1995

18.   D. Weiss, *Stempelator: A Hybrid Stemmer for the Polish Language*, Technical Report RA-002/05, Politechnika Poznańska, 2005

19.   D. Yarowsky, "Word-Sense Disambiguation Using Statistical Models of Roget's Categories Trained on Large Corpora", *Proceedings of COLING-92*, Nantes 1992

20.   L. A. Zadeh, "Fuzzy sets", *Information and Control* 8, 1965

20 Analysis of Query Logs of the Library Catalogues in the Internet Network

Kazimierz Choroś[1], Justyna Kowalska[2], Izydor Statkiewicz[3]

[1] Wroclaw University of Technology, Institute of Applied Informatics,
Wyb. S. Wyspianskiego 27, 50-370 Wroclaw, Poland
Kazimierz.Choros@pwr.wroc.pl

[2] Justyna Kowalska {dronka@poczta.fm}

[3] Wroclaw University of Technology, Main Library and Scientific Information Centre,
Wyb. S. Wyspianskiego 27, 50-370 Wroclaw, Poland
Izydor.Statkiewicz@pwr.wroc.pl

20.1 Introduction

The library catalogue is an index describing books, journals, reports etc. stored in the library. The library call numbers of the books and the positions of the books in a library store are very important for users and librarians. Such an index is very useful in an effective retrieval of relevant items in the library. The usefulness of the index is much higher if it is accessible in the Internet network.

The library Internet catalogues are accessible on the Web site of the library [2, 13, 14]. In general the user has no need to learn how to use it. The information retrieval languages of these catalogues are very simple and intuitive, frequently offering the pre-formulated query forms helping the definition of a user query reflecting potential user needs. On the other hand, the theory of information retrieval systems is generally based on the Boolean expressions of index terms using alternation, conjunction, and negation operators [4, 5, 10, 11, 12]. So, to help the user to define a query in the form of a Boolean expression the systems also offer extended retrieval methods based on the pre prepared sheets which enable the user to express his information needs by logical formula even unconsciously. The examination of the user behaviour using electronic catalogues in the Internet network is one of the most important duties of system designers and administrators [1].

229

W. Abramowicz and H.C. Mayr (eds.), Technologies for Business Information Systems, 229–240.
© 2007 *Springer.*

20.2 Search queries

Wroclaw University of Technology employs more than 2,000 academics who teach about 32,000 students at 12 faculties. The electronic library catalogues [7] started to operate in the Internet network in November 1995 and during next 7 years all information on user queries was gathered. Not only the query text was stored in system logs but also the time of its admitting and the IP number of the user's computer, etc. Because in 2003 a new catalogue system was installed, the comparative results come from the years 1996-2002. The transaction logs are one of the most effective sources of the information on user behaviour and activity [6].

20.2.1 Number of queries

Table 1 and Figure 1 present the dynamic growth of the number of user queries.

Table 1. Number of queries per year

Year	Number of queries
1996	15,230
1997	24,438
1998	38,500
1999	52,303
2000	79,393
2001	154,138
2002	15,230

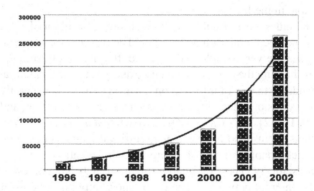

Fig. 1. Growing tendency of the number of queries

Table 2. Number of queries to a given catalogue

Catalogue	Number of queries	[%]
Books	433,314	57.89
Scientific papers WUT	153,625	20.52
Journals	87,658	11.71
Fiction books	29,956	4.00
Foreign Periodicals in Wroclaw and Opole Libraries	29,287	3.91
Electronic documents	14,645	1.96

The most popular catalogue is of course the catalogue of books, next the catalogue of the scientific papers of Wroclaw University of Technology, then the catalogue of journals (Table 2).

20.2.2 Boolean operators and parentheses

Table 3 shows that when the number of queries was increasing the use of Boolean operators was changing mainly due to the designing of pre-formulated query forms facilitating the user to express a query in the form of a Boolean expression.

Table 3. Number of queries using Boolean operators per year

Year	AND		OR		NOT		Any operator and parentheses	
	Number	[%]	Number	[%]	Number	[%]	Number	[%]
1996	7,863	51.63	301	1.98	22	0.14	275	1.81
1997	8,172	33.44	622	2.55	122	0.50	289	1.18
1998	11,705	30.40	430	1.12	96	0.25	189	0.49
1999	16,709	31.95	687	1.31	193	0.37	287	0.55
2000	13,916	17.53	4,575	5.76	558	0.70	1,005	1.27
2001	67,449	43.76	4,267	2.77	314	0.20	25,424	16.49
2002	137,385	52.87	1,982	0.76	130	0.05	18,233	7.02

The use of the negation is extremely rare. We observe that this operator, which is in general the most difficult to design and to implement in a real system, is practically not used. It may be surprising that the Boolean expressions with parentheses are used, so we cannot say that users do not formulate complex queries, although, the use of more complex queries which was leading to the application of parentheses, is not very important. It confirms the observations made for other systems [4, 5, 11].

The catalogue of the scientific papers is the one which was searched in the most sophisticated way. In Table 4 we present the percentage of simple and extended queries. Some queries expressed on a specific sheet concerning ID number were not analysed as well as those generated by external search engines. We observed that users searching in the catalogue of the scientific papers of Wroclaw University of Technology are more willing to formulate their queries in the form of complex Boolean expressions, whereas the users of the most popular catalogue of books have expressed their needs rather in a very simple way.

Table 4. Number of simple queries and extended queries in each catalogue

Catalogue	Simple Queries	[%]	Extended Queries	[%]
Books	417,731	96.6	8,622	2.0
Scientific papers WUT	93,622	61.0	37,932	24.7
Journals	75,559	86.3	10,332	11.8
Fiction books	26,540	88.7	3,085	10.3
Foreign Periodicals in Wroclaw and Opole Libraries	25,281	86.5	3,049	10.4
Electronic documents	11,971	81.8	1,733	11.8

20.2.3 Character mask technique

Table 5 contains the number of queries in which the technique of character masking of the end of search terms was used to match variant spellings. Such a technique was mainly used in search queries submitted to the catalogue of journals.

Table 5. Number of queries using character masks submitted to a given catalogue

Catalogue	Number of queries using search masks	[%]
Books	20,996	4.8
Scientific papers WUT	4,585	3.0
Journals	5,740	6.5
Fiction books	612	2.0
Foreign Periodicals in Wroclaw and Opole Libraries	2,132	0.7
Electronic documents	613	4.2

Rather very low number (less than 1%) of queries using character masks, submitted to the catalogue of foreign periodicals surely results from the low importance of mask technique in a case of non-flexible natural languages.

The number of queries using masks was growing (Table 6, but relatively such a technique becomes less popular. It seems to be caused by the fact that pre-formulated

Table 6. Numbers of queries using character masks in the years 1996-2002

Year	Number of queries with masks	[%]
1996	1,720	11.29
1997	2,019	8.26
1998	1,935	5.03
1999	2,382	4.55
2000	5,271	6.64
2001	8,365	5.43
2002	9,055	3.48

query forms offered on the Web site of the Internet library catalogues do not stimulate the technique of masking. And also the most popular search engines which create standards of search queries do not offer character masks. In consequence masking techniques become rather too specific.

The most complex queries with masks as well as parentheses and Boolean operators found in the transaction logs were as follows:

((obraz$+image$)*(przetw$+kompr$))

ˆ(rozpoznawanie+akustyk$+opty$)

(obraz$*przetwarz$+(picture$+image$)*compress$)

ˆ(akust$+(zastosowanie+rozpoznawanie))

(informator$+turysty$+przewodnik$)*(Beskid$+Karpat$+Podkarpac$)

ˆ map$

where + * ˆ stand for the alternation, conjunction and negation respectively, and the symbol $ was used for the character mask operator.

20.2.4 Specific data fields of catalogues

Next, we examined which data fields were the most attractive for users besides the obligatory title index. It is obvious that in the catalogue of books the most frequently used query was specified by an index search term expressed by an author name, whereas the second was neither the author's first name nor the call number as we expected, but the language (Table 7).

The most frequent additional search criterion used in the queries submitted to the catalogue of journals (Table 8) were terms concerning the language of journals. The number of misused criteria, inadequate for a given catalogue, is rather surprisingly high showing that users acted mechanically using specific criteria adequate for other catalogues.

Table 7. Number of queries to specific data fields of the book catalogue

Field	Content	Number of queries
an:	Author name	153,950
je:	Language	43,178
ai:	Author first name	22,923
au:	Author	15,143
sy:, sg:	Call number	10,721
rw:	Publication year	7,841
hp:	Subject term	1,428
ib:	ISBN	924
nw:	Editor	714
kr:	Country	417
other		1,638
errors:		
ae:	Author ID	393

Table 8. Number of queries to specific data fields of the journal catalogue

Field	Content	Number of queries
je:	Language	14,337
sx:	Signature	5,447
kl:	Subject classification	4,173
ed:	Electronic version	3,319
nw:	Editor	2,597
sg:	Status	1,783
is:	ISSN	1,233
kr:	Country	86
es:	Electronic version	40
sn:	Type of acquisition	27
other		1,491
errors:		
an:	Author name	1,366
ai:	Author first name	120
ae:	Author ID	74
hp:	Subject term	42
au:	Author	29

20.3 Pre-formulated query forms

When the electronic catalogues started to operate in the Internet network the users of the catalogues formulated their queries in a form of a Boolean expression without any suggestions and help. To submit a Boolean query the user was obliged to know Boolean logic as well as the formal representation of the Boolean query in the catalogues. The only help was a single and simple example of an incorrect and a simple example of a correct query in a form of a complex Boolean expression. Such a solution led to many difficulties in formulating a Boolean query, mainly for not trained users.

After few months pre-formulated query forms have been designed and implemented on the Web site of the catalogues. The pre-formulated query form is interpreted to an adequate Boolean expression, even if the user did not directly used a Boolean operator.

20.4 User Sessions

A user session is generally defined [3, 10] as a sequence of queries of a single user formulated in one search. Sessions have been recognized as a series of queries sent from the same computer, identified by the computer IP number and sent in a given time interval. We used only one criterion, time criterion to recognize the sessions, we did not analyse the change of terms used in a series of queries, although we defined such a situation as a kind of user strategy in a query refinement process.

To recognize the characteristics of the user sessions the queries presented in 2001 to the library catalogue have been examined. For every query the time between the query and the previous one was calculated if both queries were sent from the same computer. These two queries were treated as two queries of the same session if this time did not exceed a given threshold. The total time of a session has been then calculated, as well as the number of queries in one session. In the set of queries from 2001 only 6,175 sessions were recognized because the additional restriction was taken into account, the session could not last more than 3 hours. It reduced the number of session by half. The majority of long sessions were the sessions of a library service. The library workers also accessed the library catalogue in the Internet network for their internal librarian purposes and their connections lasted generally more than 10 hours a day, because the library was functioning from 8 am. to 8 pm.

The average time of a single session was 10.7 minutes. Most of them were rather short, less than 5 minutes. The diagram in Figure 2 presents the distribution of time of the user sessions. The diagram shows that the majority of the sessions were very short, 1-2 minutes, or even less than one minute. In such a short time a user is able to formulate only one short query, rather simple query expressed by a single term and then to book an item. To reformulate a query or to examine the search result much more time is needed.

Number of user sessions

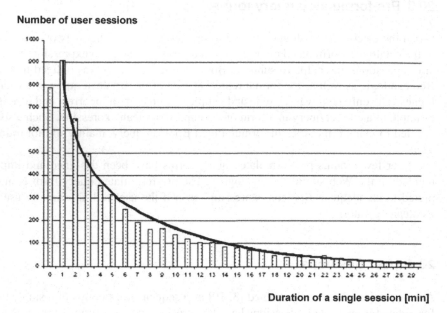

Duration of a single session [min]

Fig. 2. The distribution of the time of a single user session

The period of 10 minutes seems to be enough to make a search, examine the results and in consequence to book a retrieved item. Such sessions of about 10 minutes are 74.1% of the whole number of recognized sessions. Only 17.5% of sessions lasted longer than 15 minutes (and less than 3 hours).

The diagram in Figure 3 presents the distribution of the number of queries in a single user session. The average number of queries in a single session was 3.76. So, the average user formulates more than one query in one session. It rises a question what the strategy of formulating this sequence is.

Only in 16% of sessions we observed queries submitted to more than one catalogue (Table 9). The conclusion is that some users tried to improve their results by consulting several library catalogues.

20.5 User Strategies

Two strategies can be defined in a user behaviour: contraction strategy, i.e. the strategy leading to a more specific query, and expansion strategy, i.e. the strategy leading to a more general query. An expansion strategy, a rather rare strategy, is generally

Number of user sessions

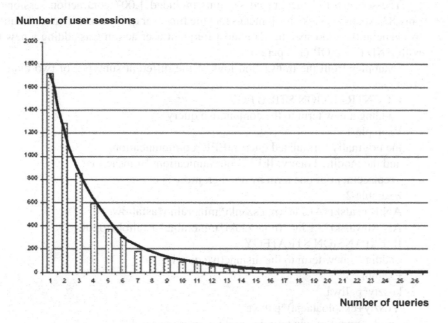

Number of queries

Fig. 3. The distribution of the number of queries in a single user session

Table 9. Number of library catalogues accessed in one session

Number of Library Catalogues	Number of Sessions	[%]
1	5,014	83.93
2	652	10.91
3	214	3.58
4	63	1.05
5	25	0.42
6	6	0.10

achieved by adding a new term to a disjunctive query. On the other hand, the contraction strategy, which was much more frequently undertaken, was observed when the user received too many items in a system response, in which case to limit the result number, the user adds a new search term to the query. But in this case the added term was in conjunction with previous terms. Unfortunately in many cases it led to a zero response. The conjunction is a very restrictive Boolean operator.

The set of 6,175 recognized sessions included 1,007 contraction sessions and only 83 expansion sessions. It means that the first user query is much more frequently too general than too specific. The most frequent user action was adding a new term with AND (*) or OR (+) operators.

Examples from the transaction logs of the different subtypes of two main user strategies:

I. CONTRACTION STRATEGY
- adding a new term to the conjunctive query
Example 1:
the originally formulated query: IEEE*communications
and the modified query: IEEE*communications*transactions
- replacement of one term by another, more specific
Example 2:
AN:Kowalski*AI:Jan*(mieszanki*mineralno*asfaltowe)
AN:Kowalski*AI:Jan*(mieszanki*mineralne*asfaltobetonowe)
II. EXPANSION STRATEGY
- adding a new term to the disjunctive query
Example 3:
koszty*paliwa
(koszty+eksploatacja)*paliwa
- replacement of one term by another, more general
Example 4:
AN:Nowak*AI:Piotr*plane
AN:Nowak*AI:Piotr*transport
The other observed actions of the users are:
- adding the category (an - author name in the example) of a search term
Example 5:
Nowak*Piotr
an:Nowak*Piotr
- auto correction of an spelling error
Example 6:
iinformation*retrieval*system
information*retrieval*system

20.6 Conclusions

The performed and presented analyses based on the examination of the transaction logs are objective as opposed to results received from for example subjective questionnaires.

Internet library catalogues are very useful for every user. The user expects the maximum of simplicity in the information retrieval language applied in the catalogue. The user tends to formulate a rather simple query, although the user being not satisfied by the system response is capable to continue his search by reformulating several times his initial query. It seems to be reasonable to maintain several specific library catalogues, because the way the user formulates the query depends on the specificity of a catalogue, although the user expects the same intuition in different catalogue retrieval languages. If not, the user can make mistakes in formulated queries using wrong data fields not adequate for a given catalogue.

The user is satisfied if the system does not force him to use complex Boolean expressions, then if he does not have to know the exact orthography of the search term, and he can use character mask techniques or browsing indexes, and finally if the ranking of the retrieved items is adequate to their relevance. It also leads to the conclusion that users should be better trained in using computer catalogues in the library. It seems that more training is necessary for users in Boolean query formulations because not all the opportunities of the computer catalogues are applied. For example, the negation operator is practically not used, although its usefulness in a query formulation cannot be denied. Also electronic help or electronic interactive assistance could be very useful in suggesting the adequate strategy in a given situation, mainly in a case the user received the empty response or the response is very large. The future solution may be an automatic enhancing of a user query as it has been proposed in [9]. The dominant role of a conjunction operator in user queries does not mean that this operator is well-known and preferred by the users. Rather, it is due to the application of pre-formulated retrieval sheets. The criteria proposed on these sheets are mostly in conjunction relations.

The information about the user behaviour gathered in the system logs during the functioning of the system is very useful not only in the controlling process but also in elaborating the system pre-formulated query forms used to facilitate the user in expressing the search query.

References

1. Browne S V, Moore J W (1996) Reuse Library Interoperability and World Wide Web, http://www.netlib.org/srwn/srwn20.ps
2. France R K, Terry N L, Fox E A, Saad R A, Zhao J (1999) Use and Usability in a Digital Library Search System, www.dlib.vt.edu/Papers/Use_usability.PDF
3. He D, Gker A, Harper D J (2002) Combining evidence for automatic Web session identification. Information Processing and Management 38:727-742
4. Jansen B J (2000) An investigation into the use of simple queries on Web IR systems Information Research. An Electronic Journal 6(1), http://jimjansen.tripod.com/academic/pubs/ir2000/ir2000.pdf
5. Jansen B J, Spink A, Saracevic T (2000) Real life, real users, and real needs: a study and analysis of user queries on the web. Information Processing and Management 36:207-227
6. Jones S, Cunningham S J, McNab R, Boddie S (2000) A transaction log analysis of a digital library. International Journal on Digital Libraries 3:152-169

7. Klesta D, Statkiewicz I (2000) Komputerowy zintegrowany system biblioteczny APIN. Elektroniczny Biuletyn Informacyjny Bibliotekarzy EBIB 10 (in Polish), http://www.oss.wroc.pl/biuletyn/ebib10/apin.html

8. Park S, Lee J H, Bae H J (2005) End user searching: A Web log analysis of NAVER, a Korean search engine. Library & Information Science Research 27:203-221

9. Poo D C C, Toh T-K, Khoo C S G (2000) Enhancing online catalog searches with an electronic referencer. Journal of Systems and Software 55:203-219

10. Silverstein C, Marais H, Henzinger M, Moricz M (1999) Analysis of a very large Web search engine query log. SIGIR Forum 33(1):6-12

11. Spink A, Cenk O H (2002) Characteristics of question format web queries: an exploratory study. Information Processing and Management 38:453-471

12. Topi H, Lucas W (2005) Mix and match: combining terms and operators for successful Web searches. Information Processing and Management 41:801-817

13. Warren P (2001) Why they still cannot use their library catalogues. Informing Science Conference, http://proceedings.informingscience.org/IS2001Proceedings/pdf/WarrenEBKWhy.pdf

14. Witten I, Cunningham S J, Rodgers B, McNab R, Boddie S (1998) Distributing Digital Libraries on the Web, CD-ROMs, and Intranets: Same information, same look-and-feel, different media. First Asia Digital Library Workshop, The University of Hong Kong, http://www.cs.waikato.ac.nz/~ihw/papers/98IHW-SJC-WR-RM-SB-Distribt.pdf

21 Business Process Retrieval of Company Policies

Jon Espen Ingvaldsen, Tarjei Lægreid, Paul Christian Sandal, Jon Atle Gulla

Norwegian University of Science and Technology
Department of Computer and Information Science
{jonespi, tarjei, paulchr, jag}@idi.ntnu.no

21.1 Introduction

In large enterprise architecture solutions corporate policies, operations, and standards are commonly described by use of graphical business process descriptions and textual governing documents. These documents are usually lengthy, and not specific to particular tasks or processes, and the user is left to read through a substantial amount of irrelevant text to find the fragments that are relevant for the execution of a specific activity. Since the users tend to use the process models as a guide in their daily work, it is often desirable to start with the activity in the process model and automatically retrieve the parts of the governing documents that pertain this activity.

Even though they document the same domain, the existence of both governing documents and graphical business process models are necessary. The expressiveness of business process models can not eliminate the importance of governing documents. Similarly, the importance of business process models can not be eliminated by giving governing documents a process oriented structure. The challenge is to find methods that enable:

1. Content consistency between the two information sources
2. Retrieval of information across both representation formats.

In this work, three different text mining approaches (Laten Semantic Indexing, Association Rules, and document expansion using WordNet) are applied to establish links between business process model elements and relevant parts of governing documents.

The techniques are thoroughly studied and implanted. The approaches are evaluated based on available documents and accompanying model fragments covering the Procurement & Logistics (P&L) area in Statoil ASA.

W. Abramowicz and H.C. Mayr (eds.), Technologies for Business Information Systems, 241–252.
© 2007 *Springer.*

The evaluation of our results indicates that the information retrieval approach to integration has potential. Of the text mining techniques under evaluation, Latent Semantic Indexing (LSI) gives the most promising results, but both this and the other techniques should be more thoroughly evaluated in a continuation of this work.

21.2 Statoil ASA

Statoil is an integrated oil and gas company with more than 25 000 employees and activities in 31 countries. The group is operator for 60 percent of all Norwegian oil and gas production. Statoil is also a major supplier of natural gas in the European market and has substantial industrial operations.

21.2.1 Business Process Model

As a tool to help managing complexity Statoil started to document the different business processes of their enterprise. The main purpose of this initiative is to change their established functional view of the enterprise areas into business processes, as part of an enterprise architecture plan for the corporation. The Statoil Business Process Model (BPM) is used to document relations between business processes, information and IT systems.

Information in Statoil is stored in a number of different systems and formats, which complicates communication between knowledge databases. This further motivates for removing redundancy in an attempt to improve the information flow between systems and databases. The aim is to have relevant information available at the right time and place in a simple way.

BPM is a top-down hierarchical model of the Statoil enterprise. At each level business processes are described by graphical business process models and related governing documents. A screenshot of the BPM showing both a graphical business process model and links to related governing documents is shown in figure 1. The graphical business process models visualize subsequent and aggregated processes / activities, involved resources (documents), events and decision points.

The governing documents are related to the graphical business process models through hyperlinks in the BPM. While the graphical models give a nice overview of the business processes in the BPM, the governing documents contains all the information (guidelines, procedures, descriptions, etc.) that are necessary for successful process execution.

Today, elements in the graphical business process models are manually related to relevant governing documents. For each process, a list of relevant governing documents is maintained. As governing documents are lengthy, include formally structured bodies of text and describe issues that are not directly relevant for the execution of specific business activities, it is in many cases bothersome to locate the fractions of text that are of importance. The links point from the graphical models to whole documents and no indication of where in the document the relevant part(s) occur is given.

Further the linking is only one-way. There are no links from the documents to the graphical models.

The BPM is not yet completed with all models and descriptions, but it is required that all business process and workflow models shall be documented in the BPM system. The vision of the BPM is that all tools, documents, descriptions, information, etc. need to carry out an activity shall be maid available from the BPM by just clicking on the activity in the graphical models.

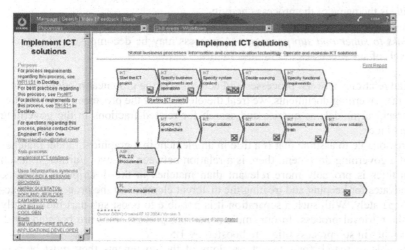

Fig. 1. A screenshot of the BPM system that shows a decomposed view of the "Implement ICT solutions" process, which is part of the main process "Information and communication technology". A description, including reference to three governing documents, for the "Implement ICT solutions" process is displayed on the left side of the figure

21.2.2 Case Study

In our work we were granted access to ten governing documents in English with related graphical business process models, all dealing with the P&L area. Independent of hierarchy levels, the content of the governing documents is structured into sections, subsections, and paragraphs. All sections and subsections contain a heading and one or more paragraphs. On the average, a governing document contains 3 792 words, 32 sections / subsections, and 160 paragraphs. In addition a few paragraphs have their own heading as well. The lengths of the different sections vary. The content is mainly pure text and point-lists, in some cases supplied with figures.

21.3 Implementation

To be able to evaluate text mining techniques for dynamic linking, a test framework has been implemented. The framework is based Lucene, which is an open source

Application Programming Interface (API) released by the Apache Software Foundation. The API contains a search engine, which offers services for text indexing and text searching.

The graphical business process models in the BPM are encoded in HTML and to be able to extract information from these models both parsing and preprocessing were necessary. The process and the activities in the models consist of three key elements which we make use of in the indexing and result ranking. That is:

1. *Title* is the name of the process / activity.
2. *Description* is a short natural language written explanation of the process.
3. *Links to super and sub processes.* A process may be decomposed into several levels of sub processes.

To find relations between processes and activities in the graphical models and sections in the governing documents, we treat the elements of the processes and activities in the graphical models as queries and search for related fractions in the governing document index.

It is reasonable to assume that if a title in an element in a graphical model matches a title of a governing document, there is a relation between the two. Further, a match between titles is probably more relevant than matches in the description contents. This motivates for keeping and treating the different elements of the processes and activities separately. With such a separation it is possible to boost sub part individually during the retrieval process. In our implementation, process titles are boosted by 2, while matches in sub process titles are boosted by 1.5.

To be able to search for relevant fractions of the documents they must be segmented prior to indexing. The governing documents related to Statoils BPM system have a common overall structure and it is reasonable to expect that the structure reflects the semantic content to some extent, and thus the explicit structure can be used as a basis for fragmentation. Each fraction of the original documents is considered as a new self-contained document with title and text. Finally, these documents are indexed by removing stop words, stemming, transforming the documents into inverted files, and storing the inverted files in the index. The inverted files are weighted by the tf-idf weighting scheme.

21.3.1 Latent Semantic Indexing

The vector space model is based on the assumption that the same terms occur in both the query and the relevant document [2]. However, in natural language texts it is common to use different terms for describing the same concepts. In an attempt to reduce this problem we have implemented a variation of LSI.

The Lucene API offers a simple way to extract the term-document frequency matrices for each indexed field. We extract the title and text fields from all documents and create one term document matrix. The term-document matrix is decomposed into three matrices by Singular Value Decomposition (SVD). The central idea is to let a matrix A represent the noisy signal, compute the SVD, and then discard small singular values of A. It can be shown that the small singular values mainly represent the noise, and thus the rank-k matrix A_k represents a filtered signal with less noise. The SVD has a variety of applications in scientific computing, signal processing, automatic control, and many other areas [6][7]. By first applying SVD, the dimensionality of our term-document matrix was reduced to from 349 to 50.

Optimally the resulting LSI-matrix should replace the original index in Lucene. This has proven to be difficult, since present and official versions of the Lucene API lack functionality for creating own indices. As an attempt to approximate the effects imposed by LSI, we instead create new pseudo documents. This is done by multiplying cells in the LSI-matrix by a constant factor to simulate term frequencies. Each term in the LSI-matrix is then added to the pseudo document the number of times it is simulated to occur. This is done for all positive values in the matrix.

These new pseudo documents, with term frequencies reflecting the LSI matrix, are then finally indexed by Lucene. The LSI process is visualized in figure 2.

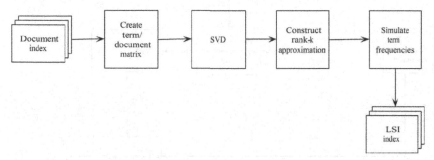

Fig. 2. Set up of the term/document matrix. Each document is a document segment from a governing document. In the created matrix, each cell corresponds to the frequency of the term in the corresponding segment. When the matrix is created, the frequencies of the title and its corresponding text are combined, e.g. a document containing the title "my title" and text "my text", then the corresponding frequencies are "my 2", "title 1", "text 1"

21.3.2 Association Rules

Our implementation of association rules mining is aimed at utilizing rules for query expansion. Since process descriptions in the graphical business process models tend to be short, a direct consequence is sparse query-vectors. Fewer words to specify the process, means fewer words to match for relevance in the document index.

If one could augment the query vector based on effective association rules, i.e. rules reflecting semantic associations in the domain of discourse, the probability of a more correct ranking could be increased and one could even get matches in documents lacking the words in the original query.

A general problem when mining text is the high number and varying quality of the extracted rules [8]. Even though the amount of rules can be limited by adjusting thresholds, the element of "random rules" is not reduced. As an attempt to limit these side effects, two main adjustments from straightforward mining in the original documents are done. First we investigate the use of sections/paragraphs (segments) as units (transactions) instead of mining whole documents.

The underlying assumption is that words occurring close to each other in a document are more likely to be somewhat related than words co-occuring at longer distance. Second we perform part-of-speech tagging and execute the association-rule algorithm on reduced text containing only nouns alone, assuming that associations between nouns have a higher probability of reflecting semantic relations than associations between other/different classes of words [12].

Our implementation is based on the Frequent Pattern Tree algorithm as it is set forth by [5], and we refer to their article for a detailed description of the algorithm.

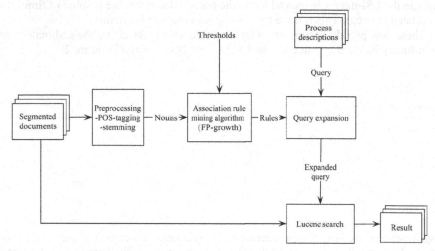

Fig. 3. Setup of the association rules implementation

Our utilization of the extracted association rules is illustrated in figure 3. The text of each section is then run through a part of speech tagger to extract the nouns. The tagger used is a stochastic tagger called QTAG and is implemented by Oliver Mason, University of Birmingham. Before the nouns are fed into the association rule algorithm they are stemmed. The mining algorithm takes as input the segments along with user-defined thresholds. To be regarded a frequent pattern, words must co-occur at a frequency within the range indicated by the thresholds. The output of the algorithm is a set of frequent patterns, or association rules. These are then used for query expansion. That is, during search all the words in the original query are looked up in the set of rules. If a word is found, the query is expanded by the associated word(s). Finally the expanded query is fed into Lucene and the search is executed.

21.3.3 Synonym and Hypernym Expansion

Equal concepts may be represented by different terms in the BPM processes and the governing documents. The two latter techniques aim at limit this problem. However, the assumption underlying these methods is that related terms co-occur more often than by chance. This is not always the case.

As an alternative we have implemented an approach that expands the document nouns with synonyms and hypernyms from the WordNet lexical database. Synonyms are concepts that have exactly the same meaning, while hypernyms are concepts (nouns) in a "is-a" relation (A is a *hypernym* of B if A is *a* (kind of) B) [10].

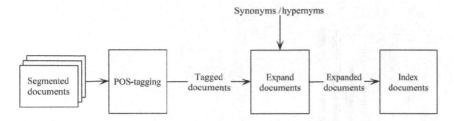

Fig. 4. Expansion of noun synonyms and hypernyms from WordNet

The term expansion is done before the governing documents are indexed. The prototype setup of the expansion is illustrated in figure 4. The following sequence is applied:

1. The documents are part-of-speech tagged to recognize nouns.
2. Each noun is looked up in WordNet, and synonym and hypernym are retrieved.
3. The documents are extended and indexed.

To test the various alternatives we create three separate indices; two for synonyms and hypernyms exclusively and one where both synonyms and hypernyms are included.

21.4 Evaluation of Results

In our evaluation we used plain Lucene search as a baseline for comparisons. Each technique is evaluated by reviewing the top five ranked items in the result sets. Seven processes from the BPM forms the test data. A Statoil employee familiar with the processes has reviewed the result sets accompanying each process and assigned scores to the result set items according to his opinion of relevance.

The scores $S_{d, expert}$ spans from 1 to 5 where 5 is most relevant. Several segments can be assigned with the same score if they are found equally relevant to the process. To make the comparison explicit we have combined his feedback with the results of the techniques. To do this we use the rank of the five topmost relevant segments of each technique and give them scores $S_{d,technique}$. The most relevant segment gets the score 5, the second gets 4, and so on. We then calculate a combined score by accumulating the scores of the top five fractions of each technique. To make the comparisons explicit we have combined his feedback with the results of the techniques.

Figure 5 shows the computed scores of each of the techniques. The first thing that should be noticed is the variance in score between the processes. This reflects the variation in the feedback from the domain expert. In fact, for process 7 none of the fractions were judged as relevant, and naturally all techniques come out with the score 0. Likewise among the fractions of process 6, only two were found relevant limiting the size of the computed score.

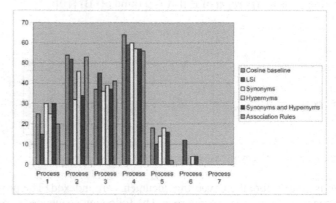

Fig. 5. The accumulated evaluation scores

On the contrary, for the processes 2-4 more than eight fractions were judged relevant, making possible higher scores. The cosine baseline generally seems to perform well, and when considering the processes as a whole no technique can be said to consistently outperform it. Neither is there any consistent pattern in what is the best technique when disregarding the baseline. If we look at the results on a per process basis, the cosine baseline is outperformed in processes 1, 3 and 6. The difference is most clear for process 3 and 6, both with the LSI implementation as the technique with the highest score.

Precision is defined as the proportion of the retrieved documents which are considered as relevant [2]. Figure 6 shows the precision of the top five fractions of each technique (i.e. percentage of the fractions also judged as relevant by the expert). Again we see that the cosine baseline performs well compared to the other techniques, and that none of the techniques consistently do better than the others. Further, the results conform well to figure 5 in that the processes with high average precision (i.e. processes 2-4) also have high average score.

Even though the extent of these evaluations is not adequate to draw any final conclusions, the following observations can be made:

The ability to find relevant information varies from process to process. Some result sets contain highly relevant fractions while others have a total lack of relevant information. Possible explanations are defective techniques, unsuitable process descriptions and lack of documents covering the process.

- None of the implemented techniques seem to consistently outperform the baseline. In defence of the techniques it should be stressed that there are several possibilities of optimization that may lead to better results.
- The main effect of applying document expansion techniques (synonyms, hypernyms and combination) seems to be an alternation of the order and not the

contents of the baseline results. This alternation generally seems to reduce the relevance scores compared to the baseline.

- The association rule technique has the most unstable effects of the techniques.
- The LSI implementation is the technique with result sets most different (low overlap) from the baseline. For some processes this gives LSI better results than the other techniques. This may indicate that LSI is capable of identifying relevant information not found by the others in particular cases.

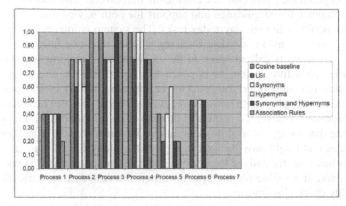

Fig. 7. The precision of the top five rank

21.5 Discussion

The results described in the previous section can be influenced and improved by several factors. The choice of number of dimensions after the SVD operation and number of included association rules are two factors that affect the result.

Another potential for improved retrieval is to make further use of existing business process model information. In the existing implementation, only the hierarchical relationships between aggregated process elements are exploited when the queries are extracted. Here, we could also make extensive use of other flow relationships, like control and resource flow. It is reasonable to believe that two subsequent model elements are somewhat related to the same domain and descriptive governing documents. Such subsequent relationships can be subsequent activities or processes relationships to resources, events and decision points.

In web based search engine solutions the ability to show all relevant documents is neither required nor feasible. Taken into account that the governing documents and the graphical business process models are business critical, it is of major importance that all information that is found to be relevant for a given business process or activity is included in the result set and shown to the user. [9] presents one alternative way of displaying relevant information on the governing documents by use of expansive sections and colour coding for visualization of relevance estimates.

21.6 Related Work

There exist several attempts to integrate some kind of business process models with underlying knowledge contained in documents, or other sources of information. These efforts show that there are several approaches for such integration. The objective of most attempts is to utilize the models to enable user-support through automatic delivery of relevant information.

EULE [11] is a implemented process-aware retrieval framework. The motivation here is to provide computer-based guidance and support for both novice and experienced office workers performing their day-today tasks. The system is integrated with the repository of the corporations' knowledge. Such repositories might be fully or partially computerized. The authors call attention to the importance of making such organizational memories an active system as opposed to a mere passive one, where manual access, e.g. through query interfaces, puts the entire responsibility on the user. Instead the user should be supplied with knowledge, even if he/she does not necessarily know that the information exists. To make this possible the system needs to know what the user is doing. Browsing a workflow diagram or a business process model are examples of interfaces that might provide such input to the system. EULE maintains process-descriptions based on formalized knowledge and data objects encoded in special clauses which make it possible for the system to perform information retrieval, deduction and validity checks just-in-time.

[1] discusses an integration of workflow management systems and agents performing information retrieval (information agents). The KnowMore project is used as an example. The target of this project is, in resemblance with EULE, to support a user performing a specific task with relevant, context-sensitive information without an explicit request from the user. To achieve this, the following features are added to conventional workflow models:

Extended specifications of complex knowledge intensive tasks, mainly describing the information need of the task, encoded as generic queries.
Context variables describing the information flow between tasks in the workflow.

These features represent the relevant context of a task and are used to instantiate the generic queries at runtime. Values assigned to the variables must be contained in a domain ontology, making reasoning and thus a more intelligent retrieval possible. When a complex task is reached, the generic query of the specific task is instantiated by the actual context. The query is then shipped to the information agent, which executes the query. Put together the system is claimed to be able to perform ontology-based, situation-specific information retrieval.

A different definition of context is adopted in [4]. The article presents an attempt to integrate workflow management systems (WFMS) and organizational memory information systems (OMIS). An implementation, called the KontextNavigator, consists of a process-oriented OMIS, in which the content is organized according to the objects of the workflow system. The context of a process in the WFMS is defined as the set of documents (in the OMIS) containing knowledge relevant to the process. This set is integrated with the WFMS through an event-driven system. When a specific event occurs at a specific process in the WFMS, the context (documents) linked to that event is automatically delivered to the user by the OMIS. How the linking is done is not described in detail. The need for interfaces to browse and store information in different contexts is mentioned by the authors. This indicates that the linking is to be done manually - demanding a considerable human effort.

[3] examine the potential of integrating text mining technology and workflow management systems in the domain of biomedical research. Even though the focus is on a specific domain, the proposed architecture is applicable in a wider range of domains.

The core of their framework is the use of web services, which enable interoperability between applications across the Internet, irrespective of platform and programming language. Three main components constitute the basis of the proposed architecture:

1. A client providing the user interface through which the user may initiate a workflow and browse the results.
2. A workflow server able to execute workflows. A workflow may consist of any number of steps. Each step might involve accessing remote information.
3. A text database server accessible to external applications through a web service interface.

The workflow server and the text database communicate through a general web services interface. The interface should as a minimum offer basic functionality such as ability to answer queries. The workflow server is responsible of query-creation and response interpretation, thus giving designers of different workflow systems the ability to influence the communication to meet the specific needs of their intended users.

When a workflow-step that demands access to the remote text database is reached, suitable text mining techniques is employed to extract query terms from the outcome of the previous steps along with surrounding context information. The query is then sent to the text database, which retrieves information found relevant to the query and returns the result. The result is then further processed by the workflow system according to the user need. Again text mining techniques are deployed.

Which text mining techniques to be used depends on the structure and amount of the information available to the specific workflow system.

21.7 Conclusion and Future Work

Both governing documents and business process models play important roles in modern enterprises. The standards for running their business operations are laid down in the governing documents by the management, and they expect their staff to follow these policies and guidelines in their daily work. The focus of these documents is on the enterprise's relationships to external entities, like customers or legal frameworks, and they are structured to ensure consistency and completeness with respect to these external aspects. Business process models, on the other hand, are structured by operational people to help the staff carry out their tasks effectively and efficiently. Unfortunately, the dynamic nature of businesses today makes it expensive or even impossible to maintain exact static correspondences between document fragments and models that are subject to continuous changes.

The approach presented here allows us dynamically to relate activities in the business process model to fragments of the governing documents at the time they are needed. This frees the organization from verifying and updating these correspondences whenever a document or business process is modified. It also allows us to find more specific information in the governing documents, as the approach actually retrieves and ranks every fragment or section of the documents relevant to the activity in the process model. This means that the users can faster check the relevant governing policies when carrying out their activities.

Plain cosine similarity based search and latent Semantic Indexing seem to give the most promising and accurate results for this particular case, but it is evident that further improvements and optimizations are needed. The feedback has increased our insight into the techniques performance and future effort will be done to improve existing approaches and to enlarge the scale of our studies.

References

1.   Abecker, A., Bernardi, A., Maus, H., Sintek, M., and Wenzel, C. Information supply for business processes: coupling workflow with document analysis and information retrieval. *Knowledge-Based Systems*, 13(5), pp. 271–284.
2.   Baeza-Yates, R. and Ribeiro Neto, B. Modern information retrieval. ACM Press Books.
3.   Gaizauskas, R., Davis, N., Demetriou, G., Guo, Y., and Roberts, I. Integrating biomedical text mining services into a distributed workflow environment. Proceedings of the third UK e-Science Programme All Hands Meeting (AHM 2004).
4.   Goesmann, T. KontextNavigator: A workflow-integrated organizational memory information system to support knowledge-intensive processes. INAP 2001, pp. 393-403
5.   Han, J., Pei, J., Yin, Y., and Mao, R. Mining frequent patterns without candidate generation: A frequent-pattern tree approach. Data Mining and Knowledge Discovery (8), pp. 53–87
6.   Hansen P.C., The truncated SVD as a method for regularization, BIT, 27, pp. 534-553.
7.   Hansen, P.C., and Jensen, S.H., FIR filter representation of reduced-rank noise reduction, IEEE Trans. Signal Proc., 46 (1998), pp. 1737-1741.
8.   Holt, J. D. and Chung, S. M. Efficient mining of association rules in text databases. Proceedings of the eighth international conference on Information and knowledge management, pp. 234–242.
9.   Ingvaldsen, J. E., Gulla, J. A., Su, X., and Rønneberg, H. "A text mining approach to integrating business process models and governing documents". OTM Workshops 2005, pp. 473–484.
10. Miller, G.A., Beckwith, R., Fellbaum, C., Gross, D., and Miller, K. Introduction to WordNet: An On-Line Lexical Database, Accessible from: www.cogsci.princeton.edu/~wn/5papers.pdf
11. Reimer, U., Margelisch, A., and Staudt, M. Eule: A knowledge-based system to support business processes. Knowledge-Based Systems, 13(5), pp. 261–269.
12. Sennelart, P. P. and Blondel, V. D. Automatic discovery of similar words. Survey of Text Mining: Clustering, Classification and Retrieval, pp. 25–43.

22 Utility of Web Content Blocks in Content Extraction

Marek Kowalkiewicz

The Poznan University of Economics, Poland
Department of Management Information Systems
M.Kowalkiewicz@kie.ae.poznan.pl

22.1 Introduction

Currently we are facing an overburdening growth of the number of reliable information sources on the Internet. The quantity of information available to everyone via Internet is dramatically growing each year [15]. At the same time, temporal and cognitive resources of human users are not changing, therefore causing a phenomenon of information overload.

World Wide Web is one of the main sources of information for decision makers (reference to my research). However our studies show that, at least in Poland, the decision makers see some important problems when turning to Internet as a source of decision information. One of the most common obstacles raised is distribution of relevant information among many sources, and therefore need to visit different Web sources in order to collect all important content and analyze it.

A few research groups have recently turned to the problem of information extraction from the Web [13]. The most effort so far has been directed toward collecting data from dispersed databases accessible via web pages (related to as data extraction or information extraction from the Web) and towards understanding natural language texts by means of fact, entity, and association recognition (related to as information extraction). Data extraction efforts show some interesting results, however proper integration of web databases is still beyond us. Information extraction field has been recently very successful in retrieving information from natural language texts, however it is still lacking abilities to understand more complex information, requiring use of common sense knowledge, discourse analysis and disambiguation techniques.

W. Abramowicz and H.C. Mayr (eds.), Technologies for Business Information Systems, 253–262.
© 2007 *Springer.*

22.1.1 Vision

Since automated information extraction do not fulfill expectations, especially when analyzing largely unstructured business documents, we believe that an interesting approach towards reducing the phenomenon of information overload is to provide methods and tools for content extraction and aggregation. One such method and tool has been proposed by Kowalkiewicz, Orlowska, Kaczmarek and Abramowicz [12].

So far the tools and methods of content extraction and aggregation do not consider an important fact. Namely the information needs are dynamically changing, and facing two information items of the same expected relevance, the relevance of one item may dramatically fall as soon as a user views the other (and acquires requested information) [21].

A problem of content aggregation methods is that the aggregation may use a limited space for presenting aggregated views. Our vision is to introduce a new concept of content utility to Web content extraction and aggregation systems that could be used as an extension of traditional relevance approach in order to present users content blocks of some significance. Such an approach would lead to optimal utilization of browser display areas.

22.1.2 Research Challenges

The research challenge of the work is to construct a strategy of assessing content block utility, ideally using already know methods originating from Information Retrieval and Economics fields.

22.1.3 Contribution

In this chapter we show how a content utility assessment could improve users' experience while fulfilling their information needs. We also draw a preliminary vision of the method. Since the chapter shows in-progress work, the discussion here should be treated as an invitation to commenting the work and possibly extending the concepts.

22.2 Web Content Extraction

Web content extraction is an interesting field, attracting many groups of researchers. Research is done as an answer to user needs, and its results are implemented in content extraction applications. In this section we analyze state of the art content extraction technologies, show results of a survey conducted among Polish managers, and describe a proof-of-concept application, myPortal, used to perform web content extraction experiments.

22.2.1 State of the Art

Content extraction is understood as extracting complex, semantically and visually distinguishable information, such as paragraphs or whole articles from the Web. It borrows from information extraction methods used in the World Wide Web environment, and especially from Web data extraction methods. The most comprehensible survey of Web data extraction tools has been provided by Laender et al. [13], there are however other ones, also relevant to our study.

The WebViews system [8] is a GUI system that allows users to record a sequence of navigation and point interesting data in order to build a wrapper. User is able to point interesting data; however it is not clear how the query to document's data is generated. The system is limited to extracting data from tables. IEPAD [6] is a system used to automatically extract repetitive subsequences of pages (such as search results). It is interesting in the context of wrapper generation and content extraction. IEPAD uses PAT trees to identify repetitive substructures and is prone to specific types of changes in subsequent substructures (for instance changing attributes of HTML tags, additional symbols between tags). Annotea [9], on the other hand, is a system designed not for content extraction, but for its annotation. The work provides a description of an approach of addressing specific parts of HTML documents. The authors present the method on XML documents, implicitly assuming that the conversion from HTML to XML representation has been done. As the authors point themselves, the method is very sensitive to changes in the document, which makes it usable only in addressing content of static documents. eShopMonitor [1] is a complex system providing tools for monitoring content of Web sites. It consists of three components: crawling system, which retrieves interesting webpages; miner, allowing users to point interesting data and then extracting the data; and reporting systems, which executes queries on extracted data and then provides user with consolidated results. The miner uses XPath expressions to represent interesting data. ANDES (A Nifty Data Extraction Systems) [16] extracts structured data using XHTML and XSLT technologies. The author of this system decomposes the extraction problem into five sub-problems: website navigation, data extraction, hyperlink synthesis, structure synthesis, data mapping, and data integration. WysiWyg Web Wrapper Factory (W4F) [18] is a set of tools for automatic wrapper generation. It provides tools for generating retrieval rules and a declarative language for building extraction rules. W4F uses a proprietary language, making it hard to integrate with other extraction systems. WebL [10] is a data extraction language. It is possible to represent complex queries (such as recursive paths and regular expressions) with it, however the language provides very limited means to address XML documents, particularly it doesn't support XSLT templates and XPath expressions. Chen, Ma, and Zhang [7] propose a system that clips and positions webpages in order to display them properly on small form factor devices. They use heuristics in order to identify potentially interesting content. Their clipping methods, according to a set of 10'000 analyzed HTML pages, behaves perfectly (no problems in page analysis and splitting) in around 55% of documents. Out of remaining 45%, some 35% percent documents cause problems in page splitting, and the final 10% generates errors in both page analysis and splitting.

Other possibly interesting systems include: WIDL [3], Ariadne [11], Garlic [17], TSIMMIS [20], XWRAP [14], and Informia [5]. It is important to note, that none of the mentioned systems was designed explicitly to extract previously defined content from dynamically changing webpages.

We have not found information on any system that would consider content utility in content extraction and aggregation. However, some approaches have been made. The most notable is a work of Anderson, Domingos, and Weld [4].

22.2.2 User Needs Specification

We have conducted a survey among Polish managers. The surveyed group included over 120 managers, undertaking Master of Business Administration studies. We asked the users several questions regarding their habits and remarks related to Internet use at workplace. The surveys were preceded by a short introduction, including overall information on web content extraction. The results of the survey, among others, showed that the Internet is an important source of information used at work (Figure 1).

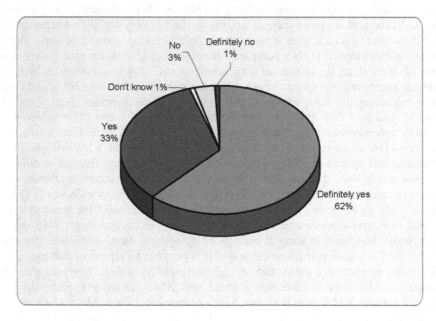

Fig. 1. *Is the Web an important source of Information you use at work?* Results of the survey distributed among Polish managers

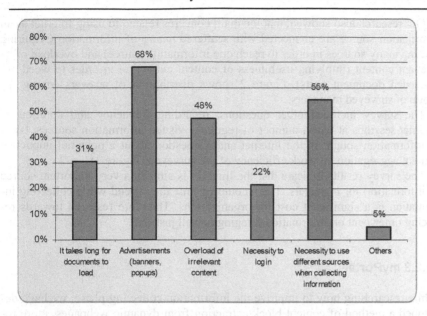

Fig. 2. *Indicate the most important problems that impede the usage of Internet as an information source (please select up to three answers).* Results of the survey distributed among Polish managers

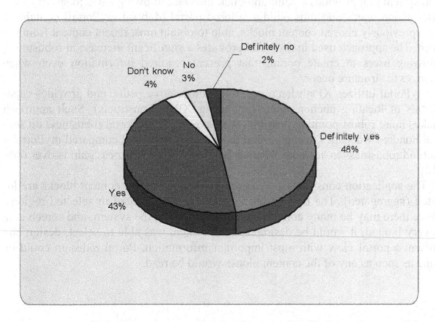

Fig. 3. *Do you think that getting a consolidated report instead of a need to search for every piece of information on the Internet would improve your efficiency?* Results of the survey distributed among Polish managers

Our research also showed, that the main concerns related to using Internet as an information source are connected with scattered nature of information (requiring visiting many sources in order to reach one information source) and overload of irrelevant content (implying usefulness of content extraction in order to weed out unneeded document parts). Figure 2 shows distribution of answers among the group of surveyed managers.

The survey included other questions, regarding frequency and duration of Internet sessions at work, number of regularly visited information sources, types of information sought in the Internet and a question about a potential impact of content aggregation on work efficiency of the surveyed (Figure 3).

The survey results indicate that the Internet is already a very important source of information for managers. The amount of time they spend while collecting information is a significant cost for organizations. Therefore research towards reducing time spent on information foraging is well justified.

22.2.3 myPortal

While researching how to improve the information collecting phase, we have developed a method of content block extraction from dynamic webpages, more robust than others available. The method has been implemented in a proof-of-concept application – myPortal [12]. MyPortal is a content extraction and aggregation system that provides a point-and-click interface allowing users to specify their information needs and thus build a tailored portal (dubbed myPortal) containing only previously chosen content blocks, able to obtain most recent content from the Web. The approach used in myPortal provides a significant increase in robustness, allowing users to create portals that present required information even when changes to structure occur.

myPortal utilizes XPath language, relies on relative paths, and provides capabilities of locating anchor points (not using XPath constructs). Such approach makes more robust pointing possible. We have tested myPortal robustness on several hundred webpages, using several thousand queries, and compared myPortal's method robustness to absolute XPath robustness. The robustness gain is over 60% [12].

The application constructs a web portal, where extracted content blocks are located (aggregated). The content blocks are currently located in selected regions. Since there may be many content block definitions in the system, and screen area is very limited, it would be desirable if the system was able to select, design and present a portal view with most important information. Portal redesign could be done as soon as any of the content blocks would be read.

22.3 Content Block Utility

22.3.1 Economical Aspects of Information Utility

Akerlof [2] was one of the first to put a stress on value of information in economical decision making. After that others – from both economics and information science – followed with important research [19]. An interesting approach to confronting economical models and the research field of information retrieval was presented by Varian [21]. He argued that the value of information can be measured: *the value of information is the increment in expected utility resulting from the improved choice made possible by better information* [21]. What is the most important conclusion for the IR community is that it is only new information that matters. Therefore acquisition of information from one document reduces relevance of another one, returned as a result of some user query. Therefore, post retrieval clustering of results may be a good approach towards evolution of IR systems by reducing the cognitive load and disambiguation. There is a number of research studies conducted in that area.

22.3.2 Content Block Utility

When considering content block extraction, one has to be aware of two facts. (1) In typical content extraction application, users are interested in different topics – their information needs are complex and most often include more than one query. (2) A typical web document consists of multiple content blocks (semantically distinguishable units), which again may be of different interest to users. A content extraction and aggregation system may extract content blocks from different web documents and place them in one view (Figure 4). Some of the content blocks may be of a higher importance to user. Some other blocks may duplicate the information.

An interesting research goal is to be able to assess the utility of content blocks. We are currently conducting studies on how to assess the "probability of relevance" in order to place content blocks in an aggregated document according to their relevance. We believe that it is possible to create a dynamic document that will change according to users' behavior (and therefore changing utility of individual content blocks).

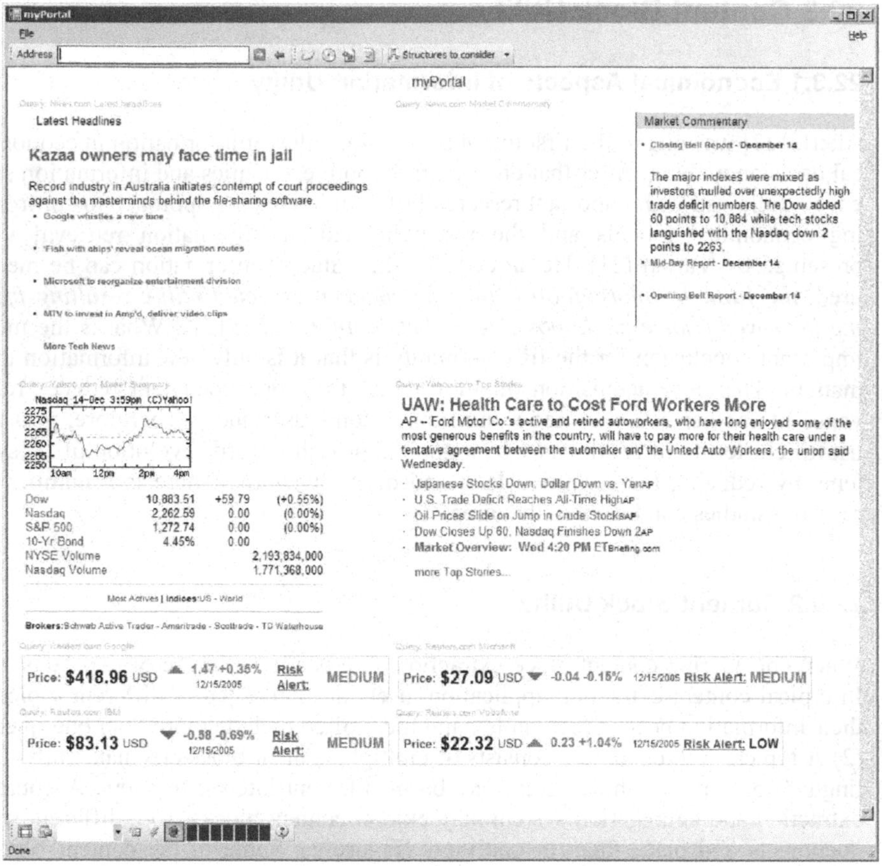

Fig. 4. A sample screen from a content extraction and aggregation system myPortal aggregating News.com, Yahoo.com and Reuters.com content blocks [12]

22.3.3 Utility Annealing

As Varian puts it [21], as soon as a user acquires information from one source, other ones, covering the same topic, become less relevant. When referring web content blocks, we call this phenomenon utility annealing. Whenever a user reads a content blocks, the aggregated document should be dynamically rearranged and most relevant content blocks should be moved to the top, while similar topics should be degraded (as their utility decreases). Such behavior requires using traditional IR methods such as assessing relevance and clustering results.

22.3.4 Utility Driven Content Block Selection and Ordering

When assessing content block utility becomes feasible, a new application of content extraction and aggregation tools emerges. It is possible that far more content blocks are extracted than can be perceived by a user in a given time. A new document, aggregating all interesting content blocks may be constructed from scratch, and provided that a limit of a document size (considering users' cognitive limitations) is given – a new document with aggregated content can be created. Only content blocks that are above a certain utility threshold will be selected and those will be ordered according to their utility and then presented to users.

22.4 Conclusions

Current web content extraction systems are not flexible enough. Even though they aim at reducing the information overload problem, there is still a lot to be done in the field. One of the approaches that may be useful in web content extraction is to construct documents aggregating different web content blocks according to their utility. No work has been done so far in the topic. We believe that after suggesting a Web content extraction method along with a prototype system that proved to be more robust than the other ones used currently, it is possible to construct a method for dynamic content aggregation based on its utility. In this chapter, after analyzing state of the art in content extraction, presenting results of our preliminary studies, we presented basic ideas underlying the concept. Further work includes development of utility assessment method and a technique for constructing dynamic aggregated documents with utility annealing. If successful, the practical implementation will be of use wherever large quantities of unstructured or semi-structured information are analyzed.

References

1. Agrawal N, Ananthanarayanan R, Gupta R, Joshi S, Krishnapuram R, Negi S (2004) The eShopmonitor: A comprehensive data extraction tool for monitoring Web sites. IBM Journal of Research and Development 5/6:679-692
2. Akerlof GA (1970) The Market for 'Lemons': Quality Uncertainty and the Market Mechanism. Quarterly Journal of Economics 3:488-500
3. Allen C (1997) WIDL: Application Integration with XML. World Wide Web Journal 4
4. Anderson CR, Domingos P, Weld DS (2001) Personalizing web sites for mobile users, In: Proceedings of the 10th international conference on World Wide Web. ACM Press: Hong Kong, pp 565-575
5. Barja ML, Bratvold T, Myllymaki J, Sonnenberger G (1998) Informia: A Mediator for Integrated Access to Heterogeneous Information Sources, In: Gardarin G, French JC, Pissinou N, Makki K, Bouganim L (eds) Proceedings of the 1998 ACM CIKM International Conference on Information and Knowledge Management. ACM Press: Bethesda, Maryland, USA, pp 234-241

6. Chang C-H, Lui S-C (2001) IEPAD: Information Extraction based on Pattern Discovery, In: Shen VY, Saito N, Lyu MR, Zurko ME (eds) Proceedings of the 10th international conference on World Wide Web. ACM Press New York: Hong-Kong, pp 681-688

7. Chen Y, Ma W-Y, Zhang H-J (2003) Detecting Web Page Structure for Adaptive Viewing on Small Form Factor Devices, In: Proceedings of the 12th International World Wide Web Conference. ACM Press New York: Budapest, Hungary, pp 225-233

8. Freire J, Kumar B, Lieuwen D (2001) WebViews: Accessing Personalized Web Content and Services, In: Shen VY, Saito N, Lyu MR, Zurko ME (eds) Proceedings of the 10th international conference on World Wide Web. ACM Press New York: Hong Kong, pp 576-586

9. Kahan J, Koivunen M-R, Prud'Hommeaux E, Swick RR (2001) Annotea: An Open RDF Infrastructure for Shared Web Annotations, In: Shen VY, Saito N, Lyu MR, Zurko ME (eds) Proceedings of the 10th international conference on World Wide Web. ACM Press New York: Hong-Kong, pp 623-632

10. Kistler T, Marais H (1998) WebL - A Programming Language for the Web, In: Proceedings of the 7th International World Wide Web Conference: Brisbane, Australia

11. Knoblock CA, Minton S, Ambite JL, Ashish N, Modi PJ, Muslea I, Philpot AG, Tejada S (1998) Modeling Web Sources for Information Integration, In: Proc. Fifteenth National Conference on Artificial Intelligence

12. Kowalkiewicz M, Orlowska M, Kaczmarek T, Abramowicz W (2006) Towards more personalized Web: Extraction and integration of dynamic content from the Web., In: Proceedings of the 8th Asia Pacific Web Conference APWeb 2006: Harbin, China

13. Laender AHF, Ribeiro-Neto BA, Silva ASd, Teixeira JS (2002) A brief survey of web data extraction tools. ACM SIGMOD Record 2:84-93

14. Liu L, Pu C, Han W (2000) XWRAP: An XML-enabled Wrapper Construction System for Web Information Sources, In: Proc. International Conference on Data Engineering (ICDE): San Diego, California

15. Lyman P, Varian HR, Swearingen K, Charles P, Good N, Jordan LL, Pal J (2003) How Much Information 2003?, School of Information Management and Systems, the University of California at Berkeley

16. Myllymaki J (2001) Effective Web Data Extraction with Standard XML Technologies, In: Shen VY, Saito N, Lyu MR, Zurko ME (eds) Proceedings of the 10th international conference on World Wide Web. ACM Press: New York, NY, USA, pp 689-696

17. Roth MT, Schwarz P (1997) Don't Scrap It, Wrap It! A Wrapper Architecture for Legacy Data Sources, In: Proceedings of the 23rd VLDB Conference.: Athens, Greece, pp 266-275

18. Sahuguet A, Azavant F (2000) WysiWyg Web Wrapper Factory (W4F), In: Mendelzon A (ed) Proceedings of the 8th International World Wide Web Conference. Elsevier Science: Toronto

19. Shapiro C, Varian HR (1999) Information rules: a strategic guide to the network economy. Harvard Business School Press: Boston, Massachusetts, USA

20. Ullman J, Chawathe S, Garcia-Molina H, Hammer J, Ireland K, Papakonstantinou Y, Widom J (1994) The TSIMMIS Project: Integration of Heterogeneous Information Sources, In: 16th Meeting of the Information Processing Society of Japan

21. Varian HR (1999) Economics and Search, In: SIGIR 1999. ACM Press: Berkeley, California, pp 1-5

23 A Comprehensive Assessment of Modern Information Retrieval Tools

Nishant Kumar[1], Jan De Beer[2], Jan Vanthienen[1], Marie-Francine Moens[2]

[1] Research Center for Management Informatics,
Katholieke Universiteit Leuven, Belgium
{nishant.kumar,jan.vanthienen}@econ.kuleuven.be
[2] Legal Informatics and Information Retrieval group,
Katholieke Universiteit Leuven, Belgium
{jan.debeer,marie-france.moens}@law.kuleuven.be

23.1 Introduction

Search tools or information retrieval tools play an important role in a wide range of information management, decision support and electronic commerce activities e.g., matching people and their products of interest on e-commerce sites, improving understanding of customer interactions, improving understanding of market research data, assisting police in obtaining knowledge from crime related unstructured data ([1]) etc. Information retrieval tools are especially important in global enterprises because of their vast amount of interconnected structured and unstructured data files available in multiple languages. With the increasing volume of information, stored in various formats and multiple languages, global enterprises throughout the world are gaining interests in powerful and reliable automated tools that turn data into useful, concise, accurate, and timely information and knowledge, and improve or assist them in information management and decision support activities. In spite of the importance of search tools in a wide variety of applications, the commercially available search tools are often poorly designed in terms of human computer interaction and also their search capabilities are limited by various factors ([2]). The problem of effective retrieval remains a challenge. These challenges ([3]) fuel academic and corporate endeavor at developing suitable tools for information exploitation. On the corporate front this constitutes a thriving business opportunity. Building and continuously adjusting these tools to fit the different and evolving customer needs requires

W. Abramowicz and H.C. Mayr (eds.), Technologies for Business Information Systems, 263–275.
© 2007 *Springer.*

much effort, time, money, vision, and expertise. For this reason, purchasing a commercial tool for intelligence analysis may prove a viable solution to many organisations. However, in general these tools are tremendously expensive, are labeled with promising marketing statements on their usefulness and abilities, have a tendency to carry their limitations and impose their view on the information management and exploitation throughout the entire operational environment in which they become employed, and their vendors are generally reluctant to provide the software free of cost for evaluation purposes.

For these and other reasons, great value may be attached to indepth (comparative) studies conducted by independent parties with sufficient domain knowledge to assess the true quality, performance, and abilities of these tools. Through our research in the INFO-NS project for the Belgian Police (BP) and this article in particular, we contribute to this line of work.

The rest of this article is organized as follows. Firstmost we describe the INFO-NS project briefly, then we elaborate on our methodology used in assessing them. The main part will be devoted to an overview of our main findings with regard to the selected tools on a number of evaluated use cases, all within the domain of search and retrieval, information extraction and link analysis from text. We end with our conclusions and mention related work for further reading.

23.2 The INFO-NS Project

The research project INFO-NS is an initiative of the Belgian Federal Police (BFP), commissioned by AGORA as part of the Belgian Science Policy[1]. It is part of the larger DOCMAN project of the BFP, which is aimed at storing the pv's (police case reports) and their base metadata in a central database and to make them accessible through the police's intranet. In this INFO-NS research project, we have investigated the applicability and quality of market-leading information retrieval tools for use within the operational environment of the BP. Special attention is given to search and retrieval, as the police is keen on having a high-quality information retrieval system.

The structured information of the BP mainly consists of detailed, structured representations of textual case reports, painstakingly derived from those reports mostly written by police officers. As the case reports, along with other types of unstructured documents, are now being centralized in a securely accessible repository, there exists a great potential for information exploitation. As one envisions the benefits, it might be possible to reduce some of the burdens and shortcomings that comes with the manual annotation and structuring of documents by trading it for open-ended search on the original, complete textual document contents.

---

[1] Visit AGORA at http://www.belspo.be/belspo/fedra/proj.asp?l=en&COD=AG/GG/101

23.3 Evaluation Methodology

23.3.1 Requirements Analysis

In order to reveal the profile of the exploitation tool desired and suitable for use within the BP, we initiated our project with a market study paired with a thorough site study. Through this survey, we learned about the different information sources, flows, systems, and uses within the operational environment of the BP.

Furthermore, through marked differences in the needs and usage patterns of information sources, we identified several user profiles, and noted down their functional requirements and priorities in great detail.

Administrator: Collects, manages, structures, and relates facts described in official documents (case reports e.g.).

Investigator: Conducts criminal investigations; their task is to compile a comprehensive report (a legal case file) describing all acts and elements part of the investigation, which will be the main source of evidence used by judicial authorities for prosecution.

Operational analyst: Examines, supports and assists criminal investigations, especially more complex ones.

Strategic analyst: Analyses security problems, their tendencies, trends, patterns, processes, novelties, etc.

From the obtained list ([4]) of fine-grained functional requirements, we were able to generalize over user profiles to a limited set of high-level *use cases*. In this article, we discuss the following four main use cases regarding the search functionality.

Free-Text Search. Search queries defined in some query language are matched against the textual contents of a document collection in order to retrieve and rank the most relevant documents (cf. web search engines, such as Google).

Metadata Search. Structured data that is associated to documents is turned into additional, searchable document fields (also called attributes, e.g. title, author, date), next to the free-text document contents.

Classification. Documents are automatically classified into either a pre-built or an automatically derived taxonomy based on content analysis and similarity.

Named Entity Extraction. Mentions of named entities are automatically recognized in text, disambiguated and classified into any of the supported entity types (e.g. persons, organisations, vehicle numbers, time).

Selection of Tools:

For the evaluation purpose, we identified 23 tools on the basis of a global overview of the market. Through matching the functional requirements and the product capabilities, we were able to further shortlist to 10 tools[2].

---

[2] Due to contractual obligations names has not been disclosed.

23.3.2 Evaluation of Selected Tools

For each of the use cases, we compiled a detailed evaluation form along with semi-automated evaluation procedures emerging from plausible and sound evaluation frameworks ([4, 5]), covering three crucial aspects of assessment.

Conformity. Conformity evaluation measures to which extent functional and technical requirements are met by the tools. As we found out that functional support is hardly a yes/no answer, exceptions, side conditions, alternative options, and remarks were noted down. This evaluation provides a clear view on the abilities, limitations, system requirements, and configuration options of the tools.

Quality. Qualitative evaluation measures the quality (such as usefulness, relevance, or accuracy) of the results as output by the tools on a number of carefully drafted test cases. As quality is often a very subjective, task- and goal-dependent concept, end users were actively involved in the evaluation process, e.g. to provide user judgments or golden standards. This evaluation provides a clear view on the qualitative capabilities of the tools.

Technical. Technical evaluation measures the allocation of system resources (such as processor, memory, diskspace, network bandwidth, runtime) by the tools on a representative set of (scalable) test cases. In addition, ease of installation and configuration, indexing statistics and errors, robustness and stability were noted down. This evaluation provides a clear view on the technical capabilities of the tools.

Test Environment:

Amongst the materials provided by the BP for the test cases is a multilingual document collection containing more than half a million documents of real-life case reports (Dutch and French) encoded in the Microsoft Word file format. This collection constitutes a representative sample of the full operational collection, which is expected to hold a number of documents that runs in the order of ten million.

All test cases were performed on a single computer, hosting both the server and client components of each tool. The machine is equipped with an Intel dual processor (2×1Ghz), 2GB (gigabytes) of volatile memory, 4GB of virtual memory, a SCSI RAID-0 disc array with separate partitions for the operating system Microsoft Windows 2003 Server (supported by all evaluated tools), the program files, and the data.

23.4 Evaluation Results

For each use case, we mention the main application purpose(s) in view of the BP's requirements, the common and differing support that is provided by the evaluated tools, followed by general findings on their qualitative assessment, and finally some suggestions for tool improvement.

23.4.1 Free-Text Search

Purpose

The basic objective of the BP in the INFO-NS project is to find a good document retrieval system to search and access the central repository of documents for operational use.

This way, documents are not just accessible through querying the corresponding structured data, but become accessible through open-ended search queries posed against the actual, complete document contents.

Support

Each tool defines a query language in which the user expresses her information needs. The language minimally supports the specification of keywords and phrases, implicitly or explicitly coined using search operators and/or modifiers (boolean, proximity, wildcard, fuzzy, lemmatization, and thesaurus operators, case sensitivity and language modifiers, etc.). In addition, conditions on metadata can be posed, and the search scope bounded by selecting any of the target document collections that were previously indexed. Each tool employs its proprietary (secret) relevance ranking model that scores each target document in accordance with the search query. The results are returned to the user and presented in (paged) document lists or navigable classification (metadata) folders, holding links to the actual documents.

At the option of the user, documents can quickly be viewed internally, typically as plain text decorated with markup and/or navigational elements surrounding (partial) matches. Consulting the documents in their original form is possible by launching external viewer applications.

No evaluated tool supported crosslingual search out-of-the-box. With crosslingual search, queries posed in one language retrieve relevant documents regardless of their content language. Integration of third-party machine translation software or crosslingual dictionaries paired with existing query expansion mechanisms may offer solutions, yet are still limited in quality and completeness.

Quality

Text extraction and markup removal was found to work fine for some of the most common document types, as tested through the 'exact search' query type supported by all tools. However, Microsoft Word page headers and footers were often discarded when indexing.

In line with the BP's requirements, due emphasis was given on fuzzy search capabilities, in order to recognize common variations, including spelling, abbreviations, phonetics, interpunction, spacing, accents and special characters, capitalization, etc. that are commonly found in case reports. The proprietary fuzzy matching algorithm of one tool was found to give excellent results on most of the variation types considered, whereas the use of the Soundex ([6]) and edit distance ([7]) operators as provided by most other tools proved to be ill-suited for most variation types. Soundex allows for some reasonable character substitution errors, but is clearly targetted at English phonetics, and does not tolerate consonant additions or removals (including abbreviations). Edit distance covers all three types of character errors (removal, insertion, and substitution), but does so in a very uniform way, assuming all character errors are independent from one another. In practice this requires large thresholds in order to cover abbreviations, interposed or omitted words, interpunction,... whereas small thresholds are desired to limit spurious matches as much as possible. Moreover, Soundex nor edit distance copes well with word reorderings, e.g. as with person names. Next to the operators' inherent shortcomings, a user's concretisation of the fuzzy search query has major impact on the quality of results. This pertains in part to a tool's conventions in tokenizing and normalizing text (e.g. with regard to accents) and whether partial string search is performed by default or only through explicit use of wildcards.

The relevance ranking model was evaluated using the *rpref* metric ([5]), a fuzzification (generalization) of the *bpref* metric ([8]) towards graded relevance assessments.In short, the metric measures the extent to which less relevant documents are ranked before higher relevant documents. Compared to a baseline *rpref* score of a random ranking model, one tool was found to consistently produce well-ranked result lists (on a scale from 0 to 100, baseline+30 up to +70) and promote a priori determined highly relevant documents, whereas other tools clearly showed variable, and some language-dependent *rpref* scores (below versus above baseline) and recall of these relevant documents. Although very interesting, we were not able to pursue evaluation metrics other than *rpref* due to time restrictions.

Given the lack of crosslingual support, language purity of the result list with regard to the search query's language (when searching against our entire multilingual collection) is considered acceptable (90% or higher on average), except for one tool (55–65%).

Technical

Base memory usage of the server (when passive) varied from 50 to 550MB (megabytes), with an additional 15 (50) MB needed whilst handling a single (fuzzy) search at a time. Query response times depend heavily on the type and complexity of the search query (use of advanced operators, e.g. fuzzy or thesaurus search requires more time), which is more pronounced in some tools than for others. For example, one tool relying mostly on meager dictionaries and simple keyword search techniques performed all queries within the second, obviously sacrificing search capabilities for speed. Indexing 1GB of Microsoft Word documents took 0.72 up to 2.12 hours, requiring 40, 50, 80 or more percent of index space, with no clear observed correlation on search quality or speed.

Suggestions

We emphasize the need for build-in support of crosslingual search, as many organisations nowadays have to deal with this problem. For the BP, tools should also be capable of handling documents containing text in different languages (hearings e.g.). Furthermore, we encourage research into and the implementation of multipurpose fuzzy search operators with user-definable threshold value, other than the rarely suitable, yet popular Soundex and edit distance operators.[3]

On the retrieval side, we encourage experimentation with alternative retrieval models, different from the keyword-based retrieval models that are implemented by all evaluated tools. Various interesting retrieval models have been proposed in the academic world, but they do not seem to find their way outside the laboratory environment. As one instance, the XML retrieval model ([9]) could be used to exploit document structure in finding relevant sections. Structure is inherent in most documents, yet ignored by most evaluated tools.

On the interface side, support for reordering result lists based on any combination of metadata is considered useful, as well as dynamically generated summaries, taking into account the user's profile and information need. Short and high-quality summaries may save a user much time in assessing the relevance of retrieved documents.

All evaluated tools implicitly assume that each document is independent from the others, where this is clearly not the case with BP's case reports. Support for logical document grouping (merging) would thus come in handy.

Lastly, all tools allow implementing user-based, document-level access policies, but none provides for fine-grained, function-driven rather than data-driven security mechanisms. The need for both kinds of security is governed by the 'need-to-know principle' as in force in the BP; officers may only access those parts of information they are entitled to for the sole purpose of carrying out their duties.

23.4.2 Metadata Search

Purpose

The BP requires the tools to include a subset of their structured data (such as PV number, police zone, date range of fact, type of document, type of crime), and considers metadata search to be an essential functionality, in combination to free-text search.

---

[3] One could think of trainable, probabilistic models in which all variation types of different content elements present in a training set of documents are covered, with probabilistic content taggers (such as POS or NERC) providing the prior probabilities for hypothesis testing in new texts. We may work this out in further research.

Support

We found sufficient and similar support for the integration of metadata in all evaluated tools through the provision of connectors to the most common types of structured data sources (such as ODBC gateways to RDBMS, or programmed plugins). These connectors synchronize with the external sources, such that the duplicated metadata residing in the tools' own searchable indices is kept consistent with the source data, disregarding some limited synchronization delays. Data mining tools offer with their tabular data structures a natural environment for working with metadata.

Standard document attributes (such as url, title, author, date, size), when available, are automatically imported by the tools. Most information retrieval tools also derive a static summary simply by extracting the most salient sentences or phrases from the text. These standard document attributes are e.g. used in search result lists, to give the user the gist of a document. Classification codes become available when indexing against one or more compiled taxonomies, and high-level document descriptors, such as entities or facts are included with the enabling of the associated tool services, if any (cf. infra).

Combinable search operators for the most common types of metadata (text, date, ordinal) are generally supported.

Quality

Due to the deterministic character of metadata search, qualitative evaluation is deemed irrelevant.

Suggestions

We suggest yielding reliably generated metadata from text using information extraction technology to reduce the burden of manual tagging and consistency problems. For the BP, given the description of case report outlines in Sect. 23.3.2, it should be possible to extract information fields (PV number, police zone,...) and identity information of victims, suspects, cars, objects, etc. in a reliable fashion.

Reordering the search result list based on any combination of metadata (e.g. police zone, date range, age group of a suspect) is a useful but not standard supported feature.

23.4.3 Classification

Purpose

Automated classification in the context of the BP can be used to organize the voluminous and heterogeneous document collection in manageable and content-specific units, reveal related and novel crimes based on their textual descriptions, or filter out relevant documents for divisions, investigators, or analysts specialized in different subject matters.

Support

We found two different approaches to automated classification in the set of evaluated tools. Document retrieval tools typically offer classification as a standard extension to search and retrieval, employing manual rule-based taxonomy construction as the underlying technology, whereas data mining tools resort to the application of standard machine learning techniques on a chosen representation of the documents. Few tools allow for a hybrid approach, with the automatic generation of editable classification rules based on sets of representative example documents.

Rule-based taxonomy construction is typically performed in a graphical user interface by a domain expert, familiar with the terminology used in the documents, as well as the tool's query language. This is because the expressivity of the rule-based classification language minimally entails classification based on literal occurrences of keywords found in the text, and is in some tools maximally extended to the entire query language. This means one can create arbitrary search queries serving as definitions for content categories.

Given a suitable representation of documents as feature vectors, one can employ supervised or unsupervised machine learning modules, that are provided in most data mining tools.In supervised classification, a classifier is trained on representatively chosen example documents for each category, and subsequently predicts the category of any newly presented document. Unsupervised classification autonomously generates (a hierarchy of) clusters of related documents based on content similarity. This technique is also used in one document retrieval tool at search time (opposed to indexing time), dynamically clustering search results using salient noun and noun groups as representations of documents and cluster labels.

Quality

Classification performance is seriously constrained by the implemented rule set and the effort that goes into it. Due to practical limitations, we were not able to draft a full rule set for each tool individually (using their distinct syntax) to seriously test their classification capabilities. Despite this fact, we can conclude - from studying the expressivity of the rule language provided - that there lies a significant gap between the lexical and semantic level of analysis, on the basis of which the tools, respectively humans are known to classify texts. This gap poses serious restrictions on what can be expected from automated classification by these tools. For example, when classifying by time of crime, a mention of '9:17am' in the text will not be recognized as belonging to the 'morning' category of the taxonomy unless explicitly coded for in the rule set, and even then it is not yet clear as to whether this mention pertains to the actual time of the crime, if any crime is described at all. Explicitely coding for all of this would require a more advanced extension of the basic rule language provided by the tools, including world knowledge.

The orientation towards simple rule languages and like rule sets, which are easier to manage, update, extend, and apply, helps to explain why none of the tools provides build-in methods for evaluating the resulting quality of classification. Sole method provided is some statistical indicators on document distribution over the taxonomy's branches, given the concern for well-balancedness of the populated taxonomy.

Implementing rule sets in practice turns out to be a painstaking activity that requires constant refinement and adaptation to cope with a constantly evolving stream of document content. Moreover, changes in the taxonomy's definition only become effective after reclassifying (often implying reindexing) the entire collection. This makes the rule-building approach practically hampered.

We tested supervised machine learning techniques (neural network and decision tree based) for a single-level taxonomy comprising three crime types (carjacking, pickpocketing, money laundering), with the term vector as traditional document representation ([10]). Even on this simple classification task, results never exceeded 82% precision and recall, which is clearly insufficient. Apparently, the traditional document representation as bag-of-words and adoption of default tool settings cannot adequately discriminate crime types in our document collection.

For practical constraints, we did not assess the quality of unsupervised machine learning techniques.

Suggestions

For the automated classification of documents, we advocate a higher-level content analysis of texts that extends the traditional, lexical (word-based) content analysis as is merely performed by all evaluated tools. In turn, this would call for the inclusion of (existing) evaluation methods to assess the quality of the resulting classification, as part of the tool's software distribution.

In some cases, documents can be more reliably classified using descriptive information units embedded in or derived from the text, rather than literal words. For example, within the BP, the main crime type can be easily derived from the PV number that is readily found in case reports using simple information extraction technology, such as regular expressions. Alternatively, this descriptor could also be (made) available as metadatum.

As with free-text search, crosslingual support is highly desired, as currently multiple rule sets have to be build and maintained in consistent manner for each language separately.

Lastly, classification is often considered a one-shot task in the evaluated tools, whereas a constantly changing content repository requires support for incremental learning, incremental taxonomy development, maintenance, and deployment, new topic signaling, and the like.

23.4.4 Named Entity Extraction

Purpose

Named entity recognition constitutes a basic operation in the structuring of texts. Its automation within the BP would e.g. tremendously aid operational analysts in the coding (schematisation) of criminal cases, sometimes covering hundreds of pages that otherwise would have to be skimmed manually for the discovery of entities of interest.

Support

Some core information retrieval tools allow the automated discovery and classification of named entities in text, amongst which person names, organisations, locations, and time instances are most commonly supported. Text mining modules of data mining tools generally incorporate this feature, whereas it forms the foundation of all tools profiled as information extraction tools.

All evaluated document retrieval tools rely largely on human editable and expandable dictionaries. Information extraction tools typically go one step further by providing human editable and expandable rule sets. A rule may be as simple as a regular expression, but may extend to incorporate lexical analysis of the source text. This way, the context of entity mentions may be used to trigger recognition or to determine their type (e.g. use of certain prepositions). We remain unsure as to which technology text mining modules resort to, but likely they use a combination of both.

Quality

We used standard measures of evaluation, namely precision, recall, and the combined F-measure ([10]) to assess the tools on a multilingual set of sample documents. We treat misalignment between extracted entity mentions and a golden standard of manually extracted mentions consistently in favour of the tools. For example, the extracted entity "South Africa" is equated with the full entity name "the Republic of South Africa", when the latter is present in the text.

Results ([11]) show high precision on the most common entity types (persons, organisations, locations), up to 97%. Recall is very poor however, less than 50%. From these findings we assume the use of rather cautious dictionaries and/or rule sets, both limited in scope and their tolerance towards typographical, compositional, and other kinds of observed variations. The latter is especially relevant given the noisiness of the texts in our collection. We also mention the problem of ambiguity, which gave rise to a number of errors, mostly when it comes to determining the entity type (e.g. locations or organisations named after persons).

Suggestions

None of the evaluated tools offers a learning approach to automated entity recognition, whereas the academic community has made much progress in this field ([12]). A line of research which is only tentatively pursued to date, but nevertheless equally important is the extraction of entities within noisy texts ([13]).

23.5 Related Work

In the past decade, many IT implementation projects have been conducted in collaboration with police forces throughout the world. Most noted are the COPLINK project of Chen et al. ([14]), and the OVER project of Oatley, Ewart & Zeleznikow ([1]), in association with the West Midlands police. Most of these projects revolve around the centralization and consolidation of various digitized information sources. Purposes range from information fusion, information sharing, improved availability of information, to advanced exploitation, for crime analysis. In the INFO-NS project, our primary purpose has been the evaluation of market-available commercial tools, for which only very limited studies exist.

Rijsbergen ([10]) has discussed evaluation techniques for measuring the performance of information retrieval tools. Related studies can be found from Lancaster ([15]), Cooper ([16]), and Ingwersen ([17]) on functional use assessment, relevance assessment, and quality evaluation, respectively, while the evaluation methodologies suggested by Elder and Abbot ([18]), Nakhaeizadeh, and Schnabl ([19]), Collier et al. ([20]) are notable.

23.6 Conclusions

In this article we have presented our general findings with regard to the state-of-the-art of a selection of market-leading tools for the exploitation of unstructured information, as was the objective of the project INFO-NS. In the areas of document retrieval, and information extraction, we have presented the support offered by these tools, reported crucial criteria and results on their qualitative assessment, and formulated recommendations on their possible improvement. We encountered many interesting aspects that are not readily found or touched upon in literature on the subject, most noticeably on the issues of privacy, security, legal aspects such as the evidential value of generated results, integration, flexibility, adaptability, and performance of exploitation tools in practical settings. We hope our work may prove useful, and inspire other researchers.

References

1. G. C. Oatley, B. W. Ewart, and J. Zeleznikow, "Decision support systems for police: Lessons from the application of data mining techniques to 'soft' forensic evidence." 2004.
2. N. J. Belkin, S. T. Dumais, J. Scholtz, and R. Wilkinson, "Evaluating interactive information retrieval systems: opportunities and challenges.," in *CHI Extended Abstracts*, pp. 1594–1595, 2004.
3. Workshop on Information Retrieval Challanges, "Challenges in information retrieval and language modeling," tech. rep., University of Massachusetts Amherst, Center for Intelligent Information Retrieval, 2002.
4. N. Kumar, J. Vanthienen, J. D. Beer, and M.-F. Moens, "Multi-criteria evaluation of information retrieval tools.," in *ICEIS (2)*, pp. 150–155, 2006.
5. J. D. Beer and M.-F. Moens, "Rpref: a generalization of bpref towards graded relevance judgments.," in *SIGIR*, pp. 637–638, 2006.
6. R. Russell and M. Odell, "Soundex," 1918.
7. V. I. Levenshtein, "Binary codes capable of correcting deletions, insertions and reversals," *Doklady Akademii Nauk SSSR*, vol. 163, no. 4, pp. 845–848, 1965.
8. C. Buckley and E. M. Voorhees, "Retrieval evaluation with incomplete information," in *Proceedings of the ACM SIGIR Annual International Conference on Information Retrieval*, vol. 27, July 2004.
9. H. Blanken, T. Grabs, H.-G. Schek, R. Schenkel, and G. Weikum, *Intelligent Search on XML Data - Applications, Languages, Models, Implementations and Benchmarks*. Springer-Verlag, 2003.
10. C. J. Van Rijsbergen, *Information Retrieval*. Butterworths London, second ed., 1979.
11. N. Kumar, J. D. Beer, J. Vanthienen, and M.-F. Moens, "Evaluation of information retrieval and text mining tools on automatic named entity extraction.," in *ISI*, pp. 666–667, 2006.
12. M.-F. Moens, *Information Extraction: Algorithms and Prospects in a Retrieval Context*. Springer-Verlag, 2006.
13. M. Chau, J. J. Xu, and H. Chen, "Extracting meaningful entities from police narrative reports," in *Proceedings of the International Conference on Intelligence Analysis*, 2005.
14. R. V. Hauck, J. Schroeder, and H. Chen, "Coplink: Developing information sharing and criminal intelligence analysis technologies for law enforcement," in *Proceedings of the National Conference for Digital Government Research*, vol. 1, pp. 134–140, May 2001.
15. F. W. Lancaster, *Information Retrieval Systems: Characteristics, Testing and Evaluation*. Wilcy, New York, 1968.
16. W. S. Cooper, "On selecting a measure of retrieval effectiveness," *Journal of the American Society for Information Science*, vol. 24, no. 2, pp. 87–100, 1973.
17. P. Ingwersen, *Information Retrieval Interaction*. London: Taylor Graham, 1992.
18. J. F. Elder and D. W. Abbott, "A comparison of leading data mining tools," tech. rep., August 1998.
19. G. Nakhaeizadeh and A. Schnabl, "Development of multi-criteria metrics for evaluation of data mining algorithms," in *Proceedings KDD-97*, AAAI Press, 1997.
20. K. Collier, B. Carey, D. Sautter, and C. Marjaniemi, "A methodology for evaluating and selecting data mining software," in *Proceedings of the International Conference on System Sciences*, 1999.

24 Polish Texts Analysis for Developing Semantic-Aware Information Systems

Jakub Piskorski, Agata Filipowska, Krzysztof Węcel, Karol Wieloch

Poznań University of Economics, Poland
Department of Management Information Systems
{J.Piskorski, A.Filipowska, K.Wecel, K.Wieloch}@kie.ae.poznan.pl

24.1 Introduction

This chapter reports on creation of a corpus of Polish free-text documents, tagged with name mentions of CIS-relevant entities, which constitutes a core resource for development and evaluation of information extraction components used within a cadastre framework.

Unstructured information in the form of free text documents is not much useful for any information system unless it is processed in desired way. The most challenging task in the domain of processing natural language documents is to structure their meaning. Systems have different requirements for the information (text) they can acquire. A text poses different language-level problems to algorithms that try to mine them. This article reports on combining requirements of an information system with language phenomena to build an information extraction resource. The end-user system is a modern Cadastral Information System. The language examined is Polish. And the result of an analysis is an annotated corpus - an important part of a mechanism feeding CIS with textual information from WWW.

The traditional cadastral information system (CIS) is a system containing mostly structured data about real estates (RE), e.g. location, ownership, value, etc. RE value is influenced by number of infrastructural, socio-economical and natural factors. We claim that an enormous amount of free-text documents, produced daily by diverse online media, contains valuable information and indicators on these factors, which are useful in the process of real-estate value estimation [Abramowicz et al., 2004].

The prerequisite for extracting structured knowledge from free-text document sources is automatic detection of references to objects, potentially relevant to

277

W. Abramowicz and H.C. Mayr (eds.), Technologies for Business Information Systems, 277–287.
© 2007 Springer.

cadastral locations, organizations, person names. Unfortunately, existing language resources for Polish are sparse and inappropriate to tackle this task (e.g. only morphologically annotated corpora are available [Przepiórkowski, 2005]). An annotated corpus with named entities is indispensable to start any endeavour in this areaThis article reports on creation of an annotated corpus for supporting development of IE tools to be utilized as submodules for automatic knowledge acquisition in CIS. In particular, we describe the DECADENT task focusing on detection of cadastre-related entities from free-text documents for Polish. Further, we discuss some corpus annotation guidelines and encountered problems. Finally, we provide some corpus statistics.

The authors are not familiar with any similar work for Polish, however we borrowed some ideas from MUC [Chinchor 1998] and ACE annotation guidelines and taxonomies [ACE], prepared for other languages and domains. Our work is also strongly related to extracting geographical references, which has been addressed in various publications [McCurley, 2001, Pouliquen et al. 2004, Amitay et al. 2004].

The rest of this paper is organized as follows. Section 2 presents basic requirements on information structures from the perspective of CIS. The requirements have a form of a virtual task called DECADENT, which is–, mainly centred around detecting name mentions. Subsequently, section 3 presents an annotation experiment that resulted with an annotated corpus. Section 4 discuses the annotation guidelines we have developed on the basis of state of the art literature and experiences during manual annotation. We end up with some conclusions in Section 5.

24.2 Basic Requirements

Development of modern Cadastral Information Systems (CIS) requires deployment of tools for automatic estimation of real estates' value which is influenced by a number of factors. After differentiation of the factors, appropriate information on certain locations needs to be acquired. Since most up-to-date information is transmitted mainly as free-text documents via online media, information extraction technology plays a key role in converting such data into valuable and structured knowledge, which facilitates automatic real-estate value estimation.

DECADENT (Detecting Cadastral Entities) task focuses on detecting mentions of CIS-relevant entities in source free-text data. We consider an entity be an object or a set of objects in the real world. Entities can be referenced in a free text by: (a) their name, (b) a common noun phrase (c) a pronoun or (d) an implicit mention in elliptical constructions (e.g., in Polish, subject is often missing in clausal constructions, but it can be inferred from the suffix of a corresponding verb form). In DECADENT task, we are only interested in recognition of entities which are explicitly referenced by their names (named entities) or by a subset of nominal constructions consisting of a common noun phrase followed by a proper name. While our task resembles more the MUC NE task [Chinchor, 1998], the NE categories are more similar to the categories of the Entity Detection Task

(EDT) introduced in ACE Program [Doddington et al., 2004]. However, DECADENT task is less complicated than EDT since the latter requires detecting mentions of any type and grouping them into full coreference chains, which is beyond the scope of our current work. In other words, we recognize text fragments which may refer to some objects in the real-world, but we do not tailor them to any concrete real-world objects.

Originally ACE program specified 7 basic categories: organizations, geopolitical entities, locations, persons, facilities, vehicles and weapons. They were used as base for specifying the DECADENT task, i.e., we have modified and adapted them to meet the needs of CIS applications. For instance, the categories: locations, facilities and geopolitical entities have been merged into one category – location, which represents entities that can be mapped onto geographical coordinates. Further, we added the category product, since product names often include valuable clues such as brand and company names, which can be utilized for inferring locations and might implicitly constitute a strong indicator of real estate price level etc. Currently, in DECADENT task, there are four main types of entities:

- Locations (LOC) (natural land forms, water bodies, geographical and political regions, man-made permanent structures, addresses, etc.)
- Organizations (ORG) (companies, government institutions, educational institutions, and other groups of people defined by an organizational structure)
- Persons (PER) (individuals or groups of humans)
- Products (PRD) (brand names, services, goods)

Clearly, LOC is the most structured of the entity types. Its main purpose is to group together entities, which are relevant for geo-indexing. Each main type is subdivided into eventually non-disjoint subtypes. The category LOC groups such entities like: natural land forms (LAN) (e.g. continent names, geographical regions), water bodies (WAT), facilities (FAC), addresses (zip codes, building numbers, geographical coordinates and URL's or e-mails), and administrative regions (ADM). Facilities (FAC) are further subdivided into: transportation hubs (TRH), transportation routes (TRR), entertainment facilities (ENT) and other utilities (UTI). Administrative regions are subdivided into: countries (CRY), provinces (PRO), counties (CNT), communes (CMN), cities (CIT), districts (DIS) and other zones (ZON). See table 3 for details.

Within ORG type, we distinguish commercial organizations (COM) (companies and some other private-owned institutions), governmental institutions (GOV) (related or are dealing with the administrative issues and other affairs of government and the state), schools, universities and research institutes (EDU), organizations related to health and care (HLT), institutions dealing with recreation or media (REC), and finally other (OTH) organizations that do not fit into any of the previous categories.

PER category groups named mentions of persons that are identified only via their first and/or second names. Titles, positions, etc. are not to be detected since this information is not necessarily of an interest in the context of CIS. Further, groups of people named after a country or likewise fall into this category too.

Entities of PRD type are to be detected due to their association with organizations that promotes them. We believe that such information might be useful for inference purposes at a later stage, as mentioned earlier. Currently, we only consider brand names (BRN).

Detecting named entities in DECADENT task consists of assigning each name mention in the source document one or possibly more tags corresponding to the type of the mentioned entity, which is accompanied by positional information. Due to eventual type ambiguities, difficulties in specifying name mention borders and subtleties of Polish, we have introduced some annotation guidelines described in more detail in the next section.

24.3 Annotation Issues

Another issue concerned assigning two competing tags for the same text fragment (a special case of overlapping annotations). The most frequent clash occurred between ORG-COM and FAC-UTI types. Inferring the right one regarding the context was hard (e.g. *Centrum Spotkania Kultur*).

This section gives a short overview of annotation guidelines and major issues we have encountered during the analysis. In particular, there are three major issues, which have to be tackled by information extraction mechanism: entity type ambiguity, specifying name mention borders, and finally inner bracketing of the matched text fragments.

24.3.1 Type ambiguity

Type ambiguity of named-entities is a well-known problem [Sundheim, 1995]. While, in most cases the type of the entities in our corpus happened to be unambiguous, some other pose problems. Usually ambiguities arise between: (a) organizations and persons, (b) brand names and organizations, and (c) locations and organization, where the latter type of ambiguity is crucial and most frequent in the context of CIS (see table 4). Consider as an example the following clauses:

(1) *Wojewódzki Szpital w Bydgoszczy nabył nową aparaturę ratunkową.*
   (Municipal Hospital in Bydgoszcz purchased an new rescue devices)
(2) *Wojewódzki Szpital w Bydgoszczy został wyremontowany.*
   (Municipal Hospital in Bydgoszcz was renovated.)
(3) *Wojewódzki Szpital w Bydgoszczy wygrał konkurs.*
   (Municipal Hospital in Bydgoszcz won a competition.)

The name *Wojewódzki Szpital w Bydgoszczy* (Municipal Hospital in Bydgoszcz) in (1) refers to the authorities of the hospital (organization), whereas in (2) it refers to the building of the hospital (location). Finally, when we disregard the context of the clause (3) appears in, it is not clear whether the name refers to the building or the authorities of the hospital. We use the following rule of thumb in such a case. If the context (either preceding or succeeding sentence or paragraph etc.) allows to unequivocally interpret the type of entity hidden behind the particular name occurrence, then a single tag should be assigned. Otherwise, if the interpretation is uncertain, two or more annotations may be assigned if necessary. We strive to solve as many type ambiguities as possible while annotating the corpus, since unambiguous information is highly relevant for automatic learning of animacy of named entities, which is a feature heavily utilized in coreference resolution approaches [Evans et al., 2000].

With respect to subtypes we decided to assign the most specific tag as far as possible. Consider as an example a private commercial educational institution which falls into either ORG-COM (commercial organization) or ORG-EDU (educational institution) class. In such a case, the more specific tag has a higher priority, i.e., ORG-EDU. This guideline is similar to the one specified in the EDT annotation guidelines of the ACE program [Doddington et al., 2004].

Ambiguities concerning tailoring particular name mentions to real-world object, e.g., there are ca. 70 cities in Poland named *Zalesie* and several companies called *POLSOFT*, are not handled within DECADENT task. Hence no attributes are produced which link text fragments to concepts.

24.3.2 Name Mentions Border Detection

Specification of what actually constitutes a name mention in Polish may be somewhat problematic. First of all, we apply the longest-match strategy, i.e., we take as many tokens which are potentially part of the name as possible, e.g., we treat the whole phrase *Akademia Ekonomiczna w Poznaniu* (The Poznań University of Economics) as a name mention since *w Poznaniu* is a part of the full name of the institution (this issue does not concern English). In cases, where it is not clear, we exclude such prepositional phrases including location names from being part of the organization name. Furthermore, in case of organization names, we disregard any common noun phrases written in lowercase letters, which preceded a proper name, as a part of the name (e.g., in *grupa kapitałowa Forum -* Holding Forum, only *Forum* is tagged), even if they could intuitively constitute a part of the full name. Contrary to this, in case of locations, we consider some nominal constructions, consisting of simple lowercased common noun phrases followed by a proper name as name mentions. Let us consider the phrase *Most Św. Rocha* which is a name of a bridge. It could be alternatively mentioned in the text as *most Św. Rocha*. Without discussing the subtleties of Polish orthography w.r.t. capitalization and the style commonly used in the newspapers etc., we decided to treat both variants as name mentions as far as the leading common noun phrases is potentially a part of the full-name (as in our example). Hence, no matter if the common noun phrase keyword being a part of the name is written in lowercase letters or starts with a capital initial letter, it is always treated as a part of a name mention. Analogously, we would annotate both *zakłady Hipolita Cegielskiego* (Hipolit Cegielski plants) and *Zakłady Hipolita Cegielskiego* as a name mention.

For solving the problem of name mention borders, we use further rules:

- If a common noun or common noun phrase keyword starts with an initial capital, is not sentence initial, and is followed by a proper name, then it is always considered to be a part of the name mention (even if one would intuitively not consider it as a part of the name), e.g. the word *Grupa* in *Grupa Kapitałowa ABC* (Capital Group ABC)
- In case of addresses all keywords, e.g. *ul., Al., al., Plac*, etc. are a part of the name mention (likewise strategy is followed for some other location subtypes)
- If deleting a lowercased common noun phrase keyword, e.g., *pomnik* in *pomnik Adama Mickiewicza* (monument of Adam Mickiewicz), results in a name (here: *Adam Mickiewicz*), which does not mach the same entity type (which is the case in our example), then such a keyword is a part of the name mention. Constructions like: *powiat Koszaliński* (county of Koszalin), *ocean Atlantycki* (Atlantic Ocean) are further examples of this type. As a counter example, consider the keyword *rzeka* (river) in *rzeka Odra*. Here, deleting *rzeka* does not change the type of *Odra* (in the same context). Hence, the keyword *rzeka* is not treated as apart of the name mention.

24.3.3 Inner Bracketing

Once name mention boundaries are identified, we eventually add some internal bracketing which reflects the inner structure of the mention to some extent. Consider the following name mentions enriched with inner bracketing.

(1) [[ul. [Jana III Sobieskiego $_{\text{PER-NAM}}$] $_{\text{LOC-FAC-TRR}}$] 10/4 $_{\text{LOC-ADR-STR}}$] (the street named after Jan III Sobieski, Polish king)

(2) [[Osiedle [Kopernika $_{\text{PER-NAM}}$] $_{\text{LOC-ADM-DIS}}$] 12/2 $_{\text{LOC-ADR-STR}}$] (the district of buildings named after Copernicus)

(3) [Zakłady [Hipolita Cegielskiego $_{\text{PER-NAM}}$] $_{\text{LOC-FAC-UTI}}$] (Hipolit Cegielski plants)

(4) [Kino [Malta $_{\text{LOC-ADM-DIS \& LOC-WAT}}$] $_{\text{LOC-FAX-ENT \& ORG-REC}}$] (cinema Malta)

(5) [Giełda Papierów Wartościowych w [Warszawie $_{\text{LOC-ADM-CIT}}$] $_{\text{ORG-COM}}$] (Warsaw Stock Exchange)

(6) [[Kulczyk $_{\text{PER-NAM}}$] Tradex $_{\text{ORG-COM}}$] (company)

(7) [fabryka [Pepsi $_{\text{ORG-COM \& PRD}}$] $_{\text{LOC-FAC-UTI}}$] (factory)

(8) [Akademia Ekonomiczna w [Poznaniu $_{\text{LOC-CIT}}$] $_{\text{ORG-EDU}}$] (university name)

A question arises, how to bracket a given name mention. Intuitively, one would only consider annotations of 'inner' entities which are related to CIS and geo-referencing. Hence, in our example only inner entities in (4, 6, 7) should be annotated, since they refer to existing locations relevant for geographical indexing (4, 7), a currently living person, known to be major investor in the city of Poznań (6), which is potentially relevant to CIS, or product brand name within the facility/organization name (7).

However, for the sake of completeness, integrity and potential utilization of the annotated corpus for other tasks (e.g., automatic induction of NE-grammar rules, evaluation of components for recognition of entities of a single type, and learning type disambiguating clues), all (or almost all) inner entities are annotated. The following table gives guidelines with examples for entity type combinations (outer – inner), for which inner bracketing is provided.

Table 1. Entity type combinations

	LOC	ORG	PER
LOC	[Ul. Biała] 13 (address)	Rondo [ONZ] (United Nations roundabout)	ul. [Jana III Sobieskiego] (street)
ORG	AE w [Poznaniu] (university name)	Wydział Prawa [UAM] (Faculty of Law of UAM)	Uniwersytet [Adama Mickiewicza] (university name)
PRD	[Warka] Strong	[Microsoft] Exchange	Piwo [Heweliusz] (beer)

Some complex nominal constructions might pose difficulties while carrying out annotations. Their inner bracketing has to be done carefully. In particular, it is important to differentiate between what we consider a full name and complex noun/prepositional phrases and appositions, which might appear tricky in some context. The following two text fragments clarify the idea:

- [*Szkoła Podstawowa im.* [*Kornela Makuszyńskiego* PER-NAM] *nr. 80 w* [*Poznaniu* LOC-ADM-CIT] ORG-EDU]
- *Siedziba* [*Microsoft* ORG-COM] *w* [*Warszawie* LOC-ADM-CIT] *w* [*Polsce* LOC-ADM-CRY]

The first one happens to be a full-name of the school (with some nested names), whereas the second one constitutes a complex noun phrase consisting of one simple noun phrase followed by two simple preposition phrases, which is unlikely to be a fullname. Hence, only *Microsoft*, *Warszawie*, and *Polsce* are tagged.

Another case touches the problem of organizations with complex structures. Consider as an example a name of an organizational unit: [*Zakład Konserwacji Zabytków* [*Wydziału Architektury* [*Politechniki Warszawskiej* ORG] ORG] ORG] ([the Unit for the Preservation of Historical Buildings and Monuments of [the Faculty of Architecture at [the Warsaw University of Technology]]]). The name of the core organization (*Politechniki Warszawskiej* – the Warsaw University of Technology) is the most relevant for CIS. As we are not interested in recognizing names of all intermediate organizational units, we decided to create only two annotations: one for the inner-most and the other for the outer-most name. In Table 2. we give some numbers of overlapping annotations with detailed information concerning pairwise type clashes (please compare Table 1). The number of overlapping annotations amounts to 210, which constitute 5% of total number of annotations.

Table 2. Overlapping annotations

	LOC	ORG	PER
LOC	60	18	6
ORG	58	23	6
PRD		38	

24.4 The Experiment

In order to be able to reason about real estates value, the CIS system needs to be supplied with diversity of documents from sources being monitored. Hence we have analysed articles from 3 different sources: (a) the real estate supplement to the on-line version of Polish daily newspaper *Rzeczpospolita* (RZ) (b) the online financial magazine *Tygodnik Finansowy* (TF), and (c) different local news portals (NP) which provide news concerning events centered around development of urban architecture. Statistics of the collected documents are given in Table 3. More fine-grained data accompanied by some examples is given in Table 4.

Table 3. Corpus statistics

Corpus	Volume (KB)	Documents	Words	Tags	Words per document	Tags per document
RZ	193	25	26750	1400	1070,00	56,00
TF	180	100	23247	1675	232,47	16,75
NP	80	31	10765	867	347,26	27,97
total:	453	156	60762	3942	389,50	25,27

Table 4. Annotation statistics and examples

Category		Total	Examples
LOC		1661	
	ADM CIT	612	Warszawa
	ADM CMN	20	gmina Warszawa Centrum
	ADM CNT	1	powiat wołomiński
	ADM CRY	207	Polska
	ADM DIS	201	Rataje
	ADM PRO	47	woj. wielkopolskie
	ADM ZON	15	Nowosolska Strefa Przemysłowa
	ADR COR	0	23° S 34 ° W
	ADR STR	35	ul. Dąbrowskiego 42
	ADR URL	51	www.archive.org
	ADR ZIP	0	61-960 Poznań
	FAC ENT	56	pomnik Rajewskiego
	FAC TRH	26	Poznań Główny
	FAC TRR	246	most św. Rocha
	FAC UTI	91	Stary Browar
	LAN	44	Dolina Nidy
	WAT	9	Kanał Ulgi

(Cont.)

Table 4. (Cont.)

ORG		1441	
	COM	1090	Elektromontaż Poznań
	EDU	31	Uniwersytet Adama Mickiewicza
	GOV	94	Urząd Miasta
	HLT	9	Szpital Powiatowy w Braniewie
	OTH	184	Unia Europejska
	REC	33	KKS Lech Poznań SA
PER		486	Witold Gombrowicz
PRD		354	Gazeta Wyborcza

The idea behind the experiment was to annotate the corpus and identify main issues related with using it as a source of semantic information to be acquired by CIS.

The corpus annotation was carried out by four people. The documents' pool was split into two parts and assigned to a different pair of annotators. The final annotation is a result of two iterations of the process consisting of three phases: (1) definition\tuning of guidelines, (2) annotation, (3) cross-validation. It turned out that ca. 10% of all tags had to be corrected and refined after the first iteration, which reflects the complexity of the annotation tasks.

For carrying out the annotation task we have chosen Callisto tool [Day et al., 2004] which supports linguistic annotation of textual sources for any Unicode-supported language and allows for defining user-defined domain and task specific tags. Callisto produces a standoff annotation in AIF (ATLAS Interchange Format) format. [Laprun et al., 2002]. AIF format, implemented as an XML application, offers good properties in respect with extensibility and facilitates widespread exchange and reuse of annotation data. jATLAS is a Java implementation of the ATLAS framework [jATLAS, 2003]. It's API provides methods for modifying and querying annotations as well as reading/writing them from/to AIF files. ATLAS data model employs an extremely general notion of annotation. An ATLAS annotation picks out a region of (possibly structured) text and associates structured information (represented as nested feature structures) to it. Further, AIF supports overlapping annotations which are crucial in the context of DECADENT task. Recently, we have find out that one of the annotation tools provided with the Ellogon platform will better suit our annotation task. Its much more comfortable w.r.t API, GUI and annotation concept wich is based on TIPSTER guidelines.

24.5 Conclusions

In the article we reported on an ongoing endeavor of creating an annotated corpus for supporting development of information extraction tools for utilization in a cadastre system for converting Polish free-text documents into structured data.

To be more precise, we have defined a CIS-relevant entity detection task, including a fine-rained taxonomy, and we elaborated on the annotation guidelines for preparation of the corpus and discussed the subtleties of the tagging process.

At present, the annotated corpus contains 156 documents (over 60.000 words). The described work is partly supported by the European Commission under the Marie Curie ToK "enIRaF" (IST-509766) and a sample the corpus will be available shortly at http://eniraf.kie.ae.poznan.pl.

Our proximate work will comprise of improving our current named-entity recognition machinery via utilization of the created corpus for automatic acquisition of NE patterns. Further, a higher-level information extraction tasks, i.e. coreference resolution task (DEMENTI – Detection of Mentions) are envisaged in the near future. In particular, an appropriate corpus with annotation of all types of mentions will be prepared on top of the one described in this paper. A long-term goal will focus on amalgamation of geo-referencing and time indexing techniques to track entity history.

The work is partly supported by the European Commission under the Marie Curie ToK "enIRaF" (IST-509766).

References

1. [Abramowicz et al., 2004] W. Abramowicz, A. Bassara, A. Filipowska, M. Wiśniewski. *eVEREst – Supporting Estimation of Real Estate Value.* Cybernetics and Systems. An International Journal 35 (7-8), 2004 , pp. 697-708, Taylor&Francis Group.
2. [ACE] ACE Program - http://projects.ldc.upenn.edu/ace/ - accessed on February 10th, 2006.
3. [Amitay et al. 2004] Einat Amitay, Nadav Har'El, Ron Sivan, Aya Soffer Web-a-where: geotagging web content. Proceedings of the 27th annual international ACM SIGIR conference on Research and development in information retrieval, 2004.
4. [Callisto] Callisto - http://callisto.mitre.org/ - accessed on February 10th, 2006.
5. [Chinchor 1998] Nancy A. Chinchor. *Overview of MUC-7.* Message Understanding Conference Proceedings, 1998 (http://www.itl.nist.gov/iaui/894.02/related_ projects/ muc/index.html).
6. [Day et al., 2004] David Day, Chad McHenry, Robyn Kozierok, Laurel Riek. *Callisto : A Configurable Annotation Workbench.* In Proceedings of LREC 2004: Fourth International Conference on Language Resources and Evaluation, Lisbon, Portugal, 2004.
7. [Doddington et al., 2004]George Doddington, Alexis Mitchell, Mark Przybocki, Lance Ramshaw, Stephanie Strassel, Ralph Weischedel. *The Automatic Content Extraction (ACE) Program - Tasks, Data, & Evaluation.* In Proceedings of LREC 2004: Fourth International Conference on Language Resources and Evaluation, Lisbon, Portugal, 2004.
8. [Evans et al., 2000] R. Evans, C. Orasan. *Improving anaphora resolution by identifying animate entities in texts.* Proceedings of the Discourse Anaphora and Reference Resolution Conference (DAARC2000), Lancaster, UK, 2000.

9.   [jATLAS, 2003]. *jATLAS, a Java implementation of the ATLAS framework.*
10.   [http://www.nist.gov/speech/atlas/jatlas/] - accessed on February 10th, 2006.
11.   [Laprun et al., 2002] Christophe Laprun, Jonathan Fiscus, Joh Garofolo, Sylvian Pajot. *A Practical Introduction to Atlas.* In Proceedings of LREC 2002: Third International Conference on Language Resources and Evaluation, La Palma, Canary Islands, Spain, 2002.
12.   [McCurley, 2001] Kevin S. McCurley. Geospatial Mapping and Navigation of the Web. WWW10, Hong Kong.
13.   [Pouliquen et al. 2004] Bruno Pouliquen, Ralf Steinberger, Camelia Ignat, Tom De Groeve. Geographical Information Recognition and Visualisation in Texts Written in Various Languages. ACM Symposium on Applied Computing, ACM 2004.
14.   [Przepiórkowski, 2005] Adam Przepiórkowski. *The IPI PAN Corpus in Numbers.* Proceedings of the 2nd Language & Technology Conference, Poznań, Poland 2005.
15.   [Sundheim, 1995] Beth M. Sundheim. Overview of results of the MUC-6 evaluation. In Proceedings of Sixth Message Understanding Conference (MUC-6). Columbia, Maryland, USA. 1995.

25 Temporalizing Ontology

Andrzej Bassara

Poznań University of Economics, Poland
Department of Management Information Systems
A.Bassara@kie.ae.poznan.pl

25.1 Introduction

Ontologies, as technology, are used to encode knowledge about world, mainly about a specific domain, and to provide common understanding of these domains. They are often considered as a common point of reference in a communication. In other words, they are "explicit specification of a conceptualization" (Gruber 1993). The word conceptualization refers to the way a certain agent or a group of agents percepts certain idea.

Ontologies are treated mostly as static entities. They are constructed once and hardly ever undergo the process of change. Unfortunately this approach is rarely correct. From the above definition at least three important sources of ontologies dynamism may be identified. Change in each of them may lead to significant changes in ontology:

- domain (external)
- conceptalization (internal)
- requirements (technical).

Domains, that are modeled are often dynamic, therefore are subject to permanent changes: new object appears, existing objects case to exist, properties of existing object are changing. (Jensen 2000) highlights following classes of applications where temporal extension is necessary:

- financial applications (portfolio management, accounting, banking)
- record-keeping applications (HR, medical-record, inventory)
- scheduling applications (airline, train, hotel reservations)
- project management

289

W. Abramowicz and H.C. Mayr (eds.), Technologies for Business Information Systems, 289–298.
© 2007 *Springer.*

- scientific applications.

The need for change may also arise not from the nature of domain but from the nature of human. In this case change in an ontology is determined by the change in conceptualization. Let us consider a concept "person in productive age". The extension of this concept depends on the definition which is changing over time and space (while is different among various countries).

The least important need for change is related to changing requirements. In this case ontologies are changed to improve system performance, reliability, or just to cover permanently changing users needs.

One may be tempted by the idea of disallowing changes. The change, however, is not to be discouraged while it is inevitable. Many software engineering (RUP (Kruchten 2003), Agile Development (Boehm & Turner 2005)) or infrastructure management (ITIL (ITIL 2000)) communities have already realized that the only solution to this problem of change is to provide formalized processes for change capture, change propagation as well as processes for releasing updated versions of a product.

Since it is unavoidable to have changes during the ontology lifecycle, the question that also must be raised is, whether it is possible to have only one conceptualization of a given domain at a given point of time. The answer to this question comes not easily and is depended on many factors, mainly the domain and ontology usage patterns being considered.

For instance, the ontology of bibliographic information used to structure books in a library may be created once for quite a long time and may be easily used by most members of the community, while the librarianship has a long lasting history and different taxonomies has been created for ages.

Contrary the ontology of content in P2P networks may be quite dynamic. This dynamism arise from the variety of content being shared. It may be even impossible to come to an agreement on one common ontology, while the community consist of users from different cultures and with different backgrounds. Or the ontology of legislature used to compare legal system of different countries over time. In this case, changes to ontology will be applied according to geographic region or time range being considered.

Summarizing, it may be stated that some information enclosed in ontology are valid only within certain scope (context). This context may be characterized by many dimensions. Above example of "person in productive age" is dependent on time and location but many more dimensions of context may be introduced. The rest of this paper will utilize time as an example dimension, which influences the overall ontology shape.

25.2 Requirements

The presented solution is part of the Black Ocean project, which aims at discovering relations between business entities. In summary, a knowledge base (KB) is constructed. This KB is permanently supplied with information on business entities. Then the filtering mechanism is used for discovering new documents that may contribute to the KB. If such a document is found, new information is extracted and added to KB. Much attention is paid to the determination of a time scope of newly added information. For instance, when it is discovered that person A works for company B, it should be stated when such a statement is true.

This approach implies that data (a.k.a. ABox) is temporal and is valid only in specific periods. The KB also learns how to structure data in new ways. If, for instance, the law has changed there may be a need for restructuring the ontology. Therefore, also the schema (a.k.a. TBox, a.k.a. Terminology) is subject to change and is valid in its own periods. The concept "a person in productive age" is still a good example.

For the purpose of the project, OWL (Bechhofer et al 2004) has been selected for the implementation. Therefore, a clarification is needed, while distinction between data and the schema is somehow sparse. We follow convention that data includes statements about individuals and relations that hold between them, everything else is enclosed in schema (the project follows OWL-DL as strictly as it is only possible, therefore sets of: classes, individuals and relations must be mutually disjoint).

From a general analysis of the problem a number of requirements for ontology temporality have been identified. Although, they are project specific, they may be applied to the vide range of other problems that involve ontology evolution in time. These requirements are related to:

- Statements temporality
- Time references
- Ontology snapshots

25.2.1 Statements Temporality

For the Black Ocean it is infeasible to have an ontology which consist of statements (facts) that are unconditionally true, which are valid at any point in time. It is necessary to have a mechanism which would allow to store in a single OWL document different perspectives on the considered domain – in this case time constitutes the perspective. Since, it is a rear case that the whole ontology is changed at once at particular point in time but the process of change is gradual, the temporality should be implemented at lower level of granularity then the whole document.

We consider a single statement (i.e. ex:subject ex: predicate ex: object, which may be translated into English as subject is in relation predicate with object) as an element which may be consider to exist in time. Basically, RDF (Hayes 2004) statements are considered to be unconditionally true, therefore there is a need to incorporate mechanism, which would allow to state that particular statement is valid only during a certain time period.

As noted before it should be considered that both data as well as the schema are temporal. In case of data the situation is rather simple. The Data Warehousing (DW) paradigm may be followed. In this case, data is never removed from DW. Each entry to the DW is described with a set of DW's dimensions, which describes precisely the situation (context) in which the data is true - for instance, to which period this data applies. The same approach may be used to describe data within OWL. Data temporality refers to the properties of individuals and existence of individuals, both of which are valid only in time ranges.

The more challenging aspect of temporality refers to the temporality of the schema. The schema (terminology) provides means for structuring data, therefore any change in schema may possibly influence ABox, and this influence is discussed in further sections.

25.2.2 Time References

Much of information available today on the Internet, which is a main source of information for the KB, is uncertain and ambiguous. Very often events (see below) that are described in news feeds do not have precisely defined time boundaries – exact start and end dates are unknown. However there usually exist many constraints that relate described events to one another, and which are sufficient for meaningful description.

Example: "Parts of the nation's midsection are cleaning up today after a strong storm system downed power lines…" cnn.com

There are two events described in the above sentence: event A – cleaning of the nation's midsection and event B – storm, which downed dower lines. No precise definition of temporal boundaries of event B is provided, but there exists constraint that states that event B took place before event A. And we also know that event A took place today with respect to information issuing date.

The designed mechanism should allow for the usage of both precisely defined time boundaries for events (absolute references, quantitative relations) as well as relatively defined boundaries by relating events to each other (relative references, qualitative relations).

25.2.3 Ontology Snapshots

The Black Ocean KB contains all data and terminology that has been put in it since the creation. That implies that the ontology consists of various very often contradictory facts, which are not suitable for direct processing. It is however assumed that at any given time there exist, so called, ontology snapshot, which is an ontology for this particular point in time and that this ontology is valid OWL-DL ontology (snapshot shall be free of any temporal extensions).

One should also be able to track changes that appear in the ontology over time. To accomplish this task presented approach should provide infrastructure for computing and presenting in formalized manner the difference between two different snapshots. This difference should consist of information that would allow for transformation from older to newer snapshot.

25.3 Sample Solution

To satisfy above requirements it is necessary to introduce a form of temporal extension, what may be accomplished by successful combination of following elements:

- theory of time
- theory of temporal incidence
- temporal qualification
- modified definition of satisfiability

Theory of time defines the structure and properties of time units being utilized. There is a number of temporal theories: instant-, interval- and instant-interval-based that may be used. The choice of particular theory is orthogonal to proposed solution therefore is not further investigated. This solution is implemented with Allen's period theory. The choice was determined by the availability of ontology of time (Time-OWL), which formalizes Allen's theory in OWL.

Theory of temporal incidence defines domain-independent truth values of fluents (a state that can assume a range of values) and events throughout the time. We impose a couple of restrictions on theory that may be used:

- fluents, in this case, may be either "on" on "off", what means that at particular point of time a single statement may hold or not. If required states may assume a range of values (for instance $<0,1>$) representing the degree of certainty that a statement holds at particular point of time. This would make the solution fuzzy-temporal extension.
- fluents must hold homogonously, i.e. if fluent holds at certain period then it also holds at every instant which is within that period, what may be formalized as: Holds(f,p) iff (Within(i,p) then Holds(f,i))
- it should address the issue of non-atomic fluents (fluents which hold on many periods/instants). For example: Holds(f, a), Holds(f, b) then depending on whether open- or closed-world assumption is used this may imply Holds(f, a $\cup$ b) or Holds(f, a $\cap$ b).
- events are not considered. The presented solution is intended to present the state of the world at different times not the process of change.

In this paper the temporal incidence is derived from the theory CD .
We propose that statements are fluents. That allow us to say that an assertions is temporal regardless the nature of assertion itself. So, for instance:

<ex:a> <ex:b> <ex:c> ~ (S)

means that above statement holds on (S), where (S) is a set of periods and instants for which the statement holds. The above preposition may state for instance that "Roman works at PUE" but also that "A is subclass of C" as well.

We also assume that if:
<ex:a> <ex:b> <ex:c> ~ (S1)
<ex:a> <ex:b> <ex:c> ~ (S2)
then
<ex:a> <ex:b> <ex:c> ~ (S1 ∪ S2)

The above abstract syntax is insufficient. We also need means to introduce the temporal extension right into the RDF model. (Reichgelt H & Villa 2005) defines four way for temporal qualification:

- temporal arguments
- temporal token arguments
- temporal reification
- temporal token reification.

Temporal qualification defines techniques for using a logic to state that statements are true/false at different times. The simplest approach would be to introduce temporal arguments. In this case a simple RDF triple subject-predicate-object could be extended to include additional arguments which would deal with time. This cannot be realized in current RDF model, which allows only for binary predicates. Hence the construction as subject-predicate-object-validityConstraints is unacceptable.

Temporal token argument uses similar approach. Every statement could contain additional argument, which would uniquely identify the statement, like subject-predicate-object-key. Then one could predicate over key, to express temporal validity constraints. This approach is unacceptable due the same reason as temporal arguments approach. This also rules out temporal token reification.

The most straightforward approach is to use temporal reification. Especially that there is direct support for reification in RDF model. Reification allows for treating statements as any other resources. In this case one can predicate directly about statements using ordinary RDF triples.

For instance:
ex:Company rdf:type rdfs:Class.

Can be reified as :
ex:r1 rdf:type ex:Company;
rdf:subject rdf:type;
rdf:predicate rdfs:Class;

Now, it is quite straightforward to state that this statement holds on certain period
ex:r1 rdf:type ex:Company;
rdf:subject rdf:type;
rdf:predicate rdfs:Class;
tr:holds ex:SomeInterval.

25.4 Temporal Statement Satisfiability

Unfortunately the semantic of the above expression is not that straightforward as it seems. The reified statement is still unconditionally true. The reifying statement cannot constraint reified statement. In this case, even if the ex:SomeInterval is empty, the statement ex:Company rdf:type rdfs:Class is true.

Therefore we need a new definition of statement satisfiaility. We need to define when temporal statement is true i.e. when an RDF/S interpretation satisfies temporal statement. To accomplish this task both definitions of interpretation and denotation introduced in RDF semantics needs to be modified.

Firstly, we have to define the time frame, which is a pair of time points and relations that holds between them (each time point is related to its predecessors and successors). We will use a linear continuous time $T = <R, <>$.

The temporal interpretation I_t is a pair $<T, Int>$ (where Int is the interpretation defined in RDF model theory) which for every $t \in T$ assigns an interpretation Int. Denotation is defined as in RDF with the exception that $I(E) = true$ at time $t \in T$ (where E is ground triple s p o.) :

if s, p and o are in V,
　　I(p) is in IP,
　　$<I(s), I(o)>$ is in IEXT(I(p)),
and there is no rs or tt in V, such as
　　$<I(rs), I(rdf:Statement)>$ is in IEXT (I(rdf:type))
　　$<I(rs), I(s)>$ is in IEXT (I(rdf: subject))
　　$<I(rs), I(p)>$ is in IEXT (I(rdf: predicate))
　　$<I(rs), I(o)>$ is in IEXT (I(rdf:object))
　　$<I(rs), I(tt)>$ is in IEXT (I(tr:holds))
or there is rs and tt in V such as
　　$<I(rs), I(rdf:Statement)>$ is in IEXT (I(rdf:type))
　　$<I(rs), I(s)>$ is in IEXT (I(rdf: subject))
　　$<I(rs), I(p)>$ is in IEXT (I(rdf: predicate))
　　$<I(rs), I(o)>$ is in IEXT (I(rdf:object))
　　$<I(rs), I(tt)>$ is in IEXT (I(tr:holds))
　　and t is within tt.
　　otherwise I(E)= false.
(naming follows RDF model theory conventions)

That implies that any RDF statement is satisfied by given interpretation if following conditions are satisfied:

- the statement is true to basic definition of interpretation and denotation
- and one of following is true:
　- the statement is not known to be reified (this breaks the monotonic assumption cause new statement may invalidate the reified statement)
　- the statement is reified and the reifying statement has no property <tr:holds>

- the statement is reified and the reifying statement has the property <tr:holds> whose object is some temporal thing (tt), that contains time point being considered (t) (definition of temporal thing as well as the time point containment conditions depends on the temporal theory and the temporal coincidence theories being used).

We also give two restrictions on statements that cannot be temporal, which refers to Resource class and concrete domains. In most cases, when an ontology is constructed there exist one concept/class that is a superclass of all concepts/classes represented in the ontology. The extension of this/concept class represents universe. In RDF such a class is named Resource. We follow the approach where particular resource exist always but can change its properties over time. Hence, statements as aaa rdf:type rdfs:Resource are atemporal.

Similar restriction refers to concrete domains. Therefore, rdfs:Datatype, rdfs:Literal, rdf:XMLLiteral cannot be objects in temporal statements.

25.5 Inference

Presented definition of interpretation does not allow for many valid interferences. Fortunately, RDF introduces also predefined, restricted vocabulary (example: rdf:type, rdfs:Resource etc.). This vocabulary has been given special meaning, what puts extra semantic conditions that interpretations must satisfy. For instance, the conditions put on rdfs:subclassOf implies that if <ex:A> rdfs:subclassOf <ex:B>., then in every interpretation the extension of class <ex:A> is the subclass of the extension of class <ex:B> (where x is in extension of class Y, when <x,Y> is in IEXT(I(rdf:type))) (for the full set of semantic constraints please refer to (Hayes 2004)).

These semantic conditions along with temporal extension introduces a whole range of valid inference rules. For instance, the above constraint allow us to conduct following reasoning:

For instance:

<ex:marek> rdf:type <ex:Worker> ~ (<1,4>)
<ex:Worker> rdfs:subclassOf <ex:Person> ~ (<1,2>)
<ex:Worker> rdf:type rdfs:Class
<ex:Person> rdf:type rdfs:Class

Implies

<ex:marek> rdf:type ex:Person ~ (<1,2>)

where <x,y> is a time period ranging from x, to y.
Table 1 contains the list of valid RDF temporal inference rules that are based on RDF inference rules. The rule naming corresponds to the one from, where names have just been prefixed with t.

Table 1. Temporal inference rules for RDFS

R. n.	if graph contains	then add
trdf1	uuu aaa yyy .~(S)	aaa rdf:type rdf:Property .~(S)
trdfs2	aaa rdfs:domain xxx .~(Sd) uuu aaa yyy .~(Ss)	uuu rdf:type xxx .~(Sd∩Ss)
trdfs3	aaa rdfs:range xxx .~(Sr) uuu aaa vvv .~(Ss)	vvv rdf:type xxx .~(Sr∩Ss)
trdfs5	uuu rdfs:subPropertyOf vvv .~(S1) vvv rdfs:subPropertyOf xxx .~(S2)	uuu rdfs:subPropertyOf xxx .~(S1∩S2)
trdfs6	uuu rdf:type rdf:Property .~(S)	uuu rdfs:subPropertyOf uuu .~(S)
trdfs7	aaa rdfs:subPropertyOf bbb .~(Sp) uuu aaa yyy .~(Ss)	uuu bbb yyy .~(Sp∩Ss)
trdfs9	uuu rdfs:subClassOf xxx .~(Sc) vvv rdf:type uuu .~(Ss)	vvv rdf:type xxx .~(Sc∩Ss)
rdfs10	uuu rdf:type rdfs:Class .~(S)	uuu rdfs:subClassOf uuu .~(S)
rdfs11	uuu rdfs:subClassOf vvv .~(S1) vvv rdfs:subClassOf xxx .~(S2)	uuu rdfs:subClassOf xxx .~(S1∩S2)
text1	uuu rdfs:domain vvv .~(Sd) vvv rdfs:subClassOf zzz .~(Sc)	uuu rdfs:domain zzz .~(Sd∩Sc)
text2	uuu rdfs:range vvv .~(Sr) vvv rdfs:subClassOf zzz .~(Sc)	uuu rdfs:range zzz .~(Sr∩Sc)
text3	uuu rdfs:domain vvv .~(Sd) www rdfs:subPropertyOf uuu .~(Sp)	www rdfs:domain vvv .~(Sd∩Sp)
text4	uuu rdfs:range vvv .~(Sr) www rdfs:subPropertyOf uuu .~(Sp)	www rdfs:range vvv .~(Sr∩Sp)

25.6 Conclusions

This approach presents means for incorporating temporal information into ontology. It may be now stated that individuals, properties of individuals as well as terminology used to describe individuals exist and can change over time. In presented examples no distinction has been made on what kind of statements are being described. This approach is general enough to provide temporality of data as well as temporality of schema.

Although the solution does not deal with aspects of undecidability of some of temporal information (it is possible to relate intervals for which boundaries are unknown), the solution is complete and provide simple means for maintaining different version of single ontology in one document.

References

1. Allen JE (1983) "Maintaining knowledge about temporal intervals", Commun. ACM 26, 11 November 1983, pp 832-843.
2. Bechhofer S, van Harmelen F, Hendler J, Horrocks I, McGuinness DL, Patel-Schneider PF, Stein LA (2004) "OWL Web Ontology Language Reference", W3C Recommendation, 10 February 2004
3. Boehm B, Turner R (2005) "Management Challenges to Implementing Agile Processes in Traditional Development Organizations", IEEE Software, September/October 2005
4. Freksa C (1992) "Temporal Reasoning Based on Semi-Intervals", Artificial Intelligence, vol. 4, issue 1, 1992, pp 1992-227
5. Gruber T (1993) "A translation approach to portable ontology specifications", Knowledge Acquisition, vol. 5, issue 2, June 1993, pp 199-220
6. Hayes P (2004) "RDF Semantics", W3C Recommendation, 10 February 2004
7. Hobbs JR, Pan F (2004) "An Ontology of Time for the Semantic Web", ACM Transactions on Asian Language Processing (TALIP): Special issue on Temporal Information Processing, Vol. 3, No. 1, March 2004, pp. 66-85.
8. Office of Government Commerce (2000), "ITIL Service Support", Stationery Office, Jun 2000
9. Jensen C (2000) "Temporal Database Management", dr.techn. thesis, April 2000
10. Kruchten P (2003) "The Rational Unified Process: an Introduction", Addison-Wesley Longman Publishing Co., Inc.. 2003
11. Reichgelt H, Villa L (2005) *Temporal Qualification in Artificial Intelligence.* Handbook of Temporal Reasoning in Artificial Intelligence. M. F. D. G. L. Vila., Elsevier Science & Technology: 167-194

26 Semantics-driven XML Data Exchange within Web-serviced Business Applications*

Jolanta Cybulka[1], Adam Meissner[1], Tadeusz Pankowski[1,2]

[1] Institute of Control and Information Engineering, Poznań University of Technology, pl. M. Skłodowskiej-Curie 5, 60-965 Poznań, Poland
{Jolanta.Cybulka,Adam.Meissner,Tadeusz.Pankowski}@put.poznan.pl

[2] Faculty of Mathematics and Computer Science, Adam Mickiewicz University, ul. Umultowska 87, 61-614 Poznań, Poland

26.1 Introduction

Many contemporary e-business applications come into being as Web-serviced systems. The technologies standing beyond such solution provide means to design collaborative and integrative, inter- and intra-organizational business applications. It appeared that in the considered framework the efficient data exchange needs the employment of their semantics specification. Therefore, the Semantic Web technologies occurred to be highly applicable, especially ontologies, natural language processing methods and knowledge representation methods, languages and tools.

The proposed methods of semantics-based exchange of data [1, 5] use the knowledge concerning the intended meaning of the whole schema (or its elements), which is obtained via some "revealing semantics" analysis of the schema, in most cases assisted by a human. The obtained semantics is usually formally specified in the form of ontology and helps to generate the data matches. There exist also the methods in which the matches are discovered by means of some heuristics and machine learning techniques [10].

The presented approach is based on the fact that Web-serviced e-business applications use XML as a standard format for data exchange (www.w3.org/TR/2004/REC-xml11-20040204/). The data are often accompanied by their schemas written in XSD (XML Schema Definition, www.w3.org/TR/2004/REC-xmlschema-0-20041028/).

---

* The work was supported in part by the Polish Ministry of Science and Higher Education under Grant N516 015 31/1553.

299

W. Abramowicz and H.C. Mayr (eds.), Technologies for Business Information Systems, 299–311.
© 2007 Springer.

Moreover, there exist some recommended XSDs for domain-oriented e-business applications, notably BMECat (www.bmecat.org), OpenTrans (www.opentrans.org) or xCBL (www.xcbl.org). For commonly accepted schemas of this kind, ontologies defining their semantics can be defined. It is convenient to embed such schema ontologies in a common foundational ontology, for it enables to obtain a set of correspondences between schema elements via some ontology-based reasoning process. The considered correspondences can be further used to generate semantics-preserving transformations of data. We propose a method to perform this task automatically using information provided by the considered schemas and the discovered set of correspondences.

In Section 2 a general structure of the process of schema- and ontology-based XML data exchange in the e-business scenario is discussed. Section 3 describes a method to generate executable schema mappings performing the transformations. In Section 4 the issues concerning ontology-based support for schema matching are presented. Section 5 contains some final remarks.

26.2 XML-structured Messages Exchange within the Web-serviced Business Applications

Many e-business applications take the form of a Web service system. There exist some specifications of such systems, for example the W3C *Web Service Architecture* (WSA, www.w3.org/TR/2004/NOTE-ws-arch-20040211/) in which the architectural model consisting of the four modules is proposed. One of them is the *message model* that contains the conceptualization of the inter-service communication. The messages can be structured in different ways but the widely used form is the XML schema. So, in this approach the automatic interoperation within the e-business service relies on the exchange of the XML data. They may be structured according to standardized e-business schemas, such as xCBL or the cataloguing schema BMECat accompanied by the business transaction schema OpenTrans. Such schemas may immediately serve as a message structure definition in the WSDL (*Web Services Description Language*, www.w3.org/TR/2005/WD-wsdl20-primer-20050510) description of a service. The analysis of existing schemas reveals that they are developed by various individual, national and public organizations, with the use of various languages, currencies, customs and national legal regulations. Thus the exchange of messages needs doing their (possibly automatic) transformations that preserve the semantics of transmitted data. On this purpose the correspondences and mappings between schemas and their elements should be discovered and formally defined.

Recall the WSDL description assume that the *interfaces* of some *services* contain the processing methods of two types of messages, where the message C_1 is structured under a schema S_1 and the other, C_2 - according to the schema S_2. Both schemas are semantically specified by means of the relevant ontologies, say O_1 and O_2. A message C_1 (the output data of some component) specified by S_1 and O_1 can play the role of the input message C_2 (to some other component) if C_1 can be converted into C_2 structured under S_2 that is specified by O_2. It means that there exists the semantic equivalency between data, based on the O_1 and O_2 alignment, i.e. there is a set of well-defined semantic functions converting C_1 to C_2 and these functions can be used to explain all steps of the conversion. The architecture of a system for such semantic data exchange is sketched in Fig. 1.

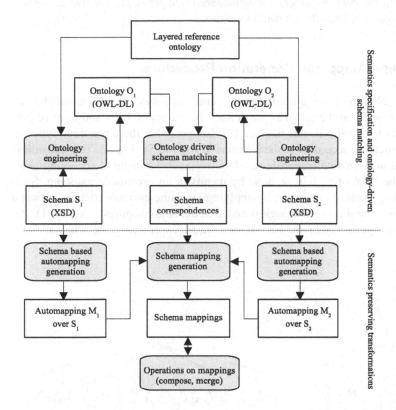

Fig. 1. The structure of a semantic XML data exchange system

The figure illustrates the two phases of XML data exchange process.

1. In the first phase, the ontologies O_1 and O_2 are specified by a knowledge engineer. The ontologies, which represent the semantics of schemas S_1 and S_2, relate to some shared reference ontology that is a layered structure consisting of a foundational ontology and some specializing core ontologies (see Section 4). Then the ontology-driven matching between the two schemas is done to obtain the correspondences between their elements (tags) or between sets of elements.

2. The obtained correspondences form the input to the schema mappings generation procedure in the second phase. This procedure relays on *automappings*, i.e. identity mappings over schemas. An automapping represents the schema and depends on constraints (keys and value dependencies) provided by the schema (see Section 3). The generated mappings between the schemas are "executable" in that they express not only relationships between schemas but also serve to transform the data instances. The considered mappings can be also composed and merged via formally defined operations.

26.3 Schema Mappings Generation Procedure

Now the problem of schema automappings and mappings generation will be addressed, provided that the schemas are defined by means of XSD and a set of correspondences between schemas is given [9]. Suppose that there are three types of messages structured according to the schemas S_1, S_2 and S_3 (Fig. 2). The semantics-preserving transformation of transferred data (instances) structured according to S_2 or S_3 into the form of S_1 will be done by means of an executable mapping. Such a mapping is generated automatically applying semantic correspondences between schemas (discovered using ontologies) and schema automappings (see Fig. 1). An automapping is generated on the basis of constraints expressed in the schema.

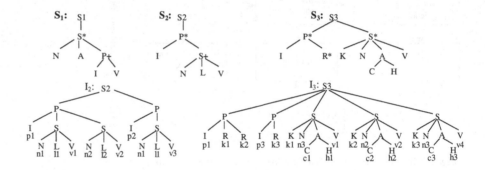

Fig. 2. Tree representation of the XML schemas and their instances

In Fig. 2 three catalog schemas are depicted having labels: *supplier (S)*, *dealer (D)*, *name (N)*, *address (A)*, *localization (L)*, *product (P)*, *identifier (I)*, *price (V)*, *manufacturer (M)*, *city (C)* and *street (H)*. Labels R and K are used to join products with their suppliers. I_2 and I_3 are the instances of S_2 and S_3, respectively. The schema S_1 does not have any materialized instance.

The part of the XSD representation of S_1 schema is given below (with `<valdep>` as a non-standard element) based on which the automapping $\mathcal{M}_1$ is generated.

```
<schema xmlns="http://www.w3.org/2001/XMLSchema">
...
  <element name="S"> <complexType> <sequence>
    <element name="N".../> <element name="A".../>
    <element ref="P"/> </sequence></complexType>
      <key name="SKey">
        <selector xpath="."/><field xpath="N"/>
      </key>
      <valdep><target name="A"/>
        <function name="a"/><source xpath="N"/>
      </valdep>
  </element>
  <element name="P"> <complexType><sequence>
    <element name="I".../> <element name="V".../>
    <element name="M".../> </sequence></complexType>
      <key name="PKey">
        <selector xpath="."/> <field xpath="I"/>
      </key>
      <valdep> <target name="V"/>
       <function name="v"/> <source xpath="I"/>
       <source xpath="N" ref="SKey"/>
      </valdep>
      <valdep> <target name="M"/>
        <function name="m"/> <source xpath="I"/>
      </valdep>
  </element>
</schema>
```

The $\mathcal{M}_1$ over S_1 is the identity mapping from the set of all instances of S_1 onto itself (the lines of the procedure are numbered for reference). It is formally defined as a quadruple $\mathcal{M} = (G, \Phi, C, \Delta)$ and generated as follows:

$\mathcal{M}_1 =$ **foreach** G_1 **where** Φ_1 **when** C_1 **exists** $\Delta_1 =$

(1) **foreach** $\$y_{S1}$ **in** $/S1$, $\$y_S$ **in** $\$y_{S1}/S$, $\$y_N$ **in** $\$y_S/N$, $\$y_A$ **in** $\$y_S/A$,
$\$y_P$ **in** $\$y_S/P$, $\$y_I$ **in** $\$y_P/I$, $\$y_V$ **in** $\$y_P/V$, $\$y_M$ **in** $\$y_P/M$,

(2) **where true**

(3) **when** $\$y_A = a(\$y_N)$, $\$y_V = v(\$y_N, \$y_I)$, $\$y_M = m(\$y_I)$
exists

(4) $F_{/S1}()$ **in** $F_{()}()/S1$

(5) $F_{/S1/S}(\$y_N)$ **in** $F_{/S1}()/S$

(6) $F_{/S1/S/N}(\$y_N)$ **in** $F_{/S1/S}(\$y_N)/N$ **with** $\$y_N$

(7) $F_{/S1/S/A}(\$y_N, \$y_A)$ **in** $F_{/S1/S}(\$y_N)/A$ **with** $\$y_A$

(8) $F_{/S1/S/P}(\$y_N, \$y_I)$ **in** $F_{/S1/S}(\$y_N)/P$

(9) $F_{/S1/S/P/I}(\$y_N, \$y_I)$ **in** $F_{/S1/S/P}(\$y_N, \$y_I)/I$ **with** $\$y_I$

(10) $F_{/S1/S/P/V}(\$y_N, \$y_I, \$y_V)$ **in** $F_{/S1/S/P}(\$y_N, \$y_I)/V$ **with** $\$y_V$

(11) $F_{/S1/S/P/M}(\$y_N, \$y_I, \$y_M)$ **in** $F_{/S1/S/P}(\$y_N, \$y_I)/M$ **with** $\$y_M$

After the variables definition (1), restrictions on them (2) are given (with **true** as "no restrictions"). The equalities in (3) reflect value dependencies (<valdep> of the XSD), where $\$y_A = a(\$y_N)$ states the dependency between the address of a supplier and its name. It means that there exists a term of the form $a()$, which represents the mapping of suppliers' names on their addresses (the definition of the a function is unimportant). The same concerns $\$y_V = v(\$y_N, \$y_I)$ and $\$y_M = m(\$y_I)$. The $F_{/S1/S}(\$y_N)$ expression is a Skolem term, where $F_{/S1/S}$ is the Skolem function name of type $/S1/S$. The value of this term is a node of the type $/S1/S$ of the newly created XML data tree. The **in** operator indicates that its left-hand side belongs to the set of nodes denoted by the right-hand side expression. The text value of a leaf node is determined by the **with** operator. A Skolem function of the type P has as arguments the key paths of the element of type P. They are defined by means of the <key> specification (e.g. I for $/S1/S/P$) and are inherited from their superelements (N for $/S1/S/P$). The key for a leaf element includes the leaf element itself, so its text value also belongs to the list of arguments (see e.g. $F_{/S1/S/P/M}(\$y_N, \$y_I, \$y_M)$).

In (4) two new nodes are created, the root $r = F_{()}()$ and the node $n = F_{/S1}()$ of the outermost element of type $/S1$. The node n is a child of the type $S1$ of r. In (5) a new node n' is created for any distinct value of $\$y_N$, each such node has the type $/S1/S$ and is a child of type S of the node created by $F_{/S1}()$ in (4). For any distinct value of $\$y_N$ in (6) also a new node n'' of type $/S1/S/N$ is created. Each such node is a child of type N of the node created by the invocation of $F_{/S1/S}(\$y_N)$ in (5) for the same value of $\$y_N$. For n'' is a leaf, its textual value is equal to the current value of $\$y_N$. The rest of the specification may be interpreted in a similar way. The automappings $\mathcal{M}_2$ and $\mathcal{M}_3$ for S_2 and S_3 can be generated by analogy.

To create mappings between schemas the correspondences between them are needed. Table 1 lists the correspondences (σ) between paths leading from the root to a leaf for S_1 and S_2, and for S_1 and S_3.

Table 1. The correspondences between maximal schema paths

$P \in S_1$	$\sigma(P) \in S_2$	$P \in S_1$	$\sigma(P) \in S_3$
$/S1/S/N$	$/S2/P/D/N$	$/S1/S/N$	$/S3/S/N$
$/S1/S/A$	$/S2/P/D/L$	$/S1/S/A$	$f_A(/S3/S/A/C, /S3/S/A/H)$
$/S1/S/P/I$	$/S2/P/I$	$f_C(/S1/S/A)$	$/S3/S/A/C$
$/S1/S/P/V$	$/S2/P/D/V$	$f_H(/S1/S/A)$	$/S3/S/A/H$
		$/S1/S/P/V$	$/S3/S/V$

For example, $\sigma(/S1/S/A) = f_A(/S3/S/A/C, /S3/S/A/H)$ denotes a $1 : n$ correspondence (one path from $S1$ corresponds to a pair of paths from $S3$). The function

f_A establishes a 1:1 correspondence between text values assigned to $/S1/S/A$, and a pair of values conforming to $/S3/S/A/C$ and $/S3/S/A/H$. If, for example, $/S1/S/A : "c1,h1"$, $/S3/S/A/C : "c1"$, and $/S3/S/A/H : "h1"$, then we have $"c1,h1" = f_A("c1","h1")$, where $P : v$ indicates that a path P has a text value v.

Having the correspondences (Table 1) and automappings is sufficient to generate mappings between schemas. Let $\mathcal{M}_1 = (G_1, \Phi_1, C_1, \Delta_1)$ and $\mathcal{M}_2 = (G_2, \Phi_2, C_2, \Delta_2)$ be the two automappings over $S1$ and $S2$, respectively. The mapping $Map(S2, S1)$ from $S2$ to $S1$ is defined as follows:

$$\mathcal{M}_{21} = Map(S_2, S_1) = (G_2, \Phi_2, C_1, \Delta_1)[\$y : P \to \$x : \sigma(P)],$$

where $[\$y : P \to \$x : \sigma(P)]$ denotes the replacement of any variable of type P (occurring in C_1, Δ_1) by the variable of type $\sigma(P)$ defined in G_2. So, we have:

$\mathcal{M}_{21}=$**foreach** $\$x_{S2}$ **in** $/S2$, $\$x_P$ **in** $\$x_{S2}/P$, $\$x_I$ **in** $\$x_P/I$, $\$x_D$ **in** $\$x_P/D$,
$\quad\quad\quad \$x_N$ **in** $\$x_D/N$, $\$x_L$ **in** $\$x_D/L$, $\$x_V$ **in** $\$x_D/V$
$\quad$ **where true**
$\quad$ **when** $\$x_L = a(\$x_N)$, $\$x_V = v(\$x_N, \$x_I)$, $\$x_M = m(\$x_I)$
$\quad$ **exists**
$\quad\quad F_{/S1}()$ **in** $F_{()}()/S1$
$\quad\quad F_{/S1/S}(\$x_N)$ **in** $F_{/S1}()/S$
$\quad\quad F_{/S1/S/N}(\$x_N)$ **in** $F_{/S1/S}(\$x_N)/N$ **with** $\$x_N$
$\quad\quad F_{/S1/S/A}(\$x_N, \$x_A)$ **in** $F_{/S1/S}(\$x_N)/A$ **with** $\$x_A$
$\quad\quad F_{/S1/S/P}(\$x_N, \$x_I)$ **in** $F_{/S1/S}(\$x_N)/P$
$\quad\quad F_{/S1/S/P/I}(\$x_N, \$x_I)$ **in** $F_{/S1/S/P}(\$x_N, \$x_I)/I$ **with** $\$x_I$
$\quad\quad F_{/S1/S/P/V}(\$x_N, \$x_I, \$x_V)$ **in** $F_{/S1/S/P}(\$x_N, \$x_I)/V$ **with** $\$x_V$
$\quad\quad F_{/S1/S/P/M}(\$x_N, \$x_I, \$x_M)$ **in** $F_{/S1/S/P}(\$x_N, \$x_I)/M$ **with** $\$x_M$

$\mathcal{M}_{21}$ converts any instance of S_2 into an instance of S_1. Moreover, all target constraints (keys and value dependencies) as well as all semantic correspondences between S_2 and S_1 are preserved.

The mapping $\mathcal{M}_{21}$ is an example of a *mapping composition*, $\mathcal{M}_{21} = \mathcal{M}_2 \bullet \mathcal{M}_1$, where σ defines a correspondence between $source(\mathcal{M}_2)$ and $source(\mathcal{M}_1)$.

Note, that while converting I_2 into I_{21}, the variable $\$y_M$ cannot be replaced. Then values of $\$y_M$ will be terms $"m(p1)"$ and $"m(p2)"$, since $\$x_I$ will be bound to $"p1"$ and $"p2"$ within I_2 (Fig. 3(a)). These terms can be resolved while merging I_{21} with I_3 (for example $"m(p1)"$ will be replaced by $"m1"$ since I_3 states that the product $"p1"$ is manufactured by $"m1"$).

To merge S_2 and S_3 under S_1, we define *merging of mappings*. Let $\mathcal{M}_{21} = (G_1, \Phi_1, C_1, \Delta_1)$, $\mathcal{M}_{31} = (G_2, \Phi_2, C_2, \Delta_2)$, $\mathcal{M}_{21}$ and $\mathcal{M}_{31}$ are defined using disjoint sets of variables, and $target(\mathcal{M}_{21}) = target(\mathcal{M}_{31})$. Then the merge of $\mathcal{M}_{21}$ and $\mathcal{M}_{31}$ is defined as the mapping:

$$\mathcal{M}_{21} \cup \mathcal{M}_{31} = (G_1 \cup G_2, \Phi_1 \wedge \Phi_2, C_1 \cup C_2, \Delta_1 \cup \Delta_2).$$

Intuitively, the obtained mapping consists of the union $G_1 \cup G_2$ of variable definitions over $source(\mathcal{M}_{21})$ and $source(\mathcal{M}_{31})$, and the conjunction $\Phi_1 \wedge \Phi_2$ of restrictions over these variables. C_1 and C_2 are defined over the same target schema and differ only in variable names. The same holds for Δ_1 and Δ_2. The result of merging I_2 and I_3 under S_1 is given in Fig. 3(b).

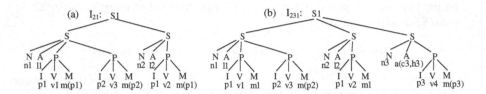

Fig. 3. Results of $I_{21} = \mathcal{M}_{21}(I_2)$ and $I_{231} = (\mathcal{M}_{21} \cup \mathcal{M}_{31})(I_2, I_3)$ transformations

Note that values of some leaf elements (M) are missed and are replaced by terms following value dependencies defined in the schema. This convention forces some elements to have the same values. A term, like "$m(p1)$" can be resolved using other mappings (see Fig. 3(b)).

26.4 Schema Correspondences Revealing through the Use of Ontologies

The most natural class of possible correspondences between the schema elements (Fig. 1) may be established on the basis of the *equivalence* and the *subsumption* relations between the ontological concepts representing schema elements. Roughly speaking, the equivalence holds between two identical concepts, while the subsumption between two concepts means that the first of them is more general then the latter (e.g. *Type* subsumes *GDT* and *HDT*, where *GDT* and *HDT* stand for gas device type and hydraulic device type, respectively). Generally, we consider the correspondence between a concept and a set of concepts, which has been previously denoted as $1 : n$ (or 1:1 when the set consists of one element). The approach does not comprise correspondences between sets of concepts since costs may exceed practical profits. The problem is computationally hard and many of its cases do not conform to the intended, intuitive meaning of the correspondence term.

The ontology is used to specify a conceptualization and takes the form of a structure consisting of *concepts* and *relations* which hold between them. The relations enable to specify the intended meaning of concepts.

We consider the layered ontological structure with the common shared (a reference) ontology on top of it (Fig. 1). This is further modularized and contains a top part representing the most general (domain independent) concepts, interrelated by the ground relations. It is referred to as the *foundational ontology* and presents the general view on reality, such as DOLCE (*Descriptive Ontology for Linguistic and Cognitive Engineering*) with the Descriptions&Situations (D&S) extension ([7, 6]). The Web-serviced systems are semantically specified by core ontologies of services such as COWS (*Core Ontology of Web Services* [8]) that specializes DOLCE and some of its extensions. It is practical to have such a layer in the reference ontology. In such reference ontology the domain ontologies may be anchored (O_1 and O_2 in Fig. 1) which materialize the semantics of data processed by the Web-serviced application. This is the case of our message structuring schemas. Additionally, we assume that for the sake of decidability and efficiency of inference methods ontologies are expressed in Description Logics (DLs) [3].

Recall the XML schemas from Fig. 2. The knowledge engineer tries to reveal the semantics lying behind the tags names and the schema composition rules in the context of the DOLCE+D&S, and decides on the choice and the definition of the ontological concepts (of O_1 and O_2) and their embodiment in the reference ontology. The concepts will be defined in OWL DL [4] and attached to the XML schema.

In DOLCE+D&S the conceptual specification of the reality may consist of the different (epistemic) layers, namely the "descriptions" (theories) and their models. The situation description should "satisfy" some real "situation". The relation of satisfaction is one of the ground relations.

The considered catalogue schemas represent somehow "frozen" real business "situations" (for example, selling and buying of goods), so the specialization of the *SituationDescription* concept is attached to it. Such a description defines a *Concept-Description* that aggregates: the action description (*Course*), the functional roles involved in the action (*Role*: *AgentiveFunctionalRole* and *Non-agentiveFunctionalRole*) and the parameters of the situation (*Parameter*). The standard ground relations connect the components of the situation description (Fig. 4).

In particular, we assume the existence of the concept *Selling* which specializes the concept *BusinessActivity*, which in turn is a specialization of the *Course*. The *Dealer* and the *Supplier* occurring in the schema are modeled as the (subject of the activity) *AgentiveFunctionalRoles* which are linked to the *Selling* by the ground *modalTarget* relation. The selling activity has also the object of the activity, the element *Product*, which is the specialization of the *Non-agentiveFunctionalRole* (also linked to the *Selling* by the *modalTarget*). The situations *Selling* have *Parameters*, i.e. some XML elements connected to the *Supplier*, the *Dealer* and the *Product*. All the *Parameters* can be assigned values coming from some *Regions* by means of the *valuedBy* ground relation. The relation *requisiteFor* binds the *Parameters* to the functional roles and the courses of events. The situation and concept description components can be also linked to the ontological entities that constitute the real situations, not mentioned here (see Fig. 4).

The semantics of various schemas may be defined by different knowledge engineers. Hence, the same "pieces of semantics" may be defined under different names

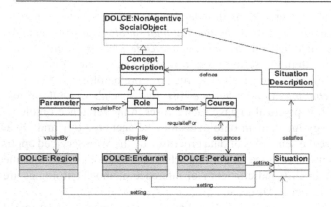

Fig. 4. The top-level of DOLCE+D&S in UML [8]

and with slightly different descriptions. Therefore, the ontology O_1 contains the following definition of the concept (class) *Supplier*:

```
<owl:Class rdf:ID="Supplier">
    <owl:unionOf rdf:parseType="Collection">
        <owl:Restriction>
          <owl:onProperty rdf:resource="&ONT;supplies" />
            <owl:allValuesFrom rdf:resource="#GDT" />
        </owl:Restriction>
        <owl:Restriction>
          <owl:onProperty rdf:resource="&ONT;supplies" />
            <owl:allValuesFrom rdf:resource="#HDT" />
        </owl:Restriction>
    </owl:unionOf>
</owl:Class>
```

The ontology O_2 might contain the following definition a concept *Dealer*: $Dealer \equiv \forall supplies.(GDT \sqcup HDT)$, in order to shorten the notation we give it as a DL formula ([3]).

The description *Supplier* symbolizes a set of individuals, who supply gas devices (*GDT*) only and also those who supply only hydraulic devices (*HDT*), while the concept *Dealer* contains individuals, who supply only one type of devices, which are either gas devices or hydraulic devices. The role *supplies* specializes the relation *requisiteFor*. The descriptions of concepts *GDT* and *HDT* are identical in both ontologies.

In order to formally specify the correspondence relationships between XML schemas we define the subsumption and the equivalence in terms of DLs. It should be remarked, that a concept in DLs is interpreted as a set of individuals and the expression $C \sqcup D$ denotes a union (in the sense of the set theory) of concepts C and D. Let

$CS = \{C_1, \ldots, C_n\}$ be a set of concepts C_i for $i = 1, \ldots, n$ and let $\bigsqcup CS = C_1 \sqcup \ldots \sqcup C_n$. A concept D (*subsumer*) *subsumes* a set of concepts CS(*subsumee*) iff $\bigsqcup CS$ is a subset of D. A set of concepts CS and a concept D are *equivalent* iff $\bigsqcup CS$ subsumes D and D subsumes $\bigsqcup CS$.

The subsumption between concepts can be established by inference methods described in [3]. For example, it can be concluded that the concept *Supplier* defined in the ontology O_1 subsumes the *Dealer* from the ontology O_2.

A subsumption not always conforms to the intuitive meaning of the correspondence intended by the user. Thus, the decision about including the particular case of subsumption to the correspondence relation in general cannot be made automatically. Moreover, when looking for the schema element, which corresponds "by subsumption" to the given element, one expects that the subsumer is possibly the most specific (i.e. the least) concept. In other words, the subsumer should directly succeed the concept modeling the considered element in the order defined by the subsumption relation. In case of the set of concepts, the subsumer should be the *least common subsumer* ([3]) of all elements included in the set. This can be retrieved from the *subsumption hierarchy*, also called the *taxonomy*. The taxonomy is a graph, which represents the partial ordering (by subsumption) of the given set of concepts. It may be constructed in many ways, assuming that a procedure of testing for the subsumption between two concepts is given. A good introduction to algorithms of computing the subsumption hierarchy contains [2]. Many of them introduce (for technical reasons) the element $\top$ (top) to the taxonomy, which may be absent in the input set of concepts. This element represents the most general concept, that is the subsumer of all considered concepts.

Summing up, we propose the simple method of establishing correspondence relationships between elements of two XML schemas, say S_1 and S_2. In the first step the taxonomy T is created for the set of concepts representing all elements of the schema S_1 and S_2. Then, the taxonomy T is taken as an input to the algorithm *FindCorresp*, which constructs the correspondence relation *Cor*. We assume that the symbol $F(C)$ for every concept C from the taxonomy T denotes a set of concepts directly subsumed by C and belonging to the other schema than C belongs to. It should be observed that C is in general the least common subsumer of $F(C)$.

Algorithm *FindCorresp*
Input: T - the taxonomy connected with elements of the schema S_1 and S_2.
Output: *Cor* - the correspondence relation between elements of S_1 and S_1.
begin
    1. Let $Cor := \emptyset$.
    2. For every concept C from T, such that $C \neq T$ and $F(C) \neq \top$
       perform 3 then end.
    3. If C is subsumed by $\bigsqcup F(C)$ then let $Cor := Cor \cup (C, F(C))$
       else let $Cor := Cor \cup Ask(C, F(C))$.
end.

The condition from the step 3 expressing that C is subsumed by $\bigsqcup F(C)$ implies the equivalence between C and $\bigsqcup F(C)$ since the subsumption in the opposite direction follows from the definition of the set $F(C)$. Therefore, if C and $F(C)$ are equivalent, then the pair $(C, F(C))$ may be added to the relation Cor. In the other case C and $F(C)$ are related only by subsumption, so their correspondence has to be verified by a human. Hence, the function Ask is called, which asks the user whether the first argument (C) corresponds to the second one, that is $F(C)$. If the answer is positive then the function returns a pair $(C, F(C))$, otherwise the value of the function Ask is $\emptyset$.

In particular case one may be interested in finding correspondences between leaves of XML schemas only. In this situation, the set of concepts for which the taxonomy is constructed (phase 1) should be restricted to leaves of the regarded schemas.

26.5 Final remarks

The problem of schema mapping is considered, which occurs in the XML structured messages exchange within Web-serviced business applications. Our solution to this problem relies on the automatic generation of semantics-preserving schema mappings. We discussed how automappings could be generated using keys and value dependencies defined in XML Schema. Constraints on values can be used to infer some missing data. Mappings between two schemas can be generated automatically from their automappings and correspondences between schemas. Automappings represent schemas, so operations over schemas and mappings can be defined and performed in a uniform way. We also outline the idea, how the ontological knowledge describing the semantics of XML schemas may be applied for finding correspondences between elements of different schemas.

References

1. Arenas M, Libkin L (2005) XML Data Exchange: Consistency and Query Answering. In: Proc. of the PODS Conference: 13–24
2. Baader F, Franconi E, Hollunder B, Nebel B, Profitlich H J (1992) An empirical analysis of optimization techniques for terminological representation systems, or: Making KRIS get a move on. In: Proc. of the 3rd Int. Conf. on Principles of Knowledge Representation and Reasoning (KR'92): 270–281
3. Baader F, McGuinness D L, Nardi D, Patel-Schneider P F (eds) (2003) The Description Logic Handbook: Theory, implementation, and applications. Cambridge University Press, Cambridge
4. McGuinness D L, Smith M K, Welty C (2004) OWL Web Ontology Language Guide, http://www.w3.org/TR/owl-guide/
5. Doan A, Noy N F, Halevy A (2004) Introduction to the Special Issue on Semantic Integration. SIGMOD Record 33(4): 11–13

6. Gangemi A, Mika P (2003) Understanding the Semantic Web through Descriptions and Situations. In: Proc. of ODBASE03, Berlin
7. Masolo C, Borgo S, Gangemi A, Guarino N, Oltramari A (2003) WonderWeb Deliverable D18; Ontology Library (final), http://wonderweb.semanticweb.org/deliverables/D18.shtml
8. Oberle D, Lamparter S, Grimm S, Vrandečić D, Staab S, Gangemi A (2005) Towards Ontologies for Formalizing Modularization and Communication in Large Software Systems,Technical Report, University of Karlsruhe, AIFB
9. Pankowski T (2006) Management of executable schema mappings for XML data exchange, LNCS 4254: 264–277
10. Rahm E, Bernstein P A (2001) A survey of approaches to automatic schema matching. The VLDB Journal 10(4): 334–350

27 An Ontological Document Management System

Eric Simon, Iulian Ciorăscu, Kilian Stoffel*

Information Management Institute, University of Neuchâtel, Switzerland,
{eric.simon,iulian.ciorascu,kilian.stoffel}@unine.ch,
http://www.unine.ch/imi

27.1 Introduction

Document Management Systems (DMS) form the cornerstone of all business and management information systems. They are sustaining the pyramid of a company's internal knowledge and are designed to provide rapid document retrieval to knowledge workers, reduce error rates, control access to documents, and significantly improve business performance [1]. Document Management Systems try to give the users control over their companies' institutionalized knowledge.

In this context, recent developments such as the Open Document Management API (ODMA [2]) for simplifying the integration and interoperability of standard desktop applications with Document Management Systems, as well as the emergence of standards for representing knowledge in open formats (e.g. OWL for ontologies [3]) change the way DMS are perceived. They are no longer mere sophisticated search engines, but have evolved into increasingly complex systems for creation, management, control and dissemination of knowledge throughout the company. The knowledge must be integrated into the companies business processes, products and services. This helps companies become more innovative and agile providers of high quality products and customer services.

Moreover, companies' web sites are often alimented by the content provided by a DMS. Especially Web sites targeting user support are based upon the companies internal DMS. This is also true for intranets providing up to date information to the companies collaborators. Most of the intra- and extranets are based on some form of Content Management Systems (CMS) [4, 5]. The goal of these systems is the collaborative creation of documents and other forms of content. This process is very closely related to document management. On the one hand the content created in

* This work was supported by the Swiss National Science Foundation, project number 200021-103551/1.

W. Abramowicz and H.C. Mayr (eds.), Technologies for Business Information Systems, 313–325.
© 2007 Springer.

a CMS is often based on existing documents and on the other hand a CMS often provides new documents that should be integrated into the DMS. Therefore a tight integration of these two systems (DMS and CMS) is very important for an efficient management of the overall information and knowledge of a company.

In this document we describe a Document Management System, based on an ontological structure of the data integrated in a Content Management System, allowing the integration of the three main components mentioned above. This architecture was motivated by the needs we identified in several projects in direct collaboration with institutions working in the health, bioinformatics, security, and linguistics domains [6]. The goal was to find a system architecture that was as open as possible to allow integration of new components as smoothly as possible. From an implementation's point of view we based our system on accepted open standards that will allow anyone interested in a similar system to replicate or use it without restriction.

The remainder of the paper is structured in the following way. In Section 27.2 we describe the overall architecture of the proposed system. In Section 27.3 we show how the integration of ontologies can greatly improve the structuring capacity of a DMS. Section 27.4 describes how within our architecture we can deal with security issues. In Section 27.5 and Section 27.6 we will describe the implementation of the system followed by an illustrative application. In the conclusion we will give some further directions.

27.2 Architecture

There are two main reasons for defining an architecture such as the one presented here:openness, in the sense of offering the possibility to integrate any existing tool, and ease of the integration of the system into an existing information management infrastructure.

As outlined in the Introduction the rough architecture of the proposed system will resemble the structure of a CMS as shown in Figure 1. On one side the system is connected to all internal and external document sources such as DMSs, file systems, data bases or other data repositories storing documents. This information is internally restructured using ontologies in order to give the user more rapid and more accurate access to their documents. The access to the system is guaranteed through a web interface as shown in Figure 1.

This architecture in three layers facilitates the integration of existing document resources through the different access mechanisms offered by each system. The integration of the system itself into an existing infrastructure is facilitated as the third layer allows a standard HTTP-integration. In the following we will give some further details on each layer. The implementation details will be given in Section 27.5.

The first layer essentially provides the data integration functionality. This is done in two different ways.

One consists of an internal database that is part of our system. If documents are uploaded and they do not belong to any existing Document Management System,

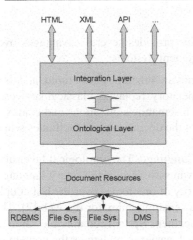

Fig. 1. The three-tier architecture

then they will be stored in the system's internal store. The functionality provided by this store corresponds roughly to that of an object oriented data base. The overall architecture is independent of the choice of this data base system. If any preferences for a given data base system exist then this system can easily be integrated as all interactions with the store are realized through standard APIs.

The other way consists of the integration of existing Document Management Systems. Our system provides an interface to integrate these systems. However, they have to provide an access mechanism to the documents and our system provides an interface to specify them. Once these specifications are given, the integration into the system is seamless. In the upload procedures the user can specify in which store he wants to have his documents and in the search process it is possible to restrict searches to certain data bases. These are the only two places where the different stores are visible.

The second layer is the heart of the system. It provides all the semantics that is added to the system through the use of ontologies. The ontologies are used to fulfill mainly three tasks. Firstly, they are used to classify documents that are added to the system. Secondly, they are used to filter the data in the system. Finally they are used to formulate queries and present the results.

The third layer is constructed in such a way that it can easily be integrated into an existing Business Information System. The integration can be realized through a standard web interface or through a web service. These are the two mechanisms currently offered. Other mechanisms can easily be added.

27.3 Ontologies

Using ontologies for the meta data repositories provides several advantages over classical approaches used in Document Management Systems:

- **Better Organization of the Data.** Ontologies are inherently structured, and they add a semantic layer over the document repository, replacing classical keyword-like meta data annotation of documents with semantic annotations and contexts. This allows a more powerful organization of the documents and facilitates scalability.
- **Increased Expressiveness of the Query Language.** The ontological layer also acts as a semantic index to enhance the expressiveness of the query language. One of the principal reasons for the popularity of ontologies over the last couple of years is their potential use for creating a semantic index for the web [7]. The basic idea for a semantic Document Management System remains the same as the one used for the web. It is however much easier to realize as the content of the document data base is known.
- **Human Readable Presentation of Search Results.** The results of the search queries are presented using the ontological relations, which allows for a presentation in context. This presentation facilitates the navigation within the results and facilitates quick drill downs. The time necessary for finding relevant documents is greatly reduced.
- **Easier Analysis of the Documents.** Often the analysis of some characteristics of documents is necessary for applying techniques of document clustering or text mining. The semantic annotation enabled by ontologies can be very useful in disambiguating terms and increasing the overall performance of these techniques. As the size of the document corpora are constantly growing text mining is becoming increasingly important and therefore it is crucial to provide efficient support for these techniques.

27.3.1 Detailed Explanation of Ontology Usage

Document Management Systems typically use RDBMS as an underlying technology for meta data storage, and indexes for efficient search. While sufficient when the structure of the data does not go beyond a tree-like classification and/or the search requirements are of a keyword based kind, this approach presents limitations as soon as the interrelations between elements are more complex or the user wants to browse the data using advanced filtering techniques. As soon as more relations between words such as synonyms, meronyms, hyponyms, are used, ontological support is needed.

Typically, the most important aspect of a Document Management System is to allow the users to quickly and efficiently find and retrieve the documents, based on different techniques:

- **Keyword Search.** This is the most obvious way of searching for information, and works very well when the user knows quite precisely what he's trying to find and the related keywords to use [8]. The idea here is to sufficiently narrow the results using a combination of keywords, so that the user can pick the desired document from a small enough list at a single glance. The problems with this technique are two-fold: first the user has to have a very precise knowledge of the representation of the meta data and the domain, and the amount of documents has to be quite small and very well categorized using the corresponding keywords. Techniques such as synonyms, pruning, ranking etc. are able to improve the results, but within limits.

- **Repository Browsing.** There is another way of searching information that is so obvious it is often omitted. If the amount of document is sufficiently small, and very well structured in form of a list or a tree, it is often easier to just browse through the entire structure to find the required document, much like someone would go through folders on a file system. The problem with such an approach is well known, as some documents tend not to be easily categorized in only one branch of a tree, and the vast amount of documents typically used in a Document Management System is usually much too large for this technique to be applicable. Still, this approach has to be implemented, as users tend to develop a kind of topological knowledge of the ontologies over time and prefer browsing to always having to enter key words and search.

- **Keyword Filtering and Browsing.** This is a combined technique aimed at narrowing down the number of presented documents by first filtering the results based on a number of keywords, or more complex expressions if necessary, and presenting the information in context, typically a tree with contextual relations (representing a portion of a graph), to allow browsing and more efficiently finding the required information. This is where ontologies are useful, as they provide the necessary semantic context in addition to the keyword index to present the data in a form suitable for browsing. Coupled with a way of exploiting the similarities between instances, either in terms of distance (see Section 27.3.2) or semantic similarities.

The approach we propose in this context is to replace the traditional indexes by an ontology layer, described in Section 27.3.3. This has the advantage to be simple in design and easy to use, while retaining the classical structure of the data itself (the documents), thus allowing to build on top of existing repositories or provide compatibility with other methods.

27.3.2 Definition of a Distance

The structuring of the concepts as ontologies allow us to very simply define distances between those concepts, depending on the application. The application of such distances is beyond the realm of this publication, but intuitively, a distance between two concepts in a tree-like structure like the one exemplified in Section 27.6 could be the number of levels between the first separation of the branch of the tree into two separate paths. With such a distance, two concepts in the same sub-category of the tree are closer to each other than two concepts in completely separate higher categories.

27.3.3 Ontology Layer

Meta data is represented as attributes of a node in a graph. A node can be a data node, a document for example, or an index node, a node of any index structure built from the data. The first type of node is straightforward, it is simply an avatar of an actual entity (document), that can be structured as a tree like in a file system. The second type of node contains additional information derived from the data, for instance an index or another ontological structured semantical information.

This way of structuring the information adds the power of inheritance of attributes and properties given by ontologies to the basic operations allowed by classical indexes. For instance, when a search is issued on a keyword index structure and the word is not found in any attribute of nodes in the corresponding level, it will be searched in all more general concepts of the structure, allowing to bring as result a superclass of documents. It is obvious how the expressiveness of the search can be increased using this technique.

Another big advantage of using ontologies is for maintainability and scalability of the overall system. Editing documents, adding new documents, coming up with new index entries can be easily envisaged, operations that are time consuming and error prone in a non hierarchical structure. Also, importing and exporting data is facilitated by the very structure of an ontological representation of meta data, which is a great advantage for the development of web services for example.

27.4 Security Management

Like every system where the public can access information that may or may not be sensitive, sooner or later restrictions on what a user is allowed or denied to do must be imposed. We propose a role-based security model which is the most elegant way of giving permissions to a user, based not on who he is, but on what role he plays in the system. Furthermore, the model is well known [9] and implemented in Zope, the framework we used for the implementation described in Section 27.5.2.

To formalize the security model we need three different notions: User, Role, and Permission. A User is a unique name given to an agent (real person or application) that interacts with the system. His possible actions are grouped into Permissions (like read/write/add or even more specific ones, like add document). While these two notions are sufficient to have a complete security model it would be a very complex and rigid one. To maintain such a system is impractical even with a small user base. A new abstraction has to be added, namely Roles that are used to group together multiple Permissions. It can also be viewed as an abstract user or a group of users.

Each user is then given one or several Roles. All permissions given to a Role are in fact given to all Users that have that role, now or in the future. Therefore the definition of a security policy for the system is split in two parts:

1. Defining Roles
2. Defining Users and assign Roles to them.

Historically, only the permissions were defined at the application design level, and the users and their assigned permissions were defined at runtime. Since the applications became more and more complex, Roles were introduced to group permissions together. The number of different permissions is set by the application and should be a tradeoff between the desired granularity of the security layer and its manageability. A very complex security layer, with many permissions is very hard to maintain and mistakes are easily made, voiding the purpose of the security layer. A better approach is to define local roles at design level and not at runtime. It depends on the logic of the application and should be carefully designed and tested before the system goes into production. Designing good Roles within a system ensures that a user having that role has the freedom to do what is supposed to do but at the same time he is also restricted to exactly these operations.

However, managing Users and their Roles is not done at the application design level but at runtime. Of course, having a good definition of Roles at the application level is not sufficient and it does not ultimately protect sensitive data if Role assignment is not correctly executed by the systems managers.

There is another important aspect of security management: authentication. It treats the problem of relating a user in the system to an actual user in the real world by some mechanism such as login/password. That part, although it can be quite complex, is not covered in this article: we will focus primarily on Roles used in a Document Management System.

27.4.1 Example

We will identify several Roles in a Document Management System. This enumeration is by no means complete, it is just to exemplify the Role concept we defined.

- **Guest User (normal user).** Can browse/search the repository (or a part of it), make personal notes, personal virtual folders, etc. There could be different categories of guest users, depending on what they can see, and how restrictive the repository is. In most cases, the guest users can see the whole repository. Depending on the repository it may be that guest users could have also write access on a personal part of the repository.
- **Editor (user with limited write access).** Like a guest user, can search/browse the repository, add new documents, update documents.
- **Supervisor (user with full write and update access).** This role has all the rights of an editor, plus they can change/update the ontological structure of the repository.

- **Administrator (almighty user).** This role has all the rights of a Supervisor, plus they can add/remove Users.

Of course this is a very simple view on the security of a Document Management System, every role can be further refined upon the needs of the system.

27.5 Implementation

In this section we show some implementation details of the system we described.

27.5.1 Implementation Platform

To implement a Semantic Document Management System we used a Content Management Framework (CMF), Zope [5]. Zope, which underlying object oriented storage had already been used successfully in related systems such as INDICO [10], provides several important parts we needed to build our prototype:

- **Web Interface Application/Service.** Since we are targeting a web interface for our system, the natural choice is a web-based CMF. It provides its own dynamic XML-based web language that makes it very easy to create dynamic web interfaces.
- **Integrated Security.** Instead of redesigning and implementing the security model from scratch we can use the already proven and tested security model provided by Zope CMF.
- **Object Oriented Storage.** Zope storage and object model follows an object oriented model and the ontological data can be mapped as such to the Zope storage model.
- **Scripting Language.** The Zope CMF uses a scripting language for doing almost all of the dynamic content generation. The scripting language, Python, is widely used and greatly facilitates the integration of external resources written in other programming languages.
- **Open Source.** Last but not least Zope is an Open Source product and therefore allows the development and installation of test systems without important up front investments. Also, it's supporting community makes it a very reliable environment.

There are several versions of Zope. At the time of the writing of this article, the stable tree is 3.x, a complete redesign over the previous 2.x branch. Although the first prototype was written using Zope 2.x, we have completely rewritten it to be a Zope 3 application.

27.5.2 Semantic Document Management System Zope Application

The Zope way of creating deployable, self-contained web portals is by using Zope Applications [5].

The base class used to keep the document repository and the classification ontologies is using ZCatalog and performs all the indexing of the repository. There are also two other important classes, one to keep an ontological object (classification) and another class to define a Document entity with all meta data and its ontological classification. Real file documents are simple Zope file objects that belongs to this Document entity.

Web interface pages are written using Zope's provided infrastructure, Zope Page Templates.

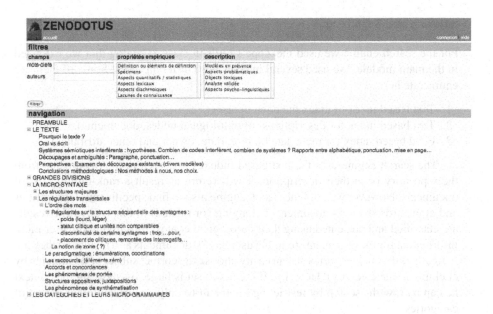

Fig. 2. A screen-shot showing the three ontologies

The entry page of the web interface shows a main categorization of documents using a tree-like ontology (see Figure 2). For every node all documents that are related to it are shown.

If there is more than one ontological categorization the user is given the possibility to browse the documents using all available ontologies. Depending on the ontology structure it can be mapped into a tree, or a list used in filtering. If a user is authenticated and has the Editor role, he has the possibility to create new document entities, or edit existing documents. By editing existing document entities he can reclassify it, change their description, meta data, or even add/delete document files. However, he cannot change the ontological classification structure unless he has the Supervisor role.

Changing the ontological classification structure will consist in most cases in adding new categories, and further refining existing ones. The categories nodes don't have any associated documents. If a category is refined the user can use filters and searches to assign the documents from the general category to the more specific categories.

It may be possible however to delete a classification node. This is a case that needs to be treated with special care because all the documents from that category should be reclassified.

Indexing and Searching

For the search engine we used the Zope's built-in class ZCatalog that we extended in the main module. We used several indexes with different types. Some of them we enumerate here:

1. Text based index to index the documents.
2. Text based index for descriptions (of ontological nodes, documents).
3. Field based index for meta data (author, date, owner and other attributes).

The search engine uses the text based indexes to search in the documents from the repository or in their description. It will return as result a rank-ordered list of documents. However we used the search engine also to find specific ontology entities and afterwards show all documents belonging (or related) to this entity. The results are classified and presented using their ontological context thus giving the user more information for the documents (e.g. If a user has 20 documents as a result and they are in totally different categories he can easily choose the correct subset of documents by clicking on the category). However, if the result set is large, by showing the context he can narrow the search by restricting the result to only one or any other subset of categories.

The meta data indexes are also used to filter documents shown in a page. This case differs from the search only by interpretation, it uses the same mechanism.

Security Implementation

Zope's internal security model includes all we described in Section 27.4 and provides even some further functionalities. In Zope the users cannot be assigned individual permissions. Zope users acquire permissions by using Roles. A Role can be assigned different permissions. Zope comes bundled with several predefined roles, however, for our project we created new roles: Guest, Editor, Supervisor just as described in the previous chapter. Zope's security model allows for further refinement by using local roles, i.e. allowing a user to have different roles depending on the location.

We also need to define permissions for the possible actions, like View, Create Document, Edit Document, Edit Ontology and assign these permissions to the corresponding roles.

We also considered using built in authentication and rely on the product logic to implement this part of the security model. But this approach is error prone and if a user succeeds in exploiting a bug in the application he would have full access to the database.

Using the underlying security model ensures data privacy on a lower level (base level) and even if a bug is found in the application, the data is still protected by Zope's security model.

27.6 Example

This architecture has already been used in web applications using the described implementation. These applications were mandates by various companies and are confidential, but one implementation is being developed as a collaboration for e-learning within our university and is described shortly below.

The system, called Zenodotus, is a knowledge repository for modern French, aimed at creating a kind of encyclopedia of articles about various aspects of the language. If we refer back to Figure 1, the user interface consists in a web application, the ontological layer refers to the supplied classifications of concepts of modern French (see below), and the document resources are the actual documents, text and sound, or records for bibliographical references.

The important part here is the classification, which is two-fold:

1. An actual table of content of all the concepts.
2. A grammatical structure, which can be further separated in two sub-categories: empirical properties and description of the concepts.

The interface allows filtered browsing in the sense explained in Section 27.3.1, using keywords and filtering over the grammatical structure to narrow down the number of results in the table of content (see Figure 2). Furthermore, one can have a look at what the main ontologies look like for this system, in the two boxes on the top part and the tree in the navigation part at the bottom. The ontology is actually more than a tree, but information about other links is then represented in context when the user selects a node, to ease the readability.

The user management is very basic in this case, with only a few users allowed to submit or modify new documents and notices. There is a mechanism of retaining the owner of a particular document to allow tracking changes, and some privileged managers have rights over the whole content.

The interface to add and edit notices and documents is straightforward, but fixed. There will certainly be the need to allow for adding new structural information (new categories) inside the interface, but currently this is done outside the system.

27.7 Conclusion and Future Work

We presented in this paper a new architecture that allows an easy integration of a semantic layer into a company's Document Management System. The semantics is added to the system through domain ontologies. The architecture is designed in such a way that the integration of existing Document Management Systems as well as other document resources is done through their own access mechanisms. On the other hand the system itself can easily be integrated in the companies information system infrastructure using open standards.

Furthermore we have presented an implementation (proof of concept) of the system using an open source framework (Zope). This implementation is used in several of our projects and is available on our web site.

As currently several implementations are being evaluated, the further improvements will essentially be based on the user feedback. Developments that have currently started are mainly dealing with two aspects, namely the improvement of the user/security management and the adaptation of our architecture for other platforms such as .NET.

Based on the experience gathered so far we know that the integration of existing document sources into our system is easy to realize and the integration of the system itself into an existing information infrastructure poses no major problems. For the project where domain ontologies were available already, the expressiveness of the DMS was greatly improved in a very short amount of time. Using standards such as OWL was of great help as large libraries of ontologies exist already. As conclusion one can say that the proposed architecture and implementation seems to overcome several of the major drawbacks of classical DMSs and can easily be integrated into en existing infrastructure.

References

1. Sutton, M.: Document Management for the Enterprise: Principles, Techniques and Applications. John Wiley & Sons, New York, NY, USA (1996)
2. AIIM International: ODMA 2.0 Specifications and Software (2005) http://ODMA.info.
3. Mc.Guinness, D.L., van Harmelen, F.: OWL Web Ontology Language W3C Recommendation (2004) http://www.w3.org/TR/owl-features/.
4. Cooper, C.: Building Websites With Plone. PACKT, UK (2004)
5. Latteier, A., Pelletier, M.: The Zope Book. New Riders (2001)
6. Ciorăscu, I., Simon, E., Stoffel, K.: An Ontological Document Management System in Zope (2005)

7. Dieter Fensel, James A. Hendler, H.L., Wahlster, W., eds.: Spinning the Semantic Web: Bringing the World Wide Web to its Full Potential. MIT Press, Boston (2003)

8. Pepe, A., Baron, T., Gracco, M., Le Meur, J.Y., Robinson, N., Simko, T., Vesely, M.: Cern document server software: the integrated digital library. ELPUB 2005 Conference (2005)

9. Abadi, M., Burrows, M., Lampson, B., Plotkin, G.: A calculus for access control in distributed systems. ACM Trans. Program. Lang. Syst. **15**(4) (1993) 706–734

10. Baron, T., Gonzalez, J.B., Le Meur, J.Y., Sanchez, H., Turney, V.: INDICO — the software behind CHEP 2004. CHEP 04 (2004)

28 Cost Estimation for Ontology Development: Applying the ONTOCOM Model

Elena Paslaru Bontas Simperl[1], Christoph Tempich[2], Malgorzata Mochol[1]

[1] Free University of Berlin, Takustr. 9, 14195 Berlin, Germany
{paslaru,mochol}@inf.fu-berlin.de
[2] Institute AIFB, University of Karlsruhe, 76128 Karlsruhe, Germany
tempich@aifb.uni-karlsruhe.de

28.1 Introduction

A core requirement for the take-up of ontology-driven technologies at industry level is the availability of proved and tested methods which allow an efficient engineering of high-quality ontologies, be that by reuse, manual building or automatic extraction methods. Several elaborated methodologies, which aid the development of ontologies for particular application requirements, emerged in the last decades. Nevertheless, in order for ontologies to be built and deployed at a large scale, beyond the boundaries of the academic community, one needs not only technologies and tools to assist the engineering process, but also means to estimate and control its overall costs. These issues are addressed only marginally by current engineering approaches, though their importance is well recognized in the community.

A first attempt to bridge this gap has been made with the ONTOCOM (**Onto**logy **Cost M**odel) approach [10], which provides an instrument to estimate the efforts involved in building, reusing and maintaining ontologies. Just as in the adjacent field of software engineering, a discipline in which cost prediction models belong to standard development environments, ONTOCOM proposes a top-down, parametric cost estimation method on the basis of pre-defined process stages and cost drivers.

ONTOCOM is based on a work breakdown structure which complies to the process model recommended by all established ontology engineering methodologies.[1] It differentiates between four main process stages: 1). **requirements analysis**; 2). **conceptualization**; 3). **implementation**; and 4). **evaluation**. For these categories,

---

[1] *cf.* [3] or [13] for recent surveys on ontology engineering methodologies.

W. Abramowicz and H.C. Mayr (eds.), Technologies for Business Information Systems, 327–339.
© 2007 *Springer.*

cost drivers influencing the required effort (in terms of person months) have been identified on the basis of a comprehensive analysis of current engineering methodologies and related case studies. Their relevance to the cost estimation issue has been confirmed by experts in the field in a comprehensive evaluation study [10]. Every cost driver is associated with effort multipliers (from *Very High* to *Very Low*), depending on the characteristics of the corresponding project setting. A first estimation of the numerical values associated with these effort multipliers was performed based on ex post analysis of different ontology engineering efforts and preliminary expert validations with very promising results [10].

This paper explains how ONTOCOM can be applied to estimate the efforts related to ontology development in arbitrary projects. For this purpose we illustrate the usage of the general-purpose model with the help of a simple example, and then describe how this model can be further refined and customized for project settings which follow a different ontology engineering methodology. The last issue is exemplified in relation to the DILIGENTmethodology, which is targeted at the construction of rapidly changing ontologies in distributed settings [14].

The remaining of this paper is organized as follows. After introducing the ONTOCOM model in Section 28.2, we demonstrate how it can be applied to estimate the costs of ontology development in Section 28.3. Section 28.4 describes the steps required to adapt the generic model to new ontology engineering methodologies. This process is exemplified for the DILIGENT methodology in Section 28.5. Section 28.6 provides a brief overview of previous work which is related to ONTOCOM, while Section 28.7 summarizes the main contributions of this paper and outlines directions of future research and development.

28.2 The Generic ONTOCOM Model

In this section we introduce the generic ONTOCOM cost estimation model. The model is generic in that it assumes a sequential ontology life cycle, according to which an ontology is conceptualized, implemented and evaluated, after an initial analysis of the requirements it should fulfill (see below). By contrast ONTOCOM does not consider alternative engineering strategies such as rapid prototyping or agile methods, which are based on different life cycles.[2] This limitation is issued in Section 28.4, which describes how the generic model should be customized to suit such scenarios.

The cost estimation model is realized in three steps. First a *top-down* work breakdown structure for ontology engineering processes is defined in order to reduce the complexity of project budgetary planning and controlling operations down to more manageable units [1]. The associated costs are then elaborated using the *parametric*

---

[2] *cf.* [3] for a discussion on the relation between this process model and the IEEE standards [5].

method. The result of the second step is a statistical prediction model (i.e. a parameterized mathematical formula). Its parameters are given start values in pre-defined intervals, but need to be calibrated on the basis of previous project data. This empirical information complemented by expert estimations is used to evaluate and revise the predictions of the initial *a-priori model*, thus creating a validated *a-posteriori model*.[3]

28.2.1 The Work Breakdown Structure

The top-level partitioning of a generic ontology engineering process can be realized by taking into account available process-driven methodologies in this field [3, 13] According to them ontology building consists of the following core steps (cf. Figure 1):
1) Requirements Analysis. The engineering team consisting of domain experts and ontology engineers performs a deep analysis of the project setting w.r.t. a set of predefined requirements. This step might also include **knowledge acquisition** activities in terms of the re-usage of existing ontological sources or by extracting domain information from text corpora, databases etc. If such techniques are being used to aid the engineering process, the resulting ontologies are to be subsequently customized to the application setting in the conceptualization/implementation phases. The result of this step is an ontology requirements specification document [12]. In particular this contains a set of competency questions describing the domain to be modeled by the prospected ontology, as well as information about its use cases, the expected size, the information sources used, the process participants and the engineering methodology.
2) Conceptualization. The application domain is modeled in terms of ontological primitives, e.g. concepts, relations, axioms.
3) Implementation. The conceptual model is implemented in a (formal) representation language, whose expressivity is appropriate for the richness of the conceptualization. If required reused ontologies and those generated from other information sources are translated to the target representation language and integrated to the final context.
4) Evaluation. The ontology is evaluated against the set of competency questions. The evaluation may be performed automatically, if the competency questions are represented formally, or semi-automatically, using specific heuristics or human judgement. The result of the evaluation is reflected in a set of modifications/refinements at the requirements, conceptualization or implementation level.

Depending on the ontology life cycle underlying the process-driven methodology, the aforementioned four steps are to be seen as a sequential workflow or as parallel activities. Methontology [4], which applies prototypical engineering principles, considers **knowledge acquisition, evaluation** and **documentation** as being complementary *support activities* performed in parallel to the main development

---

[3] *cf.* [1] for an overview of cost prediction methods for engineering projects.

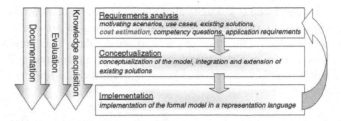

Fig. 1. Typical Ontology Engineering Process

process. Other methodologies, usually following a classical waterfall model, consider these support activities as part of a sequential engineering process. The OTK-Methodology [12] additionally introduces an initial **feasibility study** in order to assess the risks associated with an ontology building attempt. Other optional steps are **ontology population/instantiation** and **ontology evolution/maintenance**. The former deals with the alignment of concrete application data to the implemented ontology. The latter relates to modifications of the ontology performed according to new user requirements, updates of the reused sources or changes in the modeled domain. Further on, likewise related engineering disciplines, reusing existing knowledge sources—in particular ontologies—is a central topic of ontology development. In terms of the process model introduced above, **ontology reuse** is considered a **knowledge acquisition** task.

The parametric method integrates the efforts associated with each component of this work breakdown structure to a mathematical formula as described below.

28.2.2 The Parametric Equation

ONTOCOM calculates the necessary person-months effort using the following equation:

$$PM = A * Size^{\alpha} * \prod CD_i \qquad (28.1)$$

According to the parametric method the total development efforts are associated with cost drivers specific for the ontology engineering process and its main activities. Experiences in related engineering areas [1, 6] let us assume that the most significant factor is the *size of the ontology* (in kilo entities) involved in the corresponding process or process phase. In Equation 28.1 the parameter *Size* corresponds to the size of the ontology i.e. the number of primitives which are expected to result from the conceptualization phase (including fragments built by reuse or other knowledge acquisition methods). The possibility of a non-linear behavior of the model w.r.t. the size of the ontology is covered by parameter α. The constant A represents a baseline multiplicative calibration constant in person months, i.e. costs which occur "if everything is normal". The *cost drivers* CD_i have a rating level (from Very Low to

Very High) that expresses their impact on the development effort. For the purpose of a quantitative analysis each rating level of each cost driver is associated to a weight (*effort multiplier EM_i*). The *productivity range PR_i* of a cost driver (i.e. the ratio between the highest and the lowest effort multiplier of a cost driver $PR_i = \frac{max(EM_i)}{min(EM_i)}$) is an indicator for the relative importance of a cost driver for the effort estimation [1].

28.2.3 The ONTOCOM Cost Drivers

The ONTOCOM cost drivers, which are proved to have a direct impact on the total development efforts, can be roughly divided into three categories:

1) PRODUCT-RELATED COST DRIVERS account for the impact of the characteristics of the product to be engineered (i.e. the ontology) on the overall costs. The following cost drivers were identified for the task of ontology building:

• **Domain Analysis Complexity (DCPLX)** to account for those features of the application setting which influence the complexity of the engineering outcomes,

• **Conceptualization Complexity (CCPLX)** to account for the impact of a complex conceptual model on the overall costs,

• **Implementation Complexity (ICPLX)** to take into consideration the additional efforts arisen from the usage of a specific implementation language,

• **Instantiation Complexity (DATA)** to capture the effects that the instance data requirements have on the overall process,

• **Required Reusability (REUSE)** to capture the additional effort associated with the development of a reusable ontology,

• **Evaluation Complexity (OE)** to account for the additional efforts eventually invested in generating test cases and evaluating test results, and

• **Documentation Needs (DOCU)** to state for the additional costs caused by high documentation requirements.

2) PERSONNEL-RELATED COST DRIVERS emphasize the role of team experience, ability and continuity w.r.t. the effort invested in the engineering process:

• **Ontologist/Domain Expert Capability (OCAP/DECAP)** to account for the perceived ability and efficiency of the single actors involved in the process (ontologist and domain expert) as well as their teamwork capabilities,

• **Ontologist/Domain Expert Experience (OEXP/DEEXP)** to measure the level of experience of the engineering team w.r.t. performing ontology engineering activities,

• **Language/Tool Experience (LEXP/TEXP)** to measure the level experience of the project team w.r.t. the representation language and the ontology management tools,

• **Personnel Continuity (PCON)** to mirror the frequency of the personnel changes in the team.

3) PROJECT-RELATED COST DRIVERS relate to overall characteristics of an ontology engineering process and their impact on the total costs:

• **Support tools for Ontology Engineering (TOOL)** to measure the effects of using ontology management tools in the engineering process, and

• **Multisite Development (SITE)** to mirror the usage of the communication support tools in a location-distributed team.

The ONTOCOM cost drivers were defined after extensively surveying recent ontology engineering literature and conducting expert interviews, and from empirical findings of numerous case studies in the field.[4] For each cost driver we specified in detail the decision criteria which are relevant for the model user in order for him to determine the concrete rating of the driver in a particular situation. For example for the cost driver CCPLX—accounting for costs produced by a particularly complex conceptualization—we pre-defined the meaning of the rating levels as depicted in Table 1. The appropriate rating should be selected during the cost estimation procedure and used as a multiplier in equation 28.1. The concrete values of the effort multipliers have been determined during the calibration of the model, which is described in [10].

Table 1. The Conceptualization Complexity Cost Driver **CCPLX**

Rating Level	Effort multiplier	Description
Very Low	0.28	concept list
Low	0.64	taxonomy, high nr. of patterns, no constraints
Nominal	1.0	properties, general patterns available, some constraints
High	1.36	axioms, few modeling patterns, considerable nr. of constraints
Very High	1.72	instances, no patterns, considerable nr. of constraints

The decision criteria associated with a cost driver are typically more complex than in the previous example and might be sub-divided into further sub-categories, whose impact is aggregated to the final effort multiplier of the corresponding cost driver by means of normalized weights.[5]

28.3 Using the Generic Model

Starting from a typical ontology building scenario, in which a domain ontology is created from scratch by the engineering team, we simulate the cost estimation process according to the parametric method underlying ONTOCOM. Given the top-down nature of our approach this estimation can be realized in the early phases of a project, in particular after the requirements analysis has been accomplished and an initial prediction of the size of the target ontology is available. The first step of the cost estimation is the specification of the size of the ontology to be build, expressed in thousands of ontological primitives (concepts, relations, axioms and instances): if

---

[4] See [9] for a detailed explanation of the approach.

[5] Refer to http://ontocom.ag-nbi.de for a complete list of the cost drivers and the associated effort multipliers.

we consider an ontology with 1000 concepts, 200 relations (including is-a) and 100 axioms, the size parameter of the estimation formula will be calculated as follows:

$$Size = \frac{1000 + 200 + 100}{1000} = 1,3 \qquad (28.2)$$

The next step is the specification of the cost driver ratings corresponding to the information available at this point (i.e. without reuse and maintenance factors, since the ontology is built manually from scratch). Depending on their impact on the overall development effort, if a particular activity increases the nominal efforts, then it would be rated with values such as *High* and *Very High*. Otherwise, if it causes a decrease of the nominal costs, then it would be rated with values such as *Low* and *Very Low*. Cost drivers which are not relevant for a particular scenario should be rated with the nominal value 1, which does not influence the result of the prediction equation.

Assuming that the ratings of the cost drivers are those depicted in Table 2 these ratings are replaced by numerical values. The value of the DCPLX cost driver was computed as an equally weighted, averaged sum of a high-valued rating for the domain complexity, a nominal rating for the requirements complexity and a high effort multiplier for the information sources complexity (for details of other rating values see [10]):

According to the formula 28.1 ($\alpha = 1$) the estimated effort in person months would be amount to 5,6 PMs and be calculated as follows (the A parameter was set to 2.92 as described in Section 28.2):

$$PM = 2,92 * 1,3^1 * (1,26 * 1^{10} * 1,15 * 1,11 * 0,93 * 1,11 * 0,89) \qquad (28.3)$$

Table 2. Values of the cost drivers

Cost driver	Effort	Value	Cost driver	Effort	Value
Product factors			**Personnel factors**		
DCPLX	High	1,26	OCAP	High	1,11
CCPLX	Nominal	1	DCAP	Low	0,93
ICPLX	Low	1,15	OEXP	High	1,11
DATA	High	1	DEEXP	Very Low	0,89
REUSE	Nominal	1	LEXP	Nominal	1
DOCU	Low	1	TEXP	Nominal	1
OE	Nominal	1	PCON	Very High	1
Project factors					
TOOL	Very Low	1	SITE	Nominal	1

28.4 Adapting the Generic Model to Other Methodologies

ONTOCOM is intended to be applied in early stages of an ontology engineering process. In accordance to the process model introduced above the prediction of the arising costs can be performed during the feasibility study or, more reliably, during the requirements analysis. Many of the input parameters required to exercise the cost estimation are expected to be accurately approximated during this phase: the expected size of the ontology, the engineering team, the tools to be used, the implementation language etc.[6]

The high-level work breakdown structure foreseen by ONTOCOM can be further refined depending of the ontology development strategy applied in an organization or in a certain application scenario. As explained in Section 28.2.1 the generic ON-TOCOM model assumes a sequential ontology life cycle which contains only the most important management, development and support activities (cf. [3]). In case the model is applied to a different setting, the relevant cost drivers are to be aligned (or even re-defined) to the new sub-phases and activities, while the parametric equation needs to be adapted to the new activity breakdown. A detailed example of how ON-TOCOM can be applied to an ontology development methodology targeted at rapid prototyping in distributed scenarios is provided in the next section.

In order to create the cost formula for a specific ontology engineering methodology we propose the following process:

1. Select ontology engineering methodology for which the cost estimation formula should be created
2. Identify the process stages within the methodology. The estimated effort for the entire life cycle of the ontology development (PM) is then the sum of the estimated efforts for each process stage (PM_i)

$$PM = \sum_{i=0}^{n} PM_i \tag{28.4}$$

where n is the number of process stages.

The definition of process stages might differ between methodologies. In the case of ONTOCOM a process stage should have a defined starting and end point. A process stage should result in a formalized ontology.[7]

3. For each process stage identify the relevant ontology engineering activities. Map them to the corresponding cost drivers defined in ONTOCOM. If this mapping can not be directly established, check whether the activity may be generalized or

---

[6] Note that ontology engineering methodologies foresee this information to be collected in an ontology requirements document at the end of the requirements analysis phase [12].

[7] Note that according to this definition the generic cost model presented in Section 28.2 assumes an ontology engineering project consisting of a single development phase, at the end of which the prospected ontology is released.

refined and map the activity to the corresponding cost drivers. If the latter is not possible, the quality of the predictions is likely to decrease.

4. In order to derive the cost formula for a specific process stage remove the non-relevant cost drivers from the equation 28.1. The size parameter is determined by the size of the ontology built in the specific process stage.
5. Calibrate the adapted model. The generic model has been calibrated on the basis of historical project data. However, the obtained values might not be significant for the particular setting for which ONTOCOM has been adapted. Therefore, it might be of benefit to rerun this task on a relevant set of data points, collected from projects which followed the same engineering strategy.

After this optional customization step the model can be utilized for cost predictions. For this purpose the engineering team needs to specify the rating levels associated with each cost driver, as described in the previous example in Section 28.3. The values correspond to parameters in equation 28.1. The results obtained for individual stages are summed up in equation 28.4.

We now turn to an example of adapting ONTOCOM to rapid prototyping methodology.

28.5 Adapting the Generic Model to DILIGENT

28.5.1 Step 1: Select Ontology Engineering Methodology

DILIGENT stands for DIstributed, Loosely-controlled and evolvInG Engineering of oNTologies [14]. It addresses the requirements for ontology engineering in distributed knowledge management settings. For that it distinguishes two kinds of ontologies: **shared ontology** and **local ontologies**. A shared ontology is available to all users but they cannot change it directly. In order to change the shared ontology the participants obtain a copy of it and modify it in locally, obtaining a new local ontology.

28.5.2 Step 2: Identify Process Stages

A DILIGENT process comprises five main stages: (1) **build**, (2) **local adaptation**, (3) **central analysis**, (4) **central revision**, (5) **local update**. Due to space restrictions we do not provide a complete description of the methodology here but sketch the overall process and focus on a particular process stage only: *viz.* local adaptation. For a more detailed description we refer the interested reader to [14]. The detailed description gives a complete account of the different roles involved in the process, input and output factors, related activities and major decisions to be made by the actors.

Central Build The process starts by having *domain experts*, *ontology users*, and *ontology engineers* **build** an initial shared ontology.

Local Adaptation Users work with the current version of the shared ontology, adapting it to their local needs. They submit change requests to the central board in order to align their local revisions to the remotely built ontologies.

Central Analysis In order to update the shared ontology in accordance to the new user requirements a board **analyzes** the local ontologies and the associated change requests. The board tries to identify similarities in local ontologies so as to decide which changes are going to be introduced in the next version of the shared ontology.

Central Revision Once the board decides upon the changes to be made to the shared ontology, it revises and distributes it to the user community.

Local Update If a new version of the shared ontology is available, its users may **update** their own **local** ontologies accordingly. Updating may involve a re-organization of the local ontology, as only a part of the requested changes have been accepted by the engineering board. Nevertheless, using an updated version of the ontology is of benefit, as it increases the interoperability between local users.

General cost formula for DILIGENT

DILIGENT is a iterative ontology engineering methodology. The general cost formula for DILIGENT can thus be defined as:

$$ PM = PM_{CB} + \sum_{j=1}^{n} (PM_{LA_j} * m_j + PM_{CA_j} + PM_{CR_j} + PM_{LU_i} * m_j) \quad (28.5) $$

where PM_{CB}, PM_{LA_j}, PM_{CA_j}, PM_{CR_j} and PM_{LU_j} are the person months necessary for each process stage and j iterates over the total number of cycles n. The number of sites participating at the process in every cycle is captured by the variable m_j.

28.5.3 Step 3: Identify Activities and Define Mappings

As aforementioned, we exemplify this step for a single process stage of the DILIGENT methodology, namely local adaptation. The remaining process stages can be handled analogously.

In the local adaptation stage the users perform different activities in order to obtained the desired output: *local analysis of shared ontology, local specification of new requirements , ontology use, local customization of local ontology, local integration of reused ontologies to the local ontology, local modification of the local ontology, argument provision, evaluation of new local ontology* [14]. The activities are repeated in the given order until a new shared ontology is available.

Local analysis of shared ontology In this activity the users get familiar with the shared ontology. The users learn where the different concepts are located in the ontology and how they are interrelated with other concepts.

Ontology use The ontology is used in the local environment.

Specification of new requirements The local usage of the shared ontology leads to the specification of new requirements, if it does not completely represent the knowledge required by the users.

Local customization of local ontology Building an ontology is a combination of the two approaches: building from scratch and building by reuse. The local customization activity defines therefore the two sub-activities *Local modification of local ontology* and *Local integration of reused ontologies to the local ontology*.

Local modification of local ontology The local modification of the shared ontology is one option to adapt it to the local requirements.

Local integration of reused ontologies to the local ontology The second possibility to meet new local requirements of the users is to reuse external ontologies.

Argument provision The users externalize the reasons for their modeling decisions using arguments.

Evaluation of new local ontology The user evaluates his local ontology w.r.t. his local requirements. He does not evaluate the entire ontology, but only the parts relevant to him.

Documentation The ontology user documents the changes introduced into the shared ontology.

Table 3 shows the cost drivers which are relevant to each of the listed activities.

Table 3. The cost drivers relevant for the local adaptation phase

DILIGENT process		Cost factor
DILIGENT phase	DILIGENT activity	Product; Personal; Project
Local adaptation	Local analysis of shared ontology	DCPLX, OE; DECAP, DEEXP, LEXP, TEXP, PCON; TOOL
	Ontology use	DATA; DECAP, DEEXP, LEXP, TEXP; TOOL
	Specification of new requirements	DCPLX; DECAP, DEEXP, LEXP, TEXP, PCON; TOOL
	Local customization of local ontology • Local modification of local ontology • Local integration of reused ontologies to the local ontology	CCPLX,ICPLX; DEEXP, DECAP, TEXP, LEXP, PCON ; TOOL
	Argument provision	
	Evaluation of new local ontology	OE; DEEXP, DECAP, TEXP, LEXP, PCON; TOOL
	Documentation	DOCU; DEEXP, DECAP, TEXP, LEXP, PCON; TOOL

28.5.4 Step 4: Derive the Cost Formula

Just as in the previous section we restrict the example to the local adaptation phase. The formula is derived from the generic ONTOCOM formula 28.1 adapted to comply with the mapping depicted in Table 3. The equation calculates the effort required to evaluate, adapt and use the shared ontology ($Size_{LA}$ is the size of the shared ontology plus the average number of changes introduced by the users).

$$PM_{LA} = A * Size_{LA}^{\alpha} * DCPLX * CCPLX * ICPLX * DATA * OE * DOCU *$$
$$DECAP * DEEXP * LEXP * TEXP * PCON * TOOL \qquad (28.6)$$

28.5.5 Step 5: Calibration

The start values of the cost drivers may be obtained from the general ONTOCOM model. However, in order to to improve the quality of the predictions, the adapted cost model should be calibrated. In [10] we present a statistically sound method to combine the estimations calculated with the generic model with newly obtained project data in order to improve the results. A detailed description of the calibration process is out of the scope of this paper.

28.6 Related Work

Cost estimation methods have a long-standing tradition in more mature engineering disciplines such as software engineering or industrial production [1, 6, 11]. Although the importance of cost issues is well-acknowledged in the community, as to the best knowledge of the authors, no cost estimation model for ontology engineering has been published so far. Analogue models for the development of knowledge-based systems (e.g., [2]) implicitly assume the availability of the underlying conceptual structures. [8] provides a qualitative analysis of the costs and benefits of ontology usage in application systems, but does not offer any model to estimate the efforts. [7] adjusts the cost drivers defined in a cost estimation model for Web applications w.r.t. the usage of ontologies. The cost drivers, however, are not adapted to the requirements of ontology engineering and no evaluation is provided. We present an evaluated cost estimation model, introducing cost drivers with a proved relevance for ontology engineering, which can be applied in the early stages of an ontology development process.

28.7 Conclusion

Reliable methods for cost estimation are a fundamental requirement for a wide-scale dissemination of ontologies in business contexts. However, though the importance of cost issues is well-recognized in the community, no cost estimation model for ontology engineering is available so far. Starting from existing cost estimation methodologies applied across various engineering disciplines, we propose a parametric cost estimation model for ontologies by identifying relevant cost drivers having a direct impact on the effort invested in the main activities of the ontology life cycle. We explain how this model can be adapted to other ontology engineering methodologies and exemplify this with the help of the rapid prototyping method DILIGENT. In the future we intend to continue the data collection procedure in order to improve the quality of the generic model and its customizations.

Acknowledgements

This work has been partially supported by the European Network of Excellence "Knowledge Web-Realizing the Semantic Web" (FP6-507482), as part of the KnowledgeWeb researcher exchange program **T-REX**, the European project "Sekt-Semantically-Enabled Knowledge Technologies" (EU IP IST-2003-506826) and the "Knowledge Nets" project, which is part of the InterVal – Berlin Research Centre for the Internet Economy, funded by the German Ministry of Research BMBF. Further information about ONTOCOM can be found under: http://ontocom.ag-nbi.de.

References

1. B. W. Boehm. *Software Engineering Economics*. Prentice-Hall, 1981.
2. A. Felfernig. Effort estimation for knowledge-based configuration systems. In *Proc. of the 16th Int. Conf. of Software Engineering and Knowledge Engineering SEKE04*, 2004.
3. A. Gómez-Pérez, M. Fernández-López, and O. Corcho. *Ontological Engineering*. Springer, 2003.
4. A. Gomez-Perez, M. Fernandez-Lopez, and O. Corcho. *Ontological Engineering – with examples form the areas of Knowledge Management, e-Commerce and the Semantic Web*. Springer Verlag, 2004.
5. IEEE Computer Society. IEEE Standard for Developing Software Life Cycle Processes. IEEE Std 1074-1995, 1996.
6. C. F. Kemerer. An Empirical Validation of Software Cost Estimation Models. *Communications of the ACM*, 30(5), 1987.
7. M. Korotkiy. On the effect of ontologies on web application development effort. In *Proc. of the Knowledge Engineering and Software Engineering Workshop*, 2005.
8. T. Menzies. Cost benefits of ontologies. *Intelligence*, 10(3):26–32, 1999.
9. E. Paslaru Bontas and C. Tempich. How Much Does It Cost? Applying ONTOCOM to DILIGENT. Technical Report TR-B-05-20, Free University of Berlin, October 2005.
10. E. Paslaru-Bontas Simperl, C. Tempich, and Y. Sure. Ontocom: A cost estimation model for ontology engineering. In *Proceedings of the ISWC2006*, 2006. to appear.
11. R. D. Stewart, R. M. Wyskida, and J. D. Johannes. *Cost Estimator's Reference Manual*. Wiley, 1995.
12. Y. Sure, S. Staab, and R. Studer. Methodology for development and employment of ontology based knowledge management applications. *SIGMOD Record*, 31(4), 2002.
13. Y. Sure, C. Tempich, and D. Vrandecic. Ontology engineering methodologies. In *Semantic Web Technologies: Trends and Research in Ontology-based Systems*. Wiley, 2006.
14. Christoph Tempich, H. Sofia Pinto, and Steffen Staab. Ontology engineering revisited: an iterative case study with diligent. In *Proceedings of the 3rd European Semantic Web Conference, ESWC 2006*, pages 110–124, 2006.

29 Perspectives of Belief Revision in Document-driven Evolution of Ontology

Krzysztof Węcel

Poznań University of Economics, Poland
Department of Management Information Systems
K.Wecel@kie.ae.poznan.pl

29.1 Introduction and Motivation

Current trends in research point at ontologies as a way to represent information in a structured way, thus facilitating more precise querying and question answering. In a classical approach, ontologies represent a static world. Any change in the world requires a manual update of ontology what is not adequate for the fast changing business environment. On the one hand, manual modification of ontology is time-consuming and sometimes not prompt enough. On the other hand, ontology that is not up to date has little value since it does not describe the world properly. Therefore, when considering business domain, developing methodologies for automatic ontology evolution is crucial.

One of the solutions to the above mentioned problem could be maintenance by means of extracting changes from everyday business news that reflects changes in the world. Still the problem of incorporating the changes into current ontology remains. One of the approaches is belief revision, developed for past two decades, which studies processes and operations required to update a knowledge base when new fact is added. Nevertheless, in the evolution of ontology we also wish to bind changes to time, where changes are extracted from text with natural language processing techniques.

In our system, time is considered as one of the dimensions that organizes information. It orders the changes in the ontology, allows checking the validity of the facts in time and verifying consistency of ontology in time. As a result a consistent ontology for an arbitrary moment in time is maintained.

W. Abramowicz and H.C. Mayr (eds.), Technologies for Business Information Systems, 341–351.

29.2 Background and Related Work

There are several projects that deal with transformation of text into ontology, e.g. ONTOTEXT [12], Text2Onto [3], work-in-progress framework proposed by us [16]. The main problem is how to handle contradicting facts coming from different documents. One of the approaches may be belief revision.

Belief revision addresses the problem of updating a knowledge base when new information arrives and what to do when new information is contradictory with something that was considered to be true. It does not provide a single solution for integration of old and new information. There are various postulates and, depending on the required features, different sets of postulates are applied. The classical approach of belief revision is the AGM framework [1].

Basically, two kinds of changes in knowledge base are distinguished [10]:

- update, new information concerns present situation, while old beliefs are about past situation; old beliefs are updated
- revision, new information and old beliefs concern the same situation, usually producing inconsistency; when needed old beliefs are removed so that new information is inserted without causing inconsistency.

The real problem is that inconsistent knowledge base may be transformed into consistent one in many ways. The main assumption of belief revision is usually that of minimal change, although there are some authors that criticize on it [15].

Another assumption in the revision operation is that new information is always more reliable than the old knowledge base.

In the case when all beliefs refer to the same situation, the following operations are distinguished [5, 9]:

- expansion, addition of the belief without checking consistency
- contraction, removal of a belief from a knowledge base
- revision, addition of the belief while maintaining consistency
- consolidation, restoring consistency of a set of beliefs
- merging, fusion of two or more sets of beliefs while maintaining consistency; a more general operation than revision.

In the original theory, knowledge base is a deductively closed set of logical formulae. It may lead to infinite knowledge base. Hansson proposed to use set of formulas not closed under logical consequence, called a belief base [7]. It simplifies the computation complexity. Moreover, in the framework that we develop it is not justified to have an infinite knowledge base. Another argument for distinction between original beliefs and derived beliefs is that they are considered equally important while revising. In the framework we assign the credibility and therefore those beliefs are not equal. The so called original beliefs are the beliefs extracted from documents (with links to evidences in text) and some of them may be confirmed by user in during feedback process.

Another important issue is iterated revision [8]. It poses additional problems from the semantic of change point of view but is more appropriate in settings of our framework. New documents arrive steadily; beliefs should be ordered according to their entrenchment. A preference relation is taken into account for selection of new model for a knowledge base after revision. This relation (and hence which beliefs should be held and which removed) should depend not only on current knowledge base but also on the history of preceding revisions.

The basic belief revision theory need extension in that the framework we propose also considers time issues and revision of the past beliefs may also be required regardless of current knowledge about these beliefs.

29.3 Operations for Ontology Evolution

We assume that there is ontology in place, built and verified manually. Due to the still evolving world, it is not feasible to update this ontology also manually. The ontology is then extended with new concepts, instances and relations learned from filtered business news in the process of ontology learning [11].

29.3.1 Inputs

There are many approaches to ontology learning and most of them employ information extraction techniques; some rely purely on IR techniques over bag-of-words representation. Before information is extracted from Web resources, they are usually annotated based on selected ontology; hence the process of annotation and ontology learning may be merged.

When appropriate information is extracted, it should be compared to the existing knowledge. Since the knowledge may change in time, the occurrence of change should be located on time axis. Further on, we analyze how to identify a change, what modelling primitives may be affected by the change and how to present the outcomes to the user.

We may identify the following inputs for ontology evolution:

- seed ontology (domain ontology), defines core entities that should be extracted and learned from text
- language ontology, facilitates the extraction of information from text, appropriate concepts are selected for domain ontology; may be used directly to grow the seed ontology
- documents (Web resources), bring new information that has to be structured and incorporated into evolving ontology.

29.3.2 Simple Operations

Ontology should be rebuilt according to changes found in annotated documents. Moreover, documents should not only be annotated but extracted information should be stored in the database to allow further reasoning and fragments of documents should be kept in order to allow tracking of evidences.

We may look at required changes at different granularities. Belief revision is dealing with "belief" (sometimes also named a "theory"), we have triples in RDF(S) and axioms in OWL-DL ontology.

Let us start by analyzing the possible changes at the very general level. When new business documents are filtered to the system, they bring some facts. Those facts may have the following impact on a knowledge base:

- confirmation, new information confirms or supports known information, fact remains unchanged
- completion, new information adds new details about existing entity, e.g. we knew that company X is located in city Y, and the new fact is that it is located on the street Z
- contradiction, new information contradicts old information, e.g. we knew that company X had invested in Y, and the new fact is that it did not invest in Y
- correction, new information changes known facts, e.g. when company X is indeed operating in city Y, not in city Z.

There is a slight difference between contradiction and correction: the first relates to the negation of facts (A and ¬A), while the latter to the more general case of incorrect information.

When comparing to the belief revision, the following analogies may be pointed:

- confirmation does not require any change in the database; in the proposed framework it will increase the credibility of the already known facts (it should have influence on preference function for revising facts)
- completion is analogous to update; from the definition, no inconsistencies arise, and in that spirit also expansion operation may be used
- contradiction is analogous to contraction: new fact requires to remove the opposite fact from the knowledge base; depending on the credibility (entrenchment) of the new fact it will be introduced to the knowledge base or not
- correction is analogous to revision: old information has to be removed and updated one introduced into the knowledge base.

The operations mentioned above are classical in that they do not consider the temporal context.

29.3.3 Time-related Operations

Business news does not present facts in chronological order. Very often articles refer to past events. Although most of the people are interested in present situation, past states still may be significant for companies or their supervisory bodies, and consistent information about them is required. It poses serious problems to belief revision: past event may force to revise past knowledge, not only current and future events.

Time context is inherent to the evolution. Many of the facts are only valid during the limited period. In some cases the period when the information should be valid is commonly known (e.g. president of Poland is elected for five years) – additional background knowledge required, in other cases not (e.g. open period for existence of music band) – no background knowledge exists. Therefore, it is not sufficient to extract facts from the documents but also those facts should be bound to time. It requires very precise recognition of time expressions [4, 13]. Not only change has to be detected but also the time when it occurred has to be learned from the analyzed text. This information is not always explicit and tends to be ambiguous even for humans.

In the case when additional temporal context is taken into consideration, the following operations may be distinguished:

- prolongation, new information extends the temporal validity of the known fact, e.g. "the president was elected for the next term"; this is a special case of confirmation – the fact itself remains unchanged but will be valid for a longer period
- invalidation, the fact that was known to be true in the past is not true from a certain date, e.g. "the factory has just stopped producing model Q"; this is a special case of contradiction – the new fact is opposite to the existing fact; the knowledge bases changes, and history of changes is preserved
- update, new information makes known facts up-to-date, e.g. we know the turnover for May and the new fact is turnover for June; this is a special case of completion.

29.4 Framework

The proposed framework for evolution of ontology is divided into three layers: the bottom one is responsible for extraction of information from text; structured representation of the documents is stored in an internal format in the middle layer; the top layer is responsible for producing final ontology that conforms to some general and user requirements [16].

29.4.1 Layers and Evolution

From each business document several evidences for ontology evolution may be extracted. They are stored in the middle layer in the internal format. Throughout the whole process documents are annotated in each layer and therefore any kind of tool may be used to recognize named entities, contexts, or relations (modular approach).

The middle layer uses modelling primitives to represent information extracted from text. These are in the form of axioms about concepts, instances and relations with certain degree of confidence and with temporal information about their validity. We have decided to use a generic relational database model in order to store axioms. In such a way, it is possible to represent uncertainty and then produce ontology on demand according to some general requirements (e.g. consistency) and user needs (e.g. query). References of evidences back to text are also preserved in the database. Therefore, when a document is evaluated as unreliable all of its evidences should have weights lowered. Some evidences may point to several documents. Evidences collected over a longer period allow to achieve higher confidence.

Ontology is produced in the remaining layer. The three sublayers - defuzzification, snapshot, and consistency - are ordered, however, they may support each other in several iterations to produce the final ontology. Because in the internal format each axiom has a confidence level, it is not very useful for reasoning. In defuzzification, certain threshold is accepted and only the most certain axioms are an input to the next layer. Axioms have also temporal information on their validity and user might be interested only in the state of the ontology on particular date. Therefore, different versions of ontology may be created. Finally, consistency should be evaluated. Only after removing uncertainty and temporal information we are able to reason about the consistency of the ontology, when the set of axioms is fixed and any existing Description Logics reasoner may be used. If the resulting ontology is not consistent or not complete, the process of repairing ontology should be started taking into account information from two preceding sublayers. The detailed algorithms are to be developed.

29.4.2 Processes

There are four main processes in the framework. Two of them, collecting evidences and ontology evolution, are responsible for transforming crude text at the bottom into refined ontology at the top by extracting facts from text and then revising ontology. The other two processes, feedback and credibility, allow to improve the overall quality of ontology maintenance by propagating the control down the stack.

Even though the ontology produced in evolution process is consistent, it may not appropriately represent the world. Therefore, it is necessary to introduce a feedback mechanism, in which user may evaluate the truth of facts or correct the ontology. Information about acceptance or rejection of facts should be propagated back to lower layers.

First changes are introduced in defuzzification layer, when a user evaluates certain facts. The confidence level of those facts is then either one or zero (we suppose that user is sure about her statements). The change in confidence has influence on higher as well as lower layers. The impact on higher levels is reflected in new ontology that has to be built. Moreover, users may also add other axioms and correct existing ones. Finding satisfactory solution may take several iterations.

It has to be distinguished whether some of the facts from the document were false from the beginning of analyzed interval or were just updated later. In the first case, contradiction, the confidence of axioms should be lowered or the axioms should be removed (contraction). In the latter case, invalidation, the temporal validity of axiom should be updated and the new axiom added. It also has to be checked whether an axiom was correct but out of scope of the snapshot. In such case the interval in temporal relation should be extended (prolongation). More generally, another form of feedback user might give is about temporal validity of certain axioms.

29.5 Detection and Presentation of the Evolution

29.5.1 Granules of Change

In order to represent extracted information in the form of changes that may be applied to ontology, those changes should be represented in appropriate knowledge representation formalism; we need a granule of change.

In OWL-DL such granule is an axiom, e.g. "X sub-class-of Y". Therefore, new facts are transformed into appropriate axioms. By looking at basic modelling primitives, the following changes have been identified:

- class: a new class added, an existing class removed, change in hierarchy of classes, a disjoint or equivalent class defined
- instances: instance re-classified, properties of instance added or removed
- relations: domain changed, range changed, relation instances changed, value of the property changed.

Some of the axioms may not be extracted from text and therefore are not taken into account as subject to evolution, e.g. inverse object properties, sub properties. One fact may be transformed into several axioms.

After extraction of facts from text and formalization in form of axioms, it is possible to compare them to current state of knowledge base. The operations on ontology are presented in the Table 1. The notation is as follows: P, P_1, P_2 are predicates, P_{T1}, P_{T2} are temporal predicates that are valid in interval T1 and T2 respectively, meets, overlaps, before are taken from Allen's interval calculus [2].

Table 1. Operations and corresponding changing axioms

Type of change	Existing axioms	Removed axioms	Added axioms
confirmation	P(x,y)	-	-
completion	P_1(x,y)	-	P_1(x,z)$\wedge$subclassof(z,y) or P_2(x,z)
correction	P(x,y)	P(x,y)	P(x,z)

(Cont.)

Table 1. (Cont.)

Type of change	Existing axioms	Removed axioms	Added axioms
contradiction	$P(x,y)$	$P(x,y)$	-
prolongation	$P_{T1}(x,y)$	-	$P_{T2}(x,y) \wedge meets(T1,T2)$
invalidation	$P_{T1}(x,y)$	$P_{T1}(x,y)$	$P_{T2}(x,y) \wedge overlaps(T1,T2)$
update	$P_{T1}(x,y)$	-	$P_{T2}(x,z) \wedge before(T1,T2)$

When new fact arise it should be indicated how it will be handled - appropriate operation should be chosen. During confirmation operation, the confidence of the given axiom should be increased. In other cases, new axioms are introduced into ontology, which may become inconsistent. In some cases the new fact directly contradicts with a known fact, otherwise one needs a logical formalism in order to infer the contradiction.

There are different approaches to handle ontology change that may lead to inconsistency. The following major use cases has been identified in [6]:

- maintaining consistency of initially consistent ontology by applying appropriate changes
- repairing an inconsistent ontology
- reasoning with inconsistent ontology (usually on consistent sub-ontology)
- finding the right version of an ontology that is consistent.

Some approaches, like Text2Onto [3], just put the fact into the knowledge base and resolve potential contradictions when final ontology is requested. However, such an approach is not very useful for applications that require prompt action.

We claim that it is preferred to keep ontology consistent (with regards to some moment in time) in order to react properly to consecutive changes extracted from the stream of text documents. Inconsistency may be obvious, e.g. one fact says A and the other ¬A, but more often reasoning is required. We do not believe that very complex reasoning may be executed for the whole domain (with temporal logics in background, which may be undecidable). We focus only on contradicting facts with shallow reasoning. Deeper inconsistencies may be discovered just before the final ontology is created in OWL-DL, i.e. when time is not considered. There are also some approaches that allow to debug and repair an inconsistent ontology [14].

29.5.2 Temporal Axioms

Representation in form of "classic" axioms is not sufficient for business information: if it is unknown when a change occurred, it is not possible to reason about evolution. The business domain does not model a static world. Introduction of the time-related operations, like prolongation, invalidation or update, requires to extend the basic OWL formalism with *temporal axioms*, i.e. axioms that are true only in certain time interval.

Binding of axioms to time is also helpful in checking some constraints on relations, like cardinality. For example, two sentences: "Warsaw is the capital of Poland" and "Cracow is the capital of Poland" do not contradict provided that the second sentence is stated in 1500. In a static approach, it is asserted in the ontology that one country has only one capital. In the evolving world, we need to assert that a country may have only one capital at a time but several capitals throughout the whole history (not mentioning change of boarders). Generally, we have to distinguish between uniqueness (one value at a time) and universal uniqueness (one value at all). Attributes that are universally unique never change (e.g. place of birth); hence, they need not be bound to time.

The universally unique relations are particularly useful for finding contradictions in documents. In unique relations, when there are contradictory facts but stated on different dates one have to change the time validity of the first one and add another axiom with *updated* fact (e.g. when somebody changes a job). Sometimes it is not possible to give the exact date of change and therefore fuzzy representation could be used, leading to different confidence levels.

29.6 Conclusions and Future Work

This paper presented work in progress on the system that allows to extract information from a stream document for ontology evolution purposes. It focused on the evolution part which, as more than 20 years of research in belief revision shows, is not a trivial task.

What makes this framework different is the role of time. Beside simple operations: confirmation, completion, correction, contradiction, we have introduced time-related operations: prolongation, invalidation and update. Every axiom is bound to time interval and changes are resolved in accordance to their time validity. When time context is taken into account, ontology should contain information on invariability of some relations (e.g. date of birth) and cardinality in time context.

Belief revision (as a theory) was a good inspiration. Many of the problems are pointed to be irresolvable on the general level. When we look at extraction of information and ontology learning, some problems does not appear, like for example implications in knowledge base. Therefore, ontology revision for evolution should be simpler, although not ambiguous; hence feedback mechanism and user involvement.

The formalism is required in order to:

- represent extracted information in a structural way taking into account time context
- compare new facts with knowledge base
- apply changes to the ontology if necessary.

When a framework is fully developed it will allow to maintain the ontology automatically. The most promising (and one of the feasible) domain is business news.

Acknowledgement

This research project has been supported by a Marie Curie Transfer of Knowledge Fellowship of the European Community's Sixth Framework Programme under contract number MTKD-CT-2004-509766 (enIRaF – enhanced Information Retrieval and Filtering for Analytical Systems).

References

1. Alchourrón CE, Gärdenfors P, Makinson D (1985) On the logic of theory change: Partial meet contraction and revision functions. The Journal of Symbolic Logic 2:510-530
2. Allen JF, Ferguson G (1994) Actions and Events in Interval Temporal Logic. Journal of Logic and Computation 5:531-579
3. Cimiano P, Völker J (2005) Text2Onto. A Framework for Ontology Learning and Data-driven Change Discovery, In: Proceeding of NLDB'05
4. Ferro L, Gerber L, Mani I, Sundheim B, Wilson G (2005) TIDES. 2005 Standard for the Annotation of Temporal Expressions, MITRE Corporation
5. Fuhrmann A (1996) An Essay on Contraction. Studies in Logic, Language and Information. The University of Chicago Press
6. Haase P, Harmelen Fv, Huang Z, Stuckenschmidt H, Sure Y (2005) A Framework for Handling Inconsistency in Changing Ontologies. In: Gil Y, Motta E, Benjamins VR, Musen M (eds) 4th International Semantic Web Conference, ISWC 2005, Galway. Springer, LNCS, 3729
7. Hansson SO (1989) New operators for theory change. Theoria:114-133
8. Jin Y, Thielscher M (2005) Iterated Belief Revision, Revised. In: The 7th International Symposium on Logical Formalizations of Commonsense Reasoning, Corfu, Greece
9. Johnson FL, Shapiro SC (2001) Redefining Belief Change Terminology for Implemented Systems. In: Bertossi L, Chomicki J (eds) Working Notes for the IJCAI 2001 Workshop on Inconsistency in Data and Knowledge, Seattle, WA. AAAI Press, pp 11-21
10. Katsuno H, Mendelzon AO (1991) On the difference between updating a knowledge base and revising it. In: Second International Conference on Principles of Knowledge Representation and Reasoning, pp 387-394
11. Maedche A (2002) Ontology learning for the semantic Web. The Kluwer international series in engineering and computer science; SECS 665. Kluwer Academic Publishers: Boston
12. Magnini B, Negri M, Pianta E, Romano L, Speranza M, Serafini L, Girardi C, Bartalesi V, Sprugnoli R (2005) From Text to Knowledge for the Semantic Web: the ONTOTEXT Project, In: Bouquet P, Tummarello G (eds) Semantic Web Applications and Perspectives. CEUR Workshop Proceedings: Trento
13. Mani I, Pustejovsky J, Gaizauskas R (2005) The Language of Time. Oxford University Press

14. Parsia B, Sirin E, Kalyanpur A (2005) Debugging OWL ontologies, In: Proceedings of the 14th international conference on World Wide Web. ACM Press: Chiba, Japan, pp 633-640
15. Rott H (2000) Two Dogmas of Belief Revision. Journal of Philosophy 97:503-522
16. Węcel K (2006) A Framework for Document-driven Evolution of Ontology. In: Abramowicz W, Mayr HC (eds) Business Information Systems, Klagenfurt. Gesellschaft für Informatik, P-85, pp 378-391

30 Assuring Enterprise-Wide Information Quality Management Capability Maturity

Saša Baškarada, Andy Koronios, Jing Gao

Advanced Computing Research Centre
School of Computer and Information Science, University of South Australia, Mawson Lakes, SA 5095, Australia

30.1 Introduction

Contemporary enterprises have in recent times experienced significant changes, most of which have been technologically driven. The result of these gales of change has been an overabundance of information [17]. Yet such information abundance has not necessarily resulted in a more informed organization nor more effective decision making. Enterprises are now managing more information than ever before and are becoming aware of a range of information quality issues. Consequently, IQ problems abound and IQM is becoming ever more important. Many organizations recognize that they are having problems with the quality of information in their Information Systems (IS) however, they often find it difficult to assess their existing IQM capability. For that reason, we propose an IQM Maturity Model as a tool for assessing and enhancing organizational IQM Capability.

Maturity models have been very successfully used in many different disciplines, including the Capability Maturity Model (CMM) [20] and Capability Maturity Model Integration (CMMI) [5], which are heavily used in Software Engineering. Borrowing from the idea of CMMI, a similar maturity model is proposed in this chapter comprising five levels, with each level representing an evolutionary stage of IQM capability. It is thought that by separating IQ goals in a number of levels, it may be easier to achieve partial IQ objectives in an incremental way. This research adapts the Total Data Quality Management (TDQM) methodology [24] for IQ improvement and aligns the TDQM cycle stages with maturity levels. Furthermore, it endeavors to provide additional guidance by identifying specific process areas which are thought to be having an impact on IQ. Each level specifies a number of process areas which may provide a more detailed guidance for IQM.

353

W. Abramowicz and H.C. Mayr (eds.), Technologies for Business Information Systems, 353–363.
© 2007 *Springer.*

This research is still at a nascent stage and the model is now being further developed, enhanced and validated through an action research methodology in a number of asset management organizations.

30.2 Information Quality

In recent times, there has been a rapid increase in the quantity of information available to and used by organizations, as well as reliance of organizations on that information [1]. Gartner Research reports that through 2008, organizations that ignore Information Management (IM), will struggle to maintain their status in business environments [18]. However, reports from META group have indicated that 75% of companies in US have yet to implement any IQ initiative [3]. Furthermore, a study, of a major manufacturer, has found that 70% of all orders had errors [26]. Additionally, a Gartner survey shows that many financial services providers (FSPs) are experiencing operational and decision support initiatives hampered by suboptimal quality information [10], and that at least 40 percent of companies undertaking a CRM strategy are unaware of IQ problems in their environment [15]. Moreover, many organizations recognize the existence of IQ problems but do little about it because of a lack of perceived value [10]. Examples abound where impact of poor quality information has caused significant financial losses and in some cases has lead to disastrous consequences.

The impacts of poor IQ range from operational inconvenience and ill-informed decision-making to complete stoppage of business operations [1, 6, 11, 21]. Furthermore, inadequate information quality has serious implications for customer satisfaction/retention, as well as operational costs and financial reporting [15]. Thus, there is a growing need for tools and methods which can be used to assess and enhance the quality of information.

Quality has been defined by Juran [12] as "fitness for use". It implies that quality is defined by the customer, so that quality and customer satisfaction are considered as being analogous. Thus, it can also be defined as meeting or exceeding customer expectations, given that a perfectly produced product has little value if it is not what the customer wants. Furthermore, Juran [12] also coined the term "cost of quality", implying that dollar values can be associated with quality problems as well as quality management efforts. However, Crosby [8] argued that "quality is free" since all money spent on quality management is eventually saved by having less quality problems (defects). Even though, this doctrine was originally developed for the manufacturing industry, same principles have been applied to the field of Information Quality.

Common definition of IQ is also "fitness for use" [24]. "Fitness for use" however implies that the concept of IQ is subjective, which means that information with quality considered appropriate for one use may not possess sufficient quality for another use [23, 13]. Therefore, assessing IQ may be a challenging task. Additionally, even though conventional view of IQ has meant "Accuracy", a range of IQ dimensions (or quality goals), such as timeliness, completeness, relevancy and so on have been identified by Wang and Strong [25]. As a result, an IQ problem can be defined as any difficulty encountered along one or more quality dimensions that renders data completely or largely unfit for use [22].

The TDQM framework adapts Total Quality Management (TQM) principles to IQM, by drawing a correlation between traditional product manufacturing and the manufacturing of information or Information Product (IP) [24]. Therefore, the quality of resulting IP may be directly affected by the quality of processes employed in the Information System (IS). The TDQM methodology has adapted the quality improvement cycle from the manufacturing industry to IQ enhancement. TDQM applies the "Plan, Do, Check, Act" cycle from Deming's (TQM) literature [9] to IP quality improvement emphasizing that IQ improvements depend on continuous feedback to the processes producing the IP.

30.3 Capability Maturity Models

Capability Maturity Models originate from the Software Engineering discipline. The original CMM was developed by the Software Engineering Institute (SEI) at the Carnegie Mellon University (CMU) and the United States Department of Defense (US DOD), beginning in 1986. CMM has been extensively used by the US DOD to evaluate its software and system developers. It is a methodology used to develop and refine an organization's software development process by establishing a framework for continuous process improvement and defining the means to be employed to that end. CMM describes five maturity levels, which represent an evolutionary path of increasingly structured and methodically more mature processes. Even though CMM doesn't itself address any IM/IQM issues, we have adapted the CMM doctrine to IQM.

A number of IQM related maturity models have been proposed. Caballero at el. [4] employ a concept of an Information Management Process (IMP) and consider an IS as a set of IMPs. Subsequently, the maturity model is applied to each IMP. Kyung-Seok [16] describes a number of maturity stages relating to IM, showing that higher IM maturity may result in improved information quality. We have conducted a comprehensive literature review in the fields of IM and IQM and we have identified an array of process areas which are thought to be having an impact on the quality of information. In the next section, we endeavor to present those process areas and organize them into staged levels.

30.4 Rationale and Purpose

Many organizations admit to having IQ problems however they often find it difficult to assess their current IQM capability. Furthermore, many organizations are also interested in knowing how they compare to others in terms of IQM. By adapting and combining the TDQM and CMM doctrines, this chapter presents a theoretical framework that addresses these issues. Additionally, we have identified from literature and case studies, a wide range of IM and IQM process areas, which are thought to be of value to practitioners undertaking IQM initiatives, by providing additional specific guidance to the existing and well accepted TDQM methodology.

30.5 Research Methodology

This research is mainly concerned with theory building and thus it can be classified as being interpretive in nature. Interpretative research does not predefine dependent and independent variables, but focuses on the full complexity of human sense making as the situation emerges [14]. Additionally, when a subject area is not well understood, qualitative methods may be used to build theory, which then may be tested using quantitative methods such as surveys and experiments [19]. Thus, the model development can further be described as qualitative research since it is subjective, holistic, interpretative and inductive in nature. The IQM capability maturity model presented in this chapter has been developed by reviewing existing relevant literature in the domains of data and information quality, quality assurance, and maturity models [5, 7, 9, 20, 24]. Next, approximately a dozen interviews were conducted Engineering Asset Management organizations, which enabled us to gain further insights into real-world IQ issues. The theoretical framework presented in this chapter consists of concepts and their relationships, as identified from literature and interviews, which have been then further grouped and categorized. Thus, this research can be described as being interpretive, qualitative and grounded in theory.

30.6 Assuring Enterprise-Wide Information Quality Management Capability Maturity

This section presents the IQM capability maturity model based on the TDQM framework. We construct the IQM capability maturity model based on the TDQM improvement cycle by adapting the TDQM cycle into five staged maturity levels. Levels two to five represent TDQM cycle stages; whereas level one indicates that no attempts are made to manage the IQ. We then organize the process areas into five maturity levels, aiming to provide further and more specific guidance.

30.6.1 Level 1: REACTIVE

> IM/IQM processes are not standardized or documented (they are ad-hoc). There is no awareness of any IQ issues. No attempts are made to assess or enhance IQ. Organization is only reacting to IQ problems as they occur.

Database Normalization – To achieve this capability maturity level, an organization must store all its data in a normalized database.

30.6.2 Level 2: AWARE

> All IPs, together with their quality requirements, have been defined and documented. Thus, relevant IQ dimensions and required degrees of adherence have been identified.

IP & IQ Definition – All IPs, their data sources, storage media used, retrieval methods, etc. have been identified and defined by information users. Reasons for all data collection have been documented. It is also important to correctly identify and manage IQ requirements, since IQ is defined by the user ("fitness for use"). Thus the required degrees of quality conformance are being appropriately managed and recorded.

Information Products Roles and Responsibilities – Organization has clearly defined and communicated roles and responsibilities for all personnel in relation to IPs. Role descriptions outline both authority and responsibility; including definitions of skills and experience needed in the relevant position.

Information Stewardship and Ownership – This process manages information stewardship responsibilities and implements a formal stewardship program. It clearly defines responsibilities for ownership of IPs and information systems. Owners may for instance, make decisions about information classification and security.

Information Classification Scheme – A classification scheme that applies throughout the enterprise, based on the criticality and sensitivity (e.g., public, confidential, top secret, etc.) has been established. This scheme includes details about information ownership, definition of appropriate security levels and protection controls, a description of information retention and destruction requirements, criticality, sensitivity and so on.

Information Redundancy Management – It may be necessary to capture and store some information in a redundant manner. Thus, this task needs to be appropriately managed and documented.

Derived Values – Any possible derived values have been defined and documented. Values should not be entered if they can be derived from other values.

No Manual Copy – Information is entered only once into the system. It is never copied manually.

Information Dictionary and Information Syntax Rules – Information dictionary enables the sharing of information elements amongst applications and systems by providing a common understanding of information, and preventing incompatible IPs from being created.

Enforcement of Constraints on Transactional Information – Transactional information are being validated against pre-defined constraints to check for information quality (these can typically be built into a DBMS). Thus, input information is validated as close to the point of creation as possible. The goal is to reduce NULLs and default values. Referential integrity constraints may help ensure information consistency.

30.6.3 Level 3: DEFINED

> IQM is being considered as a core business activity. Organization-wide IQM initiative has been established.

Training & Mentoring – Any staff dealing with information are being appropriately trained and mentored. Standardized policies and procedures for training and mentoring are in place and are being followed.

Storage and Retention Management – Procedures for information storage and archival have been defined and implemented. They consider retrieval requirements, cost-effectiveness, security requirements and so on.

Backup (Offsite) Storage and Restoration – All critical backup media & documentation are stored offsite. Offsite arrangements are being periodically assessed for content, environmental protection, security and so on.

Information Disposal Management – Procedures to prevent access to sensitive information when they are disposed of or transferred have been defined and implemented. Such procedures ensure that information marked as deleted or to be disposed cannot be retrieved.

Information Security Requirements – Arrangements have been established to identify and apply security requirements applicable to the receipt, processing, physical storage and output of sensitive information. This includes physical records, information transmissions and any information stored offsite.

Secure IP Exchange – The transmission of any classified IPs is done via secured communication channels. Sensitive information transactions are exchanged only over a trusted path or medium with controls to provide authenticity of content, proof of submission, proof of receipt and non-repudiation of origin.

Input/Access Authorization Rules/Roles/Procedures – Only authorized staff members may perform information input/access/edits. This could be ensured through the use of various authentication mechanisms.

Information Product Version Control – Guidelines/procedures are in place (and documented), which state when/why/where/etc. different versions of IPs should be created.

Information Product Templates – A set of standard IP templates is being maintained.

Information Input Error Handling – Procedures for the correction and resubmission of information that was erroneously input are in place, documented and followed.

Roles and Responsibilities for Information Quality Management – Responsibilities for IQM have been assigned, and the quality assurance group has been provided with appropriate authority. The responsibilities and size of the quality assurance group satisfy the requirements of the organization.

Information Quality Management Project Planning – A project plan that provides a structured framework for IQM has been developed. The project scope, timelines, milestones, deliverables, and so on have been defined.

Information Consistency Assurance (Data Cleansing) – Data cleansing is a well recognized approach to IQ improvements. Many software tools are available that provide a wide range of functionalities including profiling, matching, enhancement and so on. These tools however mostly ensure information consistency, and do not necessarily enhance information accuracy.

30.6.4 Level 4: MANAGED

IQ metrics have been developed and IQ is being assessed.

Enterprise Information Architecture Model (Data Flow and Work Flow) –
An enterprise-wide information model that enables decision-supporting activities has been established and maintained. The model may facilitate the creation, use and sharing of information in a way that is flexible, functional, cost-effective, timely, secure and so on.

Meta-Information Management – Meta-information is being used to enhance information quality by providing additional information about various IPs. Not all IPs need to be meta-tagged; only the critical ones may need to have this option. Meta-information may describe various properties such as, ownership, security, edit-history and so on.

Information Processing Error Handling – Information processing error-handling procedures ensure that erroneous transactions are identified without being processed and without undue disruption of the processing of other valid transactions.

Information Quality Management Policies – A set of policies that support the IQM strategy has been developed and maintained. These policies include policy intent, roles and responsibilities, exception process, compliance approach, references to procedures, standards and guidelines.

Information Quality Management Standards and Practices –Standards, procedures and practices for IQM guiding the organization in meeting the intent of the Quality Management System (QMS) have been identified and documented. Industry best practices are being used for tailoring the organization's quality practices.

Information Quality Risk Management & Impact Assessment – IPs and IQ dimensions at risk (critical IPs) have been identified. Consequences and probabilities of IQ problems are being predicted, and acceptable levels of risk are being evaluated.

Information Quality Assessment – IQ metrics have been developed and IQ assessments are being performed.

Supplier, Input, Process, Outputs, Customer (SIPOC) Diagram – SIPOC diagrams are used to identify supplier, inputs, processes, outputs and information customers/users.

Check Sheet – Check sheets are structured forms, which are used to record IQ problems.

Statistical Control Charts for Information Quality Control – Control charts are graphs, which are used to control process variability over time. It is a statistical tool that can be used to verify the stability of processes.

Histogram – Histograms are graphs showing distribution of data points measured that fall within various class-intervals. They are used to graphically depict the variability in a process.

Pareto Chart – Pareto charts are used to analyze data about frequency of problems in a process. Thus, they may be used to prioritize problems.

30.6.5 Level 5: OPTIMIZING

> Root causes of IQ problems have been identified and impact of poor IQ has been calculated. Processes causing IQ problems are continually being improved.

Output Review and Error Handling – Procedures assure that the provider and relevant users review the accuracy of output IPs. Procedures are also in place for identification and handling of errors contained in the output.

Information Integration Management – Various IQ related problems may occur during the process of information integration. Thus, standardized policies and processes are in place to ensure that any information integration does not create further IQ problems.

Single Point of Truth (SPOT) – Information should never be duplicated (accept for backup purposes); it is recorded in only one location.

Continuous Improvement – An overall quality plan is in place, which promotes continuous improvement, and is maintained and documented.

Root Cause Analysis (RCA) – The root causes of IQ problems are being investigated and categorized. Only when it is determined why IQ problems occurred, it will be able to specify workable corrective measures that prevent future problems.

Flowchart – Flowcharts are used to graphically represent processes.

Cause-and-Effect Diagram – Also called Fishbone or Ishikawa diagram, are used to identify possible causes for a problem. It can be a useful tool for sorting causes into categories.

5 Whys – 5 Whys is a problem solving method, which is used to determine root causes of a problem. It states that five iterations of asking 'why' should be sufficient to determine the root cause of a problem.

Scatter Diagram – Scatter diagrams are used to determine if two variables are related. They can be useful in determining whether two problems, that seem to be related, both occur with the same cause.

Cost-benefit analysis – It is a technique that compares the total expected cost of an improvement initiative to the total expected benefits. Its goal is to aid in choosing the best (most profitable) option.

IQM Support for IT & Organizational Strategies – IQM initiative is aligned with IT and Organizational strategies. Thus, ensuring IQM is adding value to the organization at the strategic level.

Information Quality Accountability – This process ensures that every person is accountable for the quality of his or her work and does not send poor quality information to the next person in the process.

Audit Trail – Any IP creation, access, update, deletion, etc. must be auditable. This could be accomplished through logging of information entries/access/edits/deletes and so on.

30.7 Conclusion

In this chapter, we have presented an Information Quality Management Capability Maturity Model, basing the maturity levels on the TDQM improvement cycle. Additionally, we have identified a wide range of IM and IQM process areas, which we further organized within the maturity model. The model presented may be used by organizations to assess and enhance their IQM capability. Thus, this research contributes to the field of IQM by providing additional specific guidance to the already well accepted TDQM improvement methodology.

30.8 Future Research

This preliminary model was developed from literature and initial case-study interviews. Further research is still required to test, verify and enhance it. Where a specific new methodology or an improvement to a methodology is being studied, action research may be the only relevant research method presently available [2]. Therefore, it is intended to conduct two action research cycles in two large Australian Asset Management organizations, which will enable the researchers to test and further refine the model.

Acknowledgements

This research is conducted through the Centre for Integrated Engineering Assets Management (CIEAM). The support of CIEAM partners is gratefully acknowledged.

References

1. Ballou D, Madnick S, Wang R (2003) Special Section: Assuring Information Quality. Journal of Management Information & Systems, vol. 20, no. 3, pp. 9-11
2. Baskerville RL, Wood-Harper AT (2002) A Critical Perspective on Action Research as a Method for Information Systems Research. Qualitative Research in Information Systems, eds. MD Myers & D Avison, SAGE Publications, London, Thousand Oaks, New Delhi
3. Beg J, Hussain S, (2003) Data Quality - A problem and An Approach. Wipro Technologies
4. Caballero I, Gómez Ó, Piattini M (2004) Getting Better Information Quality by Assessing and Improving Information Quality Management. In: Proceedings of the Ninth International Conference on Information Quality (ICIQ-04), MIT, Cambridge, Massachusetts, November 5-7
5. Capability Maturity Model® Integration (CMMI). Version 1.1 (2002), Carnegie Mellon Software Engineering Institute, Pittsburgh
6. Chengalur-Smith IN, Ballou DP, Pazer HL (1999) The Impact of Data Quality Information on Decision Making: An Exploratory Analysis. IEEE Transactions on Knowledge and Data Engineering, vol. 11, no. 6, pp. 853-864
7. CobIT 4.0. (2005) The IT Governance Institute
8. Crosby P (1979) Quality is Free. McGraw-Hill, New York
9. Deming WE (1982) Out of the Crisis. MIT Press, Cambridge
10. Friedman T, Nelson S, Radcliffe J (2004) CRM Demands Data Cleansing. Gartner Research
11. Huang KT, Lee YW, Wang RY (1999) Quality Information and Knowledge. Upper Saddle River: Prentice Hall
12. Juran JM, Gryna FMJ, Bingham RS (1974) Quality Control Handbook. 3 edn, McGraw-Hill Book Co, New York, NY
13. Kahn B, Strong D, Wang R (2002) Information Quality Benchmarks: Product and Service Performance. Communications of the ACM, April, pp. 184-192
14. Kaplan B, Maxwell JA (1994) Qualitative Research Methods for Evaluating Computer Information Systems. In: Evaluating Health Care Information Systems: Methods and Applications. eds. JG Anderson, CE Aydin & SJ Jay, Sage, Thousand Oaks, CA, pp. 45-68
15. Knox M (2004) Banks and Asset Managers Are Enhancing Data Quality. Gartner Research
16. Kyung-seok R (2005) A study on data quality management maturity model. In: Proceedings of the 7th International Conference on Advanced Communication Technology, 2005, ICACT 2005
17. Lyman P, Hal RV (2003) How Much Information. retrieved from http://www.sims.berkeley.edu/how-much-info-2003 on [25th of August 2006]
18. Logan D, Newman D (2006) From IM to EIM: An Adoption Model. Gartner Research

19. Moody DL, Shanks GG (2003) Improving the quality of data models: empirical valida-
    tion of a quality management framework. Information Systems, vol. 28, no. 6, Sep-
    tember, pp. 619-650
20. Paulk MC, Curtis B, Chrissis MB, Weber CV (1993) Capability Maturity Model for
    Software. Version 1.1, Software Engineering Institute/Carnegie Mellon University
21. Redman TC (1998) The Impact of Poor Data Quality on the Typical Enterprise. Com-
    munications of the ACM, vol. 41, no. 2, February, pp. 79-82
22. Strong DM, Lee YW, Wang RY (1997) Data Quality in Context. Communications of
    the ACM, vol. 40, no. 5, May, pp. 103-110
23. Tayi GK, Ballou DP (1998) Examining Data Quality. Communications of the ACM,
    vol. 41, no. 2, February, pp. 54-57
24. Wang RYA (1998) A Product Perspective on Total Data Quality Management Com-
    munications of the ACM, vol. 41, no. 2, February, pp. 58-65
25. Wang RY, Strong D (1996) Beyond Accuracy: What Data Quality Means to Data
    Consumers. Journal of Management Information Systems, vol. 12, no. 4, pp. 5-34
26. Wang RY, Ziad M, Lee YW (2000) Data Quality. Kluwer Academic Publishers

31 Involving Users to Improve the Level of Their Satisfaction from a Software Product Designed for Public Organization

Barbara Begier

Poznan University of Technology, Pl. M. Sklodowskiej-Curie 5, Poznan, Poland

31.1 Introduction

Software applications are full of promise to improve activities in public organizations, like public administration, hospitals, social insurances, judiciary, emergency services, etc. However, results are often far away from users' expectations – it is a regular case so far that an inquirer may apply immediately for something but he/she receives a correct document in three months. There are many reasons of that. One of them is a domination of rigorous *hard methodologies* in software companies focused on making software process fast and repeatable. Those methodologies, developed to produce software for military applications, control devices, and mobile communication, don't work in the case of software systems for public organizations. First of all, an *isolation of software developers from its users* results in a low level of users' satisfaction from a software product.

Poor quality of software has its roots in the basic principle of the today's economy – the high productivity is a measure of success, also in a software production. A concentration on particular functions instead of entire business processes also underlies wrong software solutions. So yesterday's solutions are transferred into an information system. Besides that, software developers make a wrong assumption that end users are a homogenous group of people who work always perfectly. In fact, a lot of failures arise because of the mistaken data recorded in documents and databases. So called *noisy texts* are the current field of research [22]. Furthermore, too optimistic estimations concern migrations and transfers of data.

The problem is how to build-in quality into software systems developed for governmental and other public organizations. The change of technology in a public

W. Abramowicz and H.C. Mayr (eds.), Technologies for Business Information Systems, 365–377.
© 2007 *Springer.*

organization should be oriented to its *mission* which is superior to profitability of supporting tools. This mission is to provide and improve specified services for citizens who are indirect users of a software product. The software system should be designed along with a new technology and its every day usage. There is a lack of specified processes of cooperation with users.

The *level of users' satisfaction from a software product* is assumed the main measure of software quality in the presented UID (*User-Involved Development*) approach [10], which incorporates techniques derived both from hard and soft methodologies. The aim is to improve the level of average user's satisfaction. To provide it users should leave peripheries of the software process and become its *subject* [11]. The direct and indirect users are supposed to cooperate with designers to improve software quality. *Soft methodologies* include users' involvement (see section 2) but their share in the software production still remains slight. On the other hand, there is no escape from technical standards and rules of economy market. The idea of the UID derives partially from the author's experience with poor software quality and it is also a result of research concerning software quality, including quality assessment – many of the polled respondents show their willingness to influence on a software product [7]. Users take part in the specified primary and supporting processes of the UID approach. The specified infrastructure is required to realize those processes.

Developers assume that the detailed requirements are obtainable at the beginning of a product life cycle. They believe that a specification of requirements, including quality attributes, is sufficient to provide software quality. In the real life, never ending improvements are added to the software system. An essential feature of the UID approach is a *permanent feedback* from users on a software product (see section 5). This approach has been applied first to the evolutional development of software supporting specified calculations in civil engineering. After four iterations of the collaborative development including periodical assessment of software quality [8] the level of users' satisfaction from a product is much better than that at the beginning. Despite all differences between the software applied by civil engineers and those used in public organizations *the idea to incorporate direct and also indirect users* in the software process is worth working out. The quality aspects are mainly focused on the *usability* of a product assessed from the users' point of view. Examples of quality measures are given in the section 6.

People factors are usually reduced to the management of human resources in a software factory [15, 16, 27]. Users differ from developers in age, gender, skills, and personalities. Examinations in four organizations showed that 56 % of users were females in the 40 to 50 age bracket [7], while software factories are dominated by men under 35. The *competency management* in software companies should be reoriented to develop competencies which enable cooperation with users. The described approach is complementary to the recommended MDA (*Model Driven Architecture*) [24] – program authors and software users together are creators of models of future software solutions. Thus a set of competencies required in software production should also include capabilities to cooperate with people of various profession, age, culture, and gender.

31.2 Brief Survey of Users' Involvement in a Software Process to Improve Software Quality

Recommended methods to assure software quality are based on the right assumption that a good process results in a good product. Most of them refer to the ISO 9001 [20] and/or to the Capability Maturity Model (CMM) [26]. Users believe that the ISO or another certification should guarantee quality of a product. But the problem of quality is still open. Is it enough to meet standards to achieve a good process? Whose quality criteria are considered? How to improve a process to provide the software quality expected by users?

Failures in software production question a credibility of classical phases of a software development [2]. Instead of hard methodologies based on various plans and other documents, the *agile (soft) methodologies* have been developed which emphasize interactions and customer collaboration. The idea to involve users in the software process has been developed in Europe, especially in Scandinavia, since the early seventies. The Checkland's concept of soft methodologies born in the UK [13] and the Participatory Design suggested by Nygaard [30] became the flagship ideas in that area. Supporters of agile methods [1] emphasize an ecology approach [3] and human aspects of the software process. One of principles expressed in the Agile Manifesto [6, 12] states that *the most efficient and effective method of conveying information to and within a team is face-to-face conversation*. From among soft methods just the XP methodology [5] has gained a great popularity in telecommunication and aircraft industry.

The Socio-technical design [25] and the Value Sensitive Design [18] require to find an optimal solution from a social point of view. A satisfaction of an employee from his/her work is an important value there.

The User-Centered Design of web applications [21] is focused on a friendly interface of the software product. The IBM User-Centered Design incorporated in the software process [28] requires to appoint interdisciplinary teams who use techniques applied in marketing to define the target audience of the created internet application, then to build a list of their preferences, etc. The general call for a user-driven development process in web time [14] claims to respect human factors in a software process oriented to e-business and Web applications.

Specification of *use cases* expressed in UML [29] and/or creation of *prioritized and refined scenarios* [4] bring positive results. System *stakeholders* who are individuals (end users, installers, administrators, system architects, software engineers and designers) affected somehow by a software product, are engaged early in the life cycle to discover quality attributes and to develop appropriate scenarios.

Principles and general instructions of the *user-centred approach for interactive systems* have been developed in the INUSE project [19]. Software development is a collaborative process which requires multi-disciplinary teams – at least two groups are involved in a process: software designers and software users. The collaborative approach was also developed in the Memorial project [17].

Since a shortage of talents has appeared among software developers [15] thus the quality experts are expected to play a great role to provide software quality. Experts are facilitators asking stakeholders for specification and correction of scenarios, which concern typical business matters involving basic system functions. Experts also play roles of inspectors involved in the software development. Unfortunately, they slightly know the real life problems which may appear in a product exploitation. No indirect users are involved in the process.

31.3 Characteristics of the Considered Class of Software

There is no one kind of users in the case of a *software system developed for a public organization*. A *customer* or a *purchaser* is an organization (for example: hospital, ministry, Municipal Council, tax office), which orders the specified software product. The term *client* refers to the organization in which a product is installed. The words *personnel* and *employees* are synonyms in this paper. The *direct user* means any clerk, including a person holding a managerial position, who uses the considered software system at his/her work. The *indirect user* depends indirectly on the system – he/she is a patient or supplicant of the given organization. The term *users' representatives* means a set of people who represent direct and indirect users of any kind – average people as they really are. Users are various people so the representatives should be *representative* for their broad spectrum.

The top feature of a software system developed for public organizations is its relatively long life cycle. Data are maintained even longer than programs. Clerks of a given organization, not computer programmers, are the direct users. The usage and maintenance of databases and documents should stick to the safety rules recommended in the ISO standard 17799. That's assumed *a priori* that system development is carried out step by step in several years. Its evolutional development takes place till its withdraw. Changes of functionality have to keep up with the dynamically changing legislative rules, an organizational progress and new technologies. Additional source of changes comes from users' personal progress – users propose new requirements after their basic needs are satisfied, according to the hierarchy of needs described by Maslow [23].

System can be decomposed according to the maintained branch and competency structures in an organization. Software applications support an interpersonal communication and coordination of works among clerks. Software solutions have a great influence on a scope, way, deadlines, and quality of services for customers of the organization.

31.4 Conditions of Users' Reasonable Involvement

So far software developers seem to show their prejudice against less qualified, in their opinion, users. A reluctance to get involved in cooperation with users arises also due to their general criticism of unsatisfying and unreliable products – the simplest way seems to avoid contacts with software users. In turn, the users' aversion to software developers is a result of low quality of software products and an arrogance of its authors. Under some conditions these attitudes may change diametrically.

Direct users are no more supposed to adapt themselves to the software system nor to act as perfect robots. They should play an active role in a software process to provide quality of a software product which is adapted to various users' needs and capabilities. It's been assumed that a scope of requirements will grow each time after the new version of the software product is introduced. The cooperation of developers and users is not limited to the requirements phase. So software authors should not test and assess software products by themselves only. Users are periodically asked to assess software products applied in public organizations.

The representatives of *indirect users* also take part in the software process. Methods practiced in sociology should be applied to choose the representative sample of indirect users to involve them in interviews, meetings, joint reviews, questionnaires, and another forms of software assessment. Thus the quality level of services provided for citizens by a public organization using a software product is indirectly also an object of the assessment.

Software companies should be financially dependent of users' assessments of the delivered products. Direct and indirect users become conscious of their rights to assess software products and to have their influence on quality features.

Technical competencies of software developers are not sufficient in software production. Personality-based competencies essential to cooperate with users' representatives are supposed to play an important role in competency management.

Users become *the subject* of the software process. At the first glance, their capabilities to be partners of software developers during the software life cycle may seem problematic. But the estimated level of users' skills in information technologies is based on the yesterday's results of assessment. It evolves with time. Present school pupils will have no barriers to use computers at their future work and to participate in specified forms of cooperation with software developers. They will not tolerate the today's inconveniences of using imperfect software products. The role of users is more and more active in subsequent software development cycles.

31.5 Software Life Cycle and Processes in the UID Approach

The UID (*User-Involved Development*) approach has been introduced and recommended in software development [10]. It is not limited to software systems for public organizations. The model of the software life cycle in the UID approach is shown in the Figure 1. Software development is repeated and continued till the product withdraw. In the described approach two questionnaire surveys related to all potential users link the start and the end of each development cycle − first one is recommended at the very beginning to get learn users' profiles and expectations, the second one has a form of a product assessment which takes place each time the new version is introduced. Users' involvement in the software process is related to *direct and indirect users* of a product.

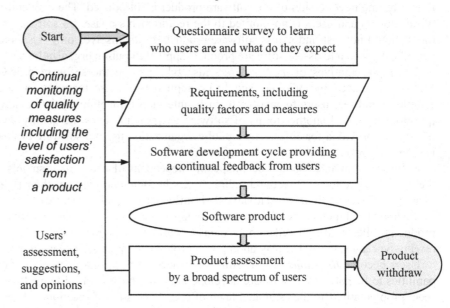

Fig. 1. The software life cycle in the UID approach

The core feature of the UID is to emphasize the *permanent feedback* between software developers and users. The users' involvement is not limited to the requirements specification. Other forms of cooperation, like a participation of delegated representatives in joint developers' team, meetings half-and-half, brain storm sessions and others, are recommended, too. Users have an influence on test plans and a design of test cases. So there are several loops of continual feedback between developers and users to provide that users' opinions are respected and considered on-line. Initial phases of software development cycle are focused on a modeling of system usage to support business processes.

The most external loop refers to an assessment of the delivered and installed product. The experience shows that many users not only give their notes to the specified software features but also include their constructive remarks in questionnaires [7, 8]. Direct and also indirect users take part in software assessment. Their expectations are considered in the entire life cycle. Results of the software assessment including users' notes, opinions, and suggestions along with other new requirements constitute an input in the next development cycle as illustrated in the Figure 2. Users enable to detect wrong solutions and lacks or in software functionality by reporting problems which occurred at their every day work. Users' presence makes available to prioritize software functions and other requirements.

Domain and quality experts are also involved in the process of quality assessment but their presence is not equivalent to users' involvement in the software process. Experts and users are different groups of people and show different competencies – experts trace a conformity with standards and similar solutions while users assess the usability of a product and its usefulness to manage regular and also untypical tasks. Indirect users assess a *level of services* provided by a given organization after its informatization.

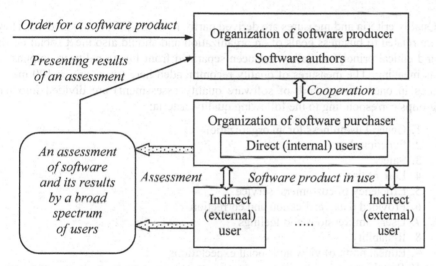

Fig. 2. Permanent feedback between software authors and users

An emphasis on *usability* of a software product is based on an assumption that any tool of work should provide its ease and improve its productivity. If new tools eliminate previous problems and a discomfort at work by reducing stress then employee's satisfaction grows. And this is an important criterion of quality of life.

The UID approach requires to expand the software process – to establish some new processes and to develop the existing ones in software production. An initial questionnaire survey to learn who users are is an example of a new process. Various subprocesses to provide the cooperation with users are required, including work in joint teams, business process modeling and analysis, software product assessment by its direct and indirect users. Users also take part in the specified, previously performed without their presence, processes – they participate in test planning and in specifying control lists for reviews and inspections.

Close relationships with users generate new requirements concerning a supporting infrastructure. The extended CRM (*Customer Relationship Management*) system is required to maintain data concerning joint activities and involved users, like delegated members of teams, participants of meetings and brain storm sessions, persons responsible for particular documents, participants of joint reviews, authors of test cases and scenarios, co-authors of check lists developed for software inspections, users taking part in an assessment of a product, etc. The prototype of such CRM system has been developed and described in [9]. The software process is monitored, controlled and modified according to the results of a product assessment – some additional activities are undertaken to avoid defects of a product.

31.6 Quality Criteria and Measures

Quality criteria and measures are derived partly from the ISO 9126 standard. They are related to business goals of an organization and should also meet social needs and ethical principles. Safety has been separated from functionality to emphasize its meaning. The measures of quality recommended here (there are ca 100 measures in one questionnaire of software quality assessment) are divided into ten groups corresponding to the following quality criteria:

1. General usefulness for an organization
2. Functionality
3. Safety
4. Ease of use
5. Efficiency of customers' service
6. Provided data verification and correction
7. Users' impressions and feelings
8. Reliability
9. Ethical point of view and social expectations
10. Portability

Examples of quality measures, specified in the fifth group from an indirect user's point of view, are the following:

5.1. An average time of performance of each specified kind of service for an inquirer's application.
5.2. The real time of data transfer from system server.
5.3. The level specifying how much activities of data acquisition and verification are time-consuming.

5.4. The total time required to fix something for a supplicant (the total time of all performed activities), for example to get an excerpt from the land register after the specified modification.

5.5. The worst time to get the correct response for each specified service of the system, for example, to get the required certificate of being able to marry from the register office (in the case of mistaken or incomplete data, changing personnel not aware of what's been done, etc.).

5.6. Real number of visits in the organization to deal with the specified business matter, for example, to get an updated excerpt from the land records.

5.7. Number of required documents and data (forms, attachments, spaces provided, etc.) which should be delivered and presented each time by an applicant (although all required data are maintained in the software system).

5.8. Level of the provided possibility to correct mistaken data immediately.

5.9. Number of words required to correct mistaken data.

5.10. Number of iterations required in the case of wrong service or mistaken data.

5.11. The ratio of the time required for service including data correction to the time of a traditional service.

5.12. Number of mistaken or incomplete data met in one day of work (an average monthly).

5.13. Number of communication errors daily.

5.14. Number of net problems (suspensions, no response, etc.) monthly.

5.15. Paper savings/wastes (the number of currently generated document pages compared with the previously printed number of pages in the same case).

5.16. Number of cases which took more than one day in service.

5.17. Number of cases which took more than one month to be completed.

All specified measures, including those given above, become items/questions in the questionnaire. Each item may have a form just of a name of this measure and then a respondent gives his/her note to it using a scale <1, 5>, where 5 means the highest value. Another solution to answer a question is to use the Likert scale – each item of the questionnaire is a statement followed by several expressions describing various possible answers of the respondent (strongly disagree, disagree, neither agree nor disagree, agree, strongly agree). The respondent is asked to indicate his/her degree of agreement with the given statement. The expected forms of answers should be carefully and precisely specified for each metric to avoid misunderstandings. Direct users give their notes or answers to all specified measures. The quoted above measures in the fifth group are also assessed by representatives of indirect users who may also assess the ninth subset of metrics.

After the specified software features are measured, a process of their refinement should be initialized if necessary. The refinement specification contains: references to the specified scenario, generated artifacts, given measures, described context, system response, unsatisfied quality attributes, sources of wrong service, their possible reasons, reported problems, possible issues and proposals of improvement. The product refinement may also involve the process improvement to avoid similar inadvertences in the next iteration of system development.

31.7 Expected Competencies and Preferred Roles in Software Production

Specified sets of competencies constitute the required competency profiles considered in the recruitment process in a software organization. Similar procedures may be applied to select an appropriate person to play the required role in team. Today's students of computer science and software engineering will be software developers in the near future. Software companies should recruit people able to work in teams, provide quality, and cooperate with users. Following this line of thought, the questionnaire survey, concerning competencies required for possible professional roles in computing, was carried out in December 2005. Just personality features were the objects of research. An initial set of competencies has been specified separately for each of eight professional roles assumed in a software company, namely: *analyst, software designer, team leader, manager, quality engineer, programmer/tester, service worker, trainer in computing.*

Participants of this survey were students of the diploma semester in the field of computer science in Poznan University of Technology. They have not been taught nor trained in competency management [31] before. Respondents had to give notes using the scale <1, 5> to competencies, listed separately in an alphabetical order for each particular professional role and possibly to add more competencies, important from their points of view. At the end of the survey respondents were asked to declare which professional role they prefer by themselves being best prepared to perform it. Some students work in software companies so the results of the survey show not only students' imagination.

As results, the four top competencies of an *analyst* are: analytical thinking, accuracy, inquisitiveness, and a capability to accept someone else's point of view. Only 8 per cent of those polled point out a competency of logical thought. A *software designer* should show subsequently: general creativity, capability to create new solutions, capability to accept someone else's point of view, goal orientation, inquisitiveness, and self-criticism. Respondents value as additional competencies: optimism, patience, and resistance to stress. The *service worker* is the only one in students' opinion who should be able to cooperate with other people and to demonstrate a personal culture and politeness. So it seems that employees who perform any other roles do not leave their office and do not speak with users. Students work individually − in their opinion only a *team leader* is supposed to show the leadership, achievement orientation, and also a capability to listen to others, to solve conflicts, and to tolerate different attitudes or behaviors. The *quality engineer* first of all should be: responsible, able to a reliable assessment, and self-reliant. The competencies of assertiveness and perceptiveness have been added to the initially specified list.

The survey has illustrated what competencies, in students' opinion, are required in software company and also what competencies have been developed by their own. It has revealed that 30 per cent of students prefer the role of an analyst and the next 19 % would like to work as the programmer/tester. No one of the respondents is going to be a quality engineer – the university education does not prepare students good enough to provide quality of software products.

31.8 Final Remarks

Users' involvement in software development does not deny a need to organize a work in software factory nor an idea of automation of the software process. The current trends in software engineering, like following the concept of Model Driven Architecture (MDA), including business modeling, creating UML models, then updating and exchanging models, and so on, do not exclude the presence of users who may participate in software modeling and development and then a software product assessment.

The proper solutions of business processes supported by the software system are the source of users' satisfaction. The question is a cost to keep users involved in a software life cycle. A high level of usability translates into high productivity. Due to the IBM experience every dollar invested in the ease of use returns $10 to $100 [28] because of the less number of failures and required modifications. Satisfied users make all business efficient and effective – customers keep cooperating with the software producer who provides collaboration resulting in high quality products.

Software systems for public organizations are built by making use of public funds. An assessment of software systems is made potentially by all taxpayers and has some indirect influence on social relationships and feelings of citizens. One may expect that investments in software systems will be better supervised by social representatives in the future than it takes place nowadays.

References

1   Agile Modeling Home Page (2005), http://www.agilemodeling.com/
2   Ambler SW (2003–2005) Phases Examined: Why Requirements, Analysis, and Design No Longer Make Sense.
    http://www.agilemodeling.com/essays/phasesExamined.htm
3   Arbaoui S, Lonchamp J, Montangero C (1999) The Human Dimension of the Software Process. In: Derniane J-C, Kaba BA, Wastell DG (eds) Software Process: Principles, Methodology, Technology. Springer, London, pp 165–200
4   Barbacci MR, Ellison R, Lattanze AJ, Stafford JA, Weinstock CB, Wood WG (August 2003) Quality Attribute Workshops (QAWs), 3rd edn. CMU/SEI-2003-TR-016, Software Engineering Institute, Pittsburgh (USA)
5   Beck K (2000) Extreme Programming Explained. Addison-Wesley, Boston (USA)
6   Beck K, Fowler M, Highsmith J, Martin RC, et al. (2001) Principles behind the Agile Manifesto. Agile Alliance, http://agilemanifesto.org/principles.html
7   Begier B (2003a) Software quality assessment by the software users. In: Problems and methods of software engineering. WNT, Warszawa - Wroclaw, pp 417–431

8   Begier B, Wdowicki J (2003b) Quality assessment of software applied in civil engineering by the users, 4th National Conference on Methods and Computer Systems in Research and Engineering MSK'03. Kraków, pp 47–552

9   Begier B (2004) Customer relationship management in software company. In: Software engineering. New challenge. WNT, Warszawa, pp 213–226

10   Begier B (2005) The UID Approach – the Balance between Hard and Soft Methodologies. In: Software Engineering: Evolution and Emerging Technologies. IOS Press, Amsterdam, pp 15–26

11   Begier B (2006) Making Users the Subject of a Software Process to Build High Quality Software for Public Organizations. In: 9th Int. Conf. on Business Inf. Systems. Lecture Notes in Informatik, Klagenfurt, pp 515–527

12   Boehm B, Turner R (2004) Balancing Agility and Discipline. Addison-Wesley, Pearson Education, Inc., Boston

13   Checkland P (1999) Soft Systems Methodology in Action. John Wiley & Sons, Chichester (UK)

14   Cloyd M H (2000) Creating a user-driven development process: in web time. 6th Conference on Human Factors & the Web. Austin, Texas

15   Curtis B, Hefley WE, Miller SA (2001) People Capability Maturity Model® (P-CMM®) Version 2.0. Software Engineering Institute, Pittsburgh (USA), http://www.sei.cmm.edu/cmm-p/

16   DeMarco T, Lister T (1987) Peopleware: Productive Projects and Teams. Dorset House, New York

17   Drozdowski K, Jarzemski J, Krawczyk H, Melzer M, Smółka M, Wiszniewski B (2004) A virtual environment supporting complex information projects. In: Software engineering. New challenges. WNT, Warszawa, pp 169–182

18   Friedman B (1997) Human Values and the Design of Computer Technology. Cambridge University Press

19   INUSE 6.2 (2002) Handbook of User-Centred Design. Nectar Project, http://www.ejeisa.com/nectar/inuse/6.2/content.htm

20   International Standard EN ISO 9001:2000 Quality management systems – Requirements. International Organization for Standardization, Genève

21   Katz-Haas R (July 1998) Ten Guidelines for User-Centered Design. Usability Interface 5, No.1, also: www.stcsig.org/usability/newsletter/9807-webguide.html, Society for Technical Communication (STC), 1998–2004

22   Kumar N, De Beer J, Van Thienen J, Moens MF (2005) Evaluation of Intelligent Exploitation Tools for Non-structured Police Information. In: Proceedings of the ICAIL 2005 Workshop on Data Mining, Information Extraction and Evidentiary Reasoning for Law Enforcement and Counter-terrorism, pp 1–7

23   Maslow A (1954) Motivation and Personality. Harper and Row, New York

24   MDA (Model-Driven Architecture). OMG Home Page: http://www.omg.org/mda/index.htm

25   Mumford E (1983) Designing Human System for New Technology – The ETHICS Method. On-line book available at: http://www.enid.u-net.com/C1book1.htm

26   Paulk MC, Weber CV, Chrissis MB (1995) The Capability Maturity Model: Guidelines for Improving the Software Process. Addison-Wesley, Reading, Massachusetts

27   Turner R, Boehm B (2003) People Factors in Software Management: Lessons from Comparing Agile and Plan-Driven Methods. Cross Talk. The Journal of Defence Software Development, December 2003, pp 4–8

28   UCD IBM (1999) User-Centered Design Process. IBM, http://www-306.ibm.com/ibm/easy/eou_ext.nsf/publish/

29   UML 2.0 (Unified Modeling Language). The Current Official Version, OMG UML^{TM} Resource Page, http://www.uml.org/#UML2.0

30   Winograd T (1996) Bringing Design to Software. Profile 14. Participatory Design, ACM Press by Addison-Wesley, New York

31   Wood R, Payne T (1998) Competency-based Recruitment and Selection. John Wiley & Sons, Chichester (UK)

32 Wrapping Semistructured Data to an Object-Oriented Model for a Data Grid*

Kamil Kuliberda[1,2], Jacek Wislicki[1,2], Radoslaw Adamus[1,2], Kazimierz Subieta[1,2]

[1] Computer Engineering Department, Technical University of Lodz, Lodz, Poland
[2] Polish-Japanese Institute of IT, Warsaw, Poland

The chapter is focused on integration of semistructured data (XML documents) in an object-oriented data grid. The presented ideas and results are a continuation of previous authors' research on relational to object-oriented model transformations with emphasis on utilization of powerful native SQL optimizers during optimization of a query expressed in the object query language (SBQL). Here, authors describe a generic procedure for semistructured data where Lore system and Lorel, its query language, are used for storing and retrieving data. The proposed architecture fully supports grid transparency and also enables actions of Lorel query optimization mechanisms. The chapter contains a description of the wrapper architecture, a query evaluation and optimization procedure and a descriptive example of these.

32.1 Introduction and Motivation

The grid technology is currently widely spread among various business data processing and service providing systems. In case of data grids (working as a single database) the main challenge is an integration of heterogeneous resources having their own storage technologies, data models and query languages. This feature can be achieved with a dedicated middleware software referred to as *wrappers*. Wrappers enable a virtual integration of distributed, heterogeneous and redundant resources and their presentation as a centralized, homogeneous and non-redundant whole. Our data grid research aims to integrate various databases, in particular relational, object-oriented, and XML data stores. The relational-to-object

* This work was supported in part by European Commission under 6. FP project eGov-Bus, IST-4-026727-ST

W. Abramowicz and H.C. Mayr (eds.), Technologies for Business Information Systems, 379–391.

wrapper is discussed in [12]. In this paper we deal with a wrapper mapping XML semistructured data into an object-oriented model available to grid users.

Semistructured data are featured by a loose model where data may have an unfixed schema and may be irregular or incomplete – these undesired features arise frequently on the Web or in applications that integrate heterogeneous resources. Thei mportant cases of semistructured data are XML or RDF files that are stored under systems such Tamino, Berkeley DB or Lore in the a so-called *parsed form*. Semistructured data can be neither stored nor queried in relational or object-oriented database management systems easily and efficiently [17]. In general, it is rather difficult to process semistructured data within a traditional strongly-typed data model requiring a predefined schema. Therefore many applications involving semistructured data do not use DBMSs, rejecting their strengths (ad-hoc queries, efficient access, concurrency control, crash recovery, security, etc.). There is however some tendency to store XML data in relational databases and access them through additional software layers or special query languages [11]. Examples of such systems are: STORED [5], Edge [6], XPERANTO [3] and Agora [14]. In some cases these systems use a sophisticated query evaluation and optimization mechanisms and our intention is to design wrappers that allow one to employ them. This frees us from any necessity to materialize the data at the side of our grid applications.

The problems of such wrappers can be subdivided into conceptual and performance issues. Conceptual problems focus on a development of a universal mechanism capable of mapping foreign data, usually with different data models, into a global view. This is especially difficult when the mapping must concern not only retrieval, but also updating. After solving the conceptual problems there are still performance problems. Both problems are much easier if one assumes some materialization (i.e. replication) of foreign data within a grid application , which is proposed e.g. in [2, 4]. During the materialization one can also provide transformin data to a desired schema and a format required by a grid application. However, a data materialization is usually impossible due to a data transmission overhead, problems with keeping consistency of materialized copies and security policies.

Therefore, we avoid materialization in favour of direct accessing a data source and exploiting a native data model and its programming interfaces such as query languages. For performance it is critical to utilize native query optimization mechanisms. Hence, during a development of a wrapper we strive to map our grid-oriented requests into optimizable queries that are to be efficiently precessed and evaluated by a local resource server.

In the proposed approach, we assume an object-oriented canonical data model similar to the CORBA, ODMG [3] or UML data models. The model is supported by SBQL, a query language of the Stack-Based Approach (SBA) [21]. SBQL has the algorithmic power of programming languages thus is powerful enough to express any required properties of a common canonical data model as well as business intentions of grid users. The clean semantics of SBQL allows to develop optimization methods comparable or more powerful in comparison to the methods applied in SQL.

Within SBA we have developed a novel mechanism of virtual updatable object-oriented views [8]. It allows achieving many forms of transparency required by grid applications. A global virtual store delivers virtual objects (defined by means of updatable views) indistinguishable for the grid users from stored objects. Our views allow full updateability of virtual objects; for details see [8, 21].

The basic assumption of the presented approach is that the local data can be described with any common data model (e.g. relational, XML, data-sheet). The paper deals with an architecture of a generic wrapper for a semistructured data model based on XML and extended through a modified data model OEM, *Object Exchange Model* [19] implemented in the database management system – Lore (*Lightweight Object Repository*) [15]. We exploit Lorel [1], the Lore's query language, supporting optimization methods for queries addressing XML and OEM [16, 17, 18]. Although queries can be optimized at the SBQL side, some optimization features, such as indices and fast joins [17, 18], can be exploited only at the Lore side. The wrapper must translate SBQL queries into Lorel queries in such a way that its optimization features are fully utilized.

Currently, we are implementing (under .NET and Java) an object-oriented platform named ODRA for Web and grid applications, thus the problem of integrating different foreign resources through wrappers is critical. With our previous experience[1] we have made the following assumptions:

1. The system will be based on our own, already implemented, object-oriented query language SBQL, which has many advantages over OQL, XQuery, SQL-99 and other languages.
2. The system will be equipped with a powerful mechanism of object-oriented virtual updatable views based on SBQL. Our views are much more powerful than e.g. SQL views, because they are defined through constructs having the computational power of programming languages. There are three basic applications of the views: (1) as integrators (mediators) making up a global virtual data and service store on top of distributed, heterogeneous and redundant resources; (2) as wrappers on top of particular local resources; (3) as customization and security facility on top of the global virtual store. A prototype implementation of SBQL views is ready [8].
3. Currently we are involved in the the European project eGov-Bus (Advanced e-Government Information Service Bus), IST-4-026727-ST, devoted to a dynamically adaptable information system supporting life events experienced by the citizen or business serviced by European government organizations. The eGov-Bus prototype must integrate distributed and heterogeneous resources that are under the control of various institutions. The project assumes an advanced object-oriented model comparable to UML and ODMG

---

[1] DBPL system to Ingres and Oracle, described in [15], and the European project ICONS, IST-2001-32429, devoted to advanced Web applications

models, thus requires more sophisticated wrappers to local data and service resources, in particular, based on relational databases and XML.

The rest of the chapter is structured as follows. Section 2 introduces the problem of processing semistructured data in a data grid. Section 3 describes the authors' idea of the grid architecture. Section 4 focuses on the architecture of a generic wrapper for semistructured data and explains the method of utilization of the Lorel optimization in the presented solution. Section 5 concludes.

32.2 Discussion on Semistructured Data Processing in a Data Grid Architecture

Integration of dozens or hundreds of servers participating in a grid requires different design processes in comparison to the situation where one object-oriented application is to be connected to a database with a semistructured data model. The common (canonical) grid database schema is a result of many negotiations and tradeoffs between business partners having incompatible (heterogeneous) data and services. This makes development of an object-semistructured wrapper much more constrained than in a non-grid case. On one hand, the wrapper should deliver the data and services according to the predefined object-oriented canonical schema. On the other hand, its back-end should work on a given semistructured data store.

The major problem with this architecture concerns how to utilize native query optimizers. As we know, the access to simple XML data is hard to optimize even through native XML query languages such as XQuery. The Lore system is designed specifically for the management of such semistructured data. The data managed by Lore may not be constrained by a schema, it may be irregular or incomplete. In general, Lore attempts to take advantage of a structure wherever it exists, but it also handles irregular data as gracefully as possible. Lore is equipped with its own data model and a query language with an optimizer designed especially for semistructured data, including a cost-based optimizer [15]. The most important for us is that Lore is fully functional and available to the public. The Lore's data model called OEM (*Object Exchange Model*) [19] is a very simple self-describing graph-based nested object model.

In all known DBMSs, the optimizer and its particular structures (e.g. indices) are transparent to the query language users. A naive implementation of a wrapper causes that it generates primitive queries in given query language such as *select * from R*, and then processes the results of such queries by DBMS QL cursors. Hence, the query optimizer has no chance to work. Our experience has shown that direct translation of object-oriented queries into Lorel is infeasible for a sufficiently general case. We propose to transform some parts of object-oriented queries in SBQL into accurate optimizable query at the Lorel side.

During querying over a wrapper, the mapping between a semistructured database and a target global object-oriented database should not involve materialization of objects on the global side, i.e. objects delivered by such a wrapper must be virtual.

The described architecture assumes that a semistructured database will be seen as a simple object-oriented database, where each labelled object between edges from OEM's labelled directed graph (available from Lore) is mapped virtually to a primitive object. Then, on such a database we define object-oriented views that convert such primitive virtual objects into complex, hierarchical virtual objects conforming to the global canonical schema, perhaps with complex repeated attributes and virtual links among the objects. Because SBQL views are algorithmically complete, we are sure that every such a mapping can be expressed.

32.3 Architecture of a Data Grid

In this section we briefly sketch the most important elements of the proposed grid architecture and situate them inside the wrapper module. The proposed grid architecture is clearly shown in Fig. 1. Our solution provides an access simplification to the distributed, heterogeneous and redundant data, constituting an interface to the distributed data residing in any local resource provider participating in a grid. The goals of the approach are to design a platform where all clients and providers are able to access multiple distributed resources without any complications concerning data maintenance and to build a global schema for the accessible data and services. The main difficulty of the described concept is that neither data nor services can be copied, replicated and maintained on the

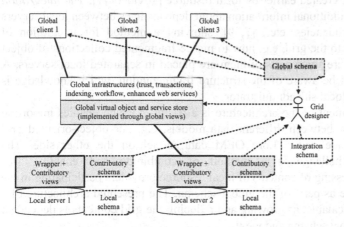

Fig. 1. The data grid architecture

global applications side (in the global schema), as they are supplied, stored, processed and maintained on their autonomous sites [9, 10].

Following Fig. 1, the elements filled in grey realize the main aspects of contribution and integration processes of the data mapping from the wrappers [9]. The central part of a grid is a *global virtual store* containing virtual objects and services. Its role is to store addresses of local servers and to process queries sent from *global client* applications, as well as to enable accessing the grid according to the trust infrastructure (including security, privacy, licensing and non-repudiation issues). It also presents business objects and services according to the *global schema*. A global schema has to be defined and agreed upon the organization that creates a grid. This is a principal mechanism enveloping all the local resources into one global data structure. Physically, it is a composition of the contribution schemata which can participate in the grid. The *global schema* is responsible for managing grid contents through access permissions, discovering resources, controlling location of resources, indexing whole grid attributes. The global schema is also used by programmers to create global client applications.

Administrators of *local servers* must define *contributory schemata* and corresponding *contributory views* [7, 9] for integrating services and objects physically available from local servers and mapping local data to the global schema. A contribution schema is created by the *grid designer* and represents the main data formalization rules for any local resource. Basing on this, local resource providers create their own contribution schemata adapted to a unique data structure present at their local sites. A *contribution view* is the query language definition of mapping the local schema to contribution schema. A well defined contribution view can become a part of the *global view*. The mapping process consists of enclosing particular contribution schemas residing in local sites into the global schema, created earlier by local resource providers [7]. The *integration schemata* contain additional information about dependencies between local servers (replications, redundancies, etc.) [7, 9], showing a method for integration of fragmented data into the grid, e.g. how to merge fragmented collections of object data structures where some parts of them are placed in separated local servers. A grid designer must be aware of the structure fragmentation, which knowledge is unnecessary for a local site administrator.

The crucial element of the architecture is a *wrapper* which enables importing and exporting data between different data models, e.g. our object-oriented grid solution at one side and a Lore OEM data model on the other side. The implementation challenge is a method of combining and enabling free bidirectional processing of contents of local resource providers participating in the global virtual store as parts of the global schema. The presented architecture of a data grid is fully scalable, as growing and reducing the grid contents is dependent on the state of global schema and views.

32.4 Wrapper

This section presents the architecture of the generic wrapper to the semistructured data stored in XML documents and querying via Lorel. Fig. 2 presents the architecture of the wrapper. Externally the data are designed according to the object-oriented model and the business intention of the *contributory schema*. This part constitutes the *front-end* of the wrapper and relies on SBQL. Internally the structures are presented in the SBA M0 model [21]. This part constitutes the *back-end* of the wrapper and is also relies on SBQL.

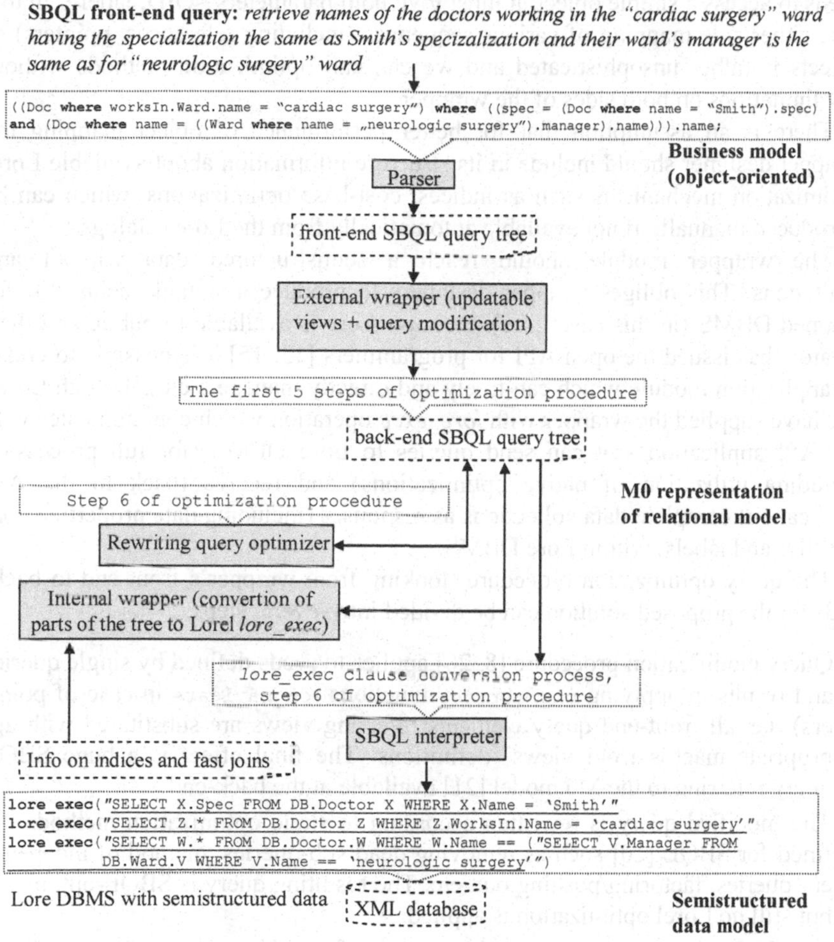

SBQL front-end query: *retrieve names of the doctors working in the "cardiac surgery" ward having the specialization the same as Smith's specialization and their ward's manager is the same as for "neurologic surgery" ward*

```
((Doc where worksIn.Ward.name = "cardiac surgery") where ((spec = (Doc where name = 'Smith").spec)
and (Doc where name = (Ward where name = „neurologic surgery").manager).name))).name;
```

Business model
(object-oriented)

Parser

front-end SBQL query tree

External wrapper (updatable
views + query modification)

The first 5 steps of optimization procedure

back-end SBQL query tree

Step 6 of optimization procedure

M0 representation
of relational model

Rewriting query optimizer

Internal wrapper (convertion of
parts of the tree to Lorel *lore_exec*)

lore_exec clause conversion process,
step 6 of optimization procedure

SBQL interpreter

Info on indices and fast joins

```
lore_exec("SELECT X.Spec FROM DB.Doctor X WHERE X.Name = 'Smith'"
lore_exec("SELECT Z.* FROM DB.Doctor Z WHERE Z.WorksIn.Name = 'cardiac surgery'"
lore_exec("SELECT W.* FROM DB.Doctor.W WHERE W.Name == ("SELECT V.Manager FROM
       DB.Ward.V WHERE V.Name == 'neurologic surgery'")
```

Lore DBMS with semistructured data   XML database

Semistructured
data model

Fig. 2. The architecture of a generic wrapper for semistructured database

The mapping between front-end and back-end is defined through updatable object views. They role is to map back-end into front-end for querying virtual objects and front-end onto back-end for updating them. The following optimization methods hold for the most often select-type queries, possibly there might be need to adjust them in case of updating or deleting queries, especially at the query modification stage. The object accessing on both sides of wrapper (front-end and back-end) is similar. At the front-end there is an object data model supported by SBQL. Each object in a database can be distinguished by a unique object identifier (*OID*). At the back-end of the wrapper there is a semistructured data model supported by Lorel. The database objects can be identified by a pair: an object identifier (OID) and a label – the name of object collection. When Lorel needs to access a simple object, it must give both parameters <OID, label>. In this case either-side mapping of various sequences (including references, pointers) of objects is rather unsophisticated and we can call optimization methods without any limitations on both sides of the wrapper.

There is an assumption that for better performance of object mapping the wrapper designer should include in its structure information about available Lorel optimization mechanisms such as indices, cost-base optimizations, which can be introduced manually if not available automatically from the Lore catalogs.

The wrapper module should reach a semistructured data without any limitations. This obliges wrapper designers to produce a suitable connector for mapped DBMS (in this case Lore). Because Lore is available to public and their creators has issued the open API for programmers [13, 15] it is possible to create an application module which can freely and directly manage a data through Lorel. We have supplied the wrapper with *lore_exec* operation which communicates with the API application – it can send queries to Lore DBMS (for full processing including utilization of native optimizations) and receive (back to the API application) complete data collections as responses (including data properties such as OIDs and labels) within Lore DBMS.

The query optimization procedure (looking from wrapper's front-end to back-end) for the proposed solution can be divided into several steps:

- Query modification procedure [8, 20] applies to seeds defined by single queries and results in applying `on_retrieve` functions (`on_navigate` in case of pointers), i.e. all front-end query elements referring views are substituted with appropriate macros from views' definitions. The final effect is a huge SBQL query referring to the M0 model [21] available at the back-end.

- The modified query is rewritten according to static optimization methods defined for SBQL [20] such as removing dead sub-queries, method of independent queries, factoring/pushing out, etc. The resulting query is SBQL-optimized, but still no Lorel optimization is applied.

- The SBQL-optimized query can be now transformed to a form that native Lorel optimization is applicable. According to the available information about Lorel optimizer, the back-end wrapper's mechanisms analyze the SBQL query in order to recognize patterns representing Lorel-optimizable queries. For instance, if for the SBQL query of the form Y **where** X == v there is a Lorel index on Y objects and their X subobjects, it is substituted (in the syntax tree) with *lore_exec* clause invoking the appropriate Lorel query:

lore_exec(``**SELECT** z.* **FROM** DB.Y z **WHERE** z.X = v'')

Any Lorel query invoked from *lore_exec* clause is assumed to be optimized efficiently and evaluated in the native Lore DBMS environment. Its result is pushed onto the SBQL query result stack in a form of Lorel tuples stored as complex binders and used for regular SBQL query evaluation and also for update and delete-type queries.

32.4.1 Optimization Example

As an optimization example consider a simple structure of labelled directed graph objects stored in the Lore. The model contains information about doctors DB.Doctor and hospital's wards DB.Ward, "DB" stands for the stub of semistructured data model depicted through labelled directed graph, see Fig. 3.

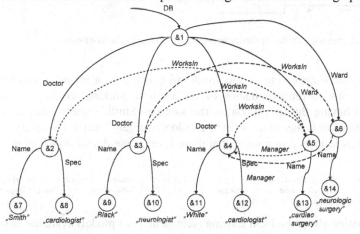

Fig. 3. The example of a semistructured data model in labelled directed graph

The semistructured schema is wrapped into an object schema shown in Fig. 4 according to the following view definitions. The DB.Doctor-DB.Ward relationship is realized with worksIn and manager virtual pointers:

```
create view DocDef {
    virtual_objects Doc {return DB.Doctor as d;}
    create view nameDef {
        virtual_objects name{return d.Name as n;}
        on_retrieve {return n;}
    }
    create view specDef {
        virtual_objects spec {return d.Spec as s;}
        on_retrieve {return s;}
```

```
      }
      create view worksInDef {
          virtual_pointers worksIn {return d.WorksIn as wi;}
          on_navigate {return wi as Ward;}
      }
  }
  create view WardDef {
      virtual_objects Ward {return DB.Ward as w;}
      create view nameDef {
          virtual_objects name {return w.Name as n;}
          on_retrieve {return n;}
      }
      create view managerDef {
          virtual_pointers manager {return w.Manager as b;}
          on_navigate {return b as Doc;}
      }
  }
```

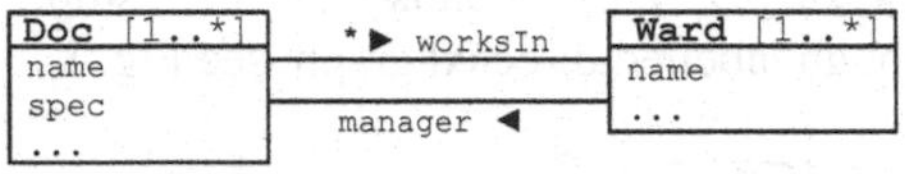

Fig. 4. Object schema used in the optimization example (wrapper's front-end)

Consider a query appearing at the front-end (visible as a business database schema) that aims to retrieve names of the doctors working in the "cardiac surgery" ward having the specialization the same as Smith's specialization and their ward's manager is the same as for "neurologic surgery" ward. The query can be formulated as follows (we assume that there is only one doctor with that name in the store):

```
((Doc where worksIn.Ward.name = "cardiac surgery") where ((spec = (Doc where
name = "Smith").spec) and (Doc where name = ((Ward where name = „neurologic
surgery").manager).name))).name;
```

The information about the local schema (semistructured model) available to the wrapper that can be used during the query optimization is that Name objects are uniquely indexed by specific Lore indexes. The transformation and optimization procedure is performed in the following steps:

1. First we introduce implicit deref (dereference) function:
```
( (Doc where worksIn.Ward.deref(name) == "cardiac surgery") where
((deref(spec) == (Doc where deref(name) == "Smith").deref(spec)) and (Doc
where deref(name) == ((Ward where deref(name) == „neurologic
surgery").manager).deref(name)))).deref(name);
```

2. Next wrapper substitutes deref with the invocation of on_retrieve function for virtual objects and on_navigate for virtual pointers:
```
((Doc where worksIn.(wi as Ward).Ward.(name.n) == "cardiac surgery") where
(((spec.s) == (Doc where (name.n) == "Smith").(spec.s)) and (Doc where
(name.n) == ((Ward where (name.n) == „neurologic surgery").manager.(b as
Doc)).(name.n)))).(name.n);
```

3. Wrapper substitute all view invocations with the queries from *sack* definitions:

```
((((DB.Doctor as d) where (d.WorksIn as wi).(wi as Ward).Ward.((w.Name as
n).n) == "cardiac surgery") where ((((d.Spec as s).s) == ((DB.Doctor as d)
where ((d.Name as n).n) == "Smith").((d.Spec as s).s) and ((DB.Doctor as d)
where ((d.Name as n).n) == (((DB.Ward as w) where ((w.Name as n).n) ==
„neurologic surgery").(w.Manager as b).(b as (DB.Doctor as d))).((d.Name as
n).n)))).((d.Name as n).n);
```

4. We remove auxiliary names s and n together with names d and w:

```
((DB.Doctor where (WorksIn as wi).(wi as Ward).Ward.Name == "cardiac
surgery") where ((Spec == (DB.Doctor where Name == "Smith").Spec and
(DB.Doctor where Name == ((DB.Ward where Name == „neurologic
surgery").(Manager as b).(b as DB.Doctor)).Name))).Name;
```

5. Next remove auxiliary names wi, Ward and b:

```
((DB.Doctor where WorksIn.Name == "cardiac surgery") where ((Spec ==
(DB.Doctor where Name == "Smith").Spec and (DB.Doctor where Name ==
((DB.Ward where Name ==„neurologic surgery").Manager).Name))).Name;
```

6. Now take common part before loop to prevent multiple evaluation of a query calculating salary value for the doctor named *Smith*:

```
(((((DB.Doctor where Name == "Smith").Spec) group as z).(((DB.Ward where
Name == „neurologic surgery").Manager) group as y).(DB.Doctor where
WorksIn.Name == "cardiac surgery") where (Spec == z and DB.Doctor.where
Name == y.Name)).Name;
```

7. Because Name objects are uniquely indexed (in path DB.Doctor), the subquery (DB.Doctor where Name == "Smith") can be substituted with *lore_exec* clause. The suchlike indexes are in path DB.Ward (see at Fig. 3) we can call more *lore_exec* clauses:

```
((((lore_exec("SELECT X.Spec FROM DB.Doctor X WHERE X.Name = 'Smith'"))
group as z).(lore_exec("SELECT Z.* FROM DB.Doctor Z WHERE Z.WorksIn.Name =
'cardiac surgery'") where (Spec == z and (lore_exec("SELECT W.* FROM
DB.Doctor.W WHERE W.Name == ("SELECT V.Manager FROM DB.Ward.V WHERE V.Name
== 'neurologic surgery'")))).Name;
```

Either of the Lorel queries invoked by *lore_exec* clause is executed in the local data resource.

32.5 Conclusions

We have shown that the presented approach to wrapping databases based on semistructured data to object-oriented business model with application of the stack-based approach and updatable views is conceptually feasible, clear and implementable. As shown in the example, a front-end SBQL query can be modified and optimized by application of appropriate SBA rules and methods within the wrapper (updatable views) and then by the native optimizers for an appropriate resource query language (i.e. Lorel). The described wrapper architecture enables building generic solutions allowing virtual representation of data stored in various resources as objects in an object-oriented model.

The semistructured to object-oriented data model wrapper together with our solution designed for relational databases [12] allow building back-ends of data grids purposed for various data sources and presenting them as a pure object-oriented business model available to grid users. The resulting database can be queried with the object query language, SBQL. Within the grid architecture a query is transformed so that at the lower (resource) grid level appropriate patterns can be found and optimizable query effectively executed in their native environment.

References

1.   Abiteboul S, Quass D,.McHugh J,.Widom J, and Wiener J (1997) The Lorel Query Language for Semistructured Data. Intl. Journal on Digital Libraries, 1(1):68-88
2.   Baru CK, Gupta A, Laudascher B, Marciano R, Papaconstantinou Y, Velikhov P, Chu V (1999) XML-based information mediation with MIX, Proc. ACM SIGMOD Conf. on Management of Data
3.   Carey M, Kiernan J, Shanmugasundaram J, Shekita E, Subramanian S (2000) XPERANTO: A Middleware for Publishing Object-Relational Data as XML Documents, Proc. of the 26th VLDB Conf.
4.   Christophides V, Cluet S and Simeon J (2000) On wrapping query languages and efficient XML integration, In Proc. of ACM SIGMOD Conf. on Management of Data
5.   Deutsch A, Fernandez M, Suciu D (1999) Storing semistructured data with STORED, Proc. of SIGMOD
6.   Florescu D, Kossman D (1999) Storing and Querying XML Data using an RDBMS. Data Engineering Bulletin, 22(3)
7.   Kaczmarski K, Habela P, Subieta K (2004) Metadata in a Data Grid Construction. 13th IEEE International Workshops on Enabling Technologies: Infrastructures for Collaborative Enterprises (WETICE-2004)
8.   Kozankiewicz H, Leszczyłowski J, Płodzień J, Subieta K (2002) Updateable Object Views. ICS PAS Reports 950
9.   Kozankiewicz H, Stencel K, Subieta K (2004) Integration of Heterogeneous Resources through Updatable Views. 13th IEEE International Workshops on Enabling Technologies: Infrastructures for Collaborative Enterprises
10. Kozankiewicz H, Stencel K, Subieta K (2005) Implementation of Federated Databases through Updateable Views. European Grid Conference
11. Krishnamurthy R, Kaushik R, Naughton JF (2003) XML-to-SQL Query Translation Literature: The State of the Art and Open Problems. Proc. of the 1st Int'l XML Database Symposium (XSym), pp.1-18
12. Kuliberda K, Wislicki J, Adamus R, Subieta K (2005) Object-Oriented Wrapper for Relational Databases in the Data Grid Architecture. OTM Workshops 2005, LNCS 3762, pp. 367-376
13. Lore DBMS Web Page: http://www-db.stanford.edu/lore/
14. Manolescu I, Florescu D, Kossmann D, Xhumari F, Olteanu D (2000) Agora: Living with XML and Relational, Proc. of the 26th VLDB Conf.
15. Matthes F, Rudloff A, Schmidt JW, Subieta K (1994) A Gateway from DBPL to Ingres. Proc. of Intl. Conf. on Applications of Databases, Vadstena, Sweden, Springer LNCS 819, pp.365-380
16. McHugh J, Abiteboul S, Goldman R, Quass D, and Widom J (1997) Lore: A DBMS for Semistructured Data. SIGMOD Record, 26(3):54-66
17. McHugh J, Widom J, Abiteboul S, Luo Q, and Rajaraman A (1998) Indexing Semistructured Data. Technical Report

18. McHugh J, Widom J (1999) Query Optimization for XML. Proc. of 25th Intl. VLDB Conf., Edinburgh, Scotland
19. Papakonstantinou Y, Garcia-Molina H, and Widom J (1995) Object exchange across heterogeneous information sources. Proc. of the 11th International Conference on Data Engineering, pp.251-260
20. Plodzien J (2000) Optimization Methods In Object Query Languages, PhD Thesis. IPIPAN, Warsaw
21. Subieta K (2004) Theory and Construction of Object-Oriented Query Languages. Editors of the Polish-Japanese Institute of Information Technology, (in Polish)

33 Script-based System for Monitoring Client-side Activity

Artur Kulpa, Jakub Swacha, Roman Budzowski

Uniwersytet Szczeciński
Instytut Informatyki w Zarządzaniu
{arturro.q@gmail.com, jakubs@uoo.univ.szczecin.pl, romek@innotech.pl}

33.1 Introduction

Gathering information on customer activity is a well established practice in e-commerce. So-called clickstreams consisting of a list of active elements clicked by website user during his session can be gathered and analyzed server-side, unfolding a pattern in user's preferences [Andersen 2000].

Another notion comes from the field of application usage study [Hilbert 2000]. In this case, any kind of trackable user-triggered event may be recorded, and then processed in order to discover high-level actions, so that application user interface may be rearranged by removing unused capabilities and making frequent actions easier to be performed.

This is also useful in e-commerce, as it is obvious that a well-designed website can generate much more profit than a badly designed one. But the detailed record of user actions also constitutes an important source of information for operational customer relationship management. It provides the sales force automation with a very precise description of customer behavior, and the customer service and support with thorough description of circumstances which led to posting an inquiry or a complaint.

However, it requires a client-side monitoring as most of the low-level activity does not have any impact on the server. In today's world of malicious spyware, web users are reluctant to install any monitoring software.

Thereinafter, we shall present a monitoring system which enables tracking many user actions that may be found useful in the study of improvement of an e-commerce website. The system does not require any additional software to be installed on the client, as all the tracking code is included in the website itself in the

393

W. Abramowicz and H.C. Mayr (eds.), Technologies for Business Information Systems, 393–402.

form of client-side scripts. Thus, a user has full knowledge on what is monitored – as the script source code is unhidden – and can easily turn off the monitoring just by changing web browser script-running options (though there is a subtler way of doing that embedded in the system).

33.2 User Activities worth Investigating

A client-side monitoring system can track a lot more than a server-side one. Not every user action can be traced even in the client system: eye movements and uttering curses being good examples of untraceable events. However, there is still a colossal amount of data which can be collected. For the sake of its simplicity and resource saving, a monitoring system should limit its surveillance to actions which record may be then found useful in practical purposes.

Such purposes are related either to system usability study or to customer research. Hereunder, some of the most popular purposes are listed:

- feature usage reports: once known, the most frequently used features should be made simpler to use, the unused features should be promoted (in case the users do not know they exist), explained (if users do not know why or how to use them), or removed (in case nobody really needs them); the simple element clicking and keystroke recording is enough to satisfy this purpose
- feature usage pattern discovery: if some features are often used together, they should be available in proximity, if some features are almost always used together, they should be composed into one new feature; in addition to standard click and keystroke events, actions like marking and clipboard operations should also be tracked for this purpose
- usage error reports: these can be helpful in improving user interface by rearranging the size and placement of visible elements, and renaming the feature captions along with adding or improving the help/hint subsystem; the basic actions of importance here are "do then undo" event patterns and also clicking on inactive web page elements
- user history reports: knowing what an individual did in the past may be helpful in personalizing the system for him/her, evaluating the customer's profitability, and – after discovering behavior patterns – grouping the users by some criteria; some sort of identification is obviously necessary here – whether user-oriented (long-term cookies and login data) or session-oriented (temporary cookies)
- browsing reports: these can show which information actually interests the user and which does not; although not a perfect measure, the time of stay on a page could give some clues on that.

33.3 Monitoring Systems Nowadays

Tracking user actions for further analysis is almost necessary in order to develop and deploy quality applications, standalone programs and web applications alike. In case of web applications it may have form of client-side or server-side monitoring.

The client-side monitoring of user actions requires either integration of monitored application with monitoring system or installation of additional program capable of recording user actions.

A good example of a client-side monitoring tool is WinTask application from TaskWare [Taskware 2005]. This application is capable of recording mouse movement and keystrokes. Every recorded sequence can be replayed later or used to produce a report. WinTask can also automatically test applications, measuring their performance in form of application response times, critical points and generated network traffic.

Fenstermacher and Ginsburg [Fenstermacher 2002] took a different approach, trying to monitor creating and accessing individual information, not individual application, so that cross-application information flows could be exposed.

Monitoring of web applications is mostly done server-side. An outgoing browser requests leave tracks in server logs. These logs can be then analyzed using data-mining applications such as OpenSource Webalizer [Webalizer 2005] which is a fast and free web server log file analysis program producing highly detailed website usage reports.

Client-side scripts can be integrated with monitored website to send information about user and viewed page to a third party server, where it is stored in a database. Existing client-side scripts are limited to tracking information which could just as well be tracked using a server-side monitoring. They come practical when a website owner does not have access to server log files or simply wants to present reliable data to others. Such script-based traffic monitoring services are offered, for instance, by gemius.pl [Gemius 2006], stat.pl [Stat.pl 2006], ShinyStat [ShinyStat 2006], OpenTracker [OpenTracker 2006] and many other providers.

Fenstermacher and Ginsburg [Fenstermacher 2003] suggested client-side monitoring framework for web browser activity. Although they described their solution as unobtrusive to users, it is based on a Python program monitoring Microsoft Internet Explorer using Component Object Model (COM) technology, and therefore it requires installing additional software. Moreover, this makes it possible only to monitor actions of clients using Windows operating system and Internet Explorer browser.

Although existing client-side scripts are limited to traffic monitoring, web browser scripting environments nowadays are complex enough to monitor practically every user action reported by web browser.

33.4 Sketch of the Script-based System

The idea at the core of the script-based monitoring system is to let a web vendor collect a detailed record of a user activity without necessity to install any software on the client system.

Another desired feature is to let the monitoring system work with existing web pages without having to alter them in a complicated way.

The system is a client-server solution, with a client being a web browser capable of running scripts.

The main problem to deal with is obtaining necessary detailed information on occurring events. This can be achieved using the Document Object Model (DOM) [Robie 2004] implemented in most web browsers, although with minor differences to the official standard.

In a DOM-compliant browser, every trackable user action leads to setting up an Event class object whose properties contain information describing the action, like the document element being the object of the action [Pfaffenberger 2004].

Every kind of DOM object available in browser is accessible using JavaScript programming environment [Goodman 2004]. This language can also be used to transmit the gathered event information to the server-side monitoring application. The server application's role is to receive the information from the client, pre-process it and then store it in a database system for further usage.

As for the server-side technology, there are many candidates like PHP, JSP, ASP or any programming language used via Common Gateway Interface (CGI). PHP5 [Coggeshall 2004] has been chosen for the experimental system implementation, as a solution which is effective, free, and popular among host providers.

The website requires a WWW server to be published. The monitoring system requires the server to be able to run server-side scripts. The experimental system implementation uses Apache server [Laurie 2002], as it has huge capabilities and perfectly cooperates with PHP5.

Data can be stored server-side in many ways. They can be saved as they come, arranged into XML documents, or passed to a database system. The latter solution makes the further processing of data much easier. Therefore, the experimental system implementation uses PostgreSQL database system [PostgreSQL 2005], because, once again, it is highly efficient, free, and easily accessible using PHP5.

33.5 Script-based Monitoring in Detail

Script-based monitoring software is based on the *Event* class objects of the Document Object Model (DOM) [Robie 2004]. As many as 25 event types (the actual number may vary between different web browsers) can be registered:

- element-related events (onclick, onchange, onfocusin, onfocusout, onselectstart, ondblclick and oncontextmenu),

- mouse events (*onmouseover, onmouseout, onmousedown, onmousewheel* and *onmouseup*),
- drag&drop events (*ondrag, ondragenter, ondrop, ondragend, ondragleave* and *ondragstart*),
- keyboard events (*onkeydown, onkeyup* and *onkeypress*),
- clipboard events (*oncopy, onpaste* and *oncut*),
- script (de-)initialization (*onload, onunload*).

The event-registering script (*eventlog.js*) is attached to the monitored HTML page via the following inclusion into the HEAD element:

```
<SCRIPT
TYPE = 'text/javascript'  SRC = '/eventlog.js'  LANGUAGE =
'JavaScript'>
</SCRIPT>
```

The *eventlog.js* file must be placed in the root directory of the WWW server. It is possible to automate the process of applying the monitoring script inclusion for the entire website with an appropriate PHP script using regular expressions.

On document loading, the browser attaches the monitoring code to the document's BODY element. It is then activated for every of the aforementioned events. Since then, every time an event is triggered after some user action, the monitoring code is executed. This is possible thanks to the 'bubbles' mechanism, by which in case of an event for any document element, its parent element is notified as well. As the BODY element is the (grand-)parent of all the rendered elements in the document, no event can evade being registered.

The proposed system does not interfere in any way with existing scripts (other tracking system or anything else), as the event handlers are not replaced – they are only wrapped with the monitoring code. Therefore, there is no need to alter the existing scripts in any way.

The information being registered by the monitoring system depends on the kind of the event. Some parts of it are common for any kind of event:

- the document's URL
- client-side date and time of the event
- kind of the event
- kind of the element which triggered the event
- NAME attribute value (provided it exists).

The remaining ones are either element type dependent:

- for INPUT elements: their type and value
- for A elements: their reference (HREF)
- for FORM elements: their action
- for other elements: first 20 characters of their content

or event type dependent:

- for clipboard events: selection and clipboard contents (partial)
- for drag&drop events: selection contents (partial)
- for keyboard events: the keystroke
- for mouse events: mouse cursor coordinates.

To provide user identification capability, a user/session registration mechanism has been built into the monitoring system. When a user enters the monitored website for the first time, two identification cookies are created. The first cookie for the purpose of session identification is temporary, valid only until the user leaves the website. The second cookie for the purpose of user identification has validity period 30 days long, thus it allows to identify users returning to the monitored website after a short period of time, but no longer than one month. The values of these cookies are attached to every of recorded event information.

In case the client browser cleans cookies after leaving the website, it will not be possible to identify the user returning to the site unless the website requires a login. In case the client browser has the cookies completely turned off, it will not be possible to continue the monitoring session when the user switches to another page on the website, limiting the session to one web page. Notice that even in this case the entire website monitoring session can usually be reconstructed later from server-side logs containing user's IP record.

The gathered information is sent to the monitoring server by setting up an asynchronous request. In case of Microsoft Internet Explorer environment 'Msxml2.XMLHTTP' ActiveX object is used for this task, whereas in Mozilla environment - 'XMLHttpRequest' object. Upon receipt of such request, the server executes a recording script written in PHP language. This script attaches the server-side date and time to the received event information and then stores it all in a PostgreSQL database system.

Communicating with the monitoring server every time an event has been triggered could noticeably slow down the browser and produce too much web traffic. In order to overcome that, the event records are merged into packets. The packet is only sent to the server when the number of stored events exceeds 20 or on the document unload event (leaving the site by the user).

All the gathered data are sent to the monitoring server using the same protocol as the remaining communication. Therefore, if the connection is secured, then the monitoring reports are sent in encrypted format. There is no possibility of sending the data from the client to anywhere outside the monitoring server domain. The gathered data are as safe as is the web server on which they are stored.

For additional security, it is possible to turn off monitoring specific kinds of events (e.g., clipboard operations) or gathering data on specific kinds of controls (e.g., input password boxes). The user can also disable the monitoring for a single web page or the entire website.

33.6 Data Encoding

A basic problem regarding the performance of the monitoring system is how to encode the gathered data so that the network connection is not slowed down considerably. All the data, both names and values, are recorded by default as text, which, given the number of monitored events and their attributes, effects in huge data packets to be transmitted to the server. This can be averted by using more efficient data encoding. We considered general purpose compression algorithm (e.g., [Swacha 2004]), but the peculiarity of monitoring system data made us convinced that devising a proprietary encoding scheme would be both more effective and much easier to implement, considering the limitations of the web browser environment.

The encoding scheme consists of several rules aimed at reducing length of the most frequent elements in the monitoring system output. The first group of rules take advantage of the names which are known to the server. Instead of being fully spelled out, they are replaced with short, mostly one letter long identifiers, readable to the server-side software as easily as plain text. The replaced names include three basic categories: data descriptors used by the monitoring system itself (e.g., 'event type', 'element type'), HTML element names (e.g., BODY, SELECT), and event names (e.g., *onmouseover*).

Another rule deals with date/time stamps attached to every event description. Every such stamp would require 12 characters to fully denote date and time. Instead, delta time encoding is used, in which the stamp is attached only to the first event in the transmitted packet; the remaining event descriptions have only short interval field containing the number of seconds that passed since the first event stored in the packet.

The remaining rules are for efficient encoding of data describing individual events. For instance, the *onmouseover* event description contains four pairs of coordinates (*EventParent, EventScreen, EventOffset, EventClient*). As the names and order of these are known, the corresponding description may be limited to 'XXpYYlXXpYYlXXpYYlXXpYY', where 'XX' and 'YY' are some numbers. Notice that characters which require special encoding when transmitted over HTTP connection (such as '=' or ';') are avoided.

33.7 Test Results

The described monitoring system was tested on two websites: www.klubinformatyka.pl and www.konferencja.org. The former is a content delivery site, therefore user activity there is rather simple and concentrated on a website navigation. The latter is the biggest Polish scientific conference catalogue and search engine, allowing user to specify search criteria, insert conferences into the catalogue and add a chosen conference to "My conferences" private repository. User activity here is much more complex with more types of actions being performed.

The monitoring scripts were installed on both websites with no special adaptation.

During one-week survey the script-based monitoring system proved its suitability in user activity tracking by managing to produce excellent detailed event reports. Although the widest range of events was reported from Internet Explorer, most important actions were also captured on FireFox (and all browsers based on Gecko engine), though lacking reporting of, for example, clipboard-related events.

The easy script configuration process with the capability of turning off or on each type of reported events separately makes it possible to focus the survey on selected features of the website.

In order to limit the impact of monitoring on the monitored system performance and generated web traffic, the packet size should be small.

After one week of monitoring, the gathered data allowed to estimate average event description packet size (see Table 1). As the results show, the packet size has been reduced by 72% on average after implementing efficient data encoding.

Table 1. Measured packet size (in bytes)

Size	Raw text	Encoded	Gain
Maximum	15385	9321	39,42%
Minimum	519	274	47,21%
Average	8122	2279	71,94%
Std. deviation	1709	473	-

The time gap between sending consecutive packets (see Table 2; very long inactivity periods are not included as they break the sessions) depends on the type of the monitored website. It gets longer for websites with more content, keeping users busy reading, thus reducing their activity.

Table 2. Time gap between packets uploads

Data	Time (s)
Average time	3
Minimum time	1
Maximum time	15

Moving the mouse across the screen over many active elements produces a packet every second. Although event descriptions are short, they sum up into huge volumes for frequently visited websites (see Table 3).

Table 3. Data transmitted to the server

	Measured	For 10 000 visits	For 100 000 visits
Raw text	307.8 MB	2.06 GB	20.62 GB
Encoded	86.4 MB	0.58 GB	5.78 GB

Frequent packet uploading could noticeably slow down the Internet connection if efficient encoding was not implemented (see Table 4). Thanks to diminishing the packet size, the proposed monitoring system can be used unobtrusively even on slow dial-up Internet connections.

Table 4. Estimated packet transmission time

	56 kbps (POTS)	128 kbps	256 kbps	512 kbps
Raw text	1.13 s	0.50 s	0.25 s	0.12 s
Encoded	0.32 s	0.14 s	0.07 s	0.03 s

33.8 Conclusions

The presented system for monitoring client-side activity is capable of monitoring a wide range of user actions performed in a web browser environment. The actions are recorded, arranged in packets, and then sent to the server to be stored and processed.

Stored information contain detailed facts about the element which triggered the event, precise date and time of the event, and identification of the document, user and session during which the event took place. Although discussing how this information can be processed is beyond the scope of this paper, it is obvious that it can at least yield valuable information on usability of particular web page elements and errors in their arrangement, thus giving hints to improve the quality of the website.

A unique feature of the described system is that it is completely script-driven on the client side, requiring no additional software to be installed on the client system. It also makes the system platform-independent as well.

The system's performance is satisfactory even on low bandwidth connections thanks to the efficient encoding of the transmitted data.

References

[Andersen 2000] J. Andersen, A. Giversen, A. H. Jensen, R. S. Larsen, T. B. Pedersen, and J. Skyt, *Analyzing Clickstreams Using Subsessions*. In *Proceedings of the Third International Workshop on Data Warehousing and OLAP*, Washington DC, November 2000, pp. 25–32.

[Coggeshall 2004] J. Coggeshall, *PHP Unleashed*, Sams Publishing, Indianapolis, 2004

[Fenstermacher 2002] K.D. Fenstermacher, M. Ginsburg, "A Lightweight Framework for Cross-Application User Monitoring", *Computer*, 35(3), 2002, pp. 51–59

[Fenstermacher 2003] K. Fenstermacher, M. Ginsburg, "Client-Side Monitoring for Web Mining", *Journal of the American Society of Information Science and Technology*, 54(7), 2003, pp. 625–637

[Gemius 2006] *Gemius*, www.gemius.pl, 2006

[Goodman 2004] D. Goodman, M. Morrison, *JavaScript Bible*, Wiley Publishing, Indianapolis, 2004

[Hilbert 2000] D. Hilbert, D.F. Redmiles, "Extracting Usability Information from User Interface Events", *ACM Computing Surveys*, Dec. 2000, pp. 384–421

[Laurie 2002] B. Laurie, P. Laurie, *Apache: The Definitive Guide*, O'Reilly Media, 2002

[OpenTracker 2006], *OpenTracker*, www.opentracker.net, 2005

[Pfaffenberger 2004] B. Pfaffenberger, S.M. Schafer, Ch. White, B. Karow, *HTML, XHTML and CSS Bible*, Wiley Publishing, Indianapolis, 2004

[PostgreSQL 2005] *PostgreSQL*, www.postgresql.org, 2005

[Robie 2004] J. Robie, S. Byrne, P. Le Hégaret, A. Le Hors, L. Wood, G. Nicol, M. Champion, *Document Object Model (DOM) Level 3 Core Specification*, http://www.w3.org/TR/2004/REC-DOM-Level-3-Core-200404077, April 2004

[ShinyStat 2006], *ShinyStat*, www.shinystat.com, 2005

[Stat.pl 2006] *Stat.pl*, www.stat.pl, 2006

[Swacha 2004] J. Swacha, The Predictive-Substitutional Compression Scheme and its Effective Implementation. In Proceedings of Data Compression Conference, IEEE Computer Society Press, Los Alamitos, 2004

[Taskware 2005], *Wintask*, www.wintask.com, 2005

[Webalizer 2005] *The Webalizer*, www.webalizer.com, 2005

34 A Security Evaluation Model for Multi-Agent Distributed Systems

Chunyan Ma, Arturo Concepcion

Computer Science Department, California State University, San Bernardino, USA
{chuma, concep}@csci.csusb.edu

34.1 Introduction

A new phase of the development of distributed system is now under way in which mobile software agent can be sent among supporting platforms. A mobile agent [6] is a program that represents a user in a computer network, and is capable of migrating autonomously from node to node, to perform computation on behalf of the user. Its tasks can range from online shopping to real-time device control to distributed scientific computing.

By using agent technology, we can move the code to the remote data. We can also send out the agent to access the remote resources without keeping the network connection alive all the time. Despite its many practical benefits, mobile agent technology results in significant new security threats due to the increased mobility. A malicious agent can corrupt information on its host and in other agents. It is even more difficult to prevent a host from changing an agent's states or even killing it. Therefore, solving the security problems of multi-agent distributed systems is crucial. It would be especially ideal if we can have a method to evaluate how secure an agent or a host is. Currently there is not much work done in this area. [1] and [2] are the few attempts to quantitatively measure the security of the mobile agent distributed systems. In this paper, we develop the security risk graph to model the system's vulnerabilities. Based on the analysis of the different security threat situations in a mobile agent system, we derive a mathematical security model for quantitatively evaluating the security of an agent-based distributed system.

This chapter is organized as follows: Section 2 gives the taxonomy of security threats for an agent-based system and describes other related works. In section 3, we will present a mathematical model for security assessment of an agent-based distributed system, followed by an example to explain how this model works. The section 4 provides the conclusions and future directions.

403

W. Abramowicz and H.C. Mayr (eds.), Technologies for Business Information Systems, 403–415.
© 2007 *Springer.*

34.2 Related Works and the Taxonomy of Security Threats for Mobile-Agent Systems

Among the different research aspects in the security issues in the agent-based systems, we are going to focus on finding the method to evaluate the security of the agent-based systems quantitatively. In this section, we are going to discuss the related works in the security evaluation of the mobile-agent systems and develop a security threats taxonomy on which we base our security model.

34.2.1 Related Works

Presently only two papers proposed security evaluation models for agent-based distributed systems. [1] proposed the idea about coefficient of malice k_i of each host and coefficient of vulnerability of an agent v and used them to calculate the probability of breaches on an agent when it is on each host as

P(breach at host i) = $1 - \exp(-\lambda_i t_i)$, where $-\lambda_i = v k_i$

t_i is the amount of time the agent spends on host i. So the agent security E is the probability of no breach at all hosts in its itinerary, $E = \exp(-\sum \lambda_i t_i)$.

[2] proposed to use the probabilistic Mean Effort To Failure (METF), as the measure of the system security. The mean effort in node j, denoted as E_j, $E_j = 1/ \sum \lambda_{jl}$. λ_{jl} is the transition rate from node j to node l, defined as $1/t$, where t is the time needed for completing the attack. Then the mean effort to failure $METF_k$ when node k is the initial node and P_{kl} is the conditional transition probability from node k to node l, is: $METF_k = E_k + \sum P_{kl} * METF_{kl}$; where $P_{kl} = \lambda_{kl} * E_k$

The model proposed in [1] did not consider the security threats of the hosts. Also the concepts of the coefficient of malice and vulnerability in [1] are not well defined. It is not clear on how to obtain the coefficient of malice and vulnerability. While in [2], the METF calculation is too complicated.

34.2.2 Taxonomy of Security Threats

Considering the consequence of the security breaches, the traditional taxonomy of the security threats identifies three main categories [3] in the ordinary distributed systems as: confidentiality, integrity and availability.

However, in the mobile-agent distributed systems, we identified a new type of security threat - repudiation, i.e., when one party in a communication exchange or transaction later denies that the transaction or exchange took place. We name this category of security threats as creditability and define the creditability as following:

- Creditability is violated when principals deny having performed a particular action.

The major elements in a mobile-agent distributed system are the agents and the hosts. When considering the actors in the mobile-agent systems, there are four main categories identified [4]: threats occurred when an agent attacks a platform; attacks against other agents; attacks the underlying network; and when a platform attacks an agent. So the security threats can be partitioned into towards the host or towards the agent subcategories. For each subcategory of the security threats, we have identified the possible security requirements when considering the consequence of the security breaches, as shown in Fig. 1.

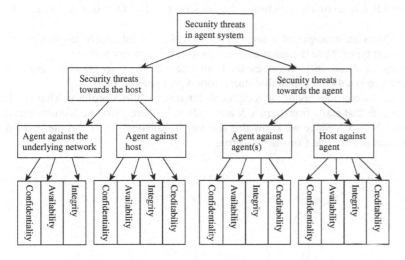

Fig. 1. Taxonomy of the security threats the agent-based systems

34.3 A Mathematical Model for Agent-based Distributed System Security Threat Evaluation

In this section, we will introduce the security risk graph based on which we will set up a mathematical model to evaluate the security of the mobile-agent systems.

34.3.1 Introduction of the Security Risk Graph

Definition 1. A vertex of a security risk graph is an agent or a host in the agent-based distributed system.

Definition 2. An edge in a security risk graph is an arc from vertex X to vertex Y, represented as (X, Y).

For each type of security threat, there is an average access time associated. We call it the transition time of a specific type of security threat.

Definition 3. Transition time is the time needed for a specific type of security threat r to succeed from one vertex to the next vertex.

By observing the systems, we can get the transition time indicating how hard for one vertex to perform one particular attack to another vertex and assign that value to the same kind of attacks identified from the system we want to analyze.

Definition 4. The weight of each edge is the transition time of each edge.

Definition 5. A directed path in a security risk graph is a sequence of vertices along with the edges in between them such that for any adjacent pair of edges $e_i e_j$, the ending vertex is e_i and the starting vertex is e_j.

Definition 6. A security risk graph of an agent-based distributed system is a directed and weighted graph G(V,E, W) where V is a set of vertices, W is the set of weights and E is a set of edges between the vertices, E = {w(u,v) | u, v $\in$ V, w$\in$W, u $\neq$ v}.

Fig. 2 shows an example of a security risk graph. The edges are labeled by the security threat types. Note B cannot gain access to E through any path.

Corollary 1. A security threat exists from one vertex X to another vertex Y whenever there is a directed path that starts from X and ends at Y.

Proof: Let us consider about the reciprocal statement of this Corollary. That is, "If there is no path that starts from vertex X and ends at Y, there exists no security threat from vertex X to Y". Since we know this reciprocal statement holds and the proof is trivial, we can deduce that Corollary 1 is true.

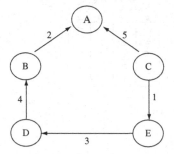

1) X can read files from Y (intercept);
2) X can guess Y's password;
3) X can get hold of Y's CPU cycle;
4) Y has no password;
5) Y uses a program owned by X.

Fig. 2. An example of a security risk graph with edges labeled by security threats

34.3.2 Security Risks Analysis

Combine the security risks related with agent against host and agent against the underlying network, we can discard all the edges from the host to agents and some of the edges between the agents that do not count for attacking the host and the underlying network. In Fig. 3, the security risks labeled in the numerical values and a prime are the security breaches to the host. Note when agent B_1 masquerade as agent A_1 to the host, we need to decide if this attack is toward agent A_1 only, the host only or both.

Definition 7. We call vertex X equals vertex Y if vertex X's behavior looks the same as vertex Y's behavior, denoted as X = Y.

Definition 8. Masquerade is the act of imitating the behavior of vertex X to vertex Y under false pretense, denoted as X(Y).

When X masquerades as Y, we have X(Y) = Y.

Definition 9. The behavior of B as seen by C is denoted as B γ C.

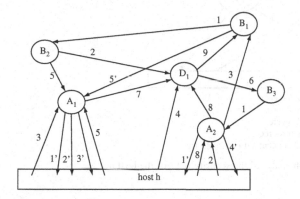

1) X can guess Y's password;
2) X can eavesdrop Y's communication with others;
3) X has write access to Y (alteration);
4) X can masquerade as another platform to Y;
5) Y uses a program owned by X;
6) X can repudiate the result from Y;
7) X can copy and replay Y's information;
8) Y has no password;
9) X can deny the service to Y;
1') X can read files from Y;
2') X can write files to Y;
3') X can get hold of Y's CPU cycle;
4') X can get hold of network resources;
5') X can masquerade as another agent Y to the platform.

Fig. 3. Security risk graph example for agent-based system

Masquerade Transition Law: If Entity A can masquerade as Entity B to Entity C, then that is an attack from Entity A to Entity C.

Proof: To C, Entity B is as itself, so B γ C = B.

When under masquerading, Entity A acts as B, so A γ C = A(B) γ C = B γ C, because A(B) = B.

So we have B γ C = A γ C = B.

Because A behaves itself to Entity C under the name of B, to obtain the privileges of C, so that is an attack from A to C.∎

Corollary 2. If a vertex A can masquerade as another vertex B to the third vertex C, then this is a security risk from A to B, also a security risk from A to C.

Proof: Because A masquerade as B, whatever A does has affected B's reputation. So it is an indirect security risk from A to B.

Also by using the masquerade transition law, we know it is a security risk from A to C.∎

Take Fig. 3 as an example, by using Corollary 2, we can isolate the security risks the host will face as in Fig. 4.

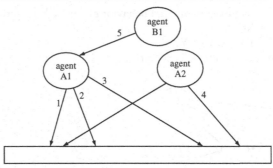

1) X can read files from Y (intercept);
2) X can write files to Y (alteration);
3) X can get hold of Y's CPU cycle;
4) X can get hold of network resources;
5) X can masquerade as another agent Y to the platform.

Fig. 4. Security risk graph analyzed the security risks of the host h

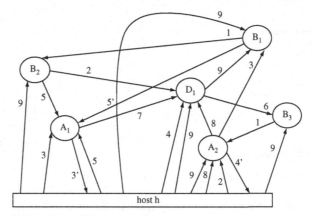

1) X can guess Y's password;
2) X can eavesdrop Y's communication with others;
3) X has write access to Y(alteration);
4) X can masquerade as another platform to Y;
5) Y uses a program owned by X;
6) X can repudiate the result from Y;
7) X can copy and replay Y's information;
8) Y has no password;
9) X can deny the service to Y;
3') X can get hold of Y's CPU cycle;
4') X can get hold of network resources;
5') X can masquerade as another agent Y to the platform.

Fig. 5. Security risk graph for agents on the platform

But for analyzing the security of the agents, we cannot just discard all the edges toward the host. Because one agent can take all host h's CPU cycles, so as to deny service to other agents, like the agent A_1 in Fig. 5. In fact, we generalize this observation into the following theorem.

Theorem 1. If an agent A on host i can take all of host i's CPU cycles, it can in turn launch denial of service attack to all of the agents running on this host except for A itself. If there are more than two agents on the same host I, they can take all of i's CPU cycles. The first one that launches the attack will succeed in the attack.

Proof: Trivial. Since all of the agents running on a host need to utilize CPU cycles for its performance. If the first agent can get hold of all CPU cycles successfully, all the other agents running on host i can not even function.

Due to the fact that an agent or a host in the agent-based systems can launch many different types of attacks, we face a problem of which one to choose for calculation.

Theorem 2. If there are several edges with the same direction from one vertex to the next in the security risk graph, the edge with the smallest transition time will be chosen in the calculation.

Proof: Without losing generality, as seen in the security risk graph (Fig. 6), suppose A is an intruder and B is a target. There are several edges from A to B, AB_1, AB_2, ..., Ab_n. Each edge has a transition time t_1, ..., t_n associated with it. Suppose $t_i = \min\{ t_1, ... t_n \}$. Since the intruders do not know the whole topology of the security risk graph. They only know the attacks that can be directly applied in a single step. So A has the options t_1, t_2, ..., t_n to attack B. From the empirical results obtained from [5], the intruder A would always try to perform the attack that takes the least time, that is t_i.■

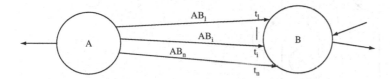

Fig. 6. Security risk graph for A as the intruder and B as the target

Theorem 3. If there is an edge from one vertex that goes back to its ancestor, then this edge would not be counted in the calculation.

Proof: From the attacker's point of view, the attacker's goal is to choose the branch that takes the least time in the security risk graph.

Case I. Edge from one vertex that goes back to its parent.

From the security risk graph in Fig. 7, we can see that the time taken from R to go all the way down to T is t (t is chosen by selecting the smallest value among different routes). But if we loop back at B_l, for route A_i - B_l, total time = $t + t_{Bli} + t_{Bil}$, where $t_{Bli} + t_{Bil} > 0$. So total time > t.

For route A_i - B_j - B_l, total time = $t + t_{Bij} + t_{Bjl} + t_{Bli}$, where $t_{Bij} + t_{Bjl} + t_{Bli} > 0$. So total time > t.

That means whatever the routes in between vertex A_i and B_l, total time > $t + t_{Bli} > t$.

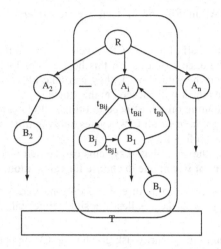

Fig. 7. Security risk graph for edge from one vertex goes back to its parent case

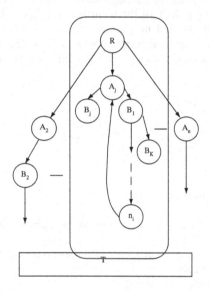

Fig. 8. Security risk graph for edge from one vertex goes back to its ancestor case

Case II. Edge from one node that goes back to its ancestor.

Similar to case I, the time taken by the branch edge from one vertex n_i goes back to its ancestor is greater than the time taken from R go all the way through A_i, n_i down to T, as in Fig. 8. If t is the time taken to loop back from n_j to A_i, $t > 0$. ∎

34.3.3 A Mathematical Security Model for Security Evaluation

In this section, we will introduce a security model for evaluating the security of agent-based distributed systems using shortest path.

Definition 10. A shortest path from vertex u to vertex v is defined as any path with weight $\delta(u, v) = \min\{w(P) \mid P(u \sim v)\}$, where $P(u \sim v)$ is the set of paths from vertex u to vertex v, and $w(P)$ is the set of weights of each path in $P(u \sim v)$.

Definition 11. Let P be a path containing vertices $v_1, v_2, \ldots v_n$, and $w(v_i, v_j)$ be the weight on the edge connecting v_i to v_j, then the length of path P is defined as

$$|P| = \sum_{i=1}^{n-1} w(v_i, v_{i+1}).$$

The time on the shortest path describes the least time the attacker will need to break into the target. If the attacker does not know the topology of the whole system, the time needed to break into the target will be definitely more than or equal to the time calculated from the shortest path. So the shortest path is a suitable measure to evaluate the system's security level.

The following algorithm based on the Dijkstra's algorithm can be used to find the security measures.

Security risks estimation algorithm:

Input: Weighted graph G, source, destination (G is the simplified graph using Theorems 2 and 3)

Output: Transition time from source to destination

Temp: temporary tree structure to hold the nodes and edges as go through graph G

1. add source, Transition time (source) = 0 to Temp
2. while (destination $\notin$ Temp)

    find edge (u, v), where:

      a. u $\in$ Temp;

      b. v $\notin$ Temp;

      c. minimize the transition time over all (u, v) satisfies a and b.

The result is, transition time = transition time(u) + w(u, v), where w(u, v) is the weight of (u, v).

Actually, Dijkstra algorithm can find the shortest path to every vertex from the source vertex. It uses the same time complexity as the one needed for just finding the shortest path to the target from the source vertex.

The shortest minimum length path between any two vertices represents the weakest security point and the longest shortest path describes the ultimate time the attacker needs to break the whole system at most.

Definition 12. The diameter of a security risk graph is the length of the longest shortest path between any two vertices.

The diameter can be used to represent the security level of the whole system because it is the least time the attacker needs to break into the whole system. If after reconfiguration, the diameter of the whole system increases, we can say that the whole system's security increases because the time needed to break into the farthest point of the system increases.

34.3.4 Illustrative Example

Now let us use the example in Fig. 3 to illustrate how this approach works. Fig. 9 shows that the edges are assigned different thicknesses to represent their weight and also to characterize the difficulty of the breaches: the thicker the edge, the easier the breach. For the convenience of calculation, we use one week as the unit of attack times. For instance, one day is approximately 0.2 week. Table 1 lists the transition time and the graph representation in the security risk graph.

Table 1. Transition time, its corresponding time in weeks, transition rate and graph representation

Transition time	Transition Time in weeks	Line type in the security risk graph
Quasi-instantaneous	0.0002	
one hour	0.02	
one day	0.2	
one week	1	
one month	5	
one year	50	

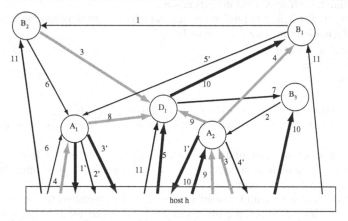

1) X can guess Y's password in one week;
2) X can guess Y's password in one month;
3) X can eavesdrop Y's communication with others (quasi-instantaneous);
4) X has write access to Y (alteration) (quasi-instantaneous);
5) X can masquerade as another platform to Y (one hour);
6) Y uses a program owned by X once in a year (one year);
7) X can repudiate the result from Y in one day (one day);
8) X can copy and replay Y's information (quasi-instantaneous);
9) Y has no password (quasi-instantaneous);
10) X can deny the service to Y in one hour;
11) X can deny the service to Y in one day;

1') X can read files from Y in one hour;
2') X can write files to Y in one day;
3') X can get hold of Y's CPU cycle in one hour;
4') X can get hold of network resources in one day;
5') X can masquerade as another agent Y to the platform in one month.

Fig. 9. Security risk graph example with weight demonstrated in different line type

Follow the security evaluation algorithm, we take B_2 as the attacker, A_2 as the target from Fig. 9 and generate the security risk graph as shown in Fig. 10.

By using Theorem 3, we can eliminate the edges B_1B_2, to get Fig. 11. Also for transition time of edge A_1Host_h, we can choose the one that gives the smallest transition time based on Theorem 2.

Following the algorithm, the example in Fig. 11 works as shown below:

1. Take the source vertex B_2 and put it in Temp. Temp = $\{B_2\}$
2. Since B_2 connects to A_1 and D_1, we mark A_1 and D_1 as candidates.
Compare $|B_2A_1| = 50$ and $|B_2D_1| = 0.0002$. Because $|B_2D_1|$ is smaller, we take D_1 into Temp. Now Temp = $\{B_2, D_1\}$ and we also get the shortest path between B_2 and D_1 is B_2D_1 with $|B_2D_1| = 0.0002$.
3. Repeat similar steps, we can get the shortest path between B_2 and B_1 is $B_2D_1B_1$ with $B_2D_1B_1 = 0.0202$. The shortest path between B_2 and B_3 is $B_2D_1B_3$ with $|B_2D_1B_3| = 0.2002$. The shortest path between B_2 and A_1 is $B_2D_1B_1A_1$ with $|B_2D_1B_1A_1| = 5.0202$. The shortest path between B_2 and $host_h$ is $B_2D_1B_1A_1host_h$ with $|B_2D_1B_1A_1host_h| = 5.0402$. The one between B_2 and A_2 is $B_2D_1B_1A_1host_hA_2$ with $|B_2D_1B_1A_1host_hA_2| = 5.0404$.

Following the method in this example, starting from each vertex, we can calculate the breach time to every other vertex respectively. The result of calculation is shown in Table 2. The breach time is represented in time duration as number of weeks.

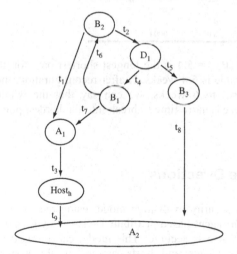

Fig. 10. Identified security risk graph for B_2 as the attacker and A_2 as the target

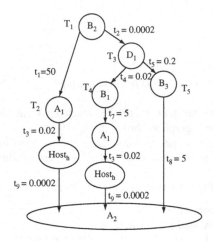

Fig. 11. Simplified security risk graph for Fig. 10 by using Theorem 2 and Theorem 3

Table 2. Breach time results (in number of weeks) calculated by using the proposed method

Start \ End	A_1	A_2	B_1	B_2	B_3	D_1	$Host_h$
A_1	---	0.0202	0.0202	0.22	0.04	0.0002	0.02
A_2	0.0202	---	0.0002	1.0002	0.04	0.0002	0.02
B_1	5	5.04	---	1	1.2002	1.0002	5.02
B_2	5.0202	5.0404	0.0202	---	0.2002	0.0002	5.0402
B_3	5.2002	5	5.0002	5.4	---	5.0002	5.2
D_1	5.02	5.0406	0.02	1.02	0.2	---	5.04
$Host_h$	0.0002	0.0002	0.0004	0.2	0.02	0.0004	---

In the above example, since $\mid B_3A_2host_hB_2 \mid$ = 5.4 is the longest shortest path for all the vertices. The diameter for this example is 5.4 weeks. If after reconfiguration, the diameter of the whole system increases to 6 weeks, we can say that the whole system's security increases because it needs more time to break into the hardest point of the system (the whole system).

34.4 Conclusions and Future Directions

In this research, we have developed a security evaluation model using the shortest path to evaluate the security levels of the agent-based distributed systems by giving a quantitative measure on how well a system is secured. This model can be used to monitor the security evolution of the agents and hosts running in the system dynamically. It can also help in the management of the system's security and performance. We can evaluate the effectiveness of different configurations by comparing the quantitative measures obtained from these different configurations.

By monitoring the system's risks, we can get the profile of the transition time of each type of security risks. We plan to use some probabilistic model to process the empirical data obtained from the observation.

Also, it would be desirable to apply some probabilistic method to the time value from the calculation so that it describes the security measure more accurately.

We plan to apply these models in Spider III, the multi-agent distributed system developed in CSUSB to study its feasibility.

Acknowledgments

The support of the National Science Foundation under the award 9810708, the Associated Students, Incorporated Research and Travel Fund and the Division of Information Resources and Technology of CSUSB are gratefully acknowledged.

References

1. Chan, A., Lyu, M.: Security Modeling and Evaluation for Mobile Code Paradigm. In: Proceedings of the Asian Computing Science Conference. (1997) 371–371
2. Concepcion, A., Ma, C.: A Probabilistic Security Model for Multi-Agent Distributed Systems. In: Proceedings of the 6th International Conference on Business Information Systems. (2003)
3. Humphries, J.: Secure Mobile Agent for Network Vulnerability Scanning. In: Proceedings of the 2000 IEEE Workshop on Information Assurance and Security. United States Military Academy, West Point, NY (2000) 6–7
4. Jansen, W., Karygiannis, T.: Mobile Agent Security. NIST Special Publication. (1999) 800–819
5. Jonsson, E., Olovsson, T.: A Quantitative Model of the Security Intrusion Process Based on Attacker Behavior. IEEE Transactions on Software Engineering. (1999)
6. Karnik, N., Tripathi, A.: Design Issues in Mobile Agent Programming Systems. (1998)

35 Industrial Application and Evaluation of a Software Evolution Decision Model

Tero Tilus[1], Jussi Koskinen[2], Jarmo J. Ahonen[3], Heikki Lintinen[4], Henna Sivula[4], Irja Kankaanpää[5]

[1] tero.tilus@jyu.fi
[2] Department of Computer Science and Information Systems, University of Jyväskylä, P.O. Box 35, 40014 Jyväskylä, Finland, koskinen@cs.jyu.fi
[3] Department of Computer Science, University of Kuopio, P.O. Box 1627, 70211 Kuopio, Finland, jarmo.ahonen@uku.fi
[4] firstname.surname@gmail.com
[5] Information Technology Research Institute, University of Jyväskylä, P.O. Box 35, 40014 Jyväskylä, Finland, irja.kankaanpaa@titu.jyu.fi

35.1 Introduction

Software maintenance and *evolution* are economically important issues [19]. The proportion of maintenance costs of the total lifecycle costs has traditionally been 50-75% in case of successful legacy systems with long lifetime [15]. *Legacy system* is an old, typically poorly documented software system, which has been implemented with old technology. It is at least partly outdated, but may contain invaluable business logic and information. According to *Lehman's first law* [14] a software system used in "real-world" environment must evolve or it will become progressively less satisfactory to its users. Therefore, during the maintenance phase, decisions have to be made concerning system evolution strategies.

Evolution strategy selections often have large-scale, long-range economical effects including changes in system maintenance costs and in possibilities to preserve the initial legacy system investment. Viable strategic options might include system modernization or system replacement.

Earlier studies conducted within our research project include theoretical analysis and comparison of many of the important methods for software modernization estimation [9], including [4,6,18,19,20,21,24,25], empirical studies, including [1,10,13], and method development [11,12]. Especially, the earlier analysis [9] reveals that more empirical studies should be conducted concerning the use and

417

W. Abramowicz and H.C. Mayr (eds.), Technologies for Business Information Systems, 417–427.

validation of the methods in this area. There is a general need to study and deal with industrial large-scale legacy systems. Especially, we are here concerned with evaluating VDM [24].

This paper is a revised and improved version of an earlier case study description which has appeared as [23]. This paper provides a more focused treatment of the application and evaluation of VDM. The paper is organized as follows. Section 2 characterizes the main principles of VDM. Section 3 describes the structure and phases of the case study applying VDM in industrial settings. Section 4 presents the results received. These include results produced by VDM and VDM's evaluation. The evaluation includes comparison with two other evaluation variants and gathered feedback from industrial experts. Finally, Section 5 summarizes the conclusions.

35.2 VDM: Value-Based Decision Model

VDM [24] is a model developed by Visaggio. It supports the selection of the most suitable software evolution strategy to be applied. Likewise as [2,17,21] it considers both economical and technical issues. It is one of the relatively well validated methods. VDM is based on a real-world renewal project on a banking system consisting of 653 programs and 1.5 MDSI.

The first step in applying VDM is to divide the system into *parts*. The division does not necessarily correspond to system components. The second step is to determine and weight metrics and to set baselines (objective-levels). Both technical and economical metrics are used. Visaggio [24] has used anomalous files, dead data, semantic redundant data etc. The metrics used within individual evaluations may vary based on their availability and suitability for the evaluation purpose. Weights are set by the model users. Baseline represents the metric threshold value which is considered to be satisfactory.

The model produces two output variables: economical value (*economic score*) and technical value (*technical score*) of the evaluated system. The received value pair is presented as a point in two-dimensional (technical, economical) space. The relative potential of the strategies can then be deduced based on the relative locations of the received points. This enables evaluation of individual changes and prioritization of system replacement, modernization and other available options. Main principles related to interpretation of the results produced by VDM are: 1) All maintenance should strive towards high economical and technical value. 2) Modernization is suitable in case of high economical and low technical value. 3) Replacement is suitable in case of low economical and technical value.

35.3 Case Study

The case study aimed at systematically evaluating one industrial legacy system regarding its possible evolution strategies based on VDM. The study was funded by National Technology Agency of Finland (TEKES) and participated industrial partners. There were three involved organizations: University of Jyväskylä; the project group implementing the study, a large Finnish software house having supplied the target system, and a large public-sector organization using the target system. About 100 work days of the project group resources were used to the planning, implementation and reporting of the case study (5/2003-3/2005).

There were six project group members and nine external experts involved to the case study. Supplier experts were: technology manager, chief of department, two communication chiefs, and two technical experts. Customer experts were two system managers. These persons participated to the case study in various workshops regarding their own areas of expertise.

35.3.1 Initiation

VDM was presented to the involved experts in two occasions (9/2003, 2/2004) and via a literary summary of its contents (11/2003). Objectives of the evaluations were determined (10/2003). VDM was considered by the involved customer experts as the most suitable evaluation method for the organizational needs.

35.3.2 Target System Characterization

Target system is a large industrial legacy system which is in constant production use. The system has been considered as a relevant target for the evaluations by the involved experts. It is a typical legacy system: implemented in relatively old technology but valuable or invaluable to the continued important business operations. The system is vital due to the large amount of specialized knowledge it contains. It also has a core-role in user organization's business. The application area is tax payment monitoring. The size of the evaluated parts was about 67 KSLOC, which represented most of the system.

35.3.3 System Division

System division is not supported by any of the methods cited earlier. Therefore, the division has been a subproblem to be solved. Our project has developed a method called MODEST [22] which is aimed at early system modernization pressure estimation. It also provides one solution to the division problem and has been applied here in that regard. The guidelines it follows regarding the division can be summarized into one central principle: *sufficient homogeneity of the values of each applied metric as such within the evaluated part*. Division was selected in workshop meetings (3-7/2004). There were two selected main parts or segments (later denoted by *A* and *B*) divided to three subparts each (*A1...A3* and *B1...B3*).

35.3.4 Calculations

Calculations were conducted at general level in three different ways. The first variant is based on VDM [24]. The other two variants are mainly based on [21], and partly on [25], and will be used in evaluating the reliability and sensitivity of the main results produced by VDM.

VDM - *Baselined evaluation* (B). Technical and economical metrics were scaled based on per-metric baselines (i.e. preset objective-levels). Strength of this variant is that it covers organization's quality policy. Weakness is that the evaluations are relatively sensitive to the expert judgments.

Relative evaluation (R). Technical metrics were scaled per size of the units (intuitively: "size-relative density").

Simplified evaluation (S). Technical metrics were weighted based on part sizes only (intuitively: "mass").

Additionally metrics were weighted according to their importance reflecting organization's quality policy. Weights were determined and preset by the involved experts based on their judgment during the measurements phase. Relative and simplified variants do not include quality objective considerations. Details of the calculations are presented in [23].

35.3.5 Selection and Definition of the Applied Metrics

The required selection of the applied metrics and their weights was achieved by applying Goal-Question-Metric (GQM) approach as presented in [3]. GQM has been applied also, e.g. in [2]. First, a goal(s) is set. Secondly, the goal is operationalized into a set of questions. Thirdly, questions are quantified in terms of metrics. Quantification into metrics was achieved during workshop meetings. These meetings were participated by experts from the involved organizations.

Some of the applied metrics were such that they were not directly suitable to be evaluated based on the calculation suggested by Visaggio. Therefore, these were evaluated according to Sneed instead. Metrics represented in the literature were somewhat adapted to increase their applicability, validity, and intuitive consistency in VDM evaluations. Relevant earlier maintenance and evolution metric surveys, classifications, and implementations include [5,6,7,8,16,20]. The selected metrics covered both technical and economical value based on both expert judgments and objective metrics. Metrics were selected and final definitions specified based on the workshop results (3-10/2004). They were used in system parts evaluations, and are detailed in [23].

35.3.6 Measurements

Measurements were planned and performed (7-12/2004) in cooperation with the project group and experts from the supplier and customer. Objective technical metrics were gathered by a technical manager and supporting personnel from the supplier and objective economical metrics by the two system managers from the customer. *Technical expert judgment* was produced by the developer team of the supplier. *Economical expert judgment* was produced by two system managers from the customer.

35.3.7 Gathered Metrics

Table 1 gathers the selected metrics, received actual and derived metrics values for the evaluated six system parts, baselines, and set weights of the metrics. "ExpertJudgment-X-Y" refers to the value of the judgment of expert X in absolute or relative terms (Y). Absolute values (A) were asked, relative values (R) were derived. Best values are written in boldface. Noteworthy are the good technical values of parts *A1* and *B1* and good economical values of parts *A1* and *A3*. As noted earlier baselines and the weights were set by the experts.

Table 1. Summary of the gathered metrics

Metric/Part	A1	A2	A3	B1	B2	B3	Baseline	Weight
Size (KSLOC)	17.8	7.2	5.8	8.3	13.0	15.8	-	-
Technical value								
ExpertJudgment-1-A	70	78	48	97	65	42	50	1.5
ExpertJudgment-1-R	113	51	25	74	77	60	50	1.5
ExpertJudgment-2-A	48	30	32	60	14	16	25	1.5
ExpertJudgment-2-R	78	20	17	46	17	23	25	1.5
Constants/KSLOC	1.7	13.2	0.7	5.4	3.1	0.1	0.2	1.0
DB-IB/KSLOC	0.0	1.0	2.7	0.0	2.6	3.0	0.1	1.0
OS-calls/KSLOC	5.6	1.1	1.5	0.0	0.1	0.1	0.1	1.0
Economical value								
ExpertJudgment-3-A	70	30	30	30	20	20	25	1.5
ExpertJudgment-3-R	40	42	53	37	16	13	25	1.5
ExpertJudgment-4-A	60	26	30	34	26	26	25	1.5
ExpertJudgment-4-R	34	36	52	41	20	16	25	1.5
Automation (%)	90	66	100	86	92	87	97	2.0
Input vol (rec./MSLOC)	579	915	5	30	345	132	100	1.0

35.4 Results

Results regarding VDM included those produced by VDM itself (4.1), VDM's evaluation (4.2), and software evolution strategy recommendations for the target system (4.3). VDM produced technical and economical scores of the evaluated system parts. Evaluation was based on sensitivity analysis and gathered feedback. Final evolution strategy recommendations were achieved based on these analyses.

35.4.1 Results produced by VDM

As noted, VDM shows the results using the four-field-square notation. The four fields are determined based on the thresholds. Figure 1 shows the results received based on the baselined (B) evaluation. This evaluation helps to identify the most valuable system parts. The figure also shows the recommended system evolution strategies for the four fields.

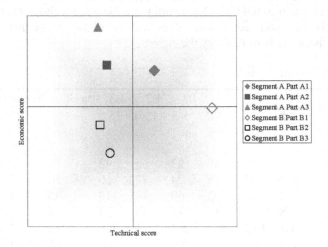

Fig. 1. Results of VDM: baselined evaluation (B)

The results suggest that default evolution strategies of the parts would be the following. Status quo, *i.e.* continued conventional maintenance for *A1* and *B1*, modernization for *A2* and *A3*, and replacement for *B2* and *B3* (however, the replacement suggestion especially for *B2* is not particularly strong). The economical value of *A2* is here increased by *A2*'s very high level of automated operation. Similarly, the economical value of *A3* is increased by its small size and high input information volume. As noted earlier, the baselined variant is most sensitive to the expert judgments. In order to study the sensitivity of these results more closely, also relative (R) and simplified (S) evaluation values were mapped.

35.4.2 VDM's Evaluation

The results produced by VDM (baselined evaluation) were compared to the results produced by relative and simplified evaluations. Table 2 characterizes the principles of using input metric values in these three variants of calculations. Only exception was that automation level is relative for all variants. Table 3 shows the final values for the six system parts calculated based on these variants. These values were received by applying the formulas presented in [23] based on the input values of Table 1 according to the main principles of Table 2. Threshold was preset by the involved experts and was used only in the baselined evaluation. It refers to a quality threshold separating good and poor systems.

Table 2. Characterization of the principles of using input metrics in the three variants of calculations

Metrics/Variant	Objective/ Technical	Objective/ Economical	Expert/ Technical	Expert/ Economical
Baselined (B)	Relative	Relative	Absolute	Relative
Relative (R)	Relative	Absolute	Absolute	Absolute
Simplified (S)	Absolute	Absolute	Relative	Absolute

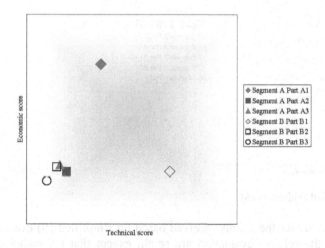

Legend:
- ◆ Segment A Part A1
- ■ Segment A Part A2
- ▲ Segment A Part A3
- ◇ Segment B Part B1
- ☐ Segment B Part B2
- ○ Segment B Part B3

Fig. 2. Results: relative evaluation (R)

Figure 2 shows the results received based on relative (R) evaluation. Sneed [21] does not use splitting of the field into squares, since there are no thresholds used. Interpretation is almost similar as in case of the previous figure. However, scores of the parts are purely relative to each others, and are here also interpreted as such. Differences of the evaluation results to the baselined evaluation are as follows.

The economic value of *A2* and *A3* is relatively much smaller. Therefore, both modernization and replacement seem to be possible options for these parts.

Table 3. Summary of the technical and economical value calculation results: VDM - baselined variant (B), relative variant (R), simplified variant (S)

Value/Part	A1	A2	A3	B1	B2	B3	Threshold
Technical-B	7.2	4.5	4.0	10.6	4.1	4.7	6
Technical-R	4.2	3.4	3.3	5.6	3.2	3.0	-
Technical-S	4.7	2.8	3.2	4.4	3.2	3.2	-
Economical-B	7.8	8.1	9.9	5.9	5.1	3.7	6
Economical-R	5.8	3.3	3.4	3.3	3.4	3.0	-
Economical-S	5.8	3.3	3.4	3.3	3.4	3.0	-

Also, the economic value of *B2* and *B3* is somewhat smaller. Therefore, it appears that the replacement is the correct strategy afterall for these parts. Technical value of *A1* is somewhat smaller, suggesting that also modernization could be a viable evolution strategy for it.

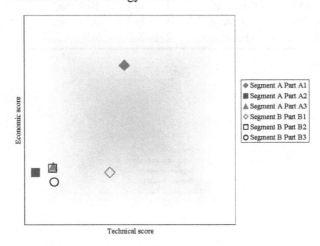

Fig. 3. Results: simplified evaluation (S)

Likewise, Figure 3 shows the results received based on simplified (S) evaluation. Differences to the relative evaluation are small, except that the technical value of parts *A2* and *B1* is smaller. This evaluation strongly suggests that some radical changes (modernization or replacement) are needed in case of part *A2*.

Additionally, feedback concerning the case study and VDM was gathered using a questionnaire. Experts from the industrial organization answered to the questions. The case study was considered successful: goals were well achieved and communication was fluent. Six persons out of the nine involved in VDM's application answered to the questions. VDM was generally considered useful, sufficiently precisely defined, and somewhat heavy to use. The results provided by it were easy to interpret, sufficiently consistent, somewhat ambiguous, possibly somewhat too abstract, definitively not too detailed, and highly reliable. The way that VDM presents its results (the four-field-square) was helping very well in forming overall view of the evaluated situation, sufficiently well in describing the state of the system and definitively not mixing or distorting issues. Application experiences suggest that VDM evaluations could benefit from more specific instructions included into the method. These should specify how to consistently utilize the classifications and how the measurements could be handled across different evaluations in practice.

35.5 Conclusions

There is a great need to have reliable decision models for supporting the selection of proper system evolution strategies. Most of the current methods, however, have insufficient empirical testing in industrial settings. One of the important and relatively well empirically validated methods is Value-Based Decision Model (VDM). It is versatile and considers both economical and technical characteristics of the legacy system to be evaluated. This paper has presented an industrial study applying and evaluating VDM. The paper also included the most essential parts of the case study underlying the evaluation. The study has been performed systematically utilizing received industrial feedback and existing methods.

The application area of the evaluated target system was tax payment monitoring. The target system was divided into subsystems, metrics were selected, and expert judgments gathered. Multiple industrial system evolution decision making experts took part to the evaluations. Subsystems were characterized based on the analyses. VDM's baselined calculations produced economical and technical values for the evaluated parts. The analyses revealed those subsystems whose economical value or technical quality need to be improved. They also provided information for the selection of suitable evolution strategies for those parts.

VDM has been evaluated. Two other calculation variants were compared to VDM. This has revealed the differences between the variants and provided information about the sensitivity of these kind of evaluations. VDM was also evaluated based on the feedback received from the industrial experts. It was considered clearly useful for its intended purpose. There were some problems confronted in its application, which have been listed in the paper. The contribution of this paper includes the received results supplementing earlier knowledge on applying VDM and highlighting issues which need to be heeded while applying it and similar methods in industrial settings.

References

1. Ahonen JJ, Sivula H, Koskinen J, Lintinen H, Tilus T, Kankaanpää I, Juutilainen P (2006) Defining the process for making software system modernization decisions. In: Münch J, Vierimaa M. (eds) Product Focused Software Process Improv - 7th Int Conf (PROFES 2006). Springer LNCS 4034, pp 5-18

2. Aversano L, Esposito R, Mallardo T, Tortorella M (2004) Supporting decisions on the adoption of re-engineering technologies. In: Proc 8th Eur Conf on Software Maintenance and Reengineering (CSMR 2004). IEEE Computer Society, pp 95–104
3. Basili VR, Caldiera G, Rombach HD (1994) The goal question metric approach. In: Encyclopedia of software engineering. Wiley.
4. Bennett K, Ramage M, Munro M (1999) Decision model for legacy systems. IEE Proceedings - Software 146 (3):153–159
5. Coleman D, Ash D, Lowther B, Oman P (1994) Using metrics to evaluate software system maintainability. Computer 27 (8):44–49
6. De Lucia A, Di Penta M, Stefanucci S, Venturi G (2002) Early effort estimation of massive maintenance processes. In: Proc Int Conf Software Maintenance - 2002 (ICSM 2002). IEEE Computer Society, pp 234–237
7. Di Lucca GA, Fasolino AR, Tramontana P, Visaggio CA (2004) Towards the definition of a maintainability model for web applications. In: Proc 8th Eur Conf Software Maintenance and Reengineering (CSMR 2004). IEEE Computer Society, pp 279–287
8. Kemerer CF (1995) Software complexity and software maintenance: a survey of empirical research. Annals of Software Engineering 1:1–22
9. Koskinen J, Lintinen H, Sivula H, Tilus T (2004) Evaluation of software modernization estimation methods using NIMSAD meta framework. Publications of the Information Technology Research Institute 15. University of Jyväskylä, Jyväskylä, Finland (Technical report)
10. Koskinen J, Ahonen JJ, Sivula H, Tilus T, Lintinen H, Kankaanpää I (2005) Software modernization decision criteria: an empirical study. In: Proc Ninth Eur Conf Software Maintenance and Reengineering (CSMR 2005). IEEE Computer Society, pp 324–331
11. Koskinen J, Ahonen JJ, Kankaanpää I, Lintinen H, Sivula H, Tilus T (2006) Checklist-based information system change decision making support method. Proc 13th Eur Conf Information Technology Evaluation (ECITE 2006). Academic Conferences Ltd. (accepted)
12. Koskinen J, Ahonen JJ, Tilus T, Sivula H, Kankaanpää I, Lintinen H, Juutilainen P (2006) Developing software evolution estimation methods for software industry. In: Kokol, P (ed) Proc 3rd IASTED Int Conf Software Eng (SE 2006). ACTA Press, pp 323-328
13. Koskinen J, Sivula H, Tilus T, Kankaanpää I, Ahonen JJ, Juutilainen P (2006) Assessing software replacement success: An industrial case study applying four approaches. In: Messnarz R. (ed) Proc 13th Conf Eur Systems and Software Process Improv and Innov (EuroSPI 2006). Springer LNCS 4257 (accepted)
14. Lehman M, Perry D, Ramil J (1998) Implications of evolution metrics on software maintenance. In: Proc Int Conf Software Maintenance - 1998 (ICSM 1998). IEEE Computer Society, pp 208–217
15. Lientz B, Swanson E (1981) Problems in application software maintenance. Communications of the ACM 24 (11):763–769
16. Oman P, Hagemeister, J (1992) Metrics for assessing a software system's maintainability. In: Proc 1992 IEEE Software Maintenance Conf (ICSM 1992). IEEE Computer Society, pp 337-344
17. Ransom J, Sommerville I, Warren I (1998) A method for assessing legacy systems for evolution. In: Proc IEEE Conf Software Re-engineering (CSMR 1998). IEEE Computer Society, pp 84–92

18. Sahin I, Zahedi F (2001) Policy analysis for warranty, maintenance, and upgrade of software systems. Journal of Software Maintenance: Research and Practice 13 (6): 469-493

19. Seacord R, Plakosh D, Lewis G (2003) Modernizing legacy systems: software technologies, engineering processes, and business practices. Addison-Wesley.

20. Sneed H (1995) Estimating the costs of software maintenance tasks. In: Proc Int Conf Software Maintenance - 1995 (ICSM 1995). IEEE Computer Society, pp 168–181

21. Sneed, H (1995) Planning the reengineering of legacy systems. IEEE Software 12 (1):24–34

22. Tilus, T, Koskinen J, Ahonen JJ, Lintinen H, Sivula H, Kankaanpää I (2005) MODEST: a method for early system modernization pressure estimation (submitted manuscript)

23. Tilus T, Koskinen J, Ahonen JJ, Lintinen H, Sivula H, Kankaanpää I (2006) Software evolution strategy evaluation: industrial case study applying value-based decision model. In: Abramowicz W, Mayer HC (eds) Proc BIS 2006 - Business Information Systems. LNI P-85, pp 543-557

24. Visaggio G (2000) Value-based decision model for renewal processes in software maintenance. Annals of Software Engineering 9:215–233

25. Warren I, Ransom J (2002) Renaissance: a method to support software system evolution. In: Proc 26th Annual Int Computer Software and Applications Conf (COMPSAC 2002). IEEE Computer Society, pp 415–420

Index

429